# Innovations in Counseling Psychology

*Developing New Roles,
Settings, Techniques*

Chris Hatcher

Bonnie S. Brooks

and Associates

# Innovations in Counseling Psychology

Jossey-Bass Publishers

San Francisco · Washington · London · 1977

INNOVATIONS IN COUNSELING PSYCHOLOGY
*Developing New Roles, Settings, Techniques*
by Chris Hatcher, Bonnie S. Brooks, and Associates

Copyright © 1977 by: Jossey-Bass, Inc., Publishers
615 Montgomery Street
San Francisco, California 94111
*&*
Jossey-Bass Limited
28 Banner Street
London EC1Y 8QE

Library of Congress Catalogue Card Number LC 77-82917

International Standard Book Number ISBN 0-87589-352-X

Manufactured in the United States of America


JACKET DESIGN BY WILLI BAUM


FIRST EDITION

*Code 7751*

The Jossey-Bass
Social and Behavioral Science Series

# Preface

Public awareness and demands for human support services have increased dramatically in the past ten years. Funding agencies, minority and special interest groups, elected public officials, and citizen groups have become far more active in questioning how these services are planned and delivered; in turn, this activity has encouraged professionals in counseling psychology to take a closer look at their established ways of functioning. While the remedial role was developing as the principal identification of the profession, a significant group of innovators were venturing into new settings and creating new educational, developmental, and preventive roles. Their work was based on a commitment to be more broadly responsive to the social, community, and institutional problems faced by client populations.

Today, the counseling psychologist faces exciting new fields of choice and direction: in role definitions, in employment settings, and in professional orientations. *Innovations in Counseling Psychology* is designed to articulate a new, nontraditional philosophical position and to illustrate this position not with model plans or pilot projects but with applications that have earned a real, functioning viability within their community. Each chapter has been specifically planned, with detailed and realistic material, to show readers how these new developments can become a part of their everyday practice and stimulate their creativity.

These directions look beyond a reactive stance and point out that intrapersonal models of psychology are not always congruent with institutional realities. Counselors working as psychoecologists and as consulting change agents have shown how to reform the system from within to make it more responsive to human needs. Holistic concepts of child growth have led to community-based parent-child education centers, psychological education curriculum development, and prevention-oriented child development specialists in elementary schools. The alternative counseling center has markedly changed social service delivery systems in the United States, defining new limits of independence and creativity. The new counselors have increased their commitments to the urban poor, black, aged, and other special groups. They know that 85 percent of traditional school counseling time is spent distributing information that could be handled by a multimedia system, and they are finding new solutions in advanced computer technology. Innovators in training settings have evolved external degree programs, competency-based training and certification applications, and retraining programs.

Robert F. Kennedy has said: "Some men see things as they are and ask, why? I dream of things that never were, and ask, why not?" *Innovations in Counseling Psychology* is designed to show how the creative ideas of others have practical significance for today and to encourage others to pursue imaginative ideas.

*September 1977*                          Chris Hatcher
                                          *San Francisco, California*

                                          Bonnie S. Brooks
                                          *El Paso, Texas*

# Contents

# The Authors

Chris Hatcher has been assistant clinical professor and director of the Family Therapy Program, Langley Porter Institute, University of California, San Francisco, since 1974. Hatcher earned his bachelor's degree in psychology at Duke University and the University of Georgia (1968) and a master's degree in psychology at the University of Georgia (1970). Pursuing interests in clinical and community psychology, he earned the Ph.D. in clinical psychology from the University of Georgia in 1972. During his internship at Letterman Medical Center, San Francisco, Hatcher became particularly interested in the study of family processes, from both therapeutic and community/educational standpoints.

In 1972 Hatcher became Director of Intern Training, Psychology Service, William Beaumont Medical Center, El Paso, Texas, and held joint faculty appointments in both the Department of Psychology and the Department of Educational Psychology and Guidance of the University of Texas at El Paso. Here he concentrated upon building an innovative community and family oriented internship, bringing the program to approval status by the American Psychological Association. He is the senior editor of *Handbook of Gestalt Therapy* (1976) and has been a training consultant to child and family agencies throughout the United States, Mexico, England, and Germany. Chris Hatcher is chairman, Mayor's Committee on Family Violence (San Francisco) and is an international consultant in hostage negotiation.

Bonnie S. Brooks is associate professor at the University of Texas at El Paso, where she has been involved in the Department of Educational Psychology and Guidance since 1968. Brooks earned a bachelor's degree in music education at Millikin University (1964) in Decatur, Illinois. Following one year of teaching public school in Peoria, Illinois, she entered Indiana University as an NDEA Fellow during the academic year 1965-1966. Brooks was awarded a master's degree in counseling in 1966; she remained at Indiana University as a counselor on the dean of students' staff. She simultaneously earned a doctoral degree in higher education (1968), with emphasis on student personnel services.

At the University of Texas at El Paso, Brooks has been instrumental in developing an active master's level counselor training program; her professional concern for counselor education is reflected by her receipt of a number of research grants, and active involvement with the Association for Counselor Education and Supervision on a state and regional basis. In the winter of 1974 she served as visiting professor of counselor education through the auspices of Ball State University in Wiesbaden, Germany, and has since become involved with counseling and international concerns. Dr. Brooks is married; her husband Bill is a professor of chemistry at the University of Texas at El Paso.

*We dedicate this book to Kara*
*and Bill, respectively—Chris and Bonnie*

Alfred S. Alschuler is professor at the Center for Humanistic Education, School of Education, University of Massachusetts, Amherst.

Ben N. Ard, Jr. is professor of counseling in the School of Education, San Francisco State University.

Charles W. Dayton is associate research scientist at the American Institutes for Research, Palo Alto, California.

David Drum is director, Office of Counseling and Student Placement, and clinical associate professor of psychology at the University of Rhode Island, Kingston.

Edward Paul Dworken is area director of Prince Georges County Model Neighborhood Community Mental Health Center, Capitol Heights, Maryland.

Howard Figler is director of counseling at Dickinson College, Carlisle, Pennsylvania.

Jo Ann Harris-Bowlsbey is associate professor of research at Western Maryland College, Westminster, Maryland.

Frederic M. Hudson is president of the Fielding Institute, Santa Barbara, California.

Allen E. Ivey is professor in the Human Relations Center, School of Education, University of Massachusetts, Amherst.

G. Brian Jones is principal research scientist at the American Institutes for Research, Palo Alto, California.

Betty Koff is instructor in nursing at Pima Community College, Tucson, Arizona.

Theodore H. Koff is associate professor of public administration at the University of Arizona, Tucson.

Peter Kuriloff is associate professor in the Program in Psychology and Education, Graduate School of Education, University of Pennsylvania, Philadelphia.

Ray N. Lowe is professor of education at DeBusk Memorial
    Center, University of Oregon, Eugene.

Julius Menaker is professor in the College of Education, Univer-
    sity of Illinois, Chicago Circle.

Carol Morse is associate coordinator of the DeBusk Memorial
    Center, University of Oregon, Eugene.

Eric Seidman is associate professor in the Department of Special
    Education, School of Education, University of Maryland,
    College Park.

David V. Tiedeman is professor in the Department of Adminis-
    tration and Services, Northern Illinois University, De
    Kalb.

# Innovations in Counseling Psychology

*Developing New Roles,
Settings, Techniques*

# 1

# New Directions

## Chris Hatcher

The field of counseling psychology has expanded rapidly and in many directions, particularly during the past decade. As public awareness of the need for human support services increased, professionals in the counseling field found it necessary to take a closer look at their established ways of functioning and to experiment with new roles and innovative approaches. But this has not occurred without considerable controversy.

Counseling psychology has traditionally been divided into three areas of general function. The first is the remedial or rehabilitative, the second the preventative, and the third the educative or developmental. Historically, the vast majority of the emphasis in counseling psychology has been on the remedial role, usually focusing on the individual's adjustment. The influence of the models of clinical psychology and psychiatry was undoubtedly very strong in shaping this focus. The remedial role, however, made the counseling psychologist an office professional whose services were devoted to a very small number of the total population. Since clients had to have problems or be in trouble to qualify for referral, a great deal of time was assigned to crisis management. Still, educational institutions, the largest employer, liked the remedial role, for it provided a convenient organizational way to deal with people identified as problems. As a result, counseling psychology learned that the way to gain status and support from the employing institutions was to define themselves more and more in the remedial role. University training programs responded by developing a body of specialized knowledge and techniques designed almost exclusively for this role.

While the remedial role was developing as the principal identification of the profession, there was a secondary, but consistent, chain of interest in the educative-developmental and preventative roles. This interest was based on a commitment of broader responsiveness to assist people in learning to deal with life development patterns and social institutions. It began in the early 1900s, with vocationally oriented services designed to provide information and support about career choices within a rapidly industrializing society. The testing movement; the limited expansion of counseling services into curriculum planning, race relations, and sensitivity training; and the humanistic psychology movement likewise grew out of a concern for a better response to increasingly complex social needs. But the counselor still existed largely as a remediator within the traditional framework of school and vocational rehabilitation settings. Slowly, professionals were beginning to realize the developmental similarities in the problems of many of their clients. They were becoming frustrated that their role did not easily permit them to do preventative work and reach larger groups of people. Experience was also showing that many minority and disenfranchised groups were not interested in these middle-class remediators in the office. The nature of their methods was excluding a significant proportion of the client population. Furthermore, counselors became more critically aware that they did not occupy a vital role organizationally. They did not have a major vote and often were not consulted in major policy decisions, even though these decisions would impact heavily on the population they were expected to serve. The counselor had become limited, usually, to a middle-level manager of specialists with little opportunity for vertical advancement in the system. An awareness of these issues began to concern a number of counseling psychologists in America in the 1960s. John Kennedy and the New Frontier, Lyndon Johnson and the Great Society, civil rights activism, and the Peace Corps symbolized a mood of utopian optimism and experimentation. At the same time, the Vietnam War was mobilizing a concern among everyone to question our conventional ways of doing things. For here was a war that most did not believe in but that the established political system seemed unable and unwilling to stop. Youth in particular were affected by these contrasts and changes, and large numbers turned to a period of drug and counterculture exploration. Some counselors decided it was time to do something and began to strike out for new ideas. But it was not easy. There was resistance on many levels within the profession. Some felt that, through the remedial role, status and position as a profession had only been recently attained and that resources should be directed toward increasing the specialized knowledge in this area. If not, the gains that had been made would be risked. Others stated that a move away from the remedial specialist emphasis would lead to a dilution of the quality of any service; that only so much could be taught, within a given time period, to a counselor in training. Even the counselors who had decided to take new directions faced conflicts within themselves. Their training had mostly prepared them for limited service and did not promote the kind of flexibility and skills necessary for creating new settings, so they had to overcome personal defensiveness and concerns about potential failure.

Despite these difficulties, the creativity, enthusiasm, and commitment of these leaders of counseling psychology led to the development of whole new developmental and preventative roles, as well as of new community-based, highly active outreach settings. At the same time, dissatisfied clinical psychologists were primarily responsible for initiating the new field of community psychology. Unfortunately, community psychology as a movement was substantially slowed in the 1970s as hard economic realities and resource shortages dramatically reduced funding sources. In addition, the increased coverage of psychological services by third-party payers, such as insurance companies and federal agencies, moved many clinical psychologists away from community psychology. While the economic situation has had an impact on counselors, the movement of exploration has gained excitement, a broad range of innovative roles, and many new members.

Today, the counseling psychologist faces exciting new fields of choice and direction in training settings, professional orientations, and employment settings. Similarly, counselor educators have become sensitive to the need for expanded flexibility in teaching, giving students a more diverse series of experiences relevant to changing roles and activities. However, the professional and resource literature in counseling psychology has been clearly and regrettably lacking in materials that are both specific and realistic with regard to current programs and concepts.

The purpose of this book is twofold. The first is to articulate a philosophical position, providing a foundation to encourage further exploration by others. The second is to illustrate this position, not with model plans or pilot projects, but with the applications that have earned a real, functioning viability within their community. Our intent is to broaden the reader's awareness of developments that go beyond the traditional school remedial or vocational remedial role orientation into the context of community-based and organizational systems settings.

In this volume, we first describe new roles for counseling psychology. David Drum and Howard Figler set the stage in the call for counselors to move out from behind their desks and office doors and carry psychology to the public, to move from the emphasis on remediation toward that of prevention. The exciting tone of the chapter is matched by practical information on how to move from reactor to initiator.

From this position, outreach counselors will come to their work with a very different system of rewards. The additional rewards will include the satisfaction of advocating institutional change and discovering that some of these changes are possible, the pleasure of seeing a well-organized plan for human service function smoothly, increased sense of worth in being able to reach larger numbers of people, and the satisfaction of training

nonprofessionals to perform as capable helpers. Next we point
out the need for school counselors to realize that intrapersonal
models of psychology are not congruent with institutional realities. These models assume, often falsely, that the individual is
"disturbed" and must be adjusted to a "normal" environment.
Instead, emotional disturbance may be viewed as an ecological
phenomenon that exists in the transactions among people. Peter
Kuriloff shows how the "psychoecologist" must take new risks
to develop the political expertise to effect positive changes in
total school environments. This is illustrated with actual case
examples, from Dottie in her initial weeks of Head Start to the
hostile aggressiveness of Tony in the eighth grade.

In Chapter Four, the activist counselor is seen in an innovative community mental health-based approach to counseling
as evolved by Edward Dworkin. Outside social action change
agents help make issues political and visible but are often
stopped at that point. This is because the target system will
work to exclude the now-identified social activist. This is the
time for the consulting change agent who works to help reform
the system from within. The change agent must know something of his self-perceptions. Is he an expert healer, idea person,
facilitator, resource generator, or social engineer? He must be
responsive to a variety of target populations, must understand
the patterns of both invited and uninvited entry, and must exit
in a manner that does not damage the changes that have taken
place. Dworkin shows how he has implemented this approach in
his personal and professional development within the setting of
a county government social service system.

Marriage and family counseling is one of the most rapidly
developing counselor roles today. Although the American Association of Marriage Counselors (now called the American
Association of Marriage and Family Counselors) was formed in
1942, it was not until the mid 1960s and early 1970s that states
began to pass specific laws on licensing and practice. While only
seven states have enacted legislation in this area, it is significant
to note that these range from the more urban, industrialized environments (California, New Jersey, and Michigan), to rural and
traditional environments (Utah and Nevada), as well as a com-

bination of urban and rural (Texas and Georgia). This indicates
a broad base of support across states with different political,
social, and interprofessional circumstances. Marriage and family
counselors now face a crucial stage in their efforts to consoli-
date the role, agree on uniform standards, and deal with challenges from older professional groups. Ben Ard, in "Marriage and
Family Counselors as Independent Professionals," traces the historical development of the field and makes a strong case for the
importance of specialty training and certification in this area.

The University of Maine's college of education graduated
588 students last June. About 150 are still looking for jobs, but
Kelly is not one of them (Gallese, 1976). Her degree is in elementary school counseling, one of the fastest growing new roles
for counselors. There are currently approximately 12,000 elementary school counselors, up from 10,000 in 1972, 6,000 in
1969, and 500 in 1963. Unlike high school counselors, whose
time is mostly devoted to problem adolescents and advising on
job opportunities and college entrance requirements, elementary school counselors try to work on prevention, aiming at
larger groups of children. We see that the skill requirements are
very different (see Eric Seidman's chapter on the work of the
Interprofessional Research Commission on pupil personnel services) and chart guidelines for a future counseling orientation
based on a holistic concept of child growth.

The next article, written by Alfred Alschuler, Allen Ivey,
and Chris Hatcher describes "psychological education," which is
perhaps one of the most important and far-reaching changes
within the educational setting. Psychological education involves
the counselor in a new preventative curriculum area in which
people learn to understand themselves and more effectively get
what they want. It aims to provide students with an increased
capacity to anticipate alternative experiences and then to develop a cognitive map or sequence in working through a set of
their personal observations. Often, this may take place through
developmental guidance experiences (DGEs) that give a format
for open discussion about all sides of an ethical or emotional
issue related to developmental tasks, rather than leading the stu-

dent to some "correct" viewpoint. The reader will find a wealth of practical examples and specific resource materials to assist them in this area, as well as an analysis of the disagreements. It must be recognized that not everybody is an enthusiastic supporter of psychological education. Some parent action groups have taken the position that schools should teach the educational basics and leave the "development of the total child" to the parents. Brookline, Massachusetts, for example, has experienced such a difference of opinion. Brookline has eight schools and nine counselors operating psychological education programs. Some parents feel that these programs infringe on family privacy by encouraging children to talk about their feelings about parents and home environment in front of others (Gallese, 1976). But the Brookline school system's director of guidance and health education says that such issues cannot be taught without looking at ethics, just as science cannot be separated from ecology. Moving beyond the schools, Ray Lowe and Carol Morse show a new functional model for child and family services. This approach, based on Adlerian concepts, focuses on multiple family groups, who meet in a community center. Rather than operating behind closed interview-room doors, families are introduced to a more open, less pathologizing way of looking at themselves with an unique design of support from other families. As Lowe and Morse describe how this idea has become a reality, we begin to see why parent-child education centers are well established at many locations in Oregon and other states.

The 1960s and 1970s have brought new awareness to the needs of people in special environments or special developmental periods. Seven of the ten largest school systems in the United States have a black student majority, even though only one of them has a black population majority. These large, urban school systems also contain a substantial minority of Mexican-Americans and Puerto Ricans. Julius Menacker, in "Student Advocacy and Environmental Change in Urban Settings," argues that traditional methods fail because they arise from middle-class assumptions. These theories are grounded in a psycho-

therapeutic foundation that places primary emphasis on improving the self-concept and self-awareness of the client through
verbal symbolization and interaction. This type of verbal ab-
straction does not mean much for the urban poor, because it is
not a valued item in their usual environment. Menacker believes
that there are viable alternatives to help the urban poor student
and presents such models as the student advocate, ombudsman,
community resource specialist, and the European educateur.
Practical examples drawn from experience in Chicago's urban
centers help the reader to see how these roles function in reality. The youth drug crisis of the late 1960s caught our established human service delivery programs unprepared. Many individuals found personal, philosophical, or political life-styles in
the drug counterculture that seemed to represent a better way
than that which they had left behind. Some, however, found
insecurity, disorientation, and exploitation by hustlers within
the movement itself. For them, drugs that promised new joy
and experience brought lasting visions of anxiety. In the traditional clinic setting, both the young person and the professional
often became hostile representatives of their own life-style
choices. From this crisis came the first alternative counseling
centers, created by people who straddled both cultures. In
"Dreams and Realities of Alternative Counseling Centers," Chris
Hatcher charts their growth and the stages in their unique organizational process and illustrates how this concept has been
applied by many other minority and special-interest groups.

Americans have always thought of themselves as youthful;
as recently as 1970 their median age was twenty-eight. The
median age will be over thirty in 1981 and forty by the year
2030, when the number of persons over sixty-five will reach
fifty-two million, or one out of every six Americans. Until recently, counseling services have not been adequately extended
to this increasing group of people because of their proximity to
death and because of the counselor's own feelings of helplessness in dealing with the end of life. Theodore Koff and Betty
Koff, in "New Horizons in Working with the Elderly," identify the eight areas of greatest risk for the older person:
retirement, poverty, relocation, protective resources, insti-

tutionalization, death and dying, grief and depression, and drug misuse and abuse. The process dynamics involved in each are discussed, and practical pathways for intervention are presented. Counseling with the aged has become one of the most rapidly expanding specialties. And, as Koff and Koff point out, the bumper sticker that proclaims "Gerontology is a sexy business" really means that there are great professional and personal rewards for those who choose this type of work.

The economic conditions of the 1970s have placed a new emphasis on career planning and vocational choice. The future shock of rapid technological advancements has shown that early career and status biases, such as a college education being desirable for all, can have severe personal and employment consequences. In high school and college settings, the complexity of contemporary job options and training pathways have mandated the introduction of computerized vocational counseling systems. In "Computer Technology in Counseling," G. Brian Jones, Jo Ann Harris-Bowlsbey, and David Tiedeman indicate that while business has revolutionized its procedures with the help of computers, education has been more resistant to the creative use of such technology. This has been true despite the fact that most counselors spend about 85 percent of their time dispensing information that could be handled by multimedia systems. But counselors and computer experts are often separated by differences in language, and the counselor also tends to see the computer as depersonalizing the individual. The authors provide a powerful assist to bridge this gap in showing how to evaluate and select a computerized program that is geared to one's own setting.

Our next chapter points beyond university, professional entry training to competency-based program planning for staff development. Dayton and Jones deal with a successful module approach, developed at the American Institutes of Research, to continuing education for staff who already occupy career positions in the counseling field.

With the increased demands of these emerging roles and trends, it is clear that the training and certification of counselors is now an even more critical issue. The number of counselor-training sites has expanded from 1 in 1906, to well over 400 in 1977. Each year some 1,500 doctorates, 17,000 master's, and an untold number of bachelor's and associate-level degrees are granted in counseling. This book deals with the critical training implications of these new roles and developments, stressing the need for innovative training and certification plans with an emphasis on competency-based education. Bonnie Brooks, in "Training Models for Tomorrow," gives a comprehensive analysis of both internal and external pressures for change: admission policies, differentiated staffing with bachelor's-degree personnel, competency-based training and certification, and special-interest group needs. Brooks feels that the periods of affluent federal funding are over and that counselor training programs must become markedly more responsive to public needs.

Many students and teachers have become dissatisfied altogether with attempts to make university campus-based training more relevant to the demands of social systems and communities. They have turned to the utilization and development of external degree programs, where competency-based measures are emphasized over the more traditional academic measure. Frederic M. Hudson has been an integral part of this movement, and his chapter provides a comprehensive review of the rewards and risks that face the interested student or teacher.

In our concluding chapter, Bonnie Brooks looks at tomorrow's directions. The clinical model as response to human problems has been validly criticized for being basically passive-reactive with a rather standardized service format. It does, however, have a clear utility, and mere simplistic rejection is not the answer. But the creative possibilities for the future lie much more in organizational and community settings, and it is here that Brooks focuses our attention.

In summary, the field of counseling psychology has changed dramatically in recent years. This text is designed to bring a new awareness of this innovative growth, which is being carried out in a variety of human support service settings. It is our hope that this will show counseling professionals that today's exciting and imaginative ideas can indeed grow to be tomorrow's realities.

# 2

# Outreach in Counseling

David Drum
Howard Figler

For the past several years, the traditional model of practice for counseling psychologists has come under serious verbal attack from some consumers, nonconsumers, and colleagues. The target of this attack is the private practice model of providing mental health services. It is a model of service that was copied from our psychiatrist colleagues and focuses exclusively on "curing problems," "reestablishing mental health," and "overcoming emotional illness."

Outreach is a total population approach to providing mental health services that offer alternatives for growth and development that are not possible within the framework of the traditional model. Advocates of the outreach approach have been calling for counselors to diminish their involvement in "treating problems" and to reinvest the energy saved in facilitation of the developmental process and in prevention of unnecessary, nonproductive life problems. The outreach approach re-

11

quires that the counselor take an active posture and not limit his work to people seeking help.

Despite the increasing emphasis on outreach skills, many graduate students and practitioners are still seeking to fully understand this rather newly established movement. We are writing this chapter on the premise that practitioners and trainers must know more about what outreach is and how one starts doing it, before they embrace these ideas within their own philosophies of what it means to be "helpful" to an individual. The purpose of this chapter is to provide an understanding of outreach by (1) reviewing the evolution of outreach activities, (2) defining and describing outreach, (3) describing a comprehensive outreach model, and (4) providing guidelines for implementing outreach programs. Throughout this article, the term *counselor* will be used to refer to all counseling psychologists, counselors, clinicians, and other mental health professionals who are employed in schools, colleges, or community agencies.

## The Evolution of Outreach Activities

Until outreach dimensions of service delivery were developed in recent years, mental health professionals and counselors relied on only one style of intervention—the private practice model of personal therapy. This model is basically passive-reactive, with a rather standardized service format. It focuses on remediation of rather severe disturbances that render a person ineffective.

In order to receive assistance from a therapist operating by the passive-reactive model, a person has to experience enough turmoil or discomfort to be motivated to seek help. In other words, a problem has to deteriorate to such a level that it becomes a painful motivating force, strong enough to compel a person to admit that his life is beyond his control. The passive-reactive model does very little to support normal growth and developmental needs, patently ignores prevention, and, in fact, depends on the deterioration of needs for its survival.

*Movement Toward Multidimensionality: Evolution of Outreach Practices.* In attempting to achieve a multidimensional service delivery system, the practice of outreach has evolved through four distinct stages.

Stage 1. The first identifiable goal of outreach was very limited and specific. It was to increase the impact and utilization of mental health services currently being offered by making them more visible. In the community mental health centers, this meant developing satellite agencies in key locations in the community, increasing publicity that described the existing programs and services, educating critical mental health referral agents about services offered, and in some cases providing transportation to the center. Psychologists working in college environments were reaching out by offering services in more naturalistic settings (student unions, residence halls, and so forth), educating campus referral agents about programs and services offered, and making materials and information about counseling programs more accessible. The focus of this first form of outreach was on the redeployment of current modes of intervention and existing services. It had a substantial effect, breaking down the myth that therapeutic services could only be offered under tight control in narrowly defined "safe" places.

Stage 2. These initial outreach efforts toward greater visibility began to blend into and form the basis for a second form of outreach. This newer type of outreach activity was aimed at improving the quality of the traditional services offered and augmenting those services with better supportive materials and personnel.

Largely as a result of the impact of the earlier outreach efforts, it became clear that helping services needed to be made more elastic to meet the needs of some people. When therapists began to function in more naturalistic settings, they rather quickly learned that there were subgroups of people in their community who virtually boycotted the services they were offering. The impact of the services their agency provided on a particular group (Mexican-Americans, Chicanos, blacks, and so on) was often embarrassingly small. It became clear that for some people the traditional style of one-to-one helping that involved going to a professional's well-appointed office, scheduling in advance, and talking rather than acting was rather

alien to the subculture of many of the people they supposedly served.

In order to affect a wider variety of constituents, mental
health workers began to diversify their services to include more
active forms of intervention, such as behavioral approaches, sensitivity groups, and self-help materials and programs. Individuals
could now elect to talk with a practitioner in a one-to-one setting or could select among other alternatives to meet their
needs. Some of the alternatives provided by outreach services
included the use of media approaches to overcome a problem. A
client could listen to a series of audio cassettes designed to overcome or control feelings of anxiety, could participate in leader-
less or peer-led group experiences, or could increase self-esteem
and make a career decision by using programmed materials
made available by the local mental health agency. None of these
forms of assistance required as large an investment of the professional's time as one-to-one therapy, and often the success of
alternate forms of intervention were comparable to one-to-one
therapy.

As a result of these first two forms of outreach activities,
it became very apparent that every community or school was
populated by people who had important mental health needs or
problems. By becoming more visible and making services more
relevant, counselors increased the number of consumers who desired to use those services and also increased their own level of
awareness that some of their services were not appropriate for
certain potential consumers. It began to become clear that there
were far more problems that needed to be resolved than there
were mental health resources available to help work toward that
end.

Stage 3. Emerging from the awareness that client needs
far outstrip both the financial and energy resources for the private practice, problem-centered models of services was the desire to find effective ways to support positive growth and development. It was from this framework that the third form of
outreach emerged. Unlike the first two types of outreach activities, which attempted to diversify the passive-reactive model of
helping in order to make it more responsive to remedial needs,

this third form represented a conceptual breakthrough and signaled a shift to an active developmental approach that stressed initiating behaviors on the part of the professional.

In this new form of outreach, the goal of the outreach worker became one of creating ways to intervene early in the developmental process to insure that normal developmental tasks and growth needs did not form the foundation for more serious problems in later life. The emphasis was shifted from remediation of problems to supporting the development of the person. Ivey (1975, pp. 529-530) graphically illustrates the need to shift the emphasis from problems to people: "Instead of looking to antiquated medical and psychological models for guidance, we should be asking our own questions. For example, what are the key developmental tasks and needed human relations skills of the American adolescent? In relying on medical and psychological models, we have tended to become problem centered rather than person centered. Clearly, a developmental framework forces all of us to change our orientation to a new, positive and dynamic framework of human development rather than human control and repair."

The revolutionary impact of becoming "person centered" rather than "problem centered" is just beginning to be experienced. Despite significant developments in programs and services, we have just begun to scratch the surface with regard to the many ways we can help people who are at developmental crossroads rather than waiting until they travel down a non-rewarding path and then helping them to recover. It is evident that helping agents must be at the crossroad—where the needs first emerge. Lawton (1970, p. 663) illustrates that most of the life decisions that a person faces take place far away from the counselor's office. He states: "Where the counselor's skills are really needed is in the life space of people who don't go to offices and who stay isolated where their problems really exist: in the homes, in the factories, in the ghettos, in the bars, the subways, the streets, the crash pads, the communes, the cafeterias, the toilets, and even the classrooms."

As a result of the shift in emphasis to being "person centered," we have been witnessing the emergence of a wide variety of new, innovative programs. These programs attempt to provide opportunity for intervention to occur while the person is at the developmental crossroads. They focus on ways to help people build in important life skills, identify and resolve important life issues, and make necessary and desired life transitions. Representative of these programs are the large number of target-focused groups that are currently being offered. Consumer response to these programs has been far in excess of what was anticipated. In a very short period of time, structured groups such as those designed to help people clarify values, become assertive, control anxiety, improve interpersonal communications skills, decide on life directions, handle loneliness, and resolve personal losses have become a permanent part of the array of services considered essential.

The successful emergence of this third form of outreach resulted in the helping services becoming truly multidimensional. Now it was possible to identify two important goals of helping: remediating existing problems and facilitating the developmental process. The existence of twin goals further required adjustments in mental health delivery systems. The intervention style appropriate for remedial intervention was of only limited relevance for facilitating development, and therefore new styles of providing services had to be developed. Among some of the new intervention methods are increasing use of paraprofessionals, offering of programs in more natural settings, reduction in the duration of the helping process, and use of educational approaches and materials.

Stage 4. Occurring somewhat parallel in time to the movement toward developmental intervention was the movement toward prevention, toward active efforts to reach individuals before they degenerate from lack of attention. Preventive outreach represents an attempt to provide intervention prior to the awareness of a need for help. In order to be preventive, an intervention must precede the emergence of a need or problem —otherwise it cannot be preventive, but can only be treatment oriented. Once a need or problem has arisen, intervention must be classified as either developmentally oriented (if shortly after origination of need) or remedially oriented (if after deterioration of the need). Preventive outreach involves developing strategies and programs that people can use to attempt to anticipate and circumvent unnecessary life hazards. Specifically, they take the form of such activities as psychological education, environmental engineering, advocacy, and consultation with human systems.

For the most part, Stage 4 outreach involves introducing changes in the school or agency, changes that will have an enduring impact on all people who pass through the institution. We are speaking of institutional change, new systems for teaching people how to grow, and such measures for helping all people within a school or agency without their having to ask for such help directly. A more explicit discussion of preventive outreach can be found in a later section of this chapter, "The Counselor as a Manager of Resources."

The Present. The regular offering of many outreach services and programs today is an indication that it has not only become accepted but is now considered part of the core of basic skills that new practitioners should have in order to be full-service professionals. Further discussion of training needs is found in another chapter of this volume. It should be pointed out that although some specific methodology and a number of practical strategies have been developed the field of preventive outreach is still in its infancy. Methods for assessment of needs and making environmental change, provision for effective consultation with community organizations and agencies, and design of more practical preventive strategies must continue to be developed.

### Outreach Defined

The term *outreach* refers to a concept that embraces a broad array of services and programs designed to extend the impact of mental health services beyond the direct remediation of seriously deteriorated problems. Literally, *outreach* means to reach out both physically and psychologically to seek additional ways to be impactive on the total population. It is the global descriptive term used to encompass a whole series of specific and unique approaches to offering mental health services. During the past few years, some of these approaches have coalesced into comprehensive helping systems, such as deliberate psychological education, paraprofessional service systems, consultation, change agentry, and structured group programs. Each of these outreach approaches has developed a working philosophy, has designed or incorporated a wide range of intervention strategies, and has acquired a substantial following of practitioners within the field of counseling.

Even though these five areas have surfaced as major outreach orientations, some forms of outreach activities have not developed into larger movements; however, they still provide important contributions as individual programs. Included in this category are interventions focusing on an individual's transactions with his living and learning environment, such as ecosystems mapping, psychoecology, and environmental engineering; interventions that are primarily preventive in nature; and interventions that center on finding new environments in which helping can take place, such as naturalistic counseling.

The practice of outreach in any setting is usually a selective blend of a number of both the major and individual approaches just mentioned. The overall outreach pattern that emerges usually depends on the degree to which the counselor desires: to vary the timing of his interventions; to expand the number of helpers involved; to diversify the methods used to intervene; to change the focus of the intervention; and to vary the setting and degree of his involvement in the actual delivery of services.

By using a pie graph analogy (see Figure 1 ) it is possible to illustrate how outreach programs vary from institution to institution. In the first example the amount of outreach provided is relatively small, and substantial emphasis is placed on continuing priority for one-to-one direct counseling services. Both the variety and depth of outreach approaches are severely restricted. The second example illustrates a situation wherein over half of the resources (time and energy) are devoted to outreach activities and therefore the depth and range of outreach approaches are greater. The third example illustrates a case in which one of the outreach dimensions is actually larger than the

**Figure 1. Examples of How a Counseling Service Might Distribute
Its Time Between Direct Service and Modes of Outreach.**

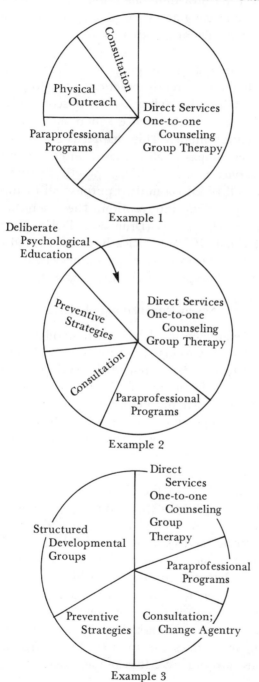

Example 1

Example 2

Example 3

emphasis placed on providing one-to-one counseling services. In this case, the counseling agency is placing a higher emphasis on structured developmental groups than on any other service variable.

We have described the range and diversity of outreach activities as they are currently practiced both to point out the depth of outreach and to clear up the misconception held by some practitioners that outreach is synonymous with only one or two intervention modes. This chapter is intended to convey that outreach encompasses all modes of intervention that move beyond the service model of private practice. Outreach philosophy links together into a unified purpose all of these diverse approaches to providing intervention. The emergence of comprehensive outreach models (Drum and Figler, 1973; Morrill, Oetting, and Hurst, 1972) has clearly demonstrated how these seemingly diverse human service approaches can and should be intertwined into a complete service delivery system.

### Seven-Dimensional Model

The seven-dimensional outreach model presented in Figure 2 provides a working structure that can be employed to illustrate the effectiveness of remedial, developmental, and preventive programs. The model identifies the seven key service variables through which the helper can vary his style of intervention. Each variable should be viewed as being a continuum with the left side representing more traditional forms of service, and points to the right indicating increasingly greater outreach orientation. In essence, the majority of interventions presented in the model are of the outreach type, and they clearly illustrate how outreach has expanded the opportunity for meaningful intervention. A therapist or agency can "stretch" its impact by offering services in as many of the thirty-five cells in the model as possible. An agency that provides interventions from only the left side of each variable is one-dimensional (remedial). In order to offer developmental and preventive assistance, it is necessary to devote resources to interventions further to the right on each variable.

The figure outlines the total structures for putting outreach methods into practice. It is an ideal, because it provides a

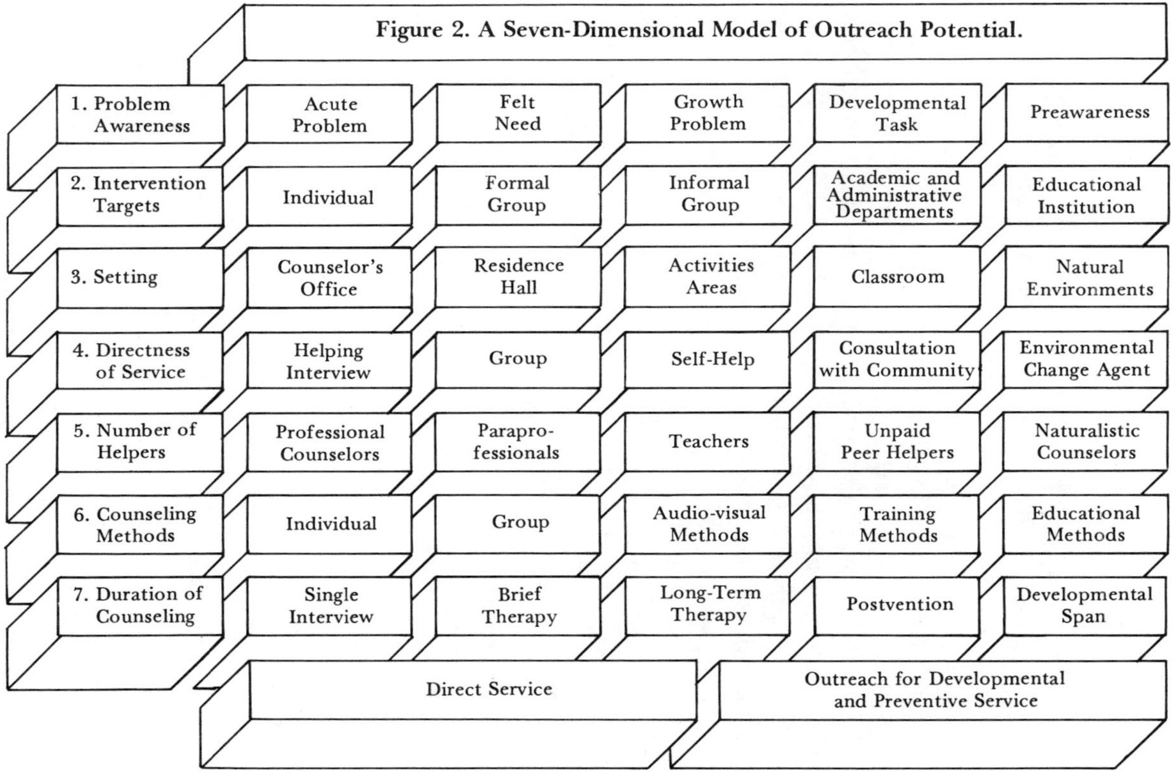

# Figure 2. A Seven-Dimensional Model of Outreach Potential.

| | | | | | | |
|---|---|---|---|---|---|---|
| 1. Problem Awareness | Acute Problem | Felt Need | Growth Problem | Developmental Task | Preawareness | |
| 2. Intervention Targets | Individual | Formal Group | Informal Group | Academic and Administrative Departments | Educational Institution | |
| 3. Setting | Counselor's Office | Residence Hall | Activities Areas | Classroom | Natural Environments | |
| 4. Directness of Service | Helping Interview | Group | Self-Help | Consultation with Community | Environmental Change Agent | |
| 5. Number of Helpers | Professional Counselors | Parapro-fessionals | Teachers | Unpaid Peer Helpers | Naturalistic Counselors | |
| 6. Counseling Methods | Individual | Group | Audio-visual Methods | Training Methods | Educational Methods | |
| 7. Duration of Counseling | Single Interview | Brief Therapy | Long-Term Therapy | Postvention | Developmental Span | |

Direct Service → Outreach for Developmental and Preventive Service structure for offering assistance to all people in a community or agency who might profit from it. In reality, there are financial and personal constraints that operate and therefore make it necessary to emphasize certain forms of intervention to the exclusion of others.

The model attempts to delineate the fullest possible range of interventions, as well as the intervention resources available to the helping agent. Even though the model was designed for use in a college or university community, it is easily adapted to other settings, especially to community mental health centers.

*Problem Awareness.* The timing of mental health intervention in relation to the origination of a need is a critical service variable. During the course of an individual's life, there are many developmental tasks that need to be satisfied in order for that person to grow and develop with some sense of self-competence. If a person does not successfully resolve important developmental tasks, those unresolved tasks often form the basis for later, more severe problems. Unfortunately, the traditional service model does not provide opportunity for intervention to occur until long after deterioration of normal developmental tasks has reached serious levels.

A full-service delivery model must provide a framework for offering assistance to individuals at several key points in time: before an individual has an awareness of a need for assistance (prevention), when he recognizes that a problem or task must be resolved in the future (developmental need), and after he is faced with an acute problem (remedial problem). As stated by the authors (1974, p. 9):

> Problem awareness . . . is one of the most graphic dimensions in this outreach model. Many counselors can vividly recall students who have made a few abortive attempts to resolve some developmental need, only to find themselves sliding backward along the [variable], into the range of acute problems.
>
> Consider the following hypothetical example of how a student's initial concern may degenerate into an acute problem. A student enrolls in your college and registers for a room in one of the resi-

dence halls. He comes from a small, isolated town
where his family and relatives have lived for years.
The environment was very supportive and made it
easy for him to acquire friends and feel part of
everything. When he arrives at the large university,
he is faced with a new developmental task—that of
developing a system of friendships or support
which provide him the nourishment and human
connection he desires. He experiences difficulty in
finding friends with whom he can relate and begins
to sense that he lacks the ability to communicate
his needs clearly. He starts to feel anxious and
alone and decides to travel home every weekend.
Soon coming back to college becomes difficult because he associates school with loneliness and feelings of alienation. After seven months of failing at
relating to his fellow students, he begins to experience considerable anguish and depression and is
unable to attend classes because he is too tired to
awaken in the morning. His feelings of failure begin
to mount, and he becomes overwhelmed and confused and panicked enough to seek out the school
counselor. He has completely regressed across the
[continuum] on problem awareness passing
through every stage until his problem became acute
and motivated him to seek out the counselor.

If it is possible for a helper to provide assistance that will allow
a person to avoid the nonproductive turmoil and energy spent
uselessly on an acute problem, he should not withhold or delay
intervention. By the same token, the therapist should not abandon his responsibility to provide remedial assistance to those
people who are already highly troubled and struggling to keep
their heads above water.

Within the past few years, workable strategies for assisting people to resolve normal growth problems and to complete
developmental tasks have been created. The technology for
helping people facilitate their own development has closed the
gap that existed between developmental theory and practice. A
large number of "person-centered" intervention strategies have
been developed, mostly in the form of structured groups, that

help people acquire important life skills, such as learning to control anxiety, assert themselves effectively, problem solve, and communicate clearly; examine and resolve critical life themes or issues that have the potential of greatly enriching or constricting the quality of their lives, such as coping with loneliness, alienation, and sexuality; and make important life transitions, such as adjusting to the death of a family member, divorce, and loss of work. With the design and implementation of developmental programs and prevention strategies, early successful intervention has become a reality.

*Intervention Targets.* Traditionally, mental health workers have viewed the individual being served as the only legitimate target of intervention. This assumption has some face validity, if the only purpose for intervention is to remediate an existing problem. But intervention aimed at facilitating the developmental process or preventing problems requires that the intervention targets be expanded to include the groups to which the individual belongs or with which he or she identifies and the environment in which the individual lives and works.

Virtually everyone belongs to some group or organization. Many formal groups and organizations have a specific need or goal, and every member of a particular group may share a common need. Where such a situation exists, it is possible to consider the group as the target of intervention, rather than the individual. By the same token, it is possible to view people who share a common need, characteristic, or way of life as constituting an "informal group." They may be viewed as a group for whom a specially designed type of intervention is appropriate because of a common need (working through a divorce, adjusting to the death of a family member), common characteristic (race, sex, age, and so on), or common style of life (hip youth, dropout, and so on).

It is possible to take one's focus entirely off the individual and center one's attempts to intervene in the agencies and institutions that have a substantial impact on the lives of the individuals who populate them. In such a situation, the target of intervention is the organization, even though the benefit accrues to individuals.

*Setting.* When counselors began to provide developmental and preventive services as well as remedial care, it became apparent that the setting where services were provided had to be expanded. The most logical extension was to try to offer services in the living environment of the consumer (residence hall, elderly housing unit, home, and so forth). Another natural extension of the setting was to consider providing services in an individual's working or learning environment (such as classroom or business). Within a short period of time, many helpers realized that services could not only be successfully provided outside of the office, but that in many cases they were more successful because they were now able to "draw the unreachables" and focus on some of the needs unique to people who lived in a certain part of the community or shared a common life-style.

The furthermost extension of the setting for mental health intervention is what we have labeled the "natural environment." Examples of the natural environment in which people often seek out understanding or help from friends are street corners, bars, and crash pads. Demonstration training programs have been instituted in which people who work in the natural environment of the helpee, such as bartenders and hairdressers, have been trained to be helping agents while on the job.

*Directness of Service.* The typical role model for someone preparing to be a helper is a therapist who provides services on a one-to-one or group therapy basis with clients who are experiencing considerable turmoil. Outreach advocates stress that we must utilize approaches that increase the ratio of clients served per hour of therapist time beyond the one client per hour ratio. It is possible that a therapist could improve this ratio by:

1. Providing self-help programs and materials that clients can use without needing continuous involvement with the helping person.
2. Offering to serve as a consultant to agencies, groups, or institutions in order to make them more responsive to the mental health needs of their members.
3. Working to identify the positive and negative elements in the community that either greatly enhance or severely constrict

individuals' growth and development. Once having identified the positive and negative elements, the therapist can work to eliminate the negative and encourage the rewarding of the positive.

As the helping agent moves from the offering of one-to-one and group counseling in his office to using self-help materials, to consulting with agencies, to becoming an environmental change agent, he is moving to less and less direct methods of providing service. Often these less direct ways of meeting needs are the most powerful.

*Number of Helpers.* It is becoming increasingly clear that it is not possible to secure enough funds to hire professional helpers to provide the wide range of remedial, developmental, and preventive services needed by people. The professional helper must work toward finding ways to involve as many non-professional helpers as possible in the helping process. During the past five years, we have witnessed a tremendous expansion in the use of peer helpers and paraprofessionals. By providing training and then capitalizing on the helping skills of paraprofessionals, the counselor can affect larger numbers of people. Many paraprofessionals are more naturally placed in the person's living environment and are therefore more likely to be present when the person is in need or is trying to make a life decision.

*Counseling Methods.* It is very important that all helping agents examine the appropriateness of the methods they use to produce change. Far too many counselors have spent a disproportionate amount of their time and effort concentrating on ways to improve individual counseling methods or techniques, to the virtual exclusion of searching for newer ways to intervene. By locking themselves into helping people who are already drowning, counselors have been spending an inordinate amount of time comparing the efficiency of the sidestroke, freestyle, and backstroke methods of rescuing struggling people and have not been attempting to alleviate the problem by looking toward radically different methods of prevention.

Outreach workers have made a modest beginning in their attempt to diversify the helping methods used by counselors.

The use of media methods of helping people (videotape, computer counseling, audio cassettes, and so on) are beginning to be widely used. Methods originally designed to train others for helping roles have had some unanticipated treatment benefits. Counselors have begun to realize that methods used to train paraprofessionals can be useful ways for helping people acquire important life skills, such as the ability to communicate, relate interpersonally, and to assert oneself. The discovery that one could actually use training methods for developing mental health services has resulted in counselors focusing on the use of educational-didactic styles of intervention.

*Duration of Counseling.* Mental health workers should look beyond the problem that a client presents and should learn to view him as a person who is in the process of developing. The traditional approach encourages the therapist to view his work as largely completed when the problem has been remediated. This process of helping does little to provide the individual with "immunity" from contracting new disorders. Outreach advocates are encouraging helpers to view clients as people who have a profile of needs rather than a "single problem." If a counselor views a person as having a profile of needs, then he will focus on ways he can intervene after resolution of a given problem (postvention) and throughout the entire developmental span of a person's life.

Through the advances of the past decade in both outreach practices and traditional services, we are beginning to witness the emergence of an increasing number of full-service professionals and comprehensive-service agencies. Outreach practices have forged a counselor who is a dramatically different person, even perhaps the antithesis, of the person who inhabited counseling offices a few years ago. He has not jettisoned or abandoned the traditional ways of providing service; rather, he has augmented those approaches with a series of new skills and ways of working. His daily work schedule now includes providing a limited number of one-to-one therapeutic sessions; managing a network of people and resources that goes well beyond the doors of the agency and impacts on the entire community; monitoring the educational and community environment; initiating institutional change; facilitating the normal growth and developmental needs of clientele; analyzing the specific needs of subgroups in his community; and developing self-help approaches or programs for people who do not want direct contact with a helping agent.

When the modes of intervention offered by the complete staff of a counseling service fill in most or all of the thirty-five cells of Figure 2 (the seven-dimensional model), then that agency is functioning as a full-service center. It is not necessary that any one individual offer all thirty-five intervention modes. However, it is desirable that a counseling service make provisions for services in virtually every cell of the model in order to fully meet the needs of people in their institution or community.

## The Counselor as a Manager of Resources

As a counselor begins to offer outreach programs and services, he will find himself working more in tandem with other helping agents and serving as a coordinator of resources. This new role of the counselor as an orchestrator of available human and material resources is dramatically altering the view of the counseling process in the minds of many people. It is apparent that if the counselor is to adopt the perspective of a full-service professional who manages resources in his efforts to deliver human services, he will have to become comfortable with certain viewpoints that run counter to the training counselors ordinarily receive. Such reversals of mind set will allow him to shed the role of the private practitioner, so that he can assume responsibility for promoting growth and development as well as continue to provide remedial therapeutic services. Examples of such restructuring include:

1. *Institutional versus Individual Focus.* While we are not suggesting that the counselor must surrender his concern for the individual, it becomes clear that much of his attention must be directed toward the entire institution, in his efforts to aid the client in the most potent possible way.

2. *Initiator versus Reactor Role.* The counselor-manager cannot afford to wait for clients to inform him that there are difficulties. Many people are neither conscious of the forces that impede their growth nor able to articulate what is happening to them. If change is to occur, it will happen because the counselor detects a need for it and takes steps to move toward a remedy, not because clients suggest that he do it.

3. *Indirect versus Direct Service.* Perhaps the majority of a counselor-manager's time will be devoted to activities that remove him from direct contact with the client but that nonetheless cast him in a helping role. Indirect service will often be more powerful than the direct helping relationship.

The current emphasis on working with "developing persons" allows the counselor to bring the helping process into full view without compromising an individual's right to confidentiality. This then frees the counselor to draw on other people in his institution or community as resources for furthering the development of the individual. It is time counselors admitted that developmental helping is no special province of the professionals in this field and that it is sheer folly to claim that only counselors are potentially effective helpers, because, first, a counseling agency will not get the staff needed to do all of the helping and provide all of the interventions required by clients; second, there are many actual and potential helpers outside of the counseling agency, and a counselor who taps into these natural resources can therefore multiply his impact; third, these people are capable of active participation in the planning and leadership of personal growth programs, or projects that represent interventions on behalf of clients; fourth, their efforts can be incorporated into their personal reward systems; and fifth, these people enjoy acting as helpers or contributors to the program because they are involved more directly and may be using skills that they had previously been leaving dormant.

If the counselor-manager wants to make an organized attempt to solicit involvement from various members of an educational or other community, here is a sequence that he might follow:

1. *Identify target population.* Identify all faculty, students, administrators, other staff, and community people.
2. *Determine skills and interests.* Ask each respondent for functional skills, specific areas of interest and experience, and degree of concern regarding problems and issues.
3. *Match skills to programs and problems.* Review the individual's skills and decide which of them might be useful in certain programs or problem areas.
4. *Encourage the participant.* Once the match is suggested between an individual's skills and a need, make direct personal contact with the person, to express personal interest and actively solicit his participation.
5. *Immediate involvement.* Begin the individual's participation in a program or project as soon as possible, so there is little time lag between his expression of interest and the reinforcement he feels from being part of the counselor's services.
6. *Ongoing training.* Make training available as it is needed by the new participant in his program, for whatever period of time he might require.
7. *Publicity.* Publicly acknowledge people who contribute their time and energy to the counseling service and its various interventions, so that others will learn of the counseling program's expanding involvement in the community and more people will be attracted to participate.

### Putting Outreach into Practice

The initial roadblock to implementation of outreach programs is what appears to be an already overburdened work schedule. Counselors and psychologists must be a little weary of having new roles suggested for them—sociologist, ecologist, consultant, and so forth. While most counselors are in agreement with the need to provide many outreach interventions, they see little hope of bringing such roles within their immediate grasp. If one is serious about adopting an outreach perspective and wants to make more than cosmetic changes in the working model, one will have to take the following sequence of initiatives.

First, one should determine the validity of outreach. Every counseling service that is considering adopting an outreach model must examine the validity of using a heavy client caseload as an excuse not to increase the range of its services. Many of the administrators who determine counseling service budgets have faced the use of similar logic several years ago, when offices such as the dean of students office asked, "How can we give housemothers additional duties in dormitories when we know they already have keys to dispense, rooms to check, students to discipline (and counsel), fire drills to organize, and many other duties that keep them fully occupied?" The question is not one of caseload but of the inherent value to the people in the institution of what one is doing. If long-term counseling cannot be afforded by an educational institution or community agency and if short-term counseling is very often only frustration for both counselor and client ("Tell me, in one hour, what I ought to do with my life"), then what should the counselor be paid to do? The counselor's presence must be justified on the basis of the contribution he makes to the growth and development of the clientele, to the organizational arrangements within the institution, and to the interactions between clients and these organizational forces.

Second, one should assess the need for outreach programs. Once having resolved the question of the legitimacy of meeting the developmental, educational, and preventive needs of clients, the counselor faces the next step, which is to assess the needs of the population he serves. Assessing needs does not have to be an elaborate process. An assessment design such as Project Upstream (Magoon, 1974) is a rather straightforward way to obtain an initial reading of existing positive and negative elements within the environment. Project Upstream utilizes a simple consensus seeking technique in which the total staff of a mental health agency are asked to reflect on the types of consumer needs either served successfully by the agency or present in the catchment area but unmet. The needs assessment phase of Project Upstream can be accomplished, in many instances, in a single day-long effort.

Third, one should articulate a philosophy of outreach.

The next step in the process of implementing outreach involves developing conceptual goals and building them into a comprehensive service philosophy that can be shared with potential consumers and decision makers. It is critically important that the programs and services offered by a counseling agency be linked together by an overall operating philosophy. When a counseling service simply adds on programs and services in a piecemeal fashion, it does little to improve its marginality within the community and thus remains vulnerable to the "meat axe" approach to budgeting. By having a clear purpose and stating the value of each outreach activity that is offered, the counselor is reminding people within the community of the validity and diversity of his or her mission.

Fourth, one should establish the range of outreach programs. Once having established a working outreach philosophy, the next important issue centers on the range of outreach services the counselor feels his service can offer. This will depend on several key variables: assessed needs, counselor skills, commitment of staff time and resources, and community resources. Each of these four major factors interact differently in any given institution, and thus in any setting a specific factor may be the most influential and important determinant of outreach capability. As an example, in many schools there are offices of institutional research that can help design and carry out needs assessment programs, while in other schools the work of conducting the needs assessment falls squarely on the counselors' shoulders. By carefully studying the interplay of these four major factors within his or her setting, a counselor can develop a realistic impression of the range of the outreach services he or she is capable of providing.

Fifth, whenever possible, the counselor should build on existing programs. Another important step to consider before designing a specific outreach program for application within one's institution is a review of already developed programs in use. Most practitioners are astounded to discover the large number of outreach programs that have been developed that could be put into use in their settings with only minor adaptations. Examples are structured groups for facilitating development, paraprofessional training programs, and consultation designs. To illustrate the transferability of outreach programs, consider the following recent developments. To date, there are at least forty different types of structured groups that have been developed into models that can be applied in a variety of educational and life settings. Some examples of transferable structured group program titles are assertion training, anxiety management, communication training, life planning, decision making, love and loving, creative risk taking, values clarification, dealing with jealousy, conscience awakening, pairing, parenting, relationship dissolution, and weight control. In the area of paraprofessional training, there are at least five major models available for professionals to choose from, as well as the existence of research on the effectiveness of those systems. A counselor who wants to begin to offer consultation services or do organizational development work can draw on resources described in *Structured Experiences for Human Relations Training* (Pfeiffer and Jones, 1975) as well as on individually designed programs used by various schools and agencies.

Sixth, the counselor should devote at least a day a week to outreach. If one is committed to the idea that some clients can be reached only through first steps taken by the counselor and if one is very much concerned about those whom one never sees, then one must clear one full day every week for the purpose of this kind of activity. If all one is committed to is the idea that "I'll do what I have to do to survive," then this is the minimum, because the growing wave of accountability will not permit a counseling center to survive on the basis of an invisible presence that caters to a small percentage of clients who badly need (and probably should pay for privately) intensive psychological services. This is the one drastic shift of behavior that will be required, because outreach cannot be done on a piecemeal, "whenever I have time" basis. The counselor must take it on faith that this outreach day will bear fruit, even though it may haunt him that certain individuals in his caseload will have to wait a bit longer for direct services. The regularity of a full day each week permits continuity for projects, enables self-monitoring of performance, and is a weekly reminder that initiatives are waiting to be taken.

If the counselor keeps a commitment to continuous outreach activity for a year or more and has a vague feeling that the rewards are beginning to appear but would like more definite signs of progress, how will he know that his outreach efforts are making a difference? Although formal evaluative criteria may be a bit muddy and inconclusive in the initial year or two, he can look for several signposts in his personal feelings and relationships day by day to discover whether the outreach impact is being felt.

The first clue may come when people begin calling to ask for help in generating ideas or programs that will help others. He will recall that in the earliest stages of outreach he had to inform everyone of what he was doing and persuade them to be interested in new services. Outreach has made a personal impact on the counselor when he looks forward more and more to the outreach day. Perhaps he is working on a continuing project that is gathering momentum or has hatched new and creative ideas that he is waiting to try out. He may even say quietly to himself that he would rather create a new style of intervention that makes a difference in the lives of many people than have five intensive therapy sessions in a given day.

As the counselor continues to reach out, he should begin to feel actually *powerful* in his new role as a shaper of the environment, rather than being relatively *powerless* in the face of forces that inhibit healthy functioning and personal growth. He may even enjoy serving on committees or community task forces, because they represent other opportunities to meet people who can help reach others directly or indirectly. He will have passed a psychic milestone in outreach when he enters a student union building or community office building and a number of people recognize who he is, are interested in talking with him (not for the purpose of therapy or counseling), and even remember what it was he was talking about the last time they met. Occasionally a person will tell the counselor of a positive program or service they have experienced in the school or community, even though this person does not know that the counselor was responsible for it. The person tells the counselor how much he or she appreciated the program, and he smiles a knowing smile, because he recalls that he had a part in making this thing happen.

## Summary

It is clear that the outreach-oriented counselor will approach his work with a drastically different reward system from that of the traditional counselor if he fully intends to diminish the direct service role in favor of providing indirect services that reach greater numbers of people. In addition to the traditional role rewards of human contact and helping relationships, he or she will anticipate the pleasure of seeing a well-organized plan function smoothly; the satisfaction of training others to perform as capable helpers; the reward of teaching life skills, resolving critical life themes, and helping with the completion of life transitions; an enhanced sense of power, in being able to affect and influence numbers of people and departments in the school and community; the satisfaction of advocating institutional change and discovering that some of these changes are possible; and, finally, the reward of contributing more directly to the health of the entire institution or community in ways that have dramatic impact on people's lives.

Just as outreach introduces a different set of rewards to the practicing counselor, so will the members of our profession be required to demonstrate a different set of skills and capabilities. In addition to the traditional interpersonal, therapeutic, and diagnostic skills, the counselor who expands his service to incorporate outreach will need to be skillful in planning, managing, persuading, politicking, speaking to groups, training, advocating, writing, and organizing people. The more that a counseling staff commits a significant proportion of its time to outreach activity, the more likely that professionals on the staff will be different people from those who might have been hired using a traditional model of helping. An altered reward system and a changed set of skills requirements will inevitably shift the criteria used in hiring and may eventually affect professional training programs.

Within three years of sustained outreach activity, it should be possible for a staff of counselors to demonstrate its capability for reaching greater numbers of people with a variety of indirect services. Administrators responsible for the financial support of counseling staffs will not fail to notice such gains and will provide strong approval for rewarding outreach-oriented counselors and attracting new ones to the staff. Outreach counselors who have the backing of their superiors will solidify their gains, and the movement of a profession from tradition-bound direct service to the wider potency of an outreach model will have become a reality.

# 3

# Counselor as Psychoecologist

## Peter Kuriloff

Current counseling practices depend heavily on the concepts and procedures of various models of psychotherapy. Such models, be they Freudian, Adlerian, Rogerian, or Skinnerian, share at least three crucial features. First, each one involves the notion of an "ill" or "disturbed" person who needs help. Second, by locating the problem within the individual, each model usually depends on the individual's cooperation in a more or less long-term effort to solve the problem either by restructuring his personality, strengthening his self-concept, or getting rid of his symptoms. Third, each model implicitly assumes a "normal" environment to which the "abnormal" individual must be adjusted.

Aubrey (1969) raised some cogent questions concerning the applicability of psychotherapy models to the practice of counseling in schools and, by implication, in such settings as colleges and employment agencies. He pointed out that counselors must operate in circumstances that differ markedly from

37

those of psychotherapists in either clinics or private practice. Beside the time pressures caused by huge caseloads and a variety of institutional demands, counselors must cope with conflicting notions of whose agents they are. This means that many of their clients come to them reluctantly or even involuntarily. When "ideal" counseling cases do present themselves, counselors usually find it difficult or impossible to schedule regular sessions over extended periods of time. What Aubrey does not mention, however, is the mounting body of evidence, supplied by such critics as Goodman (1964), Henry (1963), Jackson (1968), and Kozol (1967), that suggests that even if it were possible it might not be desirable to adjust children to the school environment.

Beside demonstrating the inappropriateness of basing counseling practice in schools on current psychotherapy models, this line of reasoning suggests a more basic point. Models are not neutral. By definition, they define who we see as the client, what we view the nature of the problem to be, and where we will attempt to solve it, as well as when and how we carry out our attempts. In this sense, models not only shape the way in which we view the world but also at least partially determine what we see and therefore how we act in it (Hanson, 1958; Kuriloff, 1970). Thus, unlike many but not all physical and biological theories (Hanson, 1958), the models we employ themselves become *events* in the field under study, so that our mere use of them has consequences for what we are trying to achieve. If, for example, we use a Freudian framework in schools, we will not only be swamped by work and faced with many unwilling and therefore highly "resistant" "patients," but we will also communicate to our colleagues in schools that we believe emotional problems are the result of "disease entities" within individuals whose only hope of "cure" is long-term psychotherapy —or, better yet, psychoanalysis. In this way, our very *language,* as well as our actions, will have a subtle impact far beyond our efforts to help any given individual. If we are serious about our Freudian model, we will work for a vast increase in the number of counselors, a restructuring of schools to allow time for us to perform our "clinical" function, and a redefinition of ourselves as agents for our student "patients." Analogous consequences can be identified for any framework we choose to employ.

If this analysis of the inappropriateness of current models is accurate, new models are needed that are not only compatible with institutional norms and expectations, as Aubrey (1969) suggests, but that also provide ways of altering and improving them. Such models should take self-conscious advantage of their own unintended consequences as they become events in the field that we, as counselors, are trying to alter. They also should include an objective or set of objectives that relates to helping people cope with, operate effectively in, and *master* their environments. White's (1959, 1960) concept of competence represents just such an objective. The concept is relevant because it is what schools are or should be about. It is also relevant because it contains implicit methodological suggestions. It takes into account the existence and importance of an inner life, is rooted in an understanding of development, and stresses the importance of acting on the environment and receiving feedback, in the form of consequences, from the environment. Practically, this means that new models must aim to foster situations in which clients can act, experience the consequences of their actions, and have an opportunity to reflect on their experiences and their feelings about them. What are the dimensions of a framework in which these aims may be achieved? Where and how can the counselor achieve them?

## Psychological Ecology

One model holding much promise can be based on a rough analogy drawn from the science of ecology. Ecology is the study of the relationship between organisms and their environment. It carries with it the connotation that living things are interrelated and interdependent in complex ways. It describes an open system capable of self-regulation and self-revitalization within broad limits (von Bertalanffy, 1968). Changes in any one element of an ecological system usually affect all other elements in complex, indeterminate ways.

The term *psychological ecology* is broad and imprecise. It

is a heuristic metaphor for the interdependencies of people and their *human* environments. The psychological ecology cannot be totally defined from a given individual's point of view; rather, it represents the confluence of all individual life spaces within a given natural setting.

Following Rhodes (1967, 1968), we maintain as a core concept of psychological ecology the idea that a disturbed person exists because someone is disturbed by him. In this sense, he may be considered *disturbing*. The disturbance is conceptualized as existing in the transaction between the person and his external environment. "It lies as much in the complementary responses and interpretations of the observer as it does in the individual's differences" (Rhodes, 1968, p. 504). Unaccustomed differences in an individual evoke resonance in the other individuals who share the same ecological system. "Strange or unorthodox behavior, such as drug addiction, alcoholism, mental illness, delinquency, and so on, becomes the releaser of corresponding excited behavior in surrounding others. This reflexive response of the family, the class, the community, or the society can take many forms. It can be retaliatory, extrusive, avoidant, and so forth" (Rhodes, 1968, p. 497).

Anthropological findings, as well as the few recorded historical cases in which such negative reactions were not forthcoming, reveal just how shared the phenomenon of disturbance is. When Pinel unchained the supposedly violent mental patients of Bicêtre at the close of the eighteenth century, they became less violent and deranged (Dumont, 1968). Similarly, Dumont (1968) reports that his study of Geel, a Belgian village that has cared for the "possessed" without using restraints for over a millenium, revealed people we would call *schizophrenic* going about their lives like other villagers. They evinced none of the disabling, dependent *incompetence* found in our hospitalized schizophrenics. Benedict's (1934) examples, drawn from many cultures, demonstrate that Geel is not unique and that the "primitive" explanatory systems of many peoples gain for their societies a flexibility in dealing with deviant behavior that our "advanced" systems fail to provide.

When the evidence just described is combined with modern findings regarding the role of disturbed family relations in mental illness (Bateson and others, 1956; Henry, 1963) and the even more important data concerning the impact of socioeconomic deprivation on the entire spectrum of human development (Eisenberg, 1962), it is no longer possible to view mental illness as something entirely endogenous to the individual. In no way does this deny the possibility that intrapsychic, organic, or learned phenomena play a role in the problem. Rather, it means that intrapersonal explanations leave out significant aspects of the problem and by their very formulation often contribute to it—sometimes actually create it. Any attempt to understand deviant behavior without taking into account the reactive processes of society will be incomplete. It follows that any treatment model based on such a narrow view cannot be fully efficacious.

## The Heuristic Value of the New Framework

The psychoecological model calls attention to the transactional nature of emotional disturbances. In doing so it emphasizes the proposition that the observer is always deeply implicated in the events observed. This implies new strategies for intervention. Within the suggested new framework, our traditional concepts take on different meaning. All disturbances become shared problems. This is true whether they represent major social problems of society or the specific "illness" of one individual. In a real sense, the theory therefore offers us a new way of thinking, perceiving, and acting.

Before illustrating its particular relevance to emotional disturbance, the general heuristic value of psychoecological theory can be demonstrated by using it to reexamine social problems of varying magnitude and gravity. In the past few years, there has been much talk about the "black problem" or the "problem of the poor." Hersch (1968) has described it as one of the major reasons for "the explosion of discontent" that occurred among mental health professionals in the 1960s. The solution we came up with was a massive attack on the conditions that breed violence and despair: "ignorance, discrimination, slums, poverty, disease, lack of jobs," as Lyndon Johnson suggested (1968). Yet all the armies of the war on poverty—from urban renewal to the Job Corps—have failed to bring the peace we so avidly desire. The reason for the failure may be as simple as one proposed by a student I once taught: "The ghettos exist because in one way or another white society profits from them." In other words, our failure stems from the way we conceive of the problem. It will be impossible to solve as long as it remains "their" problem. An ecological perspective requires us to recognize the salience of James Baldwin's argument that there is no black or white problem in this country, only an American problem. The psychologies of black and white, oppressed and oppressor, are complementary. They cannot be understood in contrast to one another because they are functionally related and similar. Both must be understood in contrast to the psychology of free people who view each other as equals (Szasz, 1967). This means that as professionals who are interested in the mental health of black people we must begin by inventing ways to change the racial prejudice that infuses the culture (U.S. Riot Commission, 1968). And perhaps we must begin this endeavor by focusing on the subtle forms of racism that infect our own psychology (see, for example, Kamin, 1974; Mercer, 1971, 1973).

The so-called welfare problem is another example of the negative effects of the conceptions held by many important people in our society, including mental health professionals. Even with the growing interest in a guaranteed annual income, welfare recipients are still treated as the objects of charity. All the weight of the individualistic cultural tradition that stresses independence and initiative has combined to remove their self-respect. They are still viewed by a large sector of society as incompetent and unable to help themselves. "Seeing" them as "helpless," we "help" by supporting and maintaining them in their dependency through programs such as Aid to Dependent Children. As in the racial question, we objectify the problem by locating it in the "outside other."

Seen through the psychoecological frame, this position is no longer feasible. An inquiry into the nature of the relationship between welfare recipients and the welfare system reveals that the characteristics of recipients the society finds most troubling are a function of the way the system deals with them! Hess (1964) has eloquently demonstrated the parallel between the manner in which the totalitarian states go about establishing their control over people and the approach of our own welfare system. Recipients are kept entirely dependent. Any initiative on their part is systematically penalized. Decisions to purchase anything out of the ordinary must be processed through the bureaucracy. Families are kept apart under the threat of loss of support. In some places, they are subjected to spot checks and nighttime raids to make sure that no man is present and no unwarranted purchases have been made. If this analysis is substantially accurate, no effort to change welfare recipients will have a chance of success unless it includes a simultaneous attempt to alter the psychology of those in charge of the welfare system.

This country is currently facing a school dropout problem that, although a phenomenon of a different order from either the race or welfare issues, is nevertheless amenable to re-examination in terms of psychoecological theory. So far, the response of school officials has been largely geared to developing special programs to identify potential dropouts and keep them in school. These programs have been coupled with a massive advertising campaign to impress children with the notion that graduation holds the key to the material treasure troves of society. (Sprinthall and Mosher, 1969, have detailed the impact of this campaign on high school students from urban, suburban, and private schools.) All of this goes on despite the fact that the last decade has seen production of scores of serious and generally scathing critiques of the public education system. Within the psychoecological model, these critiques would not go unnoticed. It would never be enough to know a child has dropped out without also asking the question "From what?" If the schools are discovered to resemble prisons in which students pass their time in essentially meaningless activities, then attempts to get those who drop out to return may be pernicious as well as useless. In order to deal effectively under current circumstances, it becomes as important to know the atmosphere

of the school and the psychology of its staff as it is to understand the psychology of the dropout. It follows that, in the long
run, interventions designed to change the school may be much
more significant than attempts to help children adapt to its
present reality. There are similar important implications when
the psychoecological model is applied to the problem of emotional disturbance in schools. These consequences become quite
clear when the model is compared to traditional frameworks in
terms of five key dimensions.

### Psychological Ecology as an Alternative to Traditional Models

First, who receives help? The traditional response is always the disturbed person. In contrast, psychoecology's emphasis on the shared, reflexive quality of problems means that not
only disturbing individuals but also those disturbed by them
must be taken into account. Reactors as well as excitors are fit
subjects for treatment. This means that responsibility, once con-
veniently located by the traditional models in the intrapersonal
domain, will come to be located in the interpersonal or public
domain.

Of course, such a stance of interpersonal or public responsibility, taken baldly and without a realistic appreciation of
the organizational needs that are met by conventional, intrapersonal conceptions of disturbance, can subject the counselor
to enormous pressures and will often fail. The natural reaction
of many teachers to a seriously disrupting student is an attempt
to remove the "culprit." Counselors often find even overt calls
for their help are covert attempts to enlist their support for the
exclusion of disturbing children. Principals, faced with harassed,
distraught teachers, sometimes join them in attempts to use
counselors in this fashion. Under certain circumstances, the
pressures on counselors can become enormous. Those who resist
risk evoking the enmity of their fellow professionals. In order to
avoid it, counselors who refuse to act as agents for removal
must offer a viable alternative that provides relief. Such an alternative, and what makes the risk worth taking, is the opportunity to help people within the system redefine disturbance in

ways that bring methods of overcoming it within their sphere of competence. To take advantage of such opportunities, counselors must not only learn as much as they can about the particular systems in which they work. They must also become sensitive politicians—in the best sense of the word. In the case studies that follow, I have tried to illustrate concretely approaches that reflect some of these skills (for a fuller treatment of the problem of organizational pressures, and the risks and opportunities inherent in them for psychoecologically oriented professionals, see Kuriloff and Kuriloff, 1972; Kuriloff, 1975).

The argument could be made that the various modern forms of behavior modification do indeed locate the "actual" origin of an individual's problem in his or her previous history of reinforcement. Treatment then represents an effort to alter the reinforcement pattern directly (through behavioral therapy) or indirectly (through consultation with parents or teachers— Tharp and Wetzel, 1969). Sophisticated behaviorists might then suggest, perhaps correctly, that the method is really interactional, since it seeks to change children's behavior by changing the way adults reward and punish them. While this method of "smuggling" help to parents and teachers while helping them change children can be useful, the mechanistic assumptions about man and woman on which it rests are a marked contrast to the "open-systems" assumptions of ecology (Allport, 1960). In place of the behaviorists' concept of interaction, with its connotation of mechanical operations suggesting simple cause-and-effect relationships within closed systems, psychoecology substitutes the term *transaction,* to approximate more closely the complex bargaining processes that characterize the relationship between individuals and their environments (Dewey and Bently, 1960).

For these reasons, I have chosen to include behavior modification within my discussion of traditional therapy models, even though in some ways it does represent a significant departure from intrapersonal frameworks.

Second, what is the nature of the disturbance? Within the psychotherapy frame, it is either viewed as the symptom of an "illness" stemming from unconscious motivations originating in the individuals' history or as a "learned habit." Consequently, while short-term efforts to relieve suffering may be necessary at times, they can never replace "cure" through personality "restructuring" or behavior modification as the ultimate goal of treatment. From a psychoecological perspective disturbance is a symptom of incompetence, where competence is defined as the ability to solve problems so they stay solved in the best interests of all those concerned. Either the excitor does not have sufficient skills to get what he wants in an appropriate, legitimate way or the reactors have not got the ability to respond in a useful fashion. Following White (1959, 1966, 1967), the assumption here is that all people have legitimate needs to affect other people and things in their environments and that legitimate ways can be found to meet these needs (Braun and Pollock, 1970). The sense of efficacy depends on executive ego functions—such as the ability to discriminate cognitively, to delay responding, to coordinate means and ends, and to control impulses (Kroeber, 1966)—which are responsible for an individual's transactions with the environment. While the short-term goal of psychoecological practice may be the interruption of exacerbating interchanges, the long-range goal is primary prevention through the education of these functions. As they are the product of learning and are themselves developed in transactions with the environment, emotional disturbance is viewed as an educational opportunity—where education is construed broadly to include psychological development.

Third, where does treatment take place? Traditional psychotherapists remove patients from their immediate environment to the mystery of the counseling office or, if they are thought to be sufficiently disturbed, to some tertiary institution. (This may be true in some behavioral approaches.) A practice that is based on psychological ecology would always take place within *natural* settings. The new practitioners would get to know people on their own terms and in their own territory. Unlike a psychotherapist, they would work with people in full view of other members of the ecology. In this sense, their practice would truly be public—exposed to their colleagues and devoid of mystery.

Fourth, when does treatment take place? Historically, counselors employing therapy models have assumed a passive role, waiting for students to seek them out. More recently, they have begun to receive students who have become so bothersome to others that they have been sent under pain of more dire punishment. Psychoecological counselors will enter into the stream of ongoing events within a given ecological system. This will put them in a position to work with situations before the situations become so agitated that an individual is expelled or has to withdraw. But the currency of such practice will be less such dramatic crises than the natural, everyday events that provide opportunities to evoke competence and enhance positive psychological development.

Fifth, how will treatment be carried out? Of course, in the intrapersonal models it involves one-to-one or group psychotherapy or behavior modification. The sufferer always remains the focus, whether the form is pure analysis or a short-term variation. In the psychoecological model, treatment becomes education. The focus is never one to one. It is always in terms of the system or subsystems. Because all individuals within a system are interrelated and because any change in one will, to a greater or lesser extent, influence all others, a major problem of such practice is to determine where a minimum input can have the maximum effect. This suggests that practitioners must know intimately the system with which they are dealing, before they can act to alter its equilibrium. Participant observation is one role that encompasses both these aspects—a way of knowing and a way of acting.

## The Psychoecological Counselor

The psychoecological counselor enters into a given ecology as an observer-participant to observe the nature of the transactions and to participate in creating ways to alter them in positive (that is, competence-enhancing) directions. Observation includes at least four separate but interrelated processes that psychoecological counselors need to acquire if they are to maximize their knowledge of a given natural setting. In an important work on the methodology of participant observation, Bruyn (1966) has argued that in order to ensure an "adequate subjectivity"—that is, a subjectivity open to self-inspection as well as to the possibility of consensual validation—observer participants must be careful to specify the context (that is, time, place, and social and physical circumstances) of their operations as well as the positive processes (language, intimacy, and modes of consensus) through which they come to know. (An argument can be made that consensually validated subjectivity or "intersubjectivity" is the only reasonable definition of objectivity— Adams, 1962.) They must monitor the negative processes (external and internal distortion) that can invalidate what they learn. Finally, in order to make meaning out of the problematic phenomena they encounter, they must be able to bring to bear knowledge of pertinent theoretical frameworks.

To specify context, observer-participants should note the different temporal phases of data gathering as they become a part of the ecology. Not only do what they learn as newcomers and what they learn as accepted members provide important points of reference for others, but the contrast itself represents information of the most profound nature. They should also pay close attention to the manner in which the people in the ecology experience their physical environment. Again, this not only supplies a reference point for cross-validation but also provides key insights into the nature of the ecology. To ensure understanding of context, observers should be especially conscious of the ways members deal with contrasting social and physical circumstances. This will enable them to check the understanding they have developed from observations of behavior in one setting—such as a classroom—against the implications of behavior evinced in other settings—such as the gym.

To recognize positive processes, observers must focus on the ways in which they experience learning the language, especially the symbolic forms that relate to the social meanings under study. This is vital because as they assume the language of those they observe their own understanding is simultaneously altered by the languages' special ways of representing life. After observers learn to "play the dozens," what they see and understand about the transaction of black ghetto youth will be light years away from what they previously understood (Foster, 1974). To be unaware of such subtle changes in one's own perception is to give up an opportunity to grasp a basic dimension of the ecology. Finally, observers should attend to the ways people they study come to agreement on social meanings. Much evidence on this is necessary before a meaning original to the ecology can be distinguished from idiosyncratic interpretations. For example, before trying to help a teacher "control" a disrupting student, it is important to observe whether a classroom's norms reflect general school-wide norms or ones that have been specifically developed within the particular room.

In order to note negative processes, observers must stay alert for signs within themselves that they are losing their neutrality in interpreting social meanings. One way they can accomplish this is to take special note of the points of similarity and difference between their needs and interest and those of the people they are studying. Another way is for observers to make every effort to specify and describe all conflicting social roles and groups so that it will be difficult for them to ignore some "unconsciously" in favor of others. It is relatively easy, for example, to become so wrapped up in a flamboyant "liberal-conservative" struggle over school discipline procedures, that one loses sight of a potentially decisive moderate majority within the faculty. But observers also must take into account signs of distortions that appear in other individuals' interpretations of social meanings and use these to adjust their own evaluation of the data. It is important to know, for example, that one subgroup of teachers within the school views the principal's introduction of a program to provide a free, nutritious breakfast as a plot to take away their preparation time.

Finally, in order to make psychological meaning out of the problematic phenomena they encounter, observers must be fully acquainted with pertinent theoretical frameworks of developmental, counseling, and educational psychology. They should consciously attempt to relate their observation to the various frames at their disposal. This will serve the dual purpose of helping them make meaning of what they see and of opening the meaning they make to the inspection of others. Beyond this, it also may help because to be aware of one's theories is to have some measure of control over their influence. Because they recognize such application as one form of implicit participation, observers who self-consciously apply various frameworks are in the enviable position of balancing their choice between those that seem to fit best and those that produce the most social good. Clearly, this depends on the values of the counselor-observer. It is an underlying premise of my argument that social scientists cannot escape making such value judgments, because their theories always become events in the field under observation and therefore influence that field. It is a virtue of the psychoecological frame that it recognizes counselor values as important ingredients of any intervention.

*Participation.* By assuming the role of observer, psychological counselors already are implicit participants in at least two related senses. First, they have accepted a conception of emotional disturbance that causes them to perceive situations differently from traditional mental health personnel. Second, the existence of these differences alone will then cause them to act differently because they will be responding to a different reality. Consequently, in the manner of self-fulfilling prophecies, the reactions they evoke will be affected and the situation transformed in subtle, perhaps unrecognizable ways (Merton, 1957; Kuriloff, 1970). Of course, assuming their practice is consistent with their theoretical assumptions, this form of participation merges into an explicit form as soon as they begin to act in their role of practitioner. Even as they begin to act, however, part of their impact—an aspect of their participation—remains on an implicit level.

In this light, the new practitioners' influence will tend to be positive if their expectations and the assumptions on which they are based, are themselves positive—that is, if they are set in a developmental frame and are consistent with the goal of fostering competence. Just how powerful a factor this can be is demonstrated by the following example.

Dottie's behavior during the first few weeks of Head Start appeared very disturbed. Her speech was garbled and when understandable often showed her thoughts to be jumbled and replete with fears and horrible fantasies. She acted like a monster, gritting her teeth, holding her arms out like two claws, and snarling almost continually. She also hit other children, disrupted their play, and could not sit still. At times she seemed in a daze, but she became a frenzy of disorganized activity during water play, painting, meals, or when her foster mother came to pick her up. She seemed especially frightened by anything that upset her routine. When the teacher had the children dictate stories, Dottie's were filled with fantasies about eating and being eaten by others, disappearing into holes and crevices, and being consumed by animals.

To the teacher, sensitive to the emotional development of her pupils, and imbued with psychodynamic concepts, Dottie's behavior seemed "psychotic" or at least "borderline." When she discovered Dottie's background, she became all the more sure of her diagnosis. Dottie had been grossly deprived as an infant. Her early home life had been extremely traumatic. She had been very neglected and had even been bitten by rats on several occasions. The spring before she began Head Start, the Division of Child Guardianship had become aware of her situation and removed her and her brother from their home. They were both placed with Mrs. T., an older woman with a firm, kind, and loving manner.

Much to the teacher's surprise, the counseling psychologist did not seem to share her deep concern over Dottie's "symptoms." Neither did he seem to agree on the necessity of a quick referral to a clinic or special school for emotionally disturbed youngsters. Rather, he began to question her about what she had observed of Dottie's behavior. When did which kinds of behaviors occur? What were the circumstances surrounding each kind? How did other children and adults react? At first, the teacher found it difficult to respond to these questions. The coherent picture of Dottie's behavior just presented is a direct result of her efforts to satisfy the psychologist. When she had finished, they both could agree that Dottie seemed quite terrified of separation, had much difficulty with handling her own impulses, and was frightened both of these and of external dangers. The psychologist then began to wonder how Dottie could be helped to feel safe, to gratify her needs in legitimate ways, to reflect on, and eventually to bring under control her impulses.

These goals implied a competence frame (Braun and Pollock, 1970). Much later, the teacher reported that the outlook and expectation they conveyed had had a profound effect on her. Although it took her many months to begin to articulate the nature of this outlook, the fact that she recognized it as a significant alternative to her assumptions was immediately apparent. Her sense of urgency regarding the referral diminished, and she began to wonder what *she* could do. Together with the psychologist, she developed a set of specific action plans. She would reassure Dottie about her safety and her ability to come and go from school without either her or it disappearing. She would help Dottie anticipate transitions by warning her in advance, recognizing how difficult she found them, and letting her know she could count on the teacher's help. In the same manner, the teacher would reflect with Dottie on her feelings before painting time and meals, offering her help if she began to feel overwhelmed by her impulses and teaching her that she could control them. With these few inputs, coupled with the persistent friendly overtures of one child, Dottie progressed to the point where by early spring she had lost all her "psychotic" symptoms.

In Dottie's case, expectation actually worked on two levels. The teacher was able to infer from the psychologist's questions and formulation of goals his assumption that Dottie's disturbing behavior could be viewed properly as an educational matter. Second, she could not help but feel his confidence in *her* ability to help Dottie through her skills and training as a teacher. While the impact of such expectations will vary with the personalities of the individuals who experience them, they cannot be discounted as an important part of the new model. To confirm this, one need only imagine the consequences of a different set of expectations in Dottie's case. Had she been defined as psychotic and removed from the class, the message to the teacher would have been "This kind of matter is beyond your depth and the competence of your job." From this position, it would not be a radical extension to argue for the separation of the educational from the psychological or even the affective. Barring this eventuality, the teacher still would have missed the opportunity to exercise her own resourcefulness and to develop it with the support and guidance of a specialist—perhaps she even would have learned to mistrust it. In either case, in contrast to the traditional practice that tends to proscribe narrowly defined areas of expertise, kept separate from each other by closely guarded professional mystiques (Bakan, 1967), the orientation of the new practice makes it possible for all individuals within a system to maintain self-concepts that include an expanding view of their personal and professional competence.

Dottie's case illustrates how an apparently severe intrapersonal problem can be solved through psychoecological intervention. I believe that any "emotional disturbance" has the potential of being solved through it. Nevertheless, there will be times when, in the best judgment of the counselor, the costs of doing so will outweigh the benefits involved. There are some situations that are of such long standing, are so complex and so potentially time consuming that they warrant the decision to remove a student to a more suitable environment. Of course, the danger is that such judgments can all too easily shade into rationalizations for giving in to the kinds of organizational pressures I have discussed both here and elsewhere (Kuriloff, 1975). Several safeguards can protect counselors from slipping into such solutions. Removals should be advocated only under the most extreme circumstances—when children's continued presence in their classroom becomes a clear and present danger—to borrow the legal standard—to themselves, or others. When such a decision is made, it should always be cast in temporary terms. These should specify to all concerned what the individual must achieve in order to return to the regular class and provide a way for him or her to learn to do it. The counselor should seek out that placement that at once provides what the child needs and is the one closest to a normal class (a resource room within the school, for example, would be more normal than a special class run by the district, which in turn would be more normal than a residential treatment center). And, once placed, the counselor should follow the child's progress to make sure he or she is returned when the preestablished criteria are met. But the psychoecologically oriented counselor's job is not finished here. The decision to remove a child can set back the whole purpose of the approach if, in the drama of removing the excitor, the counselor neglects the reactors. The goal in such unfortunate situations is to help the class, including the teacher, develop a realistic appreciation of its own limits and prepare for the reentry of the removed student as soon as possible. This is crucial, since by working with the class on reentry the counselor implicitly reaffirms the transactional view of disturbance while explicitly working to reshape those (future) transactions in more productive ways.

The influence of counselors as psychoecologists is not, of course, limited to their implicit participation. In their own approach to their work, as well as in their advice and suggestions to others, such counselors think in terms of scientific investigation. They gather data by observing and by asking pertinent questions. Almost incidentally, they direct those people they ask to what the counselors consider important and by example teach those people their way of thinking about problems the clients considered important enough to bring to them. At the same time, the counselors are actively engaged in a self-conscious attempt to make meaning of their observations. They do this, still in the presence of people with whom they are working, by considering observed phenomena in terms of various theoretical frameworks they have at their disposal. Like good natural scientists, they must be flexible enough to recognize when their observations are problematic in terms of their conceptions so they can avoid "forcing a fit." But in order to help clients change they must also see that their clients' conceptions do not adequately explain their observations (else they would need no outside help). For instance, psychoecological counselors must be able to recognize the "dead-end" quality of Aristotelian states-and-properties explanations of behavior often proffered by psychological laymen: For example, "He isn't

working *because* he *is* lazy"; "She is sad *because* it *is* her personality"; or "He *is* just a bad apple." In the case of both their
clients' conceptions and their own, the aim of this process is to
develop an idea that organizes the problematic observations in
such a manner that they do follow automatically as a matter of
course when applied. Pierce (1931) called such ideas *retroduc-
tions* and the process *retroductive.* Formulating a retroductive
idea enables the counselors to generate testable hypotheses their
clients may use in solving their own problems (Fuller, Brown,
and Peck, 1967). The process is complete when the counselors
develop action plans or ways of testing their hypotheses. They
go through the entire process in the presence of the clients they
hope to help, seeking to involve them at every stage.

The process of hypothesis testing is sometimes quite simple, involving only a way to operationalize what is already articulate in the mind of the potential reactor(s). For example, Obi
was a Nigerian child who had just entered Head Start. Her normal separation anxiety was exacerbated by her recent arrival in
a new and strange country. It manifested itself in a vague, "out-
of-it" approach to classroom activities. When her teacher re-
marked to her that she seemed to be someplace else and asked if
something was troubling her, Obi replied: "I miss my baby sister." Told about this, the psychologist suggested to the teacher
that she allow Obi to bring her sister to school for awhile, until
she became accustomed to her new environment. This was
done, and within a week or two Obi felt comfortable enough to
begin coming to Head Start alone.

Often, however, the hypothesis does involve the creation
of a genuine minitheory that renders previously baffling observations intelligible and thus approximates a true retroduction.

Because his mother was an aide in the Head Start class
closest to home, Tom was transferred to another class. He appeared to adjust to this move with a minimal amount of difficulty. Only a week or two after his arrival, he was participating
in all the classroom activities, and although he was somewhat of
"a loner" he seemed quite capable of playing with others and
making friends. Still, one peculiar behavior worried his teacher
enough to call in the psychologist. At periodic intervals, Tom

began crawling around on the floor, barking like a dog. The teacher was mystified. She could not relate the behavior to any special circumstances or events. When she tried to discuss it with the child, he became uneasy and withdrew.

The teacher and the psychologist decided to make a point of observing Tom during the following few days. They discovered that he was not as well integrated into the classroom as the teacher originally had thought. Although he worked on all the tasks, he stayed on the periphery of the social life of the room. The "playing dog" behavior seemed to occur after intensive periods of class activity in which the adults' attention had to be focused on the group. But it also occurred at times when all the adults were occupied with individual children other than Tom. So, it appeared he needed more of the teacher's attention. But what was the barking about? Still confused, the psychologist mentioned the problem to his supervisor. His response was to ask the psychologist to consider the popular imagery associated with dogs, especially puppy dogs. The notion that Tom was playing a friendly little puppy who needed to be petted, hugged, and generally "loved up" literally snapped the rest of the picture into place for the psychologist. Perhaps Tom had been more affected by the change in classrooms than either he had let on or the staff had imagined. He had not only lost the attention of his mother but also all of his old friends. Armed with this hypothesis, the psychologist suggested to the teacher that she respond to Tom's playing a dog by saying such things as: "You look like a very friendly, sad little dog who probably misses his friends at the other school." At such times she could also offer to pet him, while explaining that he was welcome in the new class and that a home would be made for him. This seemed to work, for as Tom began to feel welcome and relaxed the barking subsided.

Of course, matters are not usually resolved so easily, even when a genuine retroduction is not involved. In this case, it is often necessary to reformulate the hypothesis, often in the light of new data or changed circumstances, and to test it with a new action plan. Also, for clarity I have chosen examples that focus primarily on individual children in transaction with their teachers. How can counselors as psychoecologists proceed when the unit under observation is an entire classroom, perhaps even in relationship to other parts of the school and community?

The entire process of observation and participation through hypothesis testing in such circumstances can be illustrated by describing a typical case drawn from the combined experiences of junior high school counselors—my supervisees—interning in the Philadelphia area.

During the second month of the fall term, Miss T., an eighth-grade English teacher in her first year of teaching, came to see the counselor. She was visibly agitated and almost on the verge of tears. She explained that one of her students, Tony, was "driving [her] crazy." He was "hostile, sullen, and impossible to manage." Matters had come to a head that morning, when she had passed out mimeographed excerpts of *The Cool World* (W. Miller, 1959), a novel about the leader of a street gang. As one student read aloud, she noticed Tony playing with a Magic Marker. "Following school policy," she asked him to please hand it to her. When he refused, she reached for it and, as he backed away, brushed against him. At this he erupted into a torrent of curses, threatening to "get" her if she touched him again. Shocked both at the threat and the language, Miss T. asked Tony to go to the disciplinary room. Now, because she was sure he was seriously "disturbed," she wanted him to receive help as well as discipline.

After comforting the teacher, the counselor spent the next few days observing the class. He noted that Tony was in constant motion. Tony appeared to be both visually and auditorily hyperalert; he was distracted by the slightest noise or motion. He spent much of his time throwing spitballs, shadow boxing, and otherwise interacting with friends. If he thought he knew an answer, he simply shouted it out, seemingly unable to restrain himself. All these actions obviously irritated the teacher.

From a psychodynamic point of view, the counselor saw Tony as seriously disturbed. His behavior indicated that he was having a very difficult time controlling his impulses. His hyperalertness, his inability to delay gratification, and his action-excitement orientation all suggested that he was substituting action for anxiety and that this mode was deeply ingrained. In short, Tony looked as if he were suffering from a classic form of character disorder—a disorder with a very poor prognosis (Rexford, 1959).

In psychoecological terms, the situation looked different. The counselor knew that in Tony's environment danger was ever present. Survival—on hazardous streets, in the midst of violent gang rivalries and against a background of disorganized family life—required the development of what Malone (1966) termed a "danger orientation." And, in fact, well over half the children beside Tony displayed similar behavior. Could they all be character disordered?

Whatever the diagnosis, the psychoecological perspective suggests that such behavior is bound to have consequences for all members of the setting. As Miss T. tried to cope with it, her behavior began to mirror her pupils'. Even at the best of times, only a portion of the children really paid attention. Quite naturally, the teacher geared her lesson to this group. Because the others regularly interrupted, a self-reinforcing cycle was created in which Miss T. taught more and more to the attentive pupils, thereby evoking more and more attention-getting behavior from the "disrupters." Besides leaving her feeling defeated, frustrated, and exhausted, this daily escalation of confusion disturbed neighboring teachers. These other teachers both complained and offered advice on how Miss T. could "tighten up" by thoroughly structuring each class hour, vigorously enforcing school rules, and immediately picking up any violations.

It was natural in this situation that the Magic Marker incident would become the focus of all Miss T.'s feelings of incompetence. As soon as she noticed Tony with the Magic Marker, she felt a conflict. On the one hand, she had heard her colleagues telling her to enforce the rules "for the good of everyone" and therefore felt ashamed of her inability to handle her class. On the other hand, she felt put upon by the requirement to confiscate the marker and resentful of the explicit demand it made on her to play policeman—especially against her better judgment. What tipped the scale was her previous bad experience with Tony.

If Miss T. felt pressured, put upon, and frustrated in the context of the school, it made sense that Tony—to say nothing of the other students—might feel similarly. Perhaps Tony had the same feelings of being unable to control his life in school. Maybe both the teacher and the child had experienced similar feelings of shame in the situation.

Miss T. remembered that when she first asked Tony for the marker, he had refused, claiming vehemently that it did not belong to him. The significance of the Magic Marker now became apparent. The single most important psychoecological variable in the life of Philadelphia school children is the omnipresent street gang. Some time ago, gang members had begun building their reputations by writing their names on every available public surface in the city. Presumably, Tony was holding the marker for a fellow gang member. To have turned it over to the teacher would have violated the gang code. To have failed to retaliate when the teacher touched him would have been a further violation. Backed into a corner in front of his peers, Tony apparently had seen verbal counterattack and intransigence as the only ways to preserve his integrity.

What had seemed a simple intrapsychic problem now appeared complex indeed—but amenable to a new kind of intervention. The counselor first helped Miss T. defuse the immediate situation with Tony. This was accomplished in a short talk after school in which she explored the incident with him and discussed how both of them had become trapped as soon as he violated a school rule everyone expected her to enforce.

The counselor next helped Miss T. overcome her more general teaching problems, which, in large measure, stemmed from erroneous assumptions she held. Much of her sense of daily success was based on whether or not her pupils seemed to be paying attention. Because she assumed that if the subject matter were good enough the students would be interested, she blamed herself every time they did not pay attention; after all, she had chosen the material. The counselor helped her see how absurd it was to expect her students to pay attention all the time, especially when some could not read, many were preoccupied, and most felt unsafe.

Miss T. realized that if her students did not have to pay

attention all the time they needed appropriate ways to fade in and out. This meant making her assumptions and expectations explicit. If she wanted to make the class relevant to her students, she had to begin where they were. This meant creating an atmosphere in which it was possible to tune into their private agendas. All of these ideas involved setting clear, sensible limits. These limits went a long way toward creating a climate of psychological safety in the classroom. As the children felt more controlled and safe, they relaxed and quieted down. In turn, the teacher was able to focus on what really mattered to them.

Miss T. recognized the irony of her experience with Tony. She saw how gang codes had contributed to a breakdown of a discussion about a book chosen for its supposedly relevant treatment of gangs. She invited the counselor to lead a discussion about the incident. After analyzing with the class the nature of the impasse between the teacher and Tony, the counselor suggested they role play the situation to see if they could discover better ways to handle it. This proved as exciting as it was difficult. It also engendered a long, involved discussion about the use of markers to establish a "rep," the problem of maintaining it, and the intricacies of living within the gang code.

The following day Miss T. expanded on the discussion of gang codes by asking the students to compare their experiences with gang codes to those of the characters in *The Cool World*. Together they identified a number of problem areas that particularly concerned them. With the help of the counselor, Miss T. developed a curriculum around those areas. Consisting of readings from black literature, role playing, group fantasizing, and other affective techniques (Borton, 1970), the curriculum proved highly effective and greatly reduced the problems in the class—results consistent with those produced in other Philadelphia classrooms in which similar techniques have been employed (Newberg, Borton, and Gollub, 1971). This dampened the shock waves the class had been sending into surrounding classes. The criticism of Miss T. abated, her staff relations improved, and she grew more relaxed. The class, in turn, became more businesslike, enjoyable, and engaging.

## Conclusion

The psychoecological model is not limited to work in schools. It provides a powerful conceptual framework for mental health interventions in all institutions at all organizational levels. In college counseling, for example, an epidemic of exam anxiety can often be treated effectively by counselors' helping professors modify their unrealistic expectations. In employment counseling, a well-educated, "paranoid" blind person may show dramatic improvement once an employer is helped to overcome his prejudice.

It should be fairly obvious from these examples that the psychoecological model greatly alters the nature of counseling practice. Disturbance is not viewed as the property of an individual who is designated a "client" but as a symptom of incompetence. It indicates that people within a given setting do not have sufficient skills to get what they want from each other in legitimate ways. Because disturbance has a ripple effect, it represents an opportunity to promote change throughout the ecology.

In order to use disturbance as an opportunity, counselors as psychoecologists go about their work in the most open fashion possible. By engaging those who must carry out their hypotheses in a mutual reasoning process, counselors teach them—by example—a new way of thinking about problems that clients think are important enough to bring to them. If the action tests do not work out, counselors must be willing to develop new hypotheses. The whole approach requires their readiness to put themselves on the line by committing themselves to a tentative position.

Intervention of this kind calls for a skillful exercise of judgment in action. Unlike the work of counselors using traditional models, the work of counselors employing a psychoecological frame is immediately exposed to evaluation by other members of the ecology. The work cannot remain mysterious and esoteric. But the vulnerability this creates also brings with it a potentially substantial benefit. If the counselors' methods prove useful, the people with whom they work—children, teachers, parents, administrators—will be tempted to learn them. In fact, counselors will be eager that they do. This is what Miller (1969) meant when he advocated giving psychology away to the public. There might be no better way to multiply counselors' overall effect.

# 4

# The New Activist Counselor

## Edward Paul Dworkin

### The Activist Counselor Revisited

Over six years have passed since the publication of "The Activist Counselor" (Dworkin and Dworkin, 1971). That article, and the special issue of the *Personnel and Guidance Journal* on "Counseling and the Social Revolution" (1971) in which it appeared, represented the end of an era of social activism that characterized the 1960s. The Vietnam disaster brought to the surface many dysfunctional and repressive forces in our society that were reflected in the very institutions established to protect and care for the individual citizen. Counselors were charged with taking an active role in changing institutions, particularly their own work settings, and were asked to be more responsive to human needs. Suggested methods for doing this included social action and confrontation. These methods were highly political and visible and were guaranteed to be met with acute resistance. Counselors, counselor educators, and other caregivers resented accusations that they and the systems they represented were irrelevant and doing harm to the very persons they were trying to help. In spite of this active resistance, the activist strategies and tactics that characterized the 1960s served a very useful function in raising individual and institutional levels of consciousness and in bringing about change.

The process of helping caregivers and caregiving systems to be responsive to the publics they serve is ongoing and needs continual prodding, but it is now very clear that relevant change, which has always been the overt goal of social action, must also be brought about by working inside and with caregiving systems, as well as by working outside and against these systems. Outside social action change agents help make issues political, visible, controversial, and relevant. They often stop here, however, for once so identified a social activist change agent would be denied access into the very system he or she wishes to change.

When system pain is severe enough—which might be brought into awareness by outside forces—the time is ripe for a politically neutral and acknowledged professional change agent to help that system to reform itself from within. It is now known that changes identified and brought about by persons working within systems tend to be more stable and are often met with less resistance than changes forced on systems by outside forces. We desperately need trained professionals today who are not only skilled at bringing crises to awareness but who also can make system entry as acknowledged change agents and help these systems make appropriate modifications from within. This emerging type of change agent represents an integration of counseling-clinical, organizational, and community psychology and of community organization and other social work areas. Mental health clinicians who have moved in this direction have usually assumed the additional title of *mental health consultant.*

Even though the counseling literature is replete with alternative roles for counselors, a sound rationale exists for considering the counselor as an agent of change through mental health consultation to caregiving systems and individuals. It has always been very evident that counselors and other mental health professionals (clinical psychologists, social workers, psychiatric nurses, and psychiatrists) cannot come close to meeting the mental health needs of our country. Even if one could wave a magic wand and flood the market with excellent therapists, a vast majority of the potential client population would not seek help from them at this time. As was documented over fifteen years ago, most persons experiencing mental health problems would seek help of other significant caregivers: clergy, physicians, police, friends, and family (Gurin, Veroff, and Feld, 1960).

If counselors and other mental health professionals possess expertise, obtained through years of accumulated knowledge and training, then it certainly makes sense for them to share this expertise with those persons and systems who work with the vast majority of persons experiencing mental health problems. Primary caregivers such as clergy and police are in very strategic positions to intervene early in crises to help persons experiencing emotional pain and unclear thinking to effectively resolve these crises and thereby to help these persons to develop skills for resolving future crises more appropriately. School personnel and clergy are in key positions to provide anticipatory guidance regarding developmental crisis points in people's lives, through the curriculum and premarital counseling, respectively. It is this rationale that has given rise to the relatively recent emphasis on consultation and education as one of the required components for federally funded comprehensive community mental health centers.

The concept just presented is very threatening for many counselors and other mental health professionals, for it means taking the mystique and magic out of therapy, leaving the sanctity and safety of the office, and sharing acquired skills with others. This also mandates that counselors and other mental health professionals acquire new skills for delivering mental health programs to caregiving and other community systems. Let us suppose that a competent mental health professional works through his or her fear of and resistance toward sharing skills and expertise with other primary caregiving individuals and systems. Even if motivated to take on this new role, he or she would now be faced with new obstacles as he or she attempts to identify systems in which to intervene, make entry, and then plan, deliver, and evaluate mental health programs. The counselor-client relationship changes to the consultant-consultee relationship, which is just not analogous to the individual, family, or group therapy client system. This requires additional skill acquisition, and counselors and other mental health professionals will have to undergo additional training should they choose to move in this direction. The integration of community, organizational, and counseling and clinical psychology is now taking place in some training programs, but these programs did not exist for most mental health professionals who graduated prior to 1970.

This chapter will focus on the role of the counselor as a mental health consultant and change agent. First I will present a framework for doing consultation and change agentry with community caregiving systems and individuals. Then I will illustrate this framework by describing my work at a midwestern community mental health center, which involved the initiation of a consultation program, the development of consultation teams for delivering programs to community caregivers, and a description of one comprehensive consultation program that was delivered to three clergy groups in the county that this center served.

## Framework for Changing Systems

It is important to identify an integrated conceptual framework for changing systems through mental health consultation. Without a conceptual framework, the consultant-change agent may wander haphazardly around inside a system without having the desired impact. A review of the consultation literature makes it possible to identify four basic models of consultation (Dworkin and Dworkin, 1975). These consultation models are consultee centered, group process, social action, and ecological, exemplified by Caplan (1970), Lippitt (1959, 1969, 1971), Lippitt and Jung (1966), Lippitt, Watson, and Westley (1958), Alinsky (1970, 1972), and Kelly (1966, 1968, 1969, 1970a, 1970b). The process of consultation as identified in each of these four models is described along the following dimensions: definitions of consultation, self-perceptions of the consultant, target populations in which to intervene, factors that motivate client systems to change, strategies for making system entry, methods for conducting system diagnoses, goals of the consultation process, methods and techniques for bringing about change in the client system, how and when the consultant terminates involvement with a client system, and evaluation of the consultation effort. Table 1 presents a brief description of each of these dimensions for the four consultation models.

Based on an integration of my personal experience in doing consultation with many community caregiving systems and key concepts from the four consultation models, the following basic components of the consultation process have emerged as crucial: self-perceptions of the consultant, target populations, system entry, legitimization of the consultant and consultation process, expectations of the consultation relationship, consultant contract, use of internal consultants, diagnostic process, types of consultant interventions, power issues, termination, and evaluation of the consultation effort.

*Self-Perceptions of the Consultant.* The consultant's self-perceptions must include those of expert healer, idea person, facilitator, resource generator, social engineer, researcher, and organizer. To be effective, the consultant must relate to the client system from a variety of perspectives: as a resource generator who knows where and how to link resources, as an expert who offers solutions and imparts knowledge, and as a facilitator who can mobilize internal forces. The consultant should be aware of his or her limitations in each of these roles and be prepared to move in and out of them as the situation dictates. Most important, the consultant must continually be aware that his or her overall mission as a mental health advocate is the reduction and prevention of the incidence of new cases of mental dysfunctioning, the reduction of the duration (prevalence) of emotional impairment, and the reduction of the residue defect resulting from mental impairment. If consultants cannot relate their role as mental health professionals to the long-term positive impact on mental health prevention and promotion, then they should

**Table 1. The Consultation Process: Four Models.**

| Dimensions | Consultee Centered | Group Process | Social Action | Ecological |
|---|---|---|---|---|
| Definition of Consultation | Process of interaction between two professionals: consultant and consultee | Voluntary relationship between a helper and a help-needing system | Relationship between a community and indigenous community leaders | Relationship between a professional team and an eco-system |
| Self-Perception of the Consultant | Professional Expert Model Resource | Resource Model Facilitator Participant-Observer | Community Organizer Strategist | Researcher Planner Team member |
| Target Population | Professional caregivers | Social system or subsystem | Indigenous community leaders | Ecosystems (interrelated systems and subsystems) |
| Motivation of the Client System | Anxiety Conflict Crisis | Organizational problem: internal-external pressure "Images of potentiality" | Unmet basic human needs | Crises initiated by maladaptation or malfunction of a social system |
| Entry | Sanctioned, invited short or long term | Invited or self-initiated short or long term | Invited or uninvited long term | Invited long term |
| Diagnoses | Interview Observation Data analysis Clinical intuition | Observation Group confrontation Survey research | Informal participant-observation Personal associations | Naturalistic observation Survey research |

| | | | | |
|---|---|---|---|---|
| Overall Goals (Mission) | Increased skills Understanding Knowledge Objectivity Mastery of feelings Crisis resolution | Organizational change Mobilization of creative resources Internal consultants | Transfer of power base Fulfillment of basic human needs | Awareness of system functioning Increased coping and adaptive mechanisms |
| Techniques | Advising Teaching Skill development Theme interference reduction | Role playing Sensitivity training Deviation conference Brainstorming | Community meetings Promotion of social conflict | Research Teaching Program planning |
| Termination | Resolution of crisis | Established internal consultants Improved organizational functioning | Formation of "Peoples Organization" Appropriate strategies and tactics | Development of adaptive system-wide structures |
| Evaluation | Consultant's clinical judgment and expressed satisfaction by consultee | Collaborative subjective feedback and objective data | Subjectively determined by organizer and indigenous leaders | Formal and informal assessment procedures |

question their involvement in the consultation change process effort.

   *Target Populations.* Target populations in which the consultant-change agent can intervene consist of individuals, subsystems, systems, and ecosystems (interrelated systems and subsystems). The broad array of major caregiving systems in which the consultant can intervene includes:

1. Clergy (denominational, interdenominational, lay groups).
2. Law enforcement agencies (city, county, state, federal police).
3. Legal agencies (courts—probate, juvenile, circuit, district, federal, including judges, court referees, and probation officers; and lawyers—public defenders, prosecutors, legal aid clinics, and private practitioners).
4. Educational systems (preschool, public private k-12, community colleges, trade and technical schools, and colleges and universities).
5. Social service agencies (departments of social services, Social Security, Office of Economic Opportunity, Department of Vocational Rehabilitation, YWCA, YMCA, agricultural extension agencies).
6. Mental health systems (public and private clinics, practitioners).
7. Allied health systems (public health—especially nurses, hospitals, nursing homes, physicians, dentists).
8. Business and industry (untold opportunities here).
9. Indigenous groups (morticians, beauticians, bartenders).
10. Citizen and volunteer groups (senior citizens, Big Brothers and Sisters, Lions Clubs, service-oriented fraternities and sororities; parent-teacher organizations).

   The nature of the target population the consultant selects to change determines the goals, methods, and types of outcomes he or she can most likely obtain. Table 2, taken from Nagler and Cooper (1969) and modified by myself, presents possible goals, methods (internal and external), preventive potential, and outcomes for different client systems: individual client,

Table 2. An Intervention Model for Community Psychologists.

| Level | Target | Goal | Locus | | Preventive Potential | System Outcome |
| | | | Intramural Means | Extramural Means | | |
|---|---|---|---|---|---|---|
| I | Client or Patient | Equilibrium and/or behavior change | Client-focused clinical service | Case-centered consultation | Tertiary | Maintenance |
| II | Community Caretaker | Functioning efficiency | Case conferences with community involvement | Educational consultation and in-service training | Secondary | Modification |
| III | Social System | Institutional change | Program delivery management | Program and/or administrative consultation | Primary | Transformation |
| IV | Ecosystem | Linkage of community and institutional resources | Community/interagency coordination | Organizational and community consultation | Primary | Transformation |

Source: Nagler and Cooper (1969).

community caretaker, social system, and ecosystem (interrelation of the community and a network of social systems).

*System Entry (Invited or Uninvited).* How, when, and where does the consultant make initial entry into a client system? Should entry be invited or uninvited? Uninvited entry must be sanctioned (invited) by appropriate parties at some point early in the consultation process, or the consultant risks being asked to leave prematurely without having made the desired impact. If initial entry is invited, the consultant needs to know about: the person(s) who invited him or her (what roles they play in the client system); why they approached or selected him or her and/or others; how they and others perceive the problem and needs in the client system (acute crisis, chronic crisis, preventive, no problem); and ideas about how they might utilize the consultant. Based on answers to these questions, the consultant can decide to pursue entry conditionally or unconditionally or can decide not to accept the offer.

If consultants want to have an impact on systems, they will often have to make uninvited initial entry because a majority of the systems they want to change either are unaware of or do not sanction the use of external mental health consultants or, if they utilize consultants, want to bring them in from outside their geographical area. It is generally known that a consultant's credibility tends to be inversely related to the proximity of his or her home base, that is, the closer the geographical area where the consultant works in relation to the client system, the less his or her credibility with that client system. An important factor that works against the invited initial entry of a publicly employed mental health consultant with many help-giving systems is a consultant's identification with a public caregiving system that competes for limited funds and status with these same systems. Persons employed by other community agencies might also view the home base of the consultant as having goals that are incompatible with their goals.

Uninvited entry can be challenging and exciting, similar to a chess game where key variables are identified, a strategy and tactics are planned, and calculated moves are made. Updated files on important potential client systems will facilitate the selection and entry process. In these files can be placed news releases and literature from and/or about these systems, a record of prior contacts with them, and input from colleagues and significant others who have information about these systems. When planning uninvited initial entry, current information should be obtained about the target system from knowledgeable persons inside and outside the system regarding how key persons at various organizational levels within the targeted system (such as policy makers, managers, supervisors, and workers) view problems and needs. After scouting the system, a planning meeting with colleagues should be held, at which an entry strategy and tactics are developed, including which levels of the system to enter, whether to use direct or indirect entry, and whether to wait for an acute crisis, to bring one into awareness, or to move directly, with a well-thought-out rationale that will "hook" them into a system that is not undergoing and/or acknowledging pain.

*Legitimization of the Consultant and Consultation Process.* Who has sanctioned or legitimized the consultant (top management, policy board, program heads, supervisors, or union leaders)? Knowing where and how to obtain sanction at all appropriate levels is an important aspect of the consultation process. Mistakes in this sensitive area have accounted for a large percentage of premature terminations. I worked for more than one year with a police department, from the chief of police to officers on the beat, to obtain sanction for doing consultation, and even after that had to continue to maintain legitimacy throughout the consultation process. On another occasion, not obtaining the sanction from the head of a social service system led to a long-term failure with a program chief in that agency who very much wanted to change his service delivery program.

*Expectations of the Consultation Relationship.* Both the consultant and the client system will have expectations—they may expect the consultant to solve problems, treat cases, educate agency staff, help in future planning, and make policy more acceptable to agency staff, for example. Through experience, consultants will learn to identify and to explore their own expectations of the consultation process as well as those of the client system. Hidden and/or unclear expectations that are not identified and dealt with appropriately early in the consultation relationship may surface at a later time and have negative consequences. In an early consultation experience I had with a junior high school, the principal said he wanted teachers to develop better human relation skills. This seemed like a very worthwhile objective, for there had been some recent racial incidents in that school. Although the principal sounded sincere in his request, one could discern another subtle underlying objective: that problem teachers would be identified for further undefined action. In a diplomatic and professional manner, he was told that it would not be wise to identify individual teachers who might be racially biased, for this would undermine the consultation effort. Although he agreed, his investment level quickly diminished.

The consultant needs to be aware of grandiose and utopian expectations on his or her own part as well as on the part of the client system. Goals such as "at the end of six months staff supervisors will have solved all major issues and will relate to one another as a happy family" most likely cannot be achieved. The consultant needs to communicate that small changes in behavior should be considered indicators of success and that the client system should not expect large changes overnight. Consultants may initially select a very simple problem they know the client system can solve and let the clients experience the effects of having been successful. If they have made improvement, they might be cautioned to expect some slippage, since early behaviors that have been learned over a period of time have a tendency to reestablish themselves, no matter how dysfunctional and painful they have been.

*Consultant Contract.* It is very important for the consultant to have a clearly stated contract that covers definition of terms; statement of objectives in simple, measureable terms; methods and timetable for meeting these objectives; roles and areas of responsibility that all parties will take; renegotiation clauses; assessment procedures; and payment for services. A written letter of understanding outlining these points can be very useful. Consultants must be careful not to contract for failure by committing themselves to something they cannot deliver.

*Internal Consultants.* Within the client system, who is responsible for all phases of the consultation process? Without a sanctioned inside contact person, the likelihood of resistance to change will be increased, because of the consultant's being perceived as an outsider. Internal consultants are essential for an external consultant to make appropriate lasting interventions. It makes sense for the consultant to have a major role in selecting an internal consultant and to work closely with him or her during the initial phases of the consultation process. The intensity of the external consultant's involvement with the internal consultant can be decreased as the internal consultant develops expertise and sanction to carry on the consultation and change effort.

*Diagnostic Process.* What system and individual variables should the consultant investigate as part of the diagnostic process? Diagnosis is an ongoing process in which the consultee should be highly involved. As members of the client system gain awareness of the various forces that impinge on their system, they are more likely to channel internal resources to make desired changes. A useful diagnostic model for gaining awareness involves the identification of the control dimensions by which important system variables can be defined and described. Important system variables that consultants should understand include the overall mission of the system, rules by which the system operates, roles that members in the system take, and the relationship of the system to the other systems and greater community. The four control dimensions by which each of the system variables can be defined and described are *ascribed* (written and legally binding understandings, agreements, contracts, and policies), *attributed* (what others outside the system perceive about the system), *assumed* (what persons within the system think about various system dimensions), and *actual* the consultant's and other objective viewers' perceptions of various system dimensions). Table 3 shows how these system dimensions and the control dimensions interrelate.

Behaviors that tend to maintain problems and how indi-

**Table 3. System Awareness.**

*Control Dimensions*

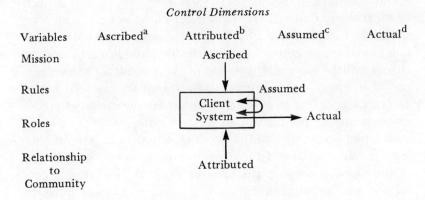

| Variables | Ascribed[a] | Attributed[b] | Assumed[c] | Actual[d] |
|---|---|---|---|---|
| Mission | | Ascribed | | |
| Rules | | | Assumed | |
| Roles | | | | Actual |
| Relationship to Community | | Attributed | | |

[a]*Ascribed:* Written legally binding understanding, agreements, contracts, policies, and so on regarding the variables.
[b]*Attributed:* Community's perception of the variables.
[c]*Assumed:* Individual consultee's perceptions of the variables.
[d]*Actual:* Consultant's perceptions of the variables.

*Source:* Prepared by Edward Dworkin and Donald Klein for Montgomery Health Department Mental Health Consultation Workshop, Rockville, Maryland (December 1975).

viduals and subgroups within the system look at system problems should be identified. The perceptions and behaviors of individuals that stop effective problem resolution can be classified into four areas: (1) denial that a problem exists when one or more problems actually are present; for example, a judge may continue to send juveniles to a detention home that is extremely contratherapeutic; (2) deemphasis of the intensity of the problem; for example, a police chief may conclude that inmates are just a little anxious and that he must be firm, when in reality the jail situation has reached an explosive stage that necessitates immediate multiple interventions; (3) denial of the solvability of the problem; for example, a majority of school personnel in a fairly conservative system may think that nothing will change in that system no matter what they do; and (4) denial of the self and/or others; for example, staff in a social service agency may think they are powerless to change a very dysfunctional system in even small ways (A. Schiff and J. Schiff, 1971).

*Consultant Interventions.* What techniques, skills, and methods should the consultant employ to most effectively and efficiently meet the contracted goals of the client system? The consultant has a broad array of techniques and methods at his or her disposal, including advising, teaching, problem solving, role modeling, group process, skill development, crisis resolution, advocacy, organizing, and survey research. The selection of consultation interventions should be based on prior training, experience, and expertise; personal style; system variables, as outlined in the contractual agreement; and outcomes of the ongoing diagnostic process. It makes little sense to use an individually oriented methodology when working with large groups or complex social systems. Conversely, it would be inappropriate to use survey research or group process techniques when working with individual consultees.

Although clinical training and therapy skills might help in diagnosing some problems in a client system, they are most often inappropriate for a mental health consultant to use directly. In many situations, a consultee attempts to bring up personal problems in the presence of a consultant, but care should be taken not to become a pseudotherapist with the consultee, because this will usually produce disastrous consequences for the consultant-consultee relationship.

*Internal Power Issues.* How will the balance of power within the client system be changed as a result of the consultation process? How can perceived lines of authority be reestablished or realigned in a functional way that will ensure the stability of the consultant's intervention? Change is initially perceived as threatening by most persons, and there is a strong tendency to return to habitual ways of behaving no matter how dysfunctional these prior behaviors have been. In dealing with power issues, the consultant might first assess the formal and informal organizational structure to determine who has authority and/or power over what and whom (accomplished in part during the initial diagnostic process). Then he or she might look

at personality dimensions relating to power and control issues
for those persons who might be most affected by the change
and/or who have the most direct influence on the change
process. During a confidential planning session, attended by the
internal consultants and the consultant, information should be
examined and strategy and tactics planned for working with key
persons for the purpose of stabilizing them and/or winning
them over as advocates of the change process. The process
should take place rather early in the consultation endeavor, in
order to maximize impact.

   *Termination.* When and how does the consultant terminate? Termination should be built into the initial phases of the
consultation process and discussed in the contractual agreement. As the consultant helps to sanction, train, and utilize
internal consultants during all phases of the consultation
process, his or her major involvement diminishes when the
client system begins to incorporate and mobilize its own internal forces for productive problem resolution. Consultants
should not terminate abruptly but should allow for a gradual
phasing out over a period of time (once a week, initially, to
every other week, to monthly, and so on). Follow-up and the
opportunity to return if requested should be built into the
initial contract. Just as individuals are encouraged to have periodic medical physicals and to see physicians in times of illness,
client systems should be encouraged to use the consultant in
this way. Ending sessions, which are very important, offer members within the client system the opportunity to give and to
receive feedback about all phases of the consultation process.
These sessions also give members an opportunity to go through
the grieving process attendant on the separation and loss of the
consultant.

   *Evaluation of the Consultation Effort.* How does the consultant and others evaluate the impact of the consultation
process? Evaluation can be conceptualized as an ongoing
process that begins prior to entry and continues after the consultant terminates. It is the process of identifying, collecting,
organizing, and disseminating information so that sound decisions can be made about what to do at every phase of the con-

sultation process (Dworkin and Walz, 1971). This does not mean that evaluation has to be a costly and an overly time-consuming process. If all members of a client system are involved in identifying, gathering, organizing, and disseminating that information with which they are familiar and have a vested interest, this becomes a significant aspect of the change process in and of itself. It helps the consultees to gain an awareness of the factors inhibiting and fostering change. It makes them active participants of the change process rather than passive recipients of other people's efforts. Evaluation should include some combination of formal methods (use of valid instruments and interviewing techniques by qualified evaluators) and informal techniques (periodic meetings where basic information is made available through existing records, and ideas shared).

## Changing Systems: Two Years in the Life of a Mental Health Consultant

So far, I have presented a rationale for the counselor as a mental health consultant and change agent and a framework for doing consultation-change agentry with community systems and individuals. Now I will illustrate the role of the mental health consultant and change agent by focusing on my own work in developing and delivering consultation programs.

*Initial Planning.* I arrived at my job at the Community Mental Health Center (referred to hereafter as the center) in September 1972, freshly graduated from a postdoctoral program and full of energy and motivation to leave my mark on the community that the center served. My only full-time work experience prior to this had been as a visiting assistant professor and director of the Counseling Laboratory, School of Education, University of Michigan. I had developed outreach programs for students with several school systems and had consulted with a local junior high school for one year, but my consultation experience with community caregiving systems had been limited.

I changed the title of my position from *Director of Consultation and Education* to *Director of Community Services,* since I thought that the former title might be perceived as threatening by many caregiving systems. The first several months on my job were spent learning about the center and the community, and the track record of the center's relationship with the community and community caregiving systems. This period was spent meeting persons from many community caregiving systems. My objectives for this period were to learn firsthand about the organization and function of major systems in the community, how they viewed the center, what they perceived as the most pressing mental health needs of the community and the populations they served, and how the center might best meet their needs. As I was new to the center and community and had the title of *Doctor,* I had little trouble in getting my foot in the door during this honeymoon period.

This experience was very educational. I discovered that our community was conservative and that there was some apprehension and overt hostility toward the center. Most important, however, a majority of the community systems I visited said they needed the support of the center. For example, the director of juvenile services complained that the center did not enforce the dictates of the court when doing therapy with juveniles. However, the court depended on the center to conduct psychosocial evaluations on many youth prior to deciding an appropriate court action. The director of juvenile services was custody oriented, while we were treatment oriented. I made a mental note that a major objective for our center's involvement with this system was to help the system move toward a more treatment-oriented model.

Based on the initial community diagnosis, a list of major community caregiving systems was developed, and for each system a rough organizational chart was prepared (if no existing one was available). Major concerns that systems expressed regarding mental health and our center were identified, and ideas were developed about how entry could be made with these systems. This was an exciting period, as most systems were receptive to me and to the idea of establishing better linkages with us. I knew almost immediately that the potential for having an impact on many caregiving systems existed and, equally important, that my work was going to be fun.

*Building a Consultation Team.* I was a staff of one in the center's consultation program and could not possibly have the desired impact unless the expertise of other center staff was utilized. I was fortunate to have many colleagues who, although initially scared and/or not interested in work that was not clinically oriented, became interested, motivated, and involved in all our consultation projects. But this did not just happen overnight; it was a planned intervention that took place gradually.

The first stage in the staff recruitment process involved obtaining the trust and confidence of center staff regarding my expertise as a consultant and clinician and as a caring person who would not take advantage of them. It was difficult for me not to come on too strong and to invade their space, for my own motivation and zeal sometimes stop me from exercising sound judgment about the time it might take others to reach the same place where I am functioning. As most of the center's staff were operating under the out-patient and drug programs, it was important to obtain the sanction and active support of the directors of these programs. The director of out-patient services and I related very positively with one another from the outset. Although he did not want to divert too many staff hours from direct clinical service, he was open to having all interested staff devote a portion of their time to consultation activities. My offer to spend a one-day equivalent doing direct treatment strengthened my position.

Unfortunately, the director of the drug program was suspicious of me from the beginning, and only after he had left for another position did I begin to make headway with staff in this program. The learnings I gleaned from my efforts to make entry with the drug program are worth discussing. Our drug program employed many paraprofessionals who identified with the youth culture and counterculture they were serving. They were suspicious of professionals, who they thought wanted to control them. They also thought that the more they were identified with the total center the more difficult it would be to make inroads with youth. Drug program personnel thought it was in their best interest to be perceived as antiestablishment. Yet, they also wanted to make entry with schools and other so-called straight community systems and therefore needed to be identified with the center. This self-made dilemma consumed substantial time and energy and detracted from the impact they could have had with key community systems. Only after another drug program director was hired, who thought that it was in the program's best interest to be identified with the center and to still demonstrate a caring attitude toward youth, did we begin to develop some excellent joint programs for police, schools, and the courts. Prior to this, however, most of the center's consultation programs were delivered by out-patient staff.

The second overlapping stage in the staff recruitment process involved the identification of staff who were interested in doing consultation with specific systems. Interested staff selected a variety of systems in which to intervene, including educational, clergy, police, courts, public health, social services, and business and industry. Once center staff had made a commitment to devote a proportion of their time to consultation activities and had received appropriate in-house sanction for this, the next stage involved skill development. This was a delicate task that had to be handled in a nonthreatening manner. We set up consultation teams that were identified with a particular target group: clergy consultation team, law enforcement consultation team, school consultation team, and so on. Each team had between three and seven members, and met periodically to plan strategies and to give and receive feedback regarding the consultation process. In addition to maintaining involvement, these teams were an excellent mechanism for informal training and supervision.

*Delivering Consultation Programs.* During my two-year tenure at the center, the consultation teams delivered an impressive array of programs to many community caregiving systems, including a few programs involving interagency coordination and cooperation. Table 4 presents the major systems in which our center intervened, including a brief statement of objectives and methods for each system.

Of the many systems in which our center intervened, one that was most successful, valuable, and personally enjoyable was the clergy. Our multifaceted interventions with the clergy sys-

Table 4. Delivering Consultation Programs.

I. *Clergy*

Objective 1: Clergy increase the quality and quantity of counseling services to their parishioners.

Methods: Counseling skill development and case consultation.

Objective 2: Clergy deliver mental health promotion and prevention programs to their congregations.

Methods: Jointly led mental health primary prevention groups and consultation.

II. *Police*

Objective 1: Police demonstrate effective crisis intervention skills.

Methods: Crisis intervention training.

Objective 2: The mental health center and sheriff's department set up a crisis intervention unit.

Methods: Program consultation.

III. *Courts*

Objective 1: Juvenile and adult probation workers increase diagnostic, referral, and counseling skills.

Methods: Counseling skill development, case consultation, jointly led therapy groups.

Objective 2: Referrals to the center from the probate court are increased, thereby reducing the number of institutional commitments from the court.

Methods: Program consultation.

Objective 3: Judges relate more closely with the center regarding pretrial evaluations and posttrial treatment.

Methods: Educational programs and program consultation.

IV. *Schools*

Objective 1: The center and the intermediate school district (ISD) increase communication and coordination of mental health services.

Methods: Center liaisons, case consultation, collaborative service delivery.

Objective 2: Preschool, elementary, and secondary school teachers increase communication and classroom management skills.

Methods: ISD and center staff offer teachers communication training.

Objective 3: An experimental psychology and mental health curriculum is implemented in one elementary and one secondary school.

Methods: The school consultation team (comprised of staff from the center and the ISD) helps local school personnel to identify, develop, and implement the psychological curriculum.

Objective 4: Parents of students increase their understanding of mental health and develop more effective communication skills with their children.

Methods: Educational programs are delivered to parent-teacher organizations by the school consultation team.

*(continued on next page)*

**Table 4 (Continued)**

---

V. *Social Services (DSS, DVR, SS, OEO, and others)*[a]

Objective 1: The center and social service agencies increase communication and coordination of services.

Methods: Educational programs, program consultation, interagency workshops.

Objective 2: Personnel from social service agencies increase diagnostic, referral, and counseling skills.

Methods: Counseling skill development, case consultation.

VI. *Allied Health (Public Health, Physicians, Hospitals, Nursing Homes)*

Objective 1: Nurses, physicians, and other health personnel are knowledgeable about and make appropriate referrals to the center.

Methods: Educational presentations and program consultation.

Objective 2: Nurses develop and increase diagnostic and counseling skills.

Methods: Counseling skill development and case consultation.

VII. *Business and Industry*

Objective 1: Business and industry are knowledgeable about and make appropriate referrals to the center.

Methods: Educational presentations.

Objective 2: Business and industry establish prevention and treatment programs in their own shops (refers to major businesses and industries).

Methods: Internal mental health specialists, program consultation, fund raising.

VIII. *Indigenous Groups (Morticians, Beauticians, Bartenders, and so on)*

Objective 1: Indigenous groups are more knowledgeable about mental illness and make appropriate referrals to human service agencies.

Methods: Educational presentations.

IX. *Citizen Groups (Rotary Clubs, Lions Clubs, and so on)*

Objective 1: Citizen groups are knowledgeable about mental health or illness and the center.

Methods: Educational presentations.

---

[a]Department of Social Services (DSS), Department of Vocational Rehabilitation (DVR), Social Security (SS), Office of Economic Opportunity (OEO).

tems in our county exemplify an application of the framework discussed in the first part of this chapter.

The county our center served was basically rural, and could be divided into three population areas: northern (several small towns and communities), central (major city-county seat, and several surrounding communities), and southern (bedroom communities serving a large city located in another state). The center was located in the major city and had one small satellite center in the northern sector. It was clear that we could not directly meet the mental health needs of our scattered rural county, let alone those of the city where we were located. In order to expand the mental health network, we decided to identify and to make entry with key caregiving groups that were already providing some form of limited counseling services in the county. Where possible, we wanted to develop and upgrade counseling skills and to link and coordinate these caregiving groups with our center.

A major caregiving group in the community was the clergy. They had congregations throughout the county and were sought out by their parishioners in times of crisis. Most had some limited training in pastoral counseling. As a group, clergy tend to be community oriented and concerned with individuals' needs. If the negative aspects—religious dogma and authoritarianism and the related use of preaching and advice giving as preferred methods for helping persons with mental health problems —can be changed to attitudes of openness, acceptance, understanding, and empathic communication, clergy can be a very potent force in the total mental health delivery system.

Since the task of developing programs with clergy involved three population centers, three clergy consultation teams were developed. One of the center's part-time counselors (Jack) also worked at a church in the northern area as a part-time clergyman. He was therefore a logical choice to be part of the clergy consultation team for this area and to take major responsibility for the identification and recruitment of clergy who had congregations there. Although there was no clergy association in the northern area, Jack was acquainted with several clergy whom he thought would be receptive to our proposed interventions. The chief pastor of Jack's church was also a member of the center's board, and another senior priest in the area had played a major role in the initial development of the center, which greatly strengthened our influence. In order to involve the schools in the northern area and to develop closer relationships with the intermediate school district, a centralized system employing school psychologists and school social workers in schools throughout the county, we recruited the school social worker assigned to that area as part of the clergy consultation team.

We set up a meeting with six clergymen who expressed an interest in linking with our center. We outlined some of our concerns regarding the mental health needs of residents of the northern area, heard about their concerns, and jointly developed a program that would begin to meet both our needs. The clergymen requested that we include some laypersons from their congregations who were motivated and already had some helping skills, plus the local police officer, who worked effectively with youth in the area. That winter, after my arrival, we delivered an eight-session program over four months on empathic communication, incorporating concepts from Parent Effectiveness Training (developed by Thomas Gordon) and transactional analysis. Time was spent during each session reviewing individual counseling cases that seminar participants presented. Based on written feedback and impressions of the clergy consultation team, this program was very successful in terms of increased skills in making appropriate referrals to the center, increased empathic communication, and establishing the beginnings of a mental health service delivery network involving the clergy, schools, police, and the center. Continued involvement was enhanced by giving participants a formal certificate of completion on completing the program, by setting up periodic educational programs, and by offering continuing case consultation through Jack.

We were fortunate to have a clergyman of a large church in the central area as chairman of our center's board. The clergy consultation team for this area, consisting of myself and two center staff, recruited him to set up a meeting with the clergy association from that area. Although we thought that our entry and delivery tasks would be facilitated through the mechanism of the clergy association, we soon discovered that the association was largely composed of well-established clergymen who led large congregations and who were more involved and interested in church politics and their own power base than in pastoral counseling. The first meeting was well attended, and we had an interesting dialogue regarding their concerns and our needs. A major concern expressed by clergy in the central area involved the lack of a coordinated network of mental health services, which prevented them from tying their congregants into an appropriate system. Although several clergy mentioned the need to upgrade their own pastoral counseling skills, they did not want to focus on this at the present time.

Although our original objective for making entry with clergy was to help them to develop and to upgrade pastoral counseling skills and to make more appropriate referrals to the center, we decided to change the focus of our intervention, especially since the problem that the clergy had pinpointed was so important. We utilized the six clergymen who wanted to work with us in this area to recruit persons from major caregiving systems: police (city, county, and state); court personnel; Department of Social Services, Division of Vocational Rehabilitation; Catholic Family Services; Child and Family Services; and board members and staff from the center. The recruitment process was very successful, because of the clergy's active role. It is difficult to turn down a sensible request from a clergyman, especially when that clergyman is your pastor.

We delivered a successful four-month, ten-session program to twenty-five community agency representatives that focused on: maximizing interagency communication and coordination of community services; changing attitudes toward mental health and illness and toward the center; and increasing empathic communication skills where appropriate (Dworkin, 1973). Even though we did not deliver the program to clergy in the central area, as originally intended, our initial entry with them was very successful and enabled us to deliver a comprehensive pastoral counseling program to them the following year.

Since we had no organized system for delivering mental health services to residents in the southern part of the county, it was essential that we involve clergy and other agencies in setting up a network of community services. Five mental health professionals were recruited for the clergy consultation team in that area: two school social workers from the intermediate school district who were servicing the local elementary schools, one social worker from Catholic Family Service, and two social workers from the center who resided in the southern area. Released time for the professionals was easily obtained because of the shared perception that there was a need for mental health programs for residents in the area. Entry was made with the clergy association in the southern sector through enlisting the assistance of a highly esteemed clergyman who was very motivated to develop mental health services for his community. After several meetings with the local clergy organization, individual and community needs were identified and translated into a mental health training program for eight clergy (including one female pastor) and five religious educators (Dworkin, 1974).

The program consisted of a series of ten three-hour sessions spanning five months. Program content included Erikson's theory of psychosocial development; crisis theory and intervention; an introduction to transactional analysis; behavioral approaches to therapy; and training in empathic communication. Counseling skills were taught by using role playing, practice exercises, small-group activities, and case studies. A variety of media were utilized: audio tapes, films, handouts, and a multimedia table. Most important, the five clergy consultation team staff developed excellent rapport with seminar participants and provided continuing case consultation after completion of the program. Participants received a formal diploma on completing the program. Formal evaluation methods revealed that the program for clergy in the southern area was very successful. Participants significantly increased their counseling caseloads, felt more effective as counselors, utilized each other as resources more, and worked more closely with other mental health professionals in the county.

The following year a meeting was held for all the clergy we had serviced from the three areas to discuss our providing them a more intense personal pastoral counseling program that focused on transactional analysis. Fifteen clergy expressed an interest in taking this program. Another staff person was recruited to help lead this program. An arrangement was made with the local community college to offer college credit for taking this program. It was a win-win situation for everyone. The community college wanted to increase its community outreach; clergy had a choice of receiving college credit for something they personally desired; and the center not only increased its mental health service capacity through upgrading pastoral counseling skills but was also reimbursed for its effort.

The program (course), which took place during twenty three-hour sessions over an eight-month period, focused on increasing counseling skills through experiential learning. Participants took turns being clients and therapists in a group setting that offered them protection and permission to experiment. Although initially threatened by the idea of discussing personal problems and/or counseling fellow clergy in the presence of their peers, most were soon actively involved in a very meaningful learning process. Judging from written and verbal feedback plus the observations of the two trainers, this was an extremely successful program. We thought that most clergy significantly developed and upgraded counseling skills and worked out some personal problems generic to their profession. We cemented a relationship between our two systems that would enable us to jointly and to confidentially expand the network of mental health services to county residents.

### Theory into Practice: Summary and Conclusions

This section will relate some of the basic components of the consultation process to the mental health consultation programs our center delivered to the clergy system. While not having some of the attributes of other formal systems such as schools, courts and social service systems, the formal and informal network of clergy throughout our county adequately serves as basis for making generalizations to other community systems.

The clergy form a very important community caretaking group that can have a noticeable impact on both the formal and informal mental health service delivery network. Viewed from ascribed, attributed, assumed, and actual points of view, the church's mission, the rules and roles by which it operates, and its relationship to the community make it an ideal system in which to intervene.

Uninvited initial entry was made by and with persons

who were acknowledged leaders within the clergy ranks. Once recruited, they helped each clergy consultation team to complete the entry process and to obtain the necessary sanction with the rest of the clergy system. Each clergy consultation team was careful to listen to the needs and concerns expressed by individual clergy prior to using the influence process to deliver programs we thought were important. In each case, verbal and written understandings were developed and shared about the types of programs we would offer them.

Within each clergy group, identified leaders and other interested clergy acted as internal consultants by helping the teams to plan and to evaluate all programs on an ongoing basis. A positive approach in working with clergy was utilized that capitalized on their strengths. The actualization of potential was emphasized, and existing skills and interests were built on, rather than focusing on deficits and weaknesses. A variety of methods were utilized that maximized skill building, attitude change, and network development. Although our programs with clergy were conducive to establishing a therapist-client relationship, we were especially careful not to become therapeutically involved with them.

Power issues were not as visible as in more structured formal organizations, since each clergy group with which we worked was interdenominational. Nonetheless, it was soon recognized that when clergy placed their counseling skills and problems out in the open for colleagues to observe, some prestige and influence might be at stake. Precautions were taken to decrease this possibility by developing a caring, trusting, and open atmosphere and by continually focusing on strengths rather than weaknesses. It was also recognized that some clergy might leave their systems after learning and experiencing therapy firsthand, and therefore the ramifications of this possibility were discussed with them. This was especially important during the second year when the clergy met as a total group for a lengthy intensive therapy learning experience.

As it was in the center's interest to maintain long-term involvement with the clergy system, termination was considered in terms of a phase-in/phase-out process, where programs and

other consultation interventions flowed smoothly and continuously together. By the end of the second year, plans had been
developed to offer clergy more intensive counseling training
programs, case consultation, jointly led therapy groups, and primary prevention programs (parent effectiveness training, premarital education, and marital enrichment). A mental health
satellite center was set up in one of the churches in the southern
sector, and plans were being developed to increase the center's
offering of direct and indirect services in churches. The primary
consultant's involvement with clergy decreased as other center
staff took greater responsibility for working with them. Final
separation from the clergy was a difficult process for all, for we
truly loved working with them.

Formal and informal evaluation were part of the entire
consultation process with all clergy groups. Written and verbal
feedback was obtained at the end of each session and was dis-
seminated to a planning team composed of both staff and clergy
representatives. Modifications based on this information were
made as needed. Formal evaluation procedures were met with
resistance by both staff and clergy. Even though formal evaluation, which utilizes a sound experimental design and valid
instrumentation, may provide consultants with useful information regarding their interventions, caution must be exercised—it
is possible to devote too much time and effort to this process.
The process may detract from the limited time a consultant has
to deliver programs and may not be perceived as important by
the very client systems the consultant wants to change. It is important to maintain an appropriate balance between formal and
informal evaluation.

This chapter has presented a rationale for the role of the
mental health consultant as a change agent and a framework for
doing consultations with community systems. Following this,
the role of the mental health consultant was illustrated by
focusing on my work with community systems—initiating a
mental health consultation program for our center, developing a
mechanism for delivering a broad array of consultation services
to many community caregiving groups and individuals with
limited resources, and delivering a comprehensive mental health

consultation program to the clergy system. I hope this chapter has stimulated the reader to consider becoming actively involved in changing systems through mental health consultation. Such involvement does not mean that the would-be counselor should give up counseling. On the contrary, counseling and other interpersonal skills are necessary for doing consultation. Counselors and other mental health professionals can have a significant impact on community caregiving systems by helping them to be more responsive to the individuals they serve.

# 5

# Marriage and Family Counselors as Independent Professionals

Ben N. Ard, Jr.

This chapter takes a brief look at the interest that various older, traditional professions have had in marriage and family counseling. Then the development of the role of marriage and family counselors will be examined, and a brief view of the major training programs offered. Next, because of the relative recency of legislation licensing marriage and family counselors, I will discuss sanctioning agencies and professional organizations, as well as some of the advantages and problems of the new role definition of marriage and family counselors. Finally, some implications for the public marketplace and credibility will be drawn.

Marriage and family counseling has emerged as an independent profession most recently in the history of the various helping professions. First, let's look at the roles of traditional professionals in marriage and family counseling. For example, ministers, rabbis, and priests have advised couples and families long before the development of professions as such. Since men of the cloth officiated at the formation of the marital union and had a major interest in social stability, they had an investment in maintaining the marriage and were sometimes consulted by people when they had problems with the marriage or family. While some clergy in more recent years may get additional professional training and provide good marriage and family counseling, unfortunately many clergy still lean more strongly toward "traditional" goals and religious values such as preventing divorces, impressing the counselees with the seriousness of marriage vows, and helping make marriage the sacred institution it once was (Kerckhoff, 1976, p. 459). Many clergy are most suspicious of the counseling done by persons not closely associated with organized religion; in other words, they tend to see counseling as religious work (Kerckhoff, 1976, p. 459).

Lawyers have always been involved in marital problems, of course, but the traditional adversary stance to which they are usually trained does not lend itself to being optimally helpful in a situation where marriage counseling might be of value. Since the lawyer has been traditionally trained in the role of adversary representation, he or she may tend to easily fall into thinking how to get the most for his or her client, rather than how to resolve some of the differences.

There are, of course, exceptions. Some lawyers are learning helping skills from marriage and family counselors and psychologists. Other lawyers are using the arbitration skills some of them have learned in their profession to assist married couples in dispute resolution, rather than always going to court and battling to get as much as possible from the "adversary." The new no-fault divorce laws in some states are doing away with the adversary stance and may be helpful in getting lawyers to change their view of their relationships with their clients.

Lawyers, as professionals, have probably nearly always been called in *after* the marital and family problems have already reached a point where conflict resolution is not very feasible and dissolution of the marriage is about the only function left to the lawyers. Most law schools today still do not train upcoming lawyers in marriage and family counseling.

Physicians, particularly the old-time country doctor who brought several generations of a family into the world, have administered much sage, although untutored, advice to their patients on family affairs. But even today courses of training in marriage and family counseling are still *not* in the course of study of most physicians. For many physicians who see sometimes forty or fifty patients a day, time for counseling just does not seem feasible, given the usual characteristics of their practice.

Clark Vincent, a behavioral scientist at Bowman-Gray School of Medicine, has noted that office overhead and the number of patients to be seen generally preclude the physician's use of the counselor's "fifty-minute hour" (Vincent, 1973, p. 3). According to Vincent, the physician simply cannot even afford many thirty-minute sessions with his patients unless he has very low overhead expenses and few patients or unless he becomes a full-time specialist counseling in sexual and marital problems and charges accordingly. Vincent suggests, however, that by serving as a "marital health consultant" in a way that is consistent with his medical practice model, the physician can be quite helpful to the patient within a period of ten to fifteen minutes (Vincent, 1973, p. 3).

The whole field of medicine is in a state of flux, with several trends in different directions. On the one hand, with increasing knowledge and technological advances, there is an increasing trend toward specialization in medicine, and the old-time country doctor as a general practitioner and in a very real sense a "family physician" is apparently dying out. The increasing numbers of physicians going into specialties have meant fewer general practitioners and fewer family physicians. And the specialization trend has probably worked against physicians becoming interested in marriage and family counseling.

However, there has also recently developed a resurgence of interest within the medical profession in "family practice" or what some see as a large-scale return to family practice, offering

a more modern, sophisticated version of the general practitioner. With this interest in some medical schools (such as Bowman-Gray, the University of Pennsylvania, the University of
California at Los Angeles, and the University of California at
San Francisco) has come considerably more behavioral science
and family therapy instruction. Some physicians in training in
such institutions are actively seeking these skills and learning
from marriage and family counselors and psychologists.

Psychiatrists deserve separate consideration from other
physicians because they have certainly seen the results of unfortunate family experiences in their particularly specialized practices over the years. But their traditional training (particularly
of the orthodox psychoanalytical variety) has usually resulted
in their seeing individuals rather than married couples or families. In fact, orthodox psychoanalytic thought has seemed to
many of its followers to preclude their even seeing or having
much, if any, contact with members of the family other than
their patient. There has been some very recent change in this
attitude on the part of those psychiatrists who have looked
beyond Freud and the identified patient and who have considered the married couple (as in sex therapy and marriage
counseling) and the whole family (as in family therapy). But the
psychiatric profession still seems largely to remain almost exclusively invested in an individual therapy model.

Social workers have traditionally been concerned with
families and have worked with environmental factors affecting
families, while psychiatrists have worked largely with intrapsychic factors in the identified patient. However, the social
worker's efforts with the family have usually been viewed as
ancillary, supplemental, or secondary to the individual therapy.
Recently psychiatric social workers have begun doing psychotherapy somewhat more independently, and some even have
started private practices on their own, although traditions of
practically endless supervision are hard to overcome in the
social work profession, which grew up, so to speak, under the
wing of psychiatry. That is, social work does not have as much
independent status as it might, due perhaps to its ancillary position to psychiatry in its formative years.

Psychologists have always been interested in normal and abnormal human behavior (perhaps more in the latter than the former, in clinical psychology), but courses in marriage or marriage counseling are still not usually offered in very many college and university psychology departments (Kimber, 1969). Such psychology departments are not preparing their graduates to deal adequately with problems faced by their clients every day.

Psychologists sometimes teach courses in these areas outside of traditional psychology departments; for example, in home economics or counseling departments. Recent developments growing out of the developments of the sex therapy movement and recent interest in the family have stimulated some psychology departments to begin to offer courses in the areas of marriage, family, and sex. And, as mentioned earlier, in the discussion of the medical profession, psychologists are now teaching courses on family therapy, sex therapy, and marriage counseling in some of the medical schools around the country.

Consequently, despite some progressive trends, there still seems to be a need for marriage and family counseling that goes beyond the services traditionally offered by some of the older professions. This would seem to explain how a new profession of marriage and family counseling has arisen. Marriage and family counselors (including sex therapists operating within this concept) need additional training beyond what has been offered in most of the traditional helping professions. Some authorities have even suggested that the routine training of the more established professions does *not* qualify persons in those professions as specialists in marriage relationships (Rutledge, 1969, p. 3).

Persons who wish to go into marriage and family counseling (or sex therapy) as qualified professionals need to get *additional* training *beyond* what they have traditionally received in their various basic professions, it would seem. Some of the early training programs in marriage and family counseling were postdoctoral (required a Ph.D. first for those candidates entering the profession) if not at least work beyond the master's (for example, at the University of Minnesota and the Merrill-Palmer Institute in Detroit).

In the 1930s and 1940s, marriage counseling as a profession began to develop in the United States (Mudd and Fowler, 1976). The American Association of Marriage Counselors (AAMC) was founded in 1942 and has always been very interdisciplinary in its membership. This small group of professional persons interested in the problems of sex and marriage were from the medical specialties, social work, psychology, and sociology. Early in the history of the AAMC, very high standards were required for membership (an M.D. or a Ph.D.).

The AAMC during the beginning years (1942-1947) concentrated its work specifically on marriage counseling. During the years 1948-1955, the AAMC joined with the National Council on Family Relations in releasing a joint statement of standards for marriage counselors and later (in 1954) also established criteria for marriage counseling training centers. During 1956-1960, three training centers were approved, namely those at the Marriage Council of Philadelphia, at the Menninger Foundation in Topeka, Kansas, and at the Merrill-Palmer Institute in Detroit.

In 1955 the AAMC membership was broken into the following categories: medicine, 31 percent (gynecology, 12 percent; general medicine, 9 percent; psychiatry, 9 percent; urology, 1 percent); 18 percent were ministers; 16 percent, social workers; 13 percent, psychologists; 11 percent, educators; 11 percent, sociologists. In 1966 the membership showed significant shifts: psychology, 26 percent; social work, 25 percent; ministry, 15 percent; education, 8 percent; medicine, 8 percent; sociology, 5 percent; law, 1 percent (Mudd and Fowler, 1976, p. 438).

In 1963 California became the first state to require licenses for those calling themselves "marriage, family, and child counselor" (the specific title used in the California law, which went into effect in 1964). It was necessary, under the law, to have a master's degree and two years of experience (B. Ard and C. Ard, 1969, pp. 399-403). Michigan followed with an act in 1966. New Jersey's law was passed in 1968, becoming effective in 1969. In 1973, Nevada and Utah passed their laws in this area (Nichols, 1976).

The enactment of state licensing laws for marriage and

family counselors was based on standards different from those of the AAMC, but appeared to be the wave of the future. Thus an historic decision was thrust on the AAMC: what to do about the AAMC minimum standards. The minimum standards of AAMC membership were revised to accept the master's degree and two years of clinical experience.

It is difficult to say why some states have passed licensing laws and others have not. It is interesting to note that the states in which licensure laws have been achieved run the gamut from urban, secularized, industrial environments (California, Michigan, and New Jersey) to rural, traditional environments (Nevada and Utah), including combinations of the two types (Georgia and Texas). Whether a state has license laws or not depends on the peculiar complex of political and interprofessional circumstances under which legislation is introduced, opposed, and implemented.

In 1970 the AAMC changed its name to the American Association of Marriage and Family Counselors. The AAMFC recognized the increasing importance of working with the total family and the burgeoning interest in family therapy.

In 1974 a challenge to the profession came in the form of an announcement by the U.S. Department of Defense that it was suspending all payments to CHAMPUS beneficiaries for treatment by marriage and family counselors (CHAMPUS is the Civilian Health and Medical Program for the Uniformed Services). Marriage and family counselors had been included since 1966. AAMFC went to work in Washington and was able to have this decision turned around by going to court. Further work is needed in the future to enable marriage and family counselors to receive third-party payments for services rendered from insurance companies, union insurance policies, Medi-Cal, Blue Cross, and Blue Shield. Obviously, this emerging profession has its work cut out for it in the future.

## Development of the Role

The development of the role of marriage and family counselor has, perhaps, not been as clear-cut as in some other professions, since marriage and family counseling is a specialized field focusing, some leaders have said, on "the marital relationship" rather than on individuals (and this in a way not done heretofore in other professions). Also, some leaders in the field have felt that marriage and family counseling as a profession in some sense may be seen as overlapping other fields such as counseling and psychotherapy; and yet leaders in the field have seen marriage and family counseling as being specifically distinct from these other fields in specialized ways (Leslie, 1964; Mace, 1974; Mudd and Fowler, 1976).

In fact, some of the existing, traditional professions have only grudgingly, if at all, recognized their own relative lack of training in marriage, sex, and family counseling and admitted that there is a growing body of qualified professionals specifically trained (with specialized, supervised experience) in marriage, family, and sex counseling. Richard Kerckhoff (1976, pp. 456-460), in a study of how the profession of marriage counseling was viewed by members of four allied professions (clergymen, physicians, social workers, and attorneys), discovered that *each* and every one of these four subsamples chose its *own* profession as *best* equipped to do marriage counseling. All four professions chose "full-time marriage counselors" as *second* best. Such empirical evidence could be supplemented by much further data that indicates that this emerging profession is still today not always received by these and other professions as a legitimate, well-trained, and qualified member of the helping professions with a particular service to provide to a public that seems to need many more helpers than the various traditional, established, helping professions have been able to provide thus far.

As sex counseling and sex therapy has developed as an even more recent subspecialty, many states do not have any laws spelling out the qualifications and requirements for holding oneself out to the public as a "sex therapist." Some physicians have once again objected to nonphysicians getting into the field, and yet many physicians themselves are poorly trained in sex therapy and often contribute to problems people have in this particular area of their lives (Mace, 1974; Comfort, 1967). As David Mace (1974, p. 8) has put it, "Either the members of the medical profession must meet the public's expectations and acquire and teach each other the skills they do not presently possess, or they must make it widely known that they claim no expertise in this area (and allow better-qualified practitioners of other disciplines to fill the need)."

But in America today there are still arguments being made by some physicians against nonphysicians who want to practice sex therapy and marriage and family counseling. Competency, not the specific degree, is the issue. Marital and sexual counseling (including premarital counseling and divorce counseling, as well as family therapy) is a developing field requiring special training and particular supervised clinical experience in order to be properly qualified, if the public is to be protected (Ard, 1974).

## Major Training Programs

The AAMFC has approved certain major training programs and clinical training centers over the years. As mentioned, some of the earlier approved training programs were located at the Marriage Council of Philadelphia (affiliated with the University of Pennsylvania School of Medicine), at the Merrill-Palmer Institute in Detroit, and at the Menninger Foundation in Topeka. Over the years, other approved graduate programs have been developed at Teachers College, Columbia University, Florida State University, the University of Minnesota, Purdue University, and the University of Southern California, to mention just a few.

Most marriage and family counselors heretofore had to get their training at such centers *in addition to,* and frequently *after,* their formal academic training. That is, the established professions did not provide the kind of specialized training needed in their routine training programs.

What, specifically, is recommended by the AAMFC for the substantive content of an approved and accredited graduate training program? As to substantive content, the AAMFC says, "The student will be exposed to the important areas of theoretical competency, including specifically personality theory, psychopathology, human sexuality, marriage and family studies, marriage counseling, and family therapy. It is expected that such exposure will include both depth and breadth, rather than being narrowly focused and that it will be flexible enough to allow for recognition of knowledge gained prior to entry into the training program and permit appropriate tailoring of academic coursework requirements and clinical experiences to meet the professional needs of individual trainees" (American Association of Marriage and Family Counselors, 1975, p. 27). In discussing the guidelines various training programs would develop their programs within, the AAMFC recommendations also state:

> Particular attention should be given to deficiencies in trainee background in the important areas of theoretical competency. The training program should possess an adequate specialized library in the areas mentioned, including the major journals, and trainees should be encouraged to study not only for background understanding and knowledge in a general sense but also for specific application to their cases and practice, working to gain an integration of theory and practice. The teaching of technique apart from a sound understanding of theory is not a desirable procedure. The [AAMFC] standards call for an introduction of a variety of theoretical viewpoints and acquainting students with the diversity of the field of marriage and family counseling substantive material rather than relying on a single theoretical viewpoint to the exclusion of appropriate acquaintance with others. While a given program may major on training practitioners to use a certain approach, it is incumbent on the program to give students adequate and unbiased exposure to the broader field of knowledge in marriage and family counseling so that the degree program is educational rather than merely an indoctrinational matter [American Association of Marriage and Family Counselors, 1975, pp. 27-28].

California, being the first state to pass a licensing law for marriage, family, and child counselors that required a master's degree as a minimum, has been developing master's degree programs in this area. But it is still relatively new as a field and new programs are still being inaugurated at this master's degree level. For example, the California Association of Marriage and Family Counselors (CAMFC) in 1975 accredited the master's degree program in counseling at San Francisco State University. This program is a two-year, sixty-semester unit program in the Department of Counseling. Other state and private universities and colleges are setting up programs that may be expected to be accredited in the future. And the University of Southern California has a doctoral program that has been approved by the AAMFC. Others in the state may have doctoral level programs fairly soon. Other AAMFC-approved programs around the country are at Syracuse University, Brigham Young University, and Colgate University.

## Sanctioning Agencies

As may be seen from the discussion in the previous section, there are several levels of sanctioning agencies with regard to marriage and family counseling. There are national organizations, state organizations, and state licensing agencies, as well as the federal government.

The AAMFC is the national organization that approves training programs (accrediting graduate training programs in colleges and universities) and clinical training centers, as well as admitting marriage and family counselors to various categories of membership (including one of approved supervisor). As has been stated elsewhere (Mudd and Fowler, 1976, p. 438), membership in the AAMFC "has come to mean, for all practical purposes, the possession of the only recognized credential in the field of professional marriage counseling, a kind of guarantee of dependable service to the general public."

The state organizations are also sanctioning agencies within the state; for example, the California Association of Marriage and Family Counselors (CAMFC) admits licensed marriage, family, and child counselors to its membership and also approves of graduate training programs in the state. CAMFC also has a code of ethics that it requires its members to follow, just as does the AAMFC. The state organization has also worked to improve the legislation applying in this area.

Each state that has a licensing law ordinarily has a licensing board; for example, in California it is the Board of Behavioral Science Examiners (1020 N Street, Sacramento, Calif. 95814). These boards, as in California, give state board written examinations, as well as arrange for oral examinations after the written examinations have been passed. Beyond this initial licensing, states have generally one of three approaches to quality control of services: professional peer review, license board investigators, or continuing education requirements for relicensure. Both professional and lay proponents of each approach continue to debate the issue heatedly.

The AAMFC usually keeps up to date on what is happening around the country regarding legislation, has even published a model law (Nichols, 1976), and is quite willing to provide professionals with whatever information they might need to get legislation started in their various states (contact AAMFC at 225 Yale Avenue, Claremont, Calif. 91711).

Another national organization, the first to certify sex therapists, is AASECT, the American Association of Sex Educators, Counselors, and Therapists (5010 Wisconsin Avenue, N.W., Suite 304, Washington, D.C. 20016). The sex therapist category of membership is available to all AASECT members whose credentials have been certified by the certification committee and approved by the board of directors as having met the standards for certification.

Another sanctioning agency of the federal government is CHAMPUS, which has been mentioned earlier; it decides which professionals shall be paid for services rendered to members of the armed services (as well as retired members of the armed services). The U.S. Department of Defense controls what payments CHAMPUS will approve.

If a national health insurance program is ever passed, it

will have great influence on who will be paid for providing what sorts of service. There is considerable maneuvering going on now among the various helping professions as to what sorts of services will be provided for and who will be paid for providing them. The areas of mental health, psychotherapy, and marriage and family counseling are specific areas where there are conflicts among several professions. The most fundamental principle that would help resolve these conflicts would be freedom of choice for clients. Such a principle would hold that clients in need of these services should have freedom of choice among qualified practitioners and not be limited to practitioners holding any one professional degree (for example, an M.D. degree).

Quality control of services is perhaps best achieved through professional peer review. Another means of assuring quality control of services offered is for continuing education to be required before relicensure is given.

### Advantages and Problems of New Role Definition

Obvious problems arise when a new profession develops among the older, more established professions. Marriage and family counseling is an emerging new profession, relatively speaking, and has had some problems because some of the older, more traditional professions have seemingly felt threatened by what may have seemed to some as a new profession moving in on the older professions.

If marriage and family counseling is seen as a form of psychotherapy, which some authorities in the field clearly state is the case (see, for example, Hudson, 1976), then practitioners in this field need to be as competently trained as anyone who does psychotherapy in any other profession. While practitioners in this field may work mainly with couples or families, it is obviously true that if one is to do premarital counseling and divorce counseling this latter sort of work is primarily with individuals.

It is true that students in training programs in this new professional area need to be trained to recognize suicidal, destructive, and psychotic individuals. Trainees need courses in

abnormal psychology and testing; these are usually routine in
most of the better training programs across the country. However, as we have seen in the earlier discussion, despite the fact
that several of the older, more established professions have
assumed that *they* were best qualified to do marriage counseling
(Kerckhoff, 1976), the routine or traditional preparation or
training in many of the older, established professions does *not*
necessarily qualify persons as specialists in marriage and family
relationships (Rutledge, 1969) or, for that matter, sex therapy.
It usually takes further training, beyond that offered in the traditional, established professions, to qualify a person to offer the
best service to the public.

One of the advantages of a newly emerging role (or new
profession) is that the ruts and limitations of older, more established professions (with their mosaic of vested interests) can be
more easily avoided. However, every new profession, after a
freely expanding beginning period, tends to evidence a tighten-
ing-up or retrenching period. This may be right around the
corner for marriage and family counseling (and particularly for
sex therapy), if it has not already arrived. For example, it may
be involved in the California experience (among the state colleges and universities) as well as in the closing down of programs
at the University of Minnesota, the Menninger Foundation, and
at the Merrill-Palmer Institute.

When family therapy first began developing with the
work of Nathan Ackerman on the East Coast and Don Jackson,
Virginia Satir, and others on the West Coast, the ambience was
enthusiastic, eager, and somewhat open. As time progressed
there has been some talk of licensing family therapists, that is,
of some means of certifying who is "in" the select inner circle
and who is "out."

In the developments regarding sex therapy since Masters
and Johnson (1970), Hartman and Fithian (1972), Helen Singer
Kaplan (1974), and others, a similar development seems to be
occurring: first openness, lots of new ideas, enthusiasm, and so
forth, and later a period of discussion of certification, licensing,
and such questions as who should be allowed to work in this
particular area of competence and advertise to the public. But

every new profession, in developing its role, experiences some growing pains. The emerging field of marriage and family counseling (including family therapy and sex therapy within the overall concept of marriage and family counseling) seems to be going through this process.

## The Public Marketplace and Credibility

Any new profession in the process of emerging on the public scene has a problem of educating the public into an awareness of what the new profession has to offer. And not all members of a newly emerging profession (as well as some members of the older, more established professions) are always careful, professional, or even professionally ethical in what they hold out to the public as their particularly qualified competencies. This is the reason why there is a need for professional organizations, codes of ethics, peer review, and licensing agencies to ride herd on the emerging profession (as well as the older ones) and to protect the public and thus ensure some credibility in what the emerging profession has to offer to the public marketplace. The questions that arise around public relations and advertising as well as professional ethics are perennial problems for all professions, of course, but are particularly so for the emerging profession of marriage and family counseling.

Ideally, the public consumers should be able to select the practitioner of their choice and have at least a portion of the cost paid for through insurance coverage (and perhaps, later, through a national health plan). But the mosaic of vested interests still prevents this ideal situation from being realized. Some insurance coverage still favors the physician, and some coverage does not even recognize marriage and family counselors as a separate profession as yet. Hopefully, if the long-term needs of the public are to be properly served, the best-qualified trained practitioners in the various areas of marriage, family, and child counseling (including sex therapy), should be able to take their rightful places alongside the other respected helping professions as members of a responsible, well-trained, competent, new profession.

# 6

# Child Development
# Consultants

## Eric Seidman

There is increasing recognition of the fact that the elementary school experience is critical in the educational process, and, consequently, greater attention is being given to programs of instruction and to the people involved in the lives of children during these years (five years to twelve years of age). A recent example of this is Public Law 94-142 (1976) mandating the integration of special school services for the handicapped, an integration that will be difficult without a reorganization.

To promote academic achievement for as many students as possible, personnel other than teachers have been employed. The nonteaching functionaries involved are known as *counselors, guidance counselors, guidance teachers, guidance directors, school psychologists, psychological examiners, pupil personnel workers, visiting teachers, helping teachers, crisis intervention teachers,* and by a number of other titles. The proliferation of these ancillary services appears to have increased in direct proportion to the growing concern of educators over the manifest deficiencies of the schools, deficiencies that preclude the attainment of stated goals. These services have become an integral part of the existing, prescribed structure of many educational systems. Their inclusion is predicated on the belief that they are necessary adjuncts to the total matrix of education that defines for the young the requisites for performing successfully in the greater society.

To function independently, adequately, and constructively as a contributing member of a democratic society is the essence of the Great American Education Dream. The educational program, then, to which all youngsters are subject is designed to equip them with the skills and knowledge that will assure the actualization of that dream.

Within the traditional educational framework, it is expected that a number of any given group of students will encounter difficulties, whether academic, social, or emotional, during the course of the formal educative process. Despite the nearly sanctified notion of individuality, the inability or unwillingness of many teachers to accept differences interferes with success in learning and creates the need for the ancillary personnel available as supportive services.

It becomes readily apparent then, that the primary purpose of the guidance and counseling services, as perceived by educators, is to help create situations or alter circumstances that will enable each child to make optimal use of whatever qualities and characteristics he or she may bring to school; to enhance the child in his or her total functioning; to be supportive of the teachers in their central roles in the school program; and, generally, to facilitate the educative process.

Children fortunate enough to have an abundance of coping skills were not blessed at birth with this attribute, nor are those devoid of these abilities simply genetically impoverished. The entire process of nurturance during the developmental years may be viewed as the primary determinant of an individual's subsequent behavioral modalities. And in the recent past, while cloaked in the psychological naiveté that obtained then, reflective of hope and optimism engendered by the stated purposes of education, it was assumed that the school would reenforce the positive antecedents and, where indicated, neutralize and negate those nonnurturing experiences that would likely preclude the expected progress toward achievement and enhancement. The advent of the practice of guidance and counseling in the elementary schools was a rather forceful suggestion that the hope and promise of the salutory effect of the school were not fulfilled.

An additional dimension of guidance and counseling functions has been the increased interest and concern regarding the ever growing numbers of children and youth who are "learning resistant," the angry, hostile, alienated academic failures. The attendant question, which becomes paramount here, relates to institutional objectives and purposes and to whether or not there is conflict or congruence with the personal objectives and goals of the children and youth who are the system's consumers.

What functions, then, are counselors to perform to facilitate the achievement of goals and objectives articulated by the institution and—perhaps less eloquently, but no less forcefully—by the student clients? The problem, as stated, assumes a complexity long ignored during the time when the principal concerns of guidance and counseling were the removal of impediments to the attainment of educational objectives. The criteria established as reference points for achievement, adjustment, and conformity are still, for the most part, culture bound. That is, practitioners in the helping professions who are involved in the problems of youngsters in the school setting see their greatest contribution as one that reduces or eliminates areas of conflict between school personnel and students. This is done, inevitably, by providing students and teachers with the appropriate experiences that will give them sufficient insight into the problem and allow them to make the necessary adjustments that will help reduce conflict. These "appropriate experiences" and the "necessary adjustments" involve preconceived notions of what is fair, right, and true.

In the recent past, there have been critical evaluations of the traditional roles and functions of pupil personnel workers (counselors, psychologists, and social workers) as well as of the training centers that define those roles (Arbuckle, 1967; Shaw, 1967; Wrenn, 1962; Seidman, 1969). Earlier, Bower (1960) set the tone for impending change when he addressed himself to the need to increase the effectiveness of the teacher-clinical staff relationships. The implementation of prevention programs, as well as the remedial action required to cope with the manifest problems of the emotionally handicapped, are hindered, he said (p. 111), by the "the quasi-competitive milieu of the mental health professions."

The slow drift toward redefining guidance and counseling has begun. The Interprofessional Research Commission on Pupil Personnel Services (IRCOPPS) project at the University of Maryland (Byrne and others, 1968) has demonstrated that a significantly altered approach to counselor training, based on the holistic concept of child growth and development, is feasible. The approach to problems encountered in the schools by both teachers and children differs from the traditional one, as does the training process itself.

Ivey and Leppaluoto (1975), delegates to a conference on the future of applied psychology, sponsored by the National Institute of Mental Health (NIMH) and the American Psychological Association (APA), attest that the guidelines established for counselor practitioners are heavily influenced by psychological models. They state that counselor training programs have been heavily influenced by the Greyston Conference on counseling psychology (Thompson and Super, 1964), which in turn had basically endorsed another APA report produced twelve years earlier (American Psychological Association, 1952). The essence of the earlier report was that the counseling psychologist is a practitioner and a scientist. The 1949 Boulder Conference clearly affirmed the scientist-practitioner model, which since then has become virtually the gospel for both clinical and counseling psychology (Raimy, 1950). The impact of these conferences on the professional practice of guidance in the United States cannot be overemphasized: The scientist-practitioner model dominates our training programs (Ivey and Leppaluoto, 1975).

The purpose of the 1973 summer conference at Vail,

Colorado, was to examine new roles and make recommendations that mandate change for the helping professions. The
implications of the issues considered led to a recognition of the
need for the related disciplines to work interdependently. This
view, in fact, verifies the interdisciplinary nature of the counseling process as conceptualized by the IRCOPPS team at the University of Maryland, or at least, a variant of that conceptualization.

The assumption established by IRCOPPS was that the
widely held view—that the great proliferation of counseling services in the schools, particularly at the elementary level, was a
measure of its success—was untenable. The validity and viability
of counseling should be determined on the basis of its purposes
and related outcomes, rather than on the basis of the number of
practitioners or the number of clients seen.

Further, the following description of the IRCOPPS project emphasizes the fact that role definition evolves and tran-
scends the professional territorial imperatives when the needs of
all the elements of the school milieu are perceived as an interrelated matrix. The child is viewed as a person in a constantly
emerging state, whose dynamics and motivating forces are
integrally related to those of the peer groups, the teachers, and
the administrators. The flux that is the educative process defies
delineation of specific and discrete vectors marking an affiliation with a particular discipline. The current reality, however, is
that elementary schools throughout the United States have been
hiring nonteaching professional personnel, serving under many
different titles and representing a number of disciplines, primarily those of psychology, counseling, and social work. These
professional positions have frequently been established in response to an urgent appeal for aid, and the well-established
model of the secondary school counselor, long an accepted feature of the body of ancillary services offered at that level, was
readily available for emulation. It is apparent, however, that the
secondary school model, which is built on the needs of adolescents faced with their unique set of social, emotional, and vocational problems, is inadequate for direct transplantation to the
elementary school level, where learning and developmental

problems are, for the most part, entirely different. When such a transplantation is attempted, it can only lead to confusion in the definition of purposes, roles, and functions for the elementary school professional.

The project reported here stemmed from a recognition of the need for substantive experiential and research data around which to construct a rational basis for functions of pupil service professionals at the elementary school level.

## The Maryland Center Project

The Interprofessional Research Commission on Pupil Personnel Services (IRCOPPS) was composed of representatives from thirteen professional organizations and was funded by the National Institute of Mental Health. It was established in 1963 to foster interprofessional cooperation and research centering on the utilization of pupil personnel service workers in the educative process. Four universities were selected as regional centers for these research activities, the University of Maryland being named as the Eastern Regional Research Center. Each center selected its own areas of pupil service research on which to focus.

The investigation conducted at the Western Regional Research Center, housed at the University of California at Los Angeles (later moved to Chico State, California), focused on broadening the role of the pupil personnel worker to act as a resource person for teachers and parents in group settings.

Another regional center, at the University of Michigan, was concerned essentially with an examination of the nature of the various disciplines' problem identification processes, screening and referral methods, and disposition of cases. The chief interest of this group was in learning how the conceptualization of the roles of the various disciplines related to an understanding of children's problems and subsequent actions taken in working with children.

At the University of Texas center, emphasis was given to experimenting with the use of pupil personnel workers exclusively as consultants to teachers. Mental health consultation techniques were taught to trained, experienced counselors and psychologists who, through sustained consultation services to teachers, could provide a positive impact on children's mental health.

It is apparent that while the programs of each center had an individual professional thrust, all defined as primary purposes conducting research on preventive mental hygiene related to schools and demonstrating efficient alternative programs of pupil personnel services.

The Maryland center undertook an extensive investigation of services at the elementary school level. The major project was concerned with the evaluation of the relative effectiveness of counselors and social workers trained and oriented in a "traditional" manner and of experimental workers known as child development consultants (CDCs). The roles and functions of the CDCs were defined as those which would help to create conditions in the school that support maximum development of all pupils and to discover and carry out those functions that lessen or remediate problems for students in need.

Although the nature of the CDCs' roles and functions was neither rigorously defined nor prescribed, regular training was provided. The CDCs met each week on campus for a two-hour seminar under the direction of the associate director of the Maryland center of IRCOPPS. The seminar topics evolved from the problems confronted by the trainees during the course of active involvement in their respective schools. The process of identification, definition, analysis, and resolution of the problems was aided by invited professionals from a number of disciplines, including medicine, psychiatry, psychology, social work, special education, and criminology. Thus the conceptual framework of the project was oriented toward providing the CDCs with a variety of role models and methodological approaches rather than any specific paradigm. Roles and functions were allowed to evolve on the basis of needs manifested by pupils or expressed by teachers and principals in the schools where the CDCs served as full-time, integral staff members.

The major intent underlying the design of the project was one of discovery; that is, the project would provide some research data potentially valuable to elementary schools making decisions on whether or not they wanted to implement various types of organization of pupil personnel services. The concept of the CDC was developed within the project, so that some schools would be staffed by workers who were relatively free from professional identifications evolved at other educational levels and in circumstances different from the elementary school environment. Thus, the role of the CDC within a school was to be evolutionary, in the sense that the functions carried out would be adaptations to existing problems and concerns. It should be noted, however, that the concept of the CDC was developed not as an ideal model but rather as a research model to aid in the generation of data and information that would later help formulate in more definitive terms the appropriate roles and functions for professional personnel workers in the elementary school.

From the point of view of evaluation, the major research problems of this project are posed in the following questions: Is pupil behavior more adaptive in experimental schools having CDCs than in comparable nonexperimental schools? Is there evidence of change in teacher behavior and attitudes in experimental schools having CDCs as contrasted with teachers in nonexperimental schools? And will experimentally evolved functions of CDCs differ from traditional patterns?

## General Plan of the Evaluation

Thirty-one schools, enrolling approximately 15,000 students and staffed by over 500 teachers, were involved in the project. Most schools participated for a period of three years, which afforded an opportunity to collect data over a sufficiently long period of time so that the development of trends could be investigated. Schools were divided into three groups. The control schools were sixteen schools having no in-school pupil personnel worker assigned; however, some services were available on request from professionals based within the school systems. The traditional worker schools were six schools having traditionally trained and oriented professional workers (counselors and social workers) assigned on an in-school basis. The CDC schools were nine schools having experimental child development consultants assigned on an in-school basis (although one CDC served two small, neighboring schools).

Table 1 shows the overall research scheme, which involved evaluation of students, teachers, and pupil personnel service workers on a large number of relevant variables. The general categories of assessment included student academic achievement as measured by standardized achievement tests; student attitudes toward themselves as learners; teacher ratings of pupil

### Table 1. Data Collection Schedule.

| Instrument | Fall 1964 | Spring 1965 | Fall 1965 | Spring 1966 | Fall 1966 | Spring 1967 |
|---|---|---|---|---|---|---|
| Perception Schedule (PS)[a] | | | | | | |
| Pupil Services Expectation Questionnaire (PSEQ) | | | Pre | | Pre | |
| Pupil Services Fulfillment Questionnaire (PSFQ) | | | | Post | | Post |
| Pupils of Unusual Concern Inventory (PUC) | | | Pre | Post | Pre | Post |
| Functions log | (Diary[b]) | | (Periodic time-sampling plan) | | | |
| Self-Concept of Ability Scale (SCA) | Pre | Post | Pre | Post | Pre | Post |
| Pupil Classroom Behavior Scale (PCBS) | Pre | Post | Pre | Post | Pre | Post |
| Lorge-Thorndike Intelligence Test (LT) | Pre | | Pre[c] | | Pre[c] | |
| Standardized Achievement Tests[d] | Pre | Post | Pre | Post | | Post |
| Dimensions of Teachers' Opinions (DOTO) | Pre | Post | Pre[c] | Post | Pre[c] | Post |
| Teacher Characteristics Schedule (TCS) | Pre | Post | Pre[c] | Post | Pre[c] | Post |

[a]Administered only once (spring 1966) to CDCs and principals of CDC schools.

[b]A daily diary was kept by workers during the trial year; analysis of these diaries resulted in the development of a standardized instrument known as the functions log.

[c]Pretest data were collected only from new participants in the project; previously tested persons were not retested at these times.

[d]At grade 2, the Metropolitan Achievement Test (MAT) was used; at grades 3 through 6, the Iowa Tests of Basic Skills (ITBS) were used.

behavior in classroom settings; teacher ratings on a variety of scales related to attitudes toward children; teacher ratings of the success of the pupil personnel services worker; and activity sheets (known as *functions logs*) maintained by the in-school workers in traditional worker and CDC schools.

Since all schools participating in the project volunteered for this involvement and since assignment to control, traditional worker, and CDC conditions could not be carried out on a random basis, there is no foundation for the use of statistical hypothesis testing procedures within the framework of this project. Most data are simply presented in the form of percentages, and the major task in interpreting these data revolves around deciding whether or not a reported difference indicates practical significance.

In summary, the general findings from the Maryland center project are as follows. First, there was no evidence for a differential effect on student achievement among the three types of schools. While minor year-to-year variations were noted, no pattern of superior academic performance could be attributed to any of the pupil personnel services arrangements.

Second, while no consistent trends were noticeable during the first two years of the project, there was evidence of a more favorable pattern of self-concept for students in schools with CDC staff during the third project year. One might speculate that a change of this type could be a necessary precursor to desirable modifications in student behavior and academic performance.

Third, teacher ratings of pupil classroom behavior showed no consistent trend during the project in any of the types of schools.

Fourth, as shown in Table 2, the presence of an in-school worker (either traditional worker or CDC) had an apparent sensitizing effect on teachers, in that larger proportions of students tended to be nominated as needing professional services, as compared to control schools. It should be noted that these results are based on teacher nominations in terms of need for services, not on actual referrals for professional assistance, since the latter would rather obviously be affected by the ready availabil-

Table 2. Percentages of Total Number of Students Identified
by Teachers as Needing Pupil Personnel Services.

| | Type of In-School Worker | | |
|---|---|---|---|
| | CDC | Traditional | None |
| Winter 1965 | 12 | 10 | 7 |
| Spring 1966 | 11 | 13 | 6 |
| Winter 1966 | 12 | 11 | 6 |
| Spring 1967 | 10 | 12 | 6 |

ity of pupil personnel services workers in the traditional worker
and CDC schools.

Fifth, when comparing traditional worker and CDC
schools, the types of concerns or problem areas that resulted in
teacher requests for assistance from an in-school worker were
highly similar and were very stable over the three-year span of
the project. Academic progress and emotional development
problem areas each accounted for approximately 25 percent of
all requests, while classroom behavior and social development
were responsible for approximately 20 percent each. The remaining 10 percent of all requests was spread over a variety of
miscellaneous categories.

Sixth, with respect to students for whom assistance was
sought from in-school workers, there was no consistent pattern
suggesting greater improvement in either the traditional worker
or CDC schools. While students referred to CDCs showed somewhat larger teacher ratings in the categories of "some" or
"much" improvement, this was not consistent for all time
periods, and the actual percentage differences were relatively
small (with the overall percentage in these improvement categories ranging between 63 percent and 76 percent).

Seventh, the results from the functions logs revealed that
in some areas the CDCs were apparently evolving a distinctive
pattern of functions that represented an integration of certain
aspects of the configurations displayed by counselors and social
workers. For simplicity, the results presented here are for workers during their second year within their assigned elementary
school. The major outcomes are described as follows.

1. CDCs and counselors were similar in that they served students representing all grade levels, 1 through 6, and both had relatively few contacts with special education students; social workers on the other hand had about 13 percent of their contacts with the special education category.
2. The functions of both CDCs and counselors were classified as involving remediation of student problems in about 50 percent of the contacts, whereas this figure was about 70 percent for social workers; consequently, social workers reported proportionately fewer contacts devoted mainly to student maintenance and enhancement.
3. Counselors in general made no visits to students' homes in order to carry out their functions; both CDCs and social workers did make home visits, and in both cases this represented about 3 percent of their functions. (In all cases, however, the vast majority of functions were performed in the school.)
4. CDCs differed from both counselors and social workers in reporting fewer functions as self-initiated (32 percent versus 44 percent and 41 percent, respectively, for counselor and social workers) and more functions as initiated by request of a school staff member (45 percent versus 31 percent for counselors and social workers). All three types of workers were essentially the same in responding to requests from parents, pupils, other workers, and miscellaneous sources.

## Conclusions

Perhaps the strongest single statement permissible on the basis of the data collected under the Maryland center project is that experimentally conceived pupil services workers who were allowed to evolve their own unique in-school roles and functions performed no worse than traditionally trained and experienced workers. Moreover, at least in terms of the criterion variables chosen for inclusion in this project, there is no clear differentiation between schools with workers and schools without workers (but having school district-based services available). Although in-school workers of all types were rated by teachers and staff members as performing well, this was not necessarily reflected in student academic achievement, ratings of student behavior, student ratings of self-concept, and other measures.

Thus we must answer in the negative to the first two research problems posed earlier: Pupil behavior was not more adaptive, and teacher behavior and attitudes did not change. Problem 3, which concerned the functions to be evolved by CDCs, is somewhat more complex. While overall the CDC resembled an elementary school counselor more closely than any other single model, there was evidence that the CDC incorporates certain functions that may make this type of worker more desirable and more adaptable than others (for example, the tendency of the CDC to make more home visits and to be more responsive to requests for initiation of services from staff members, rather than being self-initiating).

From a practical point of view, the findings suggest that a school district must first decide whether or not any in-school services at the elementary school level are necessary (beyond those available from school district-based workers) and then whether or not one specific pattern of roles and functions is more desirable than the others. While the present project cannot offer definitive answers to these questions in a specific instance, the methodology of the project may well be adaptable to local conditions. That is, taking into account local conditions and needs, workers with no particular professional allegiance could be placed in elementary schools with their training and supervision on an in-service basis. While somewhat speculative, it appears reasonable that for such workers roles would be most likely to evolve that would benefit local conditions and that these roles would differ from those studied in the present project. This procedure, while hardly a panacea, has the basic appeal of avoiding stereotypic role definitions and may lay the foundation for an interdisciplinary approach to providing pupil personnel services at the elementary school level.

The position is frequently taken that the value of counseling and the need for continued expansion of services is based on the belief that discrepant behavior is inevitably a divergence from the norm. Students who are "behavior problems" are prime candidates for referral by teachers. To a lesser degree, those students who do not perform academically in accord with the teacher's expectations and prescriptions are also candidates for "pupil personnel services" or "counseling." The gross assumption that obtains in these circumstances is that behavioral deviation and variability in the pace and style of learning are manifestations of problems in the context of the educational process. It is further assumed that "counselors" of whatever stripe can undertake some esoteric functions that hopefully will bring about an accommodation on the part of the student causing the concern. This accommodation, which is usually in the form of compliance or submission to the system, is viewed as the achievement of stability. A revised, nonstatistical concept of the norm may alter significantly teacher expectations and enable them to accept the large difference in the frequencies of the various behaviors likely to be manifested in most classrooms. This modification is predicated on the teacher's increased awareness of probable causes and potential problems.

## Beyond IRCOPPS

Despite the fact that the first two of the three major research problems addressed by IRCOPPS were answered in the negative, there is sufficient cause for optimism in the affirmation of the third statement regarding the evolutionary nature of the functions of the CDC. Professional workers with an interdisciplinary orientation can be trained in an unorthodox fashion in a relatively brief time and in such a manner that the needs of the population to be served would be met.

Beyond this, with reference to Problems 1 and 2, the scope of the counseling process must be broadened to the extent that the congruence of goals of school and pupils can be at least approximated by having the new counselor assume a child advocacy role. In addition, the new counselor must serve as an intermediary, interpretive agent for teachers with respect to patterns of causal behavior and to the interrelatedness between each child's behavior and the demands of the school.

Again, the nagging, persistent question arises regarding

the objectives and purposes of counseling. What IRCOPPS clearly demonstrated was that a child development consultant with a philosophic orientation as a habilitative change agent could perform, with skill and competence, functions similar to those of personnel workers traditionally trained and oriented toward remediation and rehabilitation. Indeed, the Maryland center staff identified as a major interest the configuration and array of services provided by the CDCs. Data provided by the functions log, an instrument designed by the staff for that purpose, indicated that both CDCs and traditional counselors performed approximately the same number of functions in a sample day. However, the variety of functions, particularly those related to working with parents and teachers, was striking in contrast to the counselors' focus on troubled children.

It appears as though the commonly accepted professional procedures, taught and reinforced in training centers for counselors and school psychologists, are designed to support, maintain, and enhance the educational system within which the student performs. Implicit in this is the fact that the success or the measure of competency of the counselors is in direct proportion to effecting an acceptable degree of conformity on the part of those students who are perceived to be in need of "help."

An examination of the academic training program for the preparation of counselors, school social workers, and school psychologists makes it immediately apparent that there is a common core of training that develops a common perspective of the functions performed by each of these specialists. Each has it within his purview that he is to aid, in cooperation with the instructional and administrative staffs, in the optimal development of all children, directly and indirectly; in the enhancement and fulfillment of all children; and in the constant search for an educative process that will be conducive to the attainment of these goals.

Gilbert Wrenn emphasizes the need for the counselor to see the whole school, the whole range of students, and the whole student and to collate and interpret this information to students, teachers, parents, and administrators. "Perhaps," he suggests, "most of all, the counselor is a human behavior consultant to teacher, administrator, and parents" (Wrenn, 1962, p. 125).

Perhaps it is of some significance at this point to restate that the counselor as conceived by IRCOPPS may be viewed as a social change agent in the broadest sense. To aid each individual child to make optimal use of whatever qualities and characteristics he or she may bring to the school does not necessitate the imposition of constraints on those with differences in pace, style, or mode of learning. To serve, as Wrenn suggests, in the capacity of a "human behavior consultant," implies a critical need to raise levels of awareness and sensitivity; only then can teachers cease to view behavioral and intellectual differences as disturbing and threatening. This, in turn, suggests that a new perspective of the education experience is required.

The counselor, then, can aid in the process of enhancing the total functioning of the child by aiding teachers, administrators, and parents to accept and value each individual with his or her differences. The counselor need no longer be, as indeed he or she currently is, an agent of the established order. Support for teachers need not take the form of inducing conforming behavior or removing a child from a group because of a specific deviancy or what may be considered a general deficiency.

The counselor can be a dynamic force in generating movement toward a more open, more humanist-oriented concept of education. The child development consultant-counselor, as child advocate, can effect a "modification of the teacher's perceptions relative to self, to his or her professional role, and to the learner's individual needs. These changes in perception would then result in behavioral adjustments with respect to quality of teacher-pupil relations, to recognition of differentiated pupil goals, and to development of processes for their implementation" (Seidman, 1969, p. 92).

Development of the child advocacy approach to the preparation of counselors in the CDC mold requires that the counselor educators revise radically the nature and sequence of courses. To fulfill the new role, skills new to the counselor training process are required. And practicum experiences, rather than occurring as culminating activities, should be ongoing, integral parts of all courses of the program. Theory and practice are melded. This approach was strongly supported by the schools that were the on-site training centers for the CDCs.

It is noteworthy that presentations of the IRCOPPS Project to the American Psychological Association (Seidman and others, 1966) and to the American Personnel and Guidance Association (Seidman and others, 1968) both elicited mixed responses. But for the most part general reactions were skeptical. Perhaps a true measure of the impact of IRCOPPS on the programs of the county school systems that participated in the project is the fact that CDCs who were the experimental subjects were incorporated into the staffs of their respective schools and continued to perform their expanded roles.

The assessment of performance has long been a core skill of counselors. Additional skills, long ignored, or considered merely peripheral, are those related to the interdisciplinary nature of the CDC. Counselors must be well grounded in the principles of normal physical and psychological growth and development. This is requisite to understanding atypical development and the stages of cognitive development. Counselors must have an understanding of and an awareness of normal crises and conflicts; this forms the basis for understanding the crises and conflicts of atypical children, particularly the behaviorally disordered. A basic premise is that to understand the exceptional child we must understand the typical child.

Another critical dimension of involvement for the new counselor is the curriculum. A knowledge of curriculum theory and the structure of learning undoubtedly can diminish the division that exists between the traditional ancillary worker and the teacher.

It appears, then, that a natural and logical extension of the child development consultant construct entails a body of skills related to child growth and development, the child's learning environment, the curriculum methods of instruction, and the teacher as a person. The conceptual development of the CDC has evolved from altered perceptions of relationships that obtain in the teaching-learning process.

Since the traditional concept of counseling is viewed as a

system maintenance service, supportive in the rehabilitative, remedial sense, it is imperative that the focus of counselor training programs be changed, for it is in the counselor education centers that the typical and traditional conceptualization of the counselor's role and functions is concretized. The resolution of crises and problems is of paramount concern. The new, and significant, modification of counselor training would not ignore the skills of crisis intervention but would merely place them in proper perspective. The major emphasis would shift from the therapeutic, remedial, and ameliorative dimensions to the role of the interventionist as a habilitative agent; the counselor would become a force in curricular modification, in teacher sensitization, and in family involvement and become an integral part of the schema of trusting relationships with the children, without which—nothing.

# 7

## Psychological Education

Alfred S. Alschuler
Allen E. Ivey
Chris Hatcher

A small group of children sit with a counselor. They are asked to tell about one thing they enjoyed during the past week. As the children share experiences, all listen attentively. The counselor is supportive but makes no value judgments. Later the children share their concerns and their enthusiasm.

A junior high school class is playing a ring toss game, in which each student decides how far to stand from the peg. The counselor notes the level of aspiration of each participant, and this information serves as the basis for discussion of achievement motivation. In this game, students learn about themselves and others.

A psychologist in a university counseling center is meeting with a group of men in a male consciousness-raising session.

126

Through contacts with women's liberation, he has become aware of the effects of sexism on males: excessive competitiveness, the exclusion of tender activities, the new demands of the "liberated woman." He wants to share his knowledge with this group and expand his own personal awareness of the effect of sexism on his own experience.

A rehabilitation counselor from a mental health unit is meeting with the board of directors of the local chamber of commerce. His concern is to facilitate job placement of a former psychiatric patient. In the past, his approach to such a situation has been to lecture and persuade. Now he is using simulation games by which the board members can come to understand the emotional experience of rehabilitation clientele. To his surprise, he finds the board responding enthusiastically to his ideas and starting to share some of their own personal concerns.

Psychological education is all of these activities and more. It is special techniques and growth centers. It is carefully designed courses that inculcate aspects of mental health and personal adjustment. It is a new curriculum area in which people learn to understand themselves and more effectively get what they want.

For practicing counselors, psychological education provides a new conception of their roles. When people hear the word *counselor,* they tend to think of a person who sits in an office and works with one person or a small group on problems in living that are brought to the counselor. Psychological education involves the counselor's taking initiative in deliberately teaching aspects of mental health to larger groups. Education, rather than remediation, is the goal.

Psychological education is a relatively new discipline, but it is already providing important levers to help counselors refocus their efforts and increase their effectiveness. Counselors support the "mental illness" focus by treating victims of inhumane institutions instead of mobilizing themselves and others to restructure learning, interpersonal and intergroup relationships, and schools so that there will be more healthy human beings and fewer casualties. It is self-condemnation to argue that counselors comprise only a small percentage of those who could rectify the situation, because it is counselors who have created an artificially scarce helping resource by placing legal restrictions on "helping" and by not teaching our colleagues, administrators, teachers, parents, and children the fundamentals of helping others. Then counselors make it doubly difficult for themselves by waiting passively for symptoms, for clients to bring problems to them, instead of actively intervening at an early stage in schools, communities, or agencies and offering programs designed to promote psychosocial health directly.

We advocate a new definition of the counselor role: that of the psychological educator who becomes actively involved in the life of institutions and teaches healthy skills to others. The principal goal of psychological education is to increase the individual's capacity to anticipate alternative experiences, to choose among them, and to find greater self-satisfaction from his choice. Within such a framework, two important factors must be recognized. First, any action represents a value that should be explored. Techniques may be neutral, but users are not. Psychological education should allow for the examination of a values continuum, not for the support of a particular world view. Philosophical or value systems beyond this should be both explicit and public. Second, the influence of group pressure to respond in one direction or another should be carefully and sensitively dealt with in each situation.

## Psychological Education Guidelines

Ivey and Alschuler (1973) have identified four basic guidelines currently being used by psychological educators in program development. First, psychological educators focus more on long-term effects than on short-term effects. Too often, in education, there is virtually no significant correlation between grades or test scores and indices of satisfaction in later life. Psychological educators need to design their courses and workshops so that the concepts and processes learned have value and utility to the student in his or her later life. One example of such a design is the "trumpet" (Weinstein and Fantini, 1970; Weinstein, 1971, 1973). Weinstein describes the process as attempting to provide the individual with a cognitive map or sequence in working through a set of personal observations. The individual is presented with models of the kinds of questions that might be asked at each phase of personal exploration. Figure 1 is a schematic overview of what the learner is exposed to.

In Weinstein's experimental "self-science education" classes, the student learns the language and skills for proceeding through the trumpet inventory responses, as he works on a variety of personal situations and themes. To illustrate the trumpet process, the following situation (Weinstein, 1973, pp. 601-602) is presented with a sample set of responses between student (S) and counselor (C):

### Inventory Responses

S: The teacher called on me today in class to explain something we had for homework.

C: [Inventorying] What happened?

S: I got so nervous I could hardly answer.

C: [Inventorying feelings] What were your feelings like?

S: I was scared as hell.

C: [Inventorying body feelings] Where in your body were you feeling the fear?

S: In my throat; it got so tight it was hard for me to talk. My hands were trembling and sweaty.

C: [Inventorying actions] What did you do?

S: I mumbled a few words, stopped, then stammered a few more. Nothing made sense.

C: [Inventorying actions] Where were your eyes looking?

S: First I looked at the teacher for a second or two, then the rest of the time I stared down at the floor.

C: [Inventorying thoughts] Do you remember what sentences you were saying to yourself at the time?

S: I was thinking about what a fool I was making out of myself

**Figure 1. The Trumpet Process.**

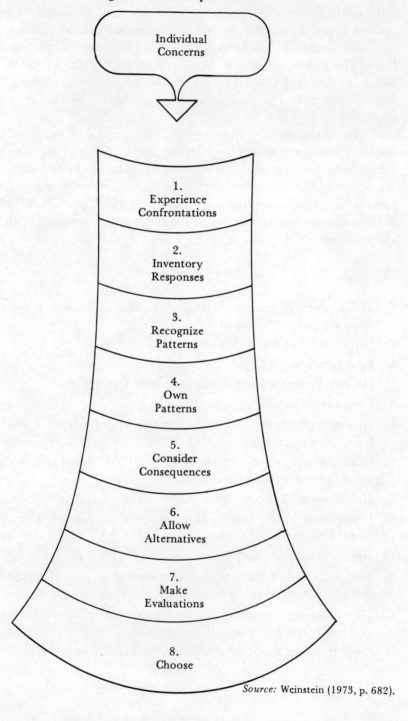

Individual
Concerns

1.
Experience
Confrontations

2.
Inventory
Responses

3.
Recognize
Patterns

4.
Own
Patterns

5.
Consider
Consequences

6.
Allow
Alternatives

7.
Make
Evaluations

8.
Choose

*Source:* Weinstein (1973, p. 682).

in front of everybody in the class, that I was going to say something so dumb everyone would laugh, and how I wished I were someplace else.

### Recognize Patterns

C: Has this ever happened to you before?

S: I'll say.

C: In what kinds of situations?

S: Whenever I have to say something in front of a group of people.

C: Is it only in school that this happens?

S: No. Sometimes at home, when we have a lot of company, I kind of stay in the background and hope that nobody asks me anything.

C: If you wanted to teach me your pattern of responding to situations like this, what kind of directions would you give me?

S: Well, first of all, I'd tell you to start imagining things the night before the day you might be called on.

C: What kinds of things?

S: Oh, imagine the teacher calls on you and you say something so stupid the whole class breaks up and starts whispering to each other about how stupid you are. Then imagine the teacher putting you down for giving such a dumb answer and then giving you a lousy mark.

C: What else would I have to do?

S: Do just what I did. When you get called on, get nervous as anything. Mumble, look down, and finally give up and don't say anything.

### Own Patterns

C: Can you tell me any way that your pattern helps you? What might it help you avoid or get? Try finishing this sentence: "By reacting this way in those situations, I avoid. . . ."

S: Well, I guess I avoid giving the wrong answers.

C:  How is avoiding giving the answers useful to you?

S:  If I don't give the answers, I can't make a mistake.

C:  And if you can't make a mistake?

S:  Then I won't do anything stupid.

C:  So you use the pattern to protect you from feeling dumb?

S:  Yeah, I guess so.

C:  Do you feel less stupid when you use the pattern?

S:  No. In fact, I think I feel more stupid.

C:  So your pattern isn't too effective in helping you get what you want?

S:  I guess not.

C:  What do you want?

S:  To feel smarter. To not feel so darn scared anytime I have to say something in front of people.

### Allow Alternatives

C:  Would you be willing to try some experiments with yourself to see if you can find anything that works a little better for you?

S:  Maybe. What kinds of experiments?

Weinstein (p. 603) then describes the student and counselor as coming up with some alternative ways to experiment with these unsatisfying feelings and responses, such as: "If I don't know an answer to a question, I will clearly say I don't know the answer, or each time I have an opportunity to say something before a group, I will practice making at least one contribution, such as telling whose opinion I agree with." After several weeks, the student and counselor again get together to look at the results of the experiments. Some traditional professionals miss the point of such experiments and comment that one could go on forever suggesting experimental responses. They fail to see that the principal focus is to teach the individual the *process* of experimentation; that the experience that results from this process helps the individual to alter old response patterns or to gain a clearer definition of his or her decision to stay with the old patterns.

A second basic guideline is that developmental theory and research suggest competences that are critical to later development and age approximations during which they are learned. For example, in their systematic review of longitudinal studies of mental health, Kohlberg, LaCrosse, and Ricks (1971) showed that the two best predictors of adult maladjustment were poor peer relationships in the first three years of school, and antisocial behavior during the second three years of school. Kolberg's (1968) continuing research into his theories of moral development have produced substantial evidence for individuals going through six ordered stages of moral judgment. Each progressive stage is characterized by increasing logic, differentiation, and broader awareness of social issues. A large number of studies by developmental psychologists indicate, surprisingly, that this progression has both cross-national and cross-cultural validity. This suggests the importance of educational attention to ego development during these critical periods, rather than concentrating social system energies on subsequent remedial help.

Using developmental theory in this way, Gum, Tamminen, and Smaby (1973) have employed structured Developmental Guidance Experiences (DGEs) to encourage open, frank discussion about all sides of ethical or value issues related to developmental tasks, rather than "leading" the students to some "correct" viewpoint. The following example is one DGE on sex role attitudes prepared for use with high school students (Gum, Tamminen, and Smaby, 1973, pp. 648-649). It begins by having the students read this story:

A young girl is deeply in love with her boyfriend, who lives across the river due to forces beyond his control. The girl's parents are very happy about this, as they do not want them to go together for various reasons. As a result of this, the girl runs away, as she wants so much to be with her love. She runs to the river and becomes aware of

the fact there is no way within her means to get
across the river and be with her boyfriend. She
soon sees a boat coming and explains her story to
the boatman. He offers to take her across, but only
if she will make love to him. Our girl does not feel
right about the proposition and runs off into the
woods to think the matter through. In the woods
she meets an old hermit, who hears her story with
attentive ears. The girl asks the hermit what she
should do in her desperation, and he says, "Do
what you think is right. I feel you will find the
right answer within yourself."

After thinking the matter through, the girl
goes back to the river, carries out the boatman's
proposition, and finally is with her love. She explains the whole story to him, and he realizes he
can no longer accept this girl after what has happened. He realizes that she does not represent the
ideals which are so important to him. He breaks off
the relationship and the girl is left alone in the
world. She finally meets up with "perfect couple,"
who listen to her story, feel very deeply for her,
and adopt her.

The students were then given the following instructions:
"Now you are to rank the people in the story (parents, girl,
boy, boatman, hermit, "perfect couple") in an order of preference you hold for them. Attempt to be as honest about your
feelings and views as possible. Try and focus on why you ranked
them as you did" (Gum, Tamminen, and Smaby, 1973, pp.
648-649). Afterward, students share and discuss their rankings,
the boy-girl relationship, and similar real-life problems. In one
follow-up of this DGE, with twenty-seven high school juniors,
the following typical answers were provided to an incomplete-
sentences questionnaire (Gum, Tamminen, and Smaby, 1973, p.
650):

DGEs gave me a chance to "find out how
my ideas differed from the kinds in class," "get to
talk and smile at someone I didn't know," "understand males more," "learn about everyone else."

During DGEs I found myself "really getting involved instead of just sitting back in a little corner," "somewhat embarrassed during the sex discussion, but I learned many things I wanted to know," "thinking about my faults and how I could improve myself," "getting wrapped up in the discussion."

I would rather participate in a DGE than "any other activity," "regular class," "have a discussion led by a person on the same thing," "sit bored listening to a lecture in other classes," "most other things," "bake cookies."

DGEs are "a lot of fun, you can really let go and say what's on your mind," "mind expanding," "nice to get to know someone without being afraid," "okay, okay," "the thing."

Developmental guidance experiences can also be effectively designed for use with younger children. One DGE for elementary school children begins with a standard-size sheet of colored construction paper cut into six odd shapes to make a puzzle. Students are divided into small groups and the groups work competitively. Then the entire class discusses what happened in the small groups—feelings, reactions to each other, and what might have been done differently. Student comments during this discussion are often like the following:  Nobody listened to my ideas, John acted like he was the only one who could do it, Mary kept putting them together in dumb ways, I wanted to be the first to get it done, I got so mad I wanted to hit Bill.  The counselor is then able to use his small-group skills to assist the students describe in full their feelings and reactions.

The third basic guideline derives from Eysenck's (1952) review of the effectiveness of various forms of psychotherapy. Eclectic procedures systematically organized to reach a specific outcome are more effective than a single procedure used to solve a variety of problems (Alschuler, 1973; Eysenck, 1961; McClelland, 1965; McClelland and Winter, 1969). What this means is that any single procedure is likely to be less effective than a combination of procedures organized into a definite curriculum to accomplish a limited, specific goal. Individual treatment, group counseling, advising, behavior therapy, Gestalt therapy, group dynamics techniques, reevaluation therapy, value clarification, and so forth, are not invalid per se; they are simply less effective than a systematic combination of several different procedures used to reach a single goal. It means also that the definition of the goal should precede the choice and sequence of methods. The obvious implication for psychological educators is that they should be open to the utility of techniques and approaches developed from various theoretical positions.

The fourth basic guideline is that the institution, school, or business needs to receive equal attention in the psychological education process. This does not mean more one-to-one counseling with administrators in addition to the students. It means developing collaborative methods to change role definitions, rules, policies, norms, and expectations that influence all people who exist in the institution. For example, if achievement motivation, communication skills, and personal responsibility for decision making are taught to students, it is important that the way in which the students learn in other classes also allows, encourages, and rewards them for acting in these ways. If the same things are taught to adults, their institution (employment office, college, business, and so on) also needs to be examined and perhaps changed. Too often effective individual training is undermined by ineffective or damaging institutions and systems. These system changes require that psychological educators have additional skills in helping organizations develop and grow.

Counselors at every level are becoming aware of their responsibility to act as consultants to classroom teachers, or to vocational rehabilitation instructors, but they are often unaware of what steps they can take to achieve a meaningful impact on the educational process. One vital role for the counselor is teaching teachers how to do psychological education in their classrooms by conducting in-service training courses and offering to teach psychological units in teachers' classrooms. Psychiatric hospitals are increasingly concerned with teaching patients "life skills," as well as with conducting the more traditional therapeutic approaches. A third role calls for the school counselor to assert a position as a full member of the curriculum development team. As Faust (1968) points out, teachers, curriculum supervisors, principals, and sometimes associate superintendents alone assume leadership in the development of curriculum. The counselor's inclusion in this process can do a great deal to sensitize the other members to a human behavior component within the regular curriculum.

Other efforts in systematic change have been described by Schmuck and Miles in *Organizational Development in Schools* (1971), by Robert Carkhuff in *The Development of Human Resources* (1971), and by Seymour Sarason in *The Creation of Settings and the Future Societies* (1972).

### Where Can You Go from Here?

Where can you go from here? This chapter has provided a basic framework, and a number of practical examples, but solid competence and sustained programs require more preparation. The sources we suggest in each of the following areas are suitable for individuals just getting into the field of psychological education.

*Activities and Exercises.* Almost all psychological educators need to develop a repertoire of games, exercises, role plays, and structured activities that can provide an experience base on which to teach the psychological lesson. The following books contain many exercises. After mastering two or three, skimming the others will quickly reveal the large overlap of activities and the many variations possible on each of the basic exercises.

First, we suggest the series of six paperbacks by Pfeiffer and Jones (1969, 1970, 1971, 1973, 1975, 1977) *Structured Experiences for Human Relations Training* (University Associates Press, Box 615, Iowa City, Iowa 52240). These six manuals contain a wealth of exercises and ideas for the development of workshops as well as psychologically oriented courses for a wide variety of age groups. Further, Pfeiffer and Jones have been quite active in conducting an excellent series of training workshops, and one may write for information in care of their publisher. In a similar vein, *Values Clarification,* by Simon, Howe, and Kirschenbaum (1972), is another very useful paperback. Its 379 pages contain seventy-nine specific techniques for extending values clarification.

Other valuable sources for exercises in psychological education include Brown, *Human Teaching for Human Learning: An Introduction to Confluent Education* (1971), and Lewis and Streetfield, *Growth Games: How to Tune In to Yourself, Your Family, and Your Friends* (1971). Some equally good sources for psychologically oriented exercises may be found in Malamud and Machover, *Toward Self-Understanding: Group Techniques in Self-Confrontation* (1965).

The National Training Labs (NTL) Institutes and Esalen have been two commonly identified leaders in small-group process in 1960s and early 70s. NTL staff Nyler, Mitchell, and Stout have drawn together material developed and field tested in numerous seminars into the *Handbook of Staff Development and Human Relations Training* (1967). While the NTL book is best suited for the educator, Schultz's *Joy* (1967), collected from his workshops at Esalen, is excellent as a first reading for students. Although *Joy* is now ten years old and has been widely read in the general population, it remains a good choice.

An important arm in psychological education for both physical and emotional health is the impact of environmental stress. New investigations in the 1970s have raised serious new questions about the mind-body dichotomy. Scientists are becoming less skeptical of the body therapists' theories on bodily tension and position as a reflection of internal psychological conflict. Jacobson's (1938) *Progressive Relaxation* is an old but classic work that provides important underpinnings for much of today's work using relaxation training. An inexpensive and more readily available introduction to Jacobson's work is his paperback book *You Must Relax* (1962). Those oriented toward body awareness owe Jacobson a great debt whether their orientation is analytic (for example, Lowen, *Physical Dynamics of Character Structure,* 1958), humanistic (for example, Gunther, *Sense Relaxation: Below Your Mind,* 1968), or behavioral (for example, Wolpe and Lazarus, *Behavior Therapy*

*Techniques,* 1968). Those interested in body work as an important part of psychological education will want to return to a detailed examination of Jacobson's studies.

The literature on altered states of consciousness and biofeedback is expanding exponentially, but most of the material available at present is highly technical. Perhaps the best source at this time is Barbara Brown's *New Mind, New Body* (1974). It should be recognized that it is relatively easy to gain a beginning understanding of biofeedback principles and techniques. However, concentrated training in instrumentation, artifact problems, and physiology is very necessary before initiating work with clients in this area.

For a more extensive listing of exercises, games, simulations, films, and growth centers where experiences such as these are offered, Canfield and Phillips, *A Guide to Humanistic Education* (1971), is a good source (Association of Humanistic Psychology, 416 Hoffman, San Francisco, Calif. 94114).

*Programs in Psychological Education.* A number of programs provide more systematic direction for organizing exercises toward specific goals. Being competent in one or more of these programs will provide models later when one attempts to combine exercises into unique programs designed to solve specific psychological problems or to develop systematic preventive developmental programs. The importance of systematic approaches to psychological education cannot be stressed too strongly, for it is the random selection of exercises without specific aims that most often results in ineffective or comical consequences. Psychological educators should have meaningful, readily transmittable rationales for all their work.

Two systematic programs in creativity stand out: Parnes's *Creative Behavior Handbook* (1967) and Gordon's *Synetics* (1961). Additional information on synetics curriculum materials is available from Synetics Educational Systems, 121 Brattle Street, Cambridge, Mass. 02138. Further information on creativity courses and methods may be obtained from the Creative Education Foundation, State University College, 1300 Elmwood Avenue, Buffalo, N.Y. 14222.

The concepts inherent in achievement motivation provide

a popular and well-researched approach to psychological education. Alschuler, Tabor, and McIntyre (*Teaching Achievement Motivation,* 1970) provide an overview of this program. Specific games to teach achievement motivation available from this publisher include "The Origami Game," "Ring Toss Game," "Who Am I?," "Aiming," and "Ten Thoughts."

For work with elementary children, the magic circle concept is particularly effective and is available in a readily usable format, as a curriculum for kindergarten through late elementary school, in Bessell's *Methods in Human Development* (1970).

Special issues of the *Counseling Psychologist* (1971, *1* [4]), "emphasizing school approaches," and of the *Personnel and Guidance Journal* (Ivey and Alschuler, 1973) providing a broader sampling, are exclusively devoted to developments in psychological education.

Other organized programs are available. Excellent programs and exercises may be found in Wells and Canfield, *About Me: A Curriculum for Developing Self-Motivation* (1970), and in Peterson, *Motivation Advance Program* (1972). Both of these are available from Combined Motivation Education Systems, 6300 River Road, Rosemont, Ill. 60018.

Dinkmeyer's *Developing Understanding of Self and Others* (American Guidance Service, Publishers' Building, Circle Elementary School Multimedia Program, 1972) is an excellent program that includes puppets, records or cassettes, discussion cards, and storybooks. The program is creatively organized around Duso the Dolphin, a wise and understanding listener. Duso is joined by Flopsie the Flounder, who is moving from indecision and dependence to more self-confidence, and Coho the Salmon, changing from insensitive to more accepting. There are, actually, two programs, one for kindergarten and lower primary and one for upper primary. The Duso programs have been field tested in 175 classrooms involving over 5,100 children in seventeen states. Hatcher, one of the coauthors of this chapter, reports excellent results in implementing the Dinkmeyer program using teachers and psychology interns.

Gestalt transactional analysis (TA) concepts are becoming increasingly important with the psychologically oriented public, but they are easier to understand than to convert or integrate with a teaching format. Most people agree that participating workshops represent the best way to learn about Gestalt therapy and transactional analysis. In the printed media, the most comprehensive Gestalt text is Hatcher and Himelstein's (1976) *Handbook of Gestalt Therapy,* which also reviews the teaching and workshop institutes throughout the United States and Canada. Of the subgroups in psychological systems, the transactional analysts have been the most active in communicating their ideas to the general public. Two of the best-received books in this area are *T.A. Games* (Bry, 1975) and *T.A. Primer* (Bry, 1973). For family education groups, Murtel James' and Dorothy Jongeward's *Transactional Analysis for Moms and Dads* (1975) is imaginatively written but benefits significantly from supplemental teaching by an instructor. Alvyn Freed's *TA for Tots* (1974) deserves a special mention. Illustrated with cartoons, it is designed to be used as a storybook or read by the kids themselves. In its fifth printing, the popularity of the book points out the strong demand for more books aimed at this level.

Behavioral approaches are not usually associated with psychological education, but the recent effort of the behavior modifiers to make their concepts clear and discernible to the layperson is in the best tradition of the psychological education movement. We believe, however, that the modification of behavior, in order to qualify as true psychological education, must be shared, rather than manipulative. Important among the many good books in this area is J. Krumboltz and H. Krumboltz's *Changing Children's Behavior* (1972). Two other helpful works for developing systematic training programs in behavioral approaches are Deibert and Harmon's *New Tools for Changing Behavior* (1973) and Carter's *Help: These Kids Are Driving Me Crazy!* (1972). Many people have founder Sulzer and Mayer's *Behavior Modification Procedures for School Personnel* (1972) especially helpful in the school situation.

A major influence in behavioral approaches to psychological education has been the work of Thomas Gordon. Gordon's books, *Parent Effectiveness Training* (1970) and *Teacher Effectiveness Training* (1975), do not present radically new approaches but do succeed in communicating child management techniques to the general reader with an unmatched excellence and clarity. Further, it is very easy for the counselor to adjust the material for teaching use in working with less educated or psychologically minded parents. Gordon's Effectiveness Training Associates have also been actively engaged for several years in conducting training workshops throughout the United States. Many professionals have found that these workshops, which include a good deal of practice time, provide the most effective medium for acquiring skills in the Parent Effectiveness Training (PET) approach.

*Transmitting Counseling Skills to People.* While based in counseling psychology and in the desire to produce better counselors, three methods of counselor training are increasingly showing themselves to be viable means of psychological education. If counseling skills are relatively easily defined, it is a short and logical extension to argue that they should be made available to the general public.

The most comprehensive statement of this position is made by Robert Carkhuff. His clear definition of helping skills should be a basic part of all psychological educators' repertoires as well as their libraries. Important foundations of Carkhuff's methods and concepts can be found in his two-volume series *Helping and Human Relations* (1969). Included in these volumes are clear definitions of his conceptual framework for facilitative human relationships. Vital extension of these basic concepts to community and societal issues, particularly those of racial relations, may be found in *The Development of Human Resources* (Carkhuff, 1971). A recent paperback, *The Art of Helping* (Carkhuff, 1973), provides a useful introduction to his concepts for the layperson, and Carkhuff plans further extensions describing his work.

Kagan's *Influencing Human Interaction* (1972), a dynamic and exciting method of counselor training using television feedback training, has proven itself as a foremost counseling construct not only to counselors and therapists but also to teachers and other groups. Kagan has produced a valuable and well-researched set of videotapes and materials that make his methods clear and learnable. Although designed originally for professionals, Kagan's materials have important implications for the psychological education movement.

A third method of imparting counseling skills to the public is represented by Ivey's *Microcounseling* (1971). The methods of microcounseling have been used to teach basic counseling and communication skills to populations as varying as medical students and psychiatric patients, parents and children, school counselors and peer counselor groups, clinical psychologists, and camp counselors. Once individuals learn basic skills, they seem able to move forward and apply these skills in a wide variety of situations. From its beginnings, microcounseling has been oriented to the counselor's role as a teacher of counseling and communication skills.

### Recent Controversies

It must be recognized that not everybody has been an enthusiastic supporter of psychological education. Some parent action groups have taken the position that schools should teach the educational basics and leave the "development of the total child" to the parents. Onalee McGraw, National Coordinator of the Coalition for Children and a member of two Maryland groups—Parents Who Care and Citizens United for Responsible Education (CURE)—has been one widely quoted promoter of this position (in Schaar, 1975). McGraw states that many children are illiterate and learning less each year and that it is time to stop attributing this to the parents and the home and start putting the blame back in the schools (Schaar, 1975).

A major focus of this concern has been directed at programs that can only be marginally classed as being psychological education. These programs sometimes take on philosophical or value positions that do not find favor with some parent and community groups. *MACOS* (*Man, A Course of Study*), an elementary school behavioral science curriculum developed with National Science Foundation funds, is an example. The *MACOS* curriculum involves instruction about behavior and values in different cultures and is designed to heighten the student's awareness that all human behavior is understandable in terms of a person's environment or circumstances. Critics reply that this produces an "anything goes" attitude that will create significant problems for the child.

In evaluating this controversy, two points are clear. First, many school systems do have real problems with students' levels of reading and math. There is little argument that we somehow must improve educational performance in this area. Second, any program that has a psychological education component must be as neutral as to values as possible and implemented on a voluntary participation basis.

Another controversy has evolved primarily out of the organizational development applications of psychological education. In particular, a number of individuals in business and organizational systems are quite aware that almost any change will produce a brief increase in employee productivity. This is the well-known Hawthorne effect. Some organizations have, unfortunately, used psychological education training programs in this way. The employees soon learn that what they were taught is not practiced in the work setting, and they tend to develop a negative attitude set toward psychological education as being two-faced or unrealistic. Of course, it is the organization, rather than the training program, that is the problem. But this still does not seem to change the employees' negative set.

Thus both organizational misuse and the *MACOS* controversy serve to remind us of the complexity of interrelationships in our society. And, rather than decrease our interest in psychological education, we should expand our practical sensitivity and research interests to include those interrelationships.

## Summary

Previously, the counselor has been defined as participating in three basic roles: the remedial or rehabilitative role, the preventive, and the educative and/or developmental. In 1976, the Professional Affairs Committee of Division 17 (Counseling

Psychology) of the American Psychological Association reexamined this definition and recommended a reordering of the three primary roles (Ivey, 1976). The committee stated that the educative and/or developmental role of the counseling psychologist must now be considered primary, with the preventive role in the secondary position. The traditional remedial and rehabilitative role is not abandoned but becomes subsumed under an enlarged definition of counseling psychology. This psychoeducational model provides a much wider area of content for functioning, and the clientele range is broadened from individuals to include families, primary groups, associational groups, institutions, and communities.

This chapter has noted that a significant number of individuals and programs are actively involved in the development, application, and evaluation of psychological education techniques. Many readers might wonder how they could possibly master this varied repertoire of skills. However, one should keep the primary aims of psychological education in mind. There are many ways to develop intentionality and growth in individuals, ranging from humanistically oriented behavior modification programs and encounter groups to large-system change efforts. All of us have our own specialties, significant experiences, and knowledge. Instead of arguing which method is "best" or "right," perhaps we could join together as colleagues and recognize that our differences in methods and concepts can actually be used to further larger mutual goals. Thus we can cherish and use our differences in attitudes, opinions, and skills. The time has come for guidance workers, psychologists, and helpers to realize that no one person or theoretical system has the answer. If we all spend time developing our own unique expertise, recognizing that everyone has something to contribute to the action, the traditional status hierarchies may disappear as counselors move toward mutuality, not only with the public but also within the helping profession.

# 8

# Parent-Child Education Centers

Ray N. Lowe
Carol Morse

This chapter describes a child guidance center that has been in operation for twenty years. While several hundred families have received assistance at the center, no less than 20,000 students have received different levels of training. Several students in advanced degree programs have gone on to establish other major centers nationally and internationally. Although the center has enjoyed enormous success, the underlying philosophy and its application to parent-teacher education is not new. The premises are those of Alfred Adler, the founder of individual psychology; the techniques are essentially those of Rudolf Dreikurs. The child guidance centers, the concern of this chapter, while a major Adlerian contribution to our time, actually represented but a small part of Adler's theoretical and therapeutic work. It was Dreikurs who introduced the child guidance notion in this country in the late 1930s. It was not until two decades later, when he began a series of summer sessions together with

146

Raymond N. Lowe at the University of Oregon in Eugene, that the major thrust began.

The Community Parent-Teacher Education Center (CP-TEC) in Eugene includes courses, counseling, and discussion groups for parents, teachers, students, and professionals who are interested in improving relationships between adults and pre- and elementary-school-age children. At CP-TEC, teacher education, counselor training, and research are combined with education and counseling. The center exists under the joint sponsorship of the University of Oregon, College of Education, and the Eugene Public Schools. The staff works closely with school personnel, physicians, court personnel, children's services, and other representatives of local agencies. Sessions are always open to the public. In short, the center is a community venture.

In the following pages, the reader is provided with a theoretical and practical orientation, some understanding of why child guidance centers remain a critical service, and an elaboration of the Adlerian approach to counseling families at a particular center, namely CP-TEC.

## The Need for a Theoretical Orientation

At the present time, there is no scientifically validated theory of human development. Of course, when one is validated, it will cease to be a theory. There are a number of theories, some more tolerated than others, that seek to explain human behavior. However, the absence of a scientifically valid theory does not preclude the counselor's or therapist's acceptance of certain observations as working hypotheses and examining their validity through his or her own experiences. A counselor undertaking a helping relationship without an awareness of the theoretical premises on which he or she is operating cannot be expected to know why his or her efforts have been effective or ineffective. The general concept of humans developing held by the counselor can contribute in considerable measure not only to his or her effectiveness but to professional development as well.

The point of view on which CP-TEC is based was actually

formulated more than fifty years ago by Viennese psychiatrist Alfred Adler in his theory of individual psychology (Bottome, 1957). Adler's position is related to a philosophy of social democracy with its implied principle of human equality and socioteleological view of human development.

From an Adlerian point of view (Ansbacher, 1956), the individual is socially embedded and can only be understood within his or her social context. Each individual strives to find a place in this context. If the individual is operating on the useful side of life, he or she will be able to bring his or her own interests into harmony with others, and "social interest" will characterize the individual's adjustment. Maladjustment is characterized by inferiority feelings, underdeveloped social interest, and uncooperative or mistaken goals of personal superiority. Problems of relationships are social problems, and since these problems arise from group interaction they must be solved within a group.

Striving (from inferiority to superiority or perfection) is the basic force behind all human activity. This striving is expressed by the individual through unique goals, which are influenced but not determined by heredity and environment. Since these goals are idealized, they remain fictional, and the individual only vaguely understands them. (Adler defines the unconscious as the unknown part of the goal.) At an early age, every individual works out a plan, a "style of life" for attempting to realize his or her fictional goals. All psychological processes of the individual are organized from the viewpoint of the style of life and ultimately of the goal (Ansbacher, 1956).

Since an understanding of these and other Adlerian propositions underlies the principles and techniques we offer at CP-TEC, an understanding of these and other Adlerian propositions is essential. The constructs of striving to find a place in the group and of goal-directed behavior, for example, are implicit in diagnosing a child's goals of misbehavior. Nevertheless, while our counselors are trained to think about theoretical dynamics, they are required to practice counseling, not psychotherapy. Adlerian psychotherapy is concerned primarily with changing the style of life of the individual; that is, changing the person's perception of how he or she sees him- or herself in relationship to others and to life in general. Adlerian counseling is essentially "counseling for minimal change" (Tyler, 1960), that is, providing information and increasing awareness without examining the style of life or restructuring the person's fundamental perceptions.

## Adler's Family Counseling Methods

By 1920 Adler was already demonstrating an educational approach to understanding personal problems and deficiencies. To bring the many factors into the open and thus be in a position to counsel effectively, children, as well as their teachers, parents, and siblings, were interviewed before groups of professional people and other parents. Originally established in schools, this procedure was used primarily as a teaching method for teachers, who observed. Since passive observers as well as participants benefited from the counseling sessions, the sessions afforded at least three opportunities: the observers learned about human psychology in general and Adler's procedures in particular; the participants benefited from the understanding they received from the counseling; and the observers increased their understanding about themselves and their families.

The school-located demonstrations were probably the first breakthrough for group counseling. Previously, counseling and therapy had been carried on in seclusion. Now the concept emerged that people's problems stem from group interaction and therefore must be solved utilizing group situations.

The revolutionary procedure of opening psychotherapeutic centers to observers was extended from the schools to community centers, principally serving parents. The centers came to be known as *Erziehungsberatungstellen,* or Centers for Guidance of Parents, or Educational Counseling Centers. In Vienna in the 1920s and early 1930s, there were about thirty centers in operation, staffed by psychiatrists, psychologists, and paraprofessionals (Lowe, 1974).

## Dreikurs' Beginnings in the United States

Although these centers were closed in the middle 1930s by the Austrian fascists, a number of Adler's students and associates established centers in the United States. An associate of Adler, Rudolf Dreikurs (McKaness, 1963), became a leading authority on Adlerian psychology and introduced his ideas in America through the Chicago Community Child Clinics, which he cofounded with Eleanore Redwin in 1939 (Dreikurs, 1959). Subsequently, a number of Adlerian community clinics were established by others, including the Community Parent-Teacher Education Center in Eugene, Oregon (Lowe, 1974).

Dreikurs clarified Adler's ideas and made a number of other contributions to individual psychology. Only three of Dreikurs' major contributions relevant to family counseling will be discussed here: the movement from an autocratic to a democratic culture of social equals (Dreikurs, 1971); goal-directed behavior (Dreikurs, 1964; Lowe, 1971); and some nonspecific principles and techniques (Dreikurs, 1964).

*Moving Toward Social Equality.* According to Dreikurs (1971), an important evolution currently is taking place in interpersonal relationships: Superiority-inferiority relationships are being replaced by democratic, egalitarian relationships. Although this trend was first evidenced in the political realm, it has pervaded the social arena as women increasingly gain equal status with men and children no longer feel inferior to adults. Wherever the evolution toward democratic relationships is manifested, traditional methods of keeping the so-called "inferior" person in line with the demands of "superiors" cannot prevail.

In the case of children, while the supremacy over children is gone, few people realized that adults can no longer *make* children do anything. Even when the idea of social equality is recognized, parents, teachers, and other professionals are ill equipped to deal with children on a democratic basis and violate the principle of mutual respect by making futile efforts to intensify their authority (with bribes, threats, rewards, or punishments) or by being permissive. Obviously these methods are ineffective, and what is required is a new tradition for working out democratic relationships, incorporating principles of in-depth psychology that explain the purposes of behaviors and the use of emotions on the parts of children and adults. Intuition, feelings, and empathy alone are pitifully inadequate guides for living and working with children, compared to a clear understanding on the part of parents and professionals of what they are doing and why. Moreover, this understanding should be based on an inclusive theory and sound principles of human behavior.

With the movement toward social equality, coupled with the impact of technology, affluence, and the reduction of the size of the family, we are preoccupied with our children as perhaps never before. Inadequate preparation has far-reaching effects. While children used to grow up as members of a natural group of brothers and sisters, children now bear the brunt of their parents' attention and lack of educational preparation. Teachers are alarmed at their inability to cope with children who misbehave or are unwilling to learn (Dreikurs, 1964), and, in fact, this inability to cope is the greatest single reason for failure among beginning teachers (Jersild, 1955). In this predicament, in which traditional methods of raising children are ineffective and new methods of democratic living are unfamiliar, parent-teacher education and counseling are mandatory.

It is most important to understand that what is advocated here is not simply more clever techniques for raising children or a new philosophical basis for child management. From an Adlerian point of view, neither are possible. Rather, our position is that, since in a democracy one cannot require another person to do anything that they are not willing to do, the concept "to make" is inappropriate. We seek to assist adults, essentially parents and teachers, in gaining practical knowledge about how to manage themselves in the multitude of conflict situations that occur in daily routine. For earlier generations, pressure from without in most cases ensured compliance with demands and with the needs of the situation. Since such pressure is no longer sufficient, parents and teachers need to provide the child with an opportunity to learn a new kind of inner stimulation toward cooperation, functioning, respecting order, and fulfilling the demands of the situation.

*Goal-Directed Behavior.* A child's behavior is the product of a dynamic, continually changing interaction between him- or herself and others. Like any human being, the child's social purpose is to become an accepted, contributing member of the group. A well-adjusted child experiences this sense of belonging and operates on the socially useful side of life. The discouraged child has experienced difficulty in achieving a sense of belonging through usefulness and participation and seeks status on the useless side of life. Difficult children are always socially discouraged children.

In instances in which the child feels inferior and doubt about having a place in the group is prolonged, he or she seeks to establish defenses that make it unnecessary for him or her to meet the requirements of the group, be it within the family, classroom, or among peers. The difficult child, believing he or she is without status, attempts to establish safeguards against further loss of prestige and against open admission of hostile intentions. Only through disturbing—often referred to as "being disturbed"—does the child feel he or she can defend him- or herself against not having a place. Here the basic desire to participate through useful contribution is sidetracked by a desire for feeling superior, gaining status, or achieving prestige. Failing in this, the child, believing he or she has no chance, gives up in despair. Thus the child's response to discouragement seems to be either to compensate by being aggressive or hostile and disturbing or to withdraw altogether, which may or may not be disturbing to those around him or her.

Dreikurs (1971) suggests that all disturbing behavior of the difficult child is directed toward one of four possible goals. These goals represent the child's perception as to how he or she must relate to the group. In his or her misbehavior, the child is either seeking simply to gain attention from others; seeking to demonstrate his or her power or superiority over others; seeking to gain revenge or punish others; or seeking to display a real or assumed disability, thus preventing his or her experiencing further discouragement by others. Difficult children operating on the useless side of life may be doing so either in an active destructive or passive destructive manner, but in either instance their behavior is the result of their evaluation of their places as they seek to relate functionally to the group.

Table 1 summarizes the child's mistaken behaviors, active and passive degrees of activity, and adult behaviors equal to the child's challenge. Before discussing procedures for counseling the difficult child, some explanation, in addition to the table, is in order.

Attention. In a typically competitive and perfectionistic atmosphere, with limited opportunities for children to make useful contributions, ambitious children are increasingly operating in ways that are disturbing to their elders. Discouraged in finding a place in the group by useful means, the child may employ attention-getting mechanisms (AGMs) in an active destructive (showing off, nagging) or in a passive destructive (nonperformance or inadequate performance) way. While AGMs may resemble the second and third goals (power and revenge), they differ in their lack of antagonism and violence. If the child's goal is simple attention, he or she stops when the goal is achieved. Because passive destructive attention-getting behaviors are less energetic than those of the attention seeker who is active destructive, they are often less disturbing to others.

Power. If the demands of an attention seeker are not met, the child may move to striving for power or superiority. Such children have discovered they can gain more attention by being difficult, often as a result of an adult attempting to subdue the annoying behavior. The children find themselves locked in a struggle for power and superiority over adults. On the active side, the children try to convince the adults that they can do what they want to and the adults will not be able to stop them. Frequently these children do the opposite of what they are told. On the passive side, they may demonstrate that adults cannot control them, by refusing to do anything. Active or passive, if the children get away with it, they have won a victory; if adults force their will on them, the children have lost, but next time they will use stronger methods and thereby gain victory. When the children's goal is power, their being difficult is more obvious, actions are more hostile, and emotions more pronounced than when attention is the goal.

Table 1. Child's Mistaken Goals.

| Goal | Active Destructive | Passive Destructive | What Child Is Saying | How Parent Feels | Child's Reaction to Correction | Appropriate Adult Behavior |
|---|---|---|---|---|---|---|
| Attention | Show off, "clown," be obtrusive, constantly ask questions | Bashful, lazy, untidy, self-indulgent, fearful, lack of concentration, eating difficulties | I only count when I am being noticed or served | Annoyed, wants to remind or coax, delighted with "good" child | Temporarily stops disturbing action when given attention | Ignore; answer or do the unexpected; give attention at pleasant time |
| Power | Resist being subdued, try to convince adults they will not be able to stop him or her, does opposite of what he or she is told | Refuse to do anything, techniques more hostile and fierce and being difficult more obvious than with simple attention | I only count when I am dominating, when you do what I want you to do. You can't make me do anything | Provoked, generally wants power, challenged: "I'll make him do it!" "You can't get away with that!" | Intensifies action when reprimanded; child wants to win, be the boss | Extricate self; act, not talk; be friendly; establish equality; redirect child's efforts into constructive channels |
| Revenge | Open warfare, attempts to hurt others, provokes others to reject him- or herself, considers being horrible a triumph | Violently passive, hate filled, deliberate and obvious withdrawal | I can't be liked; I don't have power, but I'll count if I can hurt others as I feel hurt by life | Hurt, mad: "How could she do this to me?" | Wants to get even; makes self disliked | Extricate self; win child; maintain order with minimum restraint; take time and effort to help child |
| Assumed Disability | Since the child has given up, he or she is not active | Avoidance, display inadequacy or imaginary deficiency | I can't do anything right so I won't try to do anything at all; I'm no good | Despair: "I give up." | No reprimand, therefore, no reaction; feels there is no use to try; passive | Encouragement (may take a long time); faith in child's ability |

Note: Table 1 summarizes the child's mistaken behaviors and adult behaviors equal to the child's challenge. Note that the goals may be expressed in an active or passive way and there is a progression from less difficult levels to more difficult levels. In the case of passive destructive goals, frequently the child "gives up" at the attention-getting level and proceeds to Goal 4, where he or she hopes people will leave him or her alone.

Revenge. The struggle between adults and children for power may intensify as adults try every conceivable means to subjugate the culprit. The mutual antagonism and hatred may become so strong that no pleasant experience is left to maintain a feeling of belonging, friendliness, or cooperation, and the child then seeks revenge. Discouraged in bids for attention and power and feeling completely ostracized and disliked, the child finds gratification only in hurting others and getting even for being hurt by them. Active children may be violent and vicious; they know where it hurts most and take advantage of the vulnerability of their opponents. Convinced that nobody likes them, they provoke anyone with whom they come in contact to reject them. Children who are passive do not engage in open warfare, but rather become violently passive; they are enraged in their hate-filled, deliberate, and obvious withdrawal from relationships with others. Passive children are usually more difficult to encourage than active children.

Assumed Disability. Children who are easily discouraged frequently try to display an inadequacy with, or more often without, any real justification. They assume real or imaginary deficiencies as a means to safeguard their prestige. These children have what Adler called an "inferiority complex," in contrast with inferiority feelings, which tend to motivate a person in an active rather than a passive manner. The children are so sure that they will fail that they will avoid situations where failure and inadequacy might become obvious. The children prefer and apparently find it more acceptable to their own self-respect to pretend to be inadequate rather than to risk the chance of *being found out* to be inadequate. Since children who have assumed a disability have given up, they are always passive rather than active.

*Nonspecific Techniques for Improving Relationships.* When adults and children are in cooperative social relationships, they each have responsibilities and rights. Contrary to what many may think, the major responsibility of an individual is to cooperate in the attainment of the group's goal, initially to the goals of the family. The notion of an individual fully functioning outside the group is foreign to Adlerian thinking. Mutual respect, based on the assumptions of equality, is the inalienable right of all human beings. In the context of the family, mutual respect means that no unreasonable request should be made of any family member; neither the parent or child should be a slave or a tyrant. For example, for the family to expect one member to do most of the work even though others are capable does not show respect for that person. The mother in some families is a slave. She shows no respect for herself, and the others take cruel advantage of her.

While some semblance of respect is accorded to adults in some families, children are frequently not accorded respect. Even though children are generally mentally and physically inferior to adults, they have a right to be respected. Treating a child as a toy, an idiot, or royalty is probably just as harmful as treating him or her as "bad" because they are all false. Mutual respect means honest evaluation and treatment of the child. Parents ought to view the child as an immature human being who should be accorded full respect. Lying to him or her, whether about the stork, other people, or their role in life, shows disrespect and harms the child. Neglect or overprotection are equally bad—both give the child an unreal picture of life and do not prepare him or her for successful living.

Mutual respect is the basis for all constructive change in the family. Change can be brought about by consistently implementing Dreikursian techniques. Some of the nonspecific techniques include (Dreikurs, 1964):

Encouragement. Children misbehave only if they are discouraged and believe they cannot succeed by useful means. Encouragement implies faith and respect for children as they are and communicates belief in their natural strengths and abilities, not their "potentialities."

Natural Consequences. In using this technique, parents allow children to experience the direct consequences of their own behavior. Children learn to respect reality and its demands when parents refrain from protecting them from unpleasant consequences of their own behavior. In short, resolution to a problem is between the children and the situation.

Logical Consequences. In contrast to natural consequences, wherein the child experiences the consequences of behaviors directly (for example, falling down and "feeling" pain), logical consequences involve two or more people wherein some form of understanding, agreement, and possibly negotiation is required. In short, agreement is essential to the point that the consequence is logical to the situation. For example, when an individual comes home late for supper, he or she is not scolded or reprimanded; rather, it is understood that supper is not available.

A word of caution is appropriate here. One must be very careful in applying natural and logical consequences in that they do not become techniques of punishment. If they are used for this purpose, the original intent will be lost.

Action Instead of Words. Corrective measures consisting of "talk" are ineffective, especially in conflict situations. Children no longer listen—they have become "mother deaf." Usually children already know what is expected, and it is unnecessary to explain what they have heard repeatedly. Talking should be restricted to friendly conversations, not used as a means of discipline. Effective action in moments of conflict can consist of natural consequences, physical aggression, or self-removal from the scene.

Efficacy of Withdrawal. When the child demands undue attention or tries to become involved in a power contest, withdrawing from the scene is a most effective instructional tactic. It is no longer effective for the child to lose his or her temper if there is no audience; nor is there any satisfaction in being annoying if nobody attends. Withdrawal is not surrender; on the contrary, it is effective counteraction in which the child does not "get by" with bids for undue attention or power.

Take Time for Training. Teaching a child essential skills or habits requires definite instruction. Training should occur at calm times, regularly, and not in moments of conflict or company. Attention should be given to one training area at a time. Taking time for training saves time in the long run, since less time will be spent correcting an untrained child.

Firmness Without Domination. While firmness gains the child's respect, domination may contribute to rebellion. Firmness indicates action, refusal to give in to the child's undue demands. Domination implies concern with what the child does and the adult's efforts to impose his or her will on the child. An adult has the right to take a firm position, but a child has the right to decide what he or she will do.

## Adlerian Family Counseling

This theoretical and practical orientation and some understanding as to why child guidance centers remain a critical service provide the reader with background for the following elaboration of the Adlerian approach to family counseling at a particular center, CP-TEC.

*Characteristics of the Counseling Approach.* The typical procedure for "dealing with" children is to do something *to* them, or *at* them, or *for* them. The schoolteacher may suggest that the parents be less rigidly insistent on scheduled periods of homework; a principal may urge the teacher to change his or her method of disciplining the child, glasses may be prescribed, or a different set of playmates may be located. All these efforts are done *to* or *for* the child. What we suggest is that the counseling process be one in which more adequate solutions are sought *with* the child.

Because the problems of one child stem primarily from interpersonal relationships within his or her family, we deal with all family members. The "family" might include one or both parents, grandparents, any other adult in the immediate family or living in the home, siblings, and, in some cases, a babysitter. The procedure for dealing with the whole family is based on the idea that in order to understand the child, we must understand the dynamics of the interplay in the family. Improving the relationships between child and parents and among siblings is the primary objective of counseling. Without this improvement, it is impossible to alter the child's behavior, approaches to social living, and concept of him- or herself in relation to others.

While a number of people may be involved in the counseling process, the focus of attention is directed toward the parents. The parents generally stimulate the problem, not the child.

The child responds in his or her own way to the experiences to which he or she is exposed. Younger children, particularly, do not change easily as long as the parents' attitudes and approaches to the child do not change. If there are other children in the family, all siblings are included in the counseling process, not just the child presenting the problem. The child's problems are closely related to the behavior of all other children in the family. To deal adequately with the behavior of any one sibling, the interrelationships, lines of alliance, competition, and the antagonisms of the entire group must be understood.

The problems of the child are frankly discussed with him or her, regardless of age. If the child understands the words, he or she can also understand the psychological dynamics they describe. Contrary to widespread belief, young children show an amazing keenness in grasping and accepting psychological explanations. In general, it takes much longer for a parent to understand the psychological dynamics of the problem.

In the sessions, each case is discussed openly in front of other parents, teachers, students, and visitors attending. Since many parents participate simultaneously, this procedure might be called *group counseling*. It is assumed that many parents gain greater insight into their own situation by listening to the discussion of similar problems of other parents. In this way, an influence is exerted beyond the scope of individual counseling, and the whole community is directed toward a better approach to understanding children. In fact, it is for the purpose of involving the entire community that this counseling program is located in an elementary school, which is a logical neighborhood setting where all may attend.

Normally, problems of children are reflections of a disturbed parent-child relationship. The counselor is confronted with these disturbed relationships and must approach them from both the child's and the parents' positions. Working with only the parents or only the child is a handicap. The speed and course of counseling depend on the receptivity of parents and children alike.

*Principal Assumptions.* The program discussed here is based on a number of assumptions, the principal one being that if a child is psychologically deficient in his or her sociopersonal relationships during the early years, these deficiencies will continue in later life. Working with a child's family and teachers in an "open" setting can contribute much toward the improvement of their relationships. Other assumptions include the following. First, many parents seeking to improve their relationships with their children can profit from information that may preclude the need for later therapy. Second, teachers attending may observe the dynamics of human interaction and thereby gain meaningful experiences as they relate to developing a better understanding of children's behavior as well as their own. Third, "open" sessions make it possible for many parents and teachers to profit from the concerns of a few. Fourth, reaching larger numbers at early stages is less expensive, is preventative, and requires the professional services of fewer specialists. And, fifth, most parents and teachers have difficulty with children not because they or the children are psychologically sick but because the vast majority of *all* adults are ignorant of how to live with children.

*The Center Staff.* The operation of the center would be impossible without the support of its fifteen to twenty staff people. Normally a staff of four to six would be adequate to conduct a center. In Eugene, because of its university affiliation, a larger staff is required.

The center staff operates on a democratic model, and keeping the center running efficiently is everyone's job. In addition to the Saturday morning center sessions, the staff meets on Friday regarding the business and procedural operations of the center and on Saturday afternoon for purposes of staffing cases and developing concepts and skills. Group processes are an important aspect of the staff's working relationship. Just as an orchestra practices together to play a concert, the staff practices together to work smoothly as a team.

The center coordinator facilitates the overall functioning of the center. He is assisted in administrative details, instruction, counseling, and counselor training by one or more associate coordinators. The associate coordinators also work with students, teachers, and parent-study groups. Counselors in training assist with many of the activities. Other support services are afforded by the role-playing director, who offers a systematic program in which parents or children can role play or "try out" alternative behaviors, and by the playroom director, who provides child care and observational experiences during the counseling sessions. Role-playing and playroom reports are contributed regularly to the counseling sessions.

The parent study-group leader provides a program of parent education. Attending a parent group is a condition of counseling, but many parents who are not being counseled also participate. Parents coming to the center are typically greeted by the secretary-receptionist or the intake interviewer, who interviews and schedules families for counseling. Paralleling the parent study groups are teacher study groups. Under the leadership of a member of the center staff, teachers meet, in much the same manner as the parents, to discuss Adlerian and Dreikursian principles about managing themselves while working with children.

*The Counseling Session.* Normally, the sessions are held on Saturday mornings, which seem to be the best time for allowing parents, teachers, and others interested to attend. Parents come for counseling for the purpose of learning to understand their children and how to deal with them. They need the knowledge of adequate approaches rather than changes in their own psychological makeup. They come for counseling, not psychotherapy. They view the counselor as a guide, consultant, and "teacher," not as a psychotherapist.

The counselor's basic premise in his or her approach can be stated tersely. While the primary concern is with the immediate concern and its improvement, the ultimate hope is that the parents will acquire a more adequate approach to dealing with children. Briefly, the counselor interprets the dynamics of the family situation to the parents and reveals to the child the child's own goals. The assumption here is that more effective corrective measures can be undertaken if the counselor utilizes a "goal-directed" or "behavior is purposeful" approach. Once the goals of the child are determined, specific measures can be undertaken by the parents and the teachers.

As in all counseling interviews, the art of listening is of utmost importance. Essential to determining the goals of children is an understanding of the family constellation, family atmosphere, and the methods of child training. In stating their problems, the parents reveal trends in their own personalities that give clues not only for diagnostic impressions of the parents but also to the interrelations in the family. In observing the interactions of the parents, one can easily recognize the dominant one, the overly eager member, the overambitious one, the disciplinarian, the one who is unsure of him- or herself, the one concerned with prestige, the overprotective one, or the too-demanding one.

In an initial interview, the parents are asked to name all those who make up the "family," the family constellation. As the parents name both adults and children and their ages, the counselor begins "guessing" about family dynamics. The parent is asked to describe each child in general terms. If the general descriptions do not prompt the parents to describe the problem child, the counselor asks the parent to name the child of most concern and to describe the kinds of behaviors that are disturbing.

After allowing the parents to state their overall problems, the counselor usually attempts to obtain some further general information. Typical questions that are asked at this stage of the counseling are "What do you think is the reason for your child's behavior?" "What have you been advised to do and by whom?" "What do you think is the right way to handle this problem?" "What have you actually done to correct this problem?" "What success have you had?" The purpose is to give the parents every opportunity to express themselves, to encourage them to go on, to make them feel that they will be listened to with understanding, and to help other members in the group avoid errors of snap judgments.

After the parents have gone on for a while, perhaps five to ten minutes, the parents are asked to describe a typical day in their family life. The interview is structured to facilitate understanding the relationship with the children and especially the so-called problem child or children. For example: "Tell me about how the children get up in the morning," "Any problem about dressing?" "How does breakfast go?" "How is going to school in the morning accomplished?" "What do you know about his (or her) school behavior?" "How about playing with other children?" "Any difficulties about eating lunch?" "How do the children get along with each other?" "Any problems with television?" "Any difficulties with supper?" "How about going to bed, washing, cleaning teeth, taking baths?" "Does she have any problems sleeping at night?"

During the interview about the family routine, if any problems are raised the question is asked, "And what do *you* do about it?" As the parents respond, the counselor gains an understanding of the parents' attitudes toward the children's behavior and what methods of training the parents use.

The counselor may feel that one or both of the parents are falling for the tricks of the child who is looking for recognition and is demanding excessive attention or may tentatively decide that the child is attempting to gain power, that the parents are slaves of the child, that they are engaged in a power contest with him or her, or that the parents' high standards are demoralizing and discouraging. In short, a diagnosis or working hypothesis is tentatively made. All recommendations depend on an accurate diagnosis, and one can be wrong despite all precautions. If the counselor has an hypothesis, additional information will usually confirm or deny its validity. When confirmed, all concerned are more certain of the final diagnosis and subsequent recommendations. If denied, subsequent working hypotheses must be established.

After about forty-five minutes, parents are asked to leave the room, and the children are asked to come in. It is necessary to send parents from the room because, in our experience, the presence of parents often precludes children expressing themselves. The dynamics that result in parents continuing to correct children in the counseling session are the same that underlie the disruptive relationships at home. Before parents leave, they may be asked to predict how the children will behave. Parents usually have the option of watching their children being interviewed on closed-circuit television and are frequently surprised at their behavior. Children are also given the same option of watching parents being counseled, but most elect to remain in the playroom.

During the period after the parents leave and before the children arrive from the playroom, the counselor may say to the group something of a predictive nature about the child's or children's behavior or alert them to various kinds of behavior that the children may demonstrate. Some children come forward, shake hands, smile, and talk freely about their parents and life in general in the easiest and most facile manner. Others are sullen and refuse to participate at all. There are children who show unusual behavior. Children run in, walk in politely, refuse to sit down, push each other off the bench, or help each other on. Others sit down with their backs to the group or refuse to communicate except with gestures, frowns, and smiles. All types of behavior are grist to the counselor's mill; they are considered as they relate to the nature of the problem expressed earlier by the parents.

An important distinction needs to be made here: Parents are counseled; children are interviewed. To the reader oriented to the notion of "total family counseling," an explanation is in order. We would be misleading if we created the impression that the purpose of interviewing the children is counseling. We do not counsel children, because we assume that changes in children striving to belong will take place only if the atmosphere in which they are living changes. The counseling setting for children is not appropriate to gaining changes in their behavior. Whatever encouragement may be conveyed to the child in a counseling setting is lost unless fundamental changes in the relationship are initiated and maintained by parents at home or teachers in the classroom. It is in these principal settings that a sustaining relationship is maintained. The purpose of this interview is for validation of information provided by the parents and other adults.

And why not counsel all members of the family at the same time? Again, probably because we do not believe there is much to be gained from counseling children. Children are not autonomous; they are without skills or maturity to effect constructure change in the family atmosphere. In our culture, this skill is reserved for adults.

Some clarification of counseling children before a large audience is also in order. When the child and siblings enter the counseling room for the first time, they are confronted with a group of strangers whom they have not met before. While this situation is "strange" to them, the effect of the strangeness is both profound and extremely helpful. Contrary to the assumption that children are not themselves in a perplexing atmosphere, we have found repeatedly that they express themselves more accurately in this unfamiliar setting than in the familiar surrounding of their homes or schools, where they may hide behind well-established patterns of behavior.

There is a strong interaction between the children and the audience. Both contribute greatly, to their mutual benefit. Most impressive is the realization by the adults of how much more easily the children understand the nature of their troubles and problems than do their parents. Parents often strongly resist any interpretations differing from preconceived explanations for their children's behavior. Children's relative sensitivity to psychological understanding and their response to psychological interpretation contrast impressively with the obvious lack of similar qualities in their parents.

The counselor seeks to put the children at ease by asking general questions that indicate interest in them and their problems. Preliminary questions for children are brief and direct. One may ask, "What is your name?" "Robert." "How are things going at home?" "Fine." "Do you know why you are here?" "No." Then an explanation is usually given, followed by a discussion about what mothers, fathers, or teachers have said.

The children give short answers, and, as far as they are concerned, there may be no problem. Children are usually verbal optimists. However, the counselor is interested in the child's self-concept. Typical questions are "Are you a big girl or a little girl?" "What gets Mommy upset?" "Why does your mother bring you here?" "What do you want to become?" "Who are your friends?" "What do you like to do?" "Who is the boss in the family?"

After the children have been interviewed, they return to the playroom and the parents are called back. In their presence, the counselor asks the playroom worker to report his or her observations of the children and of how the children relate to other children and to the group. This information supplements that obtained by the counselor from the intake interviewer, from the parents, and from the children. The playroom worker's reports are of great importance as they indicate to what extent changes are occurring in the children's behavior. In those instances where role playing is used, a report is requested from the person conducting this activity. Also, at this time reports are received from others who have some responsible relationship to the children. These are usually teachers, but may be juvenile workers, social workers, public health nurses, or others.

Now comes the period when the parents are to be given systematic explanations of the dynamics of the child's behavior and specific recommendations. Generally, the counselor is concerned with handling only one aspect of the child's behavior, usually the problem considered most pressing by the parents. It is best to limit the number of interpretations and suggestions. The impact of too many new ideas and suggestions for dealing with children may be too much for a parent to understand and accept. If too much is given, the parent may become confused and discouraged, feel inadequate, and make no effort to change at all. Consequently, it is very important to limit discussion and to point out that all human beings make mistakes and that in order to learn the use of new methods, one has to have the courage to make them.

The counselor is sensitive to the parents' feelings in order to phrase comments. Generally, the counselor's instructions tend to be first of a negative, "don't" type, and then of the positive, "do" type, because the parent first has to stop what he or she is doing wrong before he or she can begin to do what should be done. For example, the counselor may say, "It seems to me there might be some other ways in getting done the things you try to do; maybe you could stop talking so much." Among the most usual suggestions are "stop nagging," "stop bribing," "stop preaching," "stop promising," "stop discouraging," "stop threatening," "stop complaining," "stop comparing," and the like. These "don't's" should be illustrated with concrete examples gained from the interview so that the parent can really grasp what he or she should not do, rather than interpret the "don't's" as criticisms. The counselor's attitude must reflect that there are no stars for being right and there is no stigma in being wrong; that in fact everyone attending, including the counselor, is at the center to learn. Furthermore, the counselor must be supportive of the parents. Encouragement for a discouraged parent is as equally important as encouragement for a discouraged child. Without encouragement, neither insight or constructive change is possible.

If the counselor's hypothesis, explanations of the child's dynamics and behavior, and nonspecific recommendations have been in the right direction, the specific recommendation will "make sense" to the parents. In addition to monitoring the counseling session as it proceeds, the counselor can check out his or her hypothesis and interactions with the parent and a co-counselor, the observer who recorded the session, or other staff members who meet after Saturday sessions for purposes of staff development. Frequently, the audience or parent study group leader also offers questions or information that the counselor can use in deciding whether the session was "on target." An advantage to the center's group approach to family counseling is that involving a number of helpers tends to minimize the tendency of a counselor to view family interaction in line with a private or mistaken hypothesis. All of these attempts, however, are only educated guesses. Effectiveness is better assessed when in subsequent sessions the parent is able to report how the information was actually used in improving family relationships.

The parents are urged to sit in the audience during the intervening weeks until the subsequent interview sessions. Other parents look forward to the follow-ups because they "identify" with the family. The "mutual support" is readily felt whether the parents are experiencing "success" or "failure." It is a great source of satisfaction to parents to see how things often improve, to watch a family change from a state of disorganization to a well-integrated and even happy family.

In the follow-up interview, the parents are usually asked what they have learned in the first interview, what has happened since the first interview, and what do they think about what has happened. The counselor reviews the previous session from the recorder's report and may check, point by point, to see whether the recommendations agreed to were followed, such as not nagging, allowing the child more responsibility, avoiding interference in their squabbles, starting a family council, letting the child learn by natural consequences, providing the children an adequate allowance, helping them to budget money, and so on.

Generally, parents who are able to follow directions report some partial improvement after the first interview. It is not unusual, however, for them to state that the experience was quite difficult and that the children took advantage of the new situation, were resistant, and so forth. Nevertheless, parents who follow the recommendations usually feel encouraged. They begin to benefit from listening to the recommendations developed with other parents. This, coupled with the counseling, makes it possible for them to handle other problems more adequately. Sometimes, dramatic changes are reported in the children's behavior, and the whole family tone seems to have improved. On the other hand, some parents are not able to adhere to recommendations. In such instances, the counselor has the problem of attempting to assist such parents in gaining self-confidence so that they will be able to put into effect new methods, regardless of the attitudes of family and friends who disapprove. In this regard, other parents can be of great help, since those being counseled feel supported by the group and have confidence in the opinions of fellow parents, who frequently give dramatic information as to their success.

At this point, the session moves along the same lines as the initial interview: The children are interviewed, pertinent reports are given, the session is summarized, and new recommendations are made. It is not unusual for a family to be well into this new direction for dealing with problems after the sixth or eighth session.

In some cases, parents show little behavioral evidence of progress. A parent may, for example, follow suggestions without understanding the principles involved. In this case, it is particularly essential that parent education complement the counseling process. Or, for example, a parent may report little progress, "but I am trying." "Trying" is sometimes offered by parents as an excuse. Generally, behind the excuse is a fear of failure, of looking like a bad or ineffective parent. The counselor must then be firm but kind in suggesting that the parent quit "trying" and start acting, while supporting the parent by offering reassurance that the center is not asking for proof of success or failure, but for an honest attempt at working toward improving family relationships. For the "yes, but" parent, it is most important that he or she realize the dynamics of what is going on. A simple interjection might be "Excuse me, I don't understand your expression, 'yes, but.' Could you help me with this?" The intention is that the parent become aware that he or she does not really believe in what he or she heard ("yes") but rather is offering counterreasons why the idea will not work ("but"). For the few cases where parents appear unable to profit from the discussions, referral for psychotherapy may be made. While we acknowledge that we do not know all the answers, we can say that we do have a frame of reference that can be of considerable help in many cases.

Many of the principles suggested to parents apply to all human relationships, not only to those between parents and children. Parents who learn to become effective in dealing with their children often find they can improve their relationship with their spouses by using similar approaches. Naturally, even the best methods do not prevent conflict or guarantee success. But a parent who is acquainted with these principles and who knows what to do and why is in a better position to deal with a given situation effectively and for the best interest of the child.

### Other Adlerian Family Counseling Centers

In 1958 there were twelve family counseling centers designed and functioning along the lines described herein. All were in the greater Chicago area and all were under the egis of the Alfred Adler Institute, of which Rudolf Dreikurs was the founder and director. Many forms of parent education beginning at the institute were widespread, but Adlerian Child Guidance Centers, as they were called then, were few in number. With the development of an Adlerian program at the University of Oregon, coupled with the efforts for family counseling centers made by Dreikurs during his many visits here, additional centers began. Because Dreikurs attracted students to the university from all over the world, it was but a short time before centers began appearing in the remotest of areas. Today the number is not known, but it is estimated that there are close to 200, some associated with other universities where University of Oregon graduates have located, others with churches, institutes, and county agencies. It is as if Adler had come into his time through those who have been profoundly influenced by his ideas.

## Conclusion

The recognition of children's goals is an important prerequisite for improving adult-child relationships. The knowledge of children's goals permits a viable approach and above all prevents unwitting acceptance of the children's provocations, which only increases their maladjustment and difficulty. Doing what the children expect confirms their belief that their disturbing approaches are effective. Counseling as described herein implies an exploration of the children's family situations, the dynamics of their relationships with their parents and siblings, the methods by which they were raised, the situations that influenced the atmosphere in which they live, and some understanding of processes of encouragement.

The setting in which counseling and education takes place must facilitate these ideas being readily available to large numbers of people. The notions underlying the organization and administration of the Community Parent-Teacher Education Center provides such a setting. That this method and vehicle are valuable is attested to by the several hundred institutes, workshops, and centers currently being conducted both in this and many other countries. Adler's school-located centers, probably the first breakthrough in group counseling, have now emerged internationally as a major technique and procedure for approaching solutions to people's problems in our time.

# 9

# Student Advocacy and Environmental Change in Urban Settings

## Julius Menacker

This chapter speaks to the counseling needs of a specific population within a specific environmental and institutional context. The population addressed is the urban adolescent, who is typically poor and a member of a minority group. The environmental context is the inner city, which is characterized by crowded conditions, deteriorated housing, and a high level of crime. The institutional context is the inner-city school, which typically mirrors the environmental situation.

In 1970, seven of the ten largest school systems had a black student majority, even though only one of them (Washington, D.C.) had a black population majority (Meranto, 1970). There is also a significant number of Latinos, primarily Mexican-Americans and Puerto Ricans, enrolled in urban schools, and lesser numbers of poor Appalachian whites and native Americans (Indians). These groups, taken together, represent

171

the "culturally different" population that increasingly predominates within urban public education.

The traditional theories and techniques of school counseling that were developed by and for the white middle class have proven ineffective in meeting the personal, social, and psychological needs of this new urban student clientele. Counselors are no more guilty of failure in this regard than are their colleagues in teaching and school administration. Indeed, the same charge can be made for almost all social services reaching into the inner cores of American cities. An important reason for the failure of these social services to significantly help the urban poor and minorities is that their theories and procedures arise from middle-class assumptions and values. Improvements in the effectiveness of helping professions for urban minorities occur in proportion to the degree to which traditional practice is modified to meet the special conditions and characteristics of those groups.

### Characteristics of Urban Poor Minority Students

The assignment of general characteristics to even a single identifiable ethnic group is in itself a very tentative and risky task. This is so because there are more differences *within* any ethnic group than *between* ethnic groups. Therefore, attempting to assign characteristics common to the several distinct groups comprising the urban poor minority population may seem presumptuous. However, some generalized, tentative statements are necessary in order to formulate helping responses that begin to meet their needs more adequately than traditional practice. The characteristics identified are limited to those which have implications for school counseling.

1. They tend to depend more on concrete than on symbolic, abstract experience in guiding their behavior (Gordon, 1967).
2. "They are less able than their middle-class counterparts to make use of conventional verbal symbols in representing and interpreting their feelings, their experiences and the objects in their environment" (Gordon, 1967). This is not to say they are deficient in verbal representational ability. Rather, their mode is simply different from the conventional pattern.

3. These children commonly have a general attitude of passivity and defeatism in relation to the traditional helping institutions of society. Intermittent displays of defiance and self-assertion serve to highlight the general attitude of defeatism, rather than to replace it (Menacker, 1974).

4. The pattern of reinforcement to which they respond is one of the immediate, concrete rewards, with a lower order of value placed on deferred and intrinsic reinforcement (Menacker, 1974).

These are general tendencies that seem to exist among the poor minorities that constitute a large proportion of urban public schools. Not all minority poor conform to these characteristics. However, the majority exhibit most of them (those who do not conform to these general tendencies need not overly concern the counselor). Those exhibiting these characteristics represent the population most in need of help and most poorly served by traditional counseling practice.

## Changing the Theoretical Bases of Urban School Counseling

Traditional models of school counseling, whether labeled *directive* or *nondirective, developmental* or *psychoanalytical, client-centered, behavioral, trait factor,* or various other titles, have a common base. They are firmly grounded in a psychotherapeutic foundation that places primary emphasis on improving the self-concept and self-awareness of the client through verbal interaction techniques. Rogers (1962, p. 428) captured the essence of this psychologically based traditional approach: "The purpose of guidance counseling is to enhance the personal development, the psychological growth toward a socialized maturity, of its clients."

These traditional, psychologically based techniques rely on passive verbal interactions to effect psychological changes in the client that contribute to his or her ability to grow in more emotionally, intellectually, and socially wholesome ways. The failure of this approach for the urban poor minority student is related to the characteristics indicated earlier. They do not respond well to symbolic, abstract stimulants to behavior and cannot easily relate to unfamiliar verbal symbolization. Yet these are exactly the means employed to help them! The traditional approach of placing the counselor in a passive verbal role, in which client activity is the key to beneficial change, further emphasizes the counterproductivity of standard psychological practice. Characteristically, the urban poor minority client is passive and defeatist regarding such institutions as the school. He or she is also more easily motivated by immediate, concrete reinforcement than by abstract, deferred reinforcement. Yet, the typical counselor-client relationship expects words to replace concrete reality and change a lifetime of conditioning.

Another problem in reliance on psychotherapeutic skill as the basis of school counseling is that the typical school counselor is not well trained for this function. The usual master's program has a course or two on counseling techniques, along with one on theories of personality or a similar topic. Most programs are not sufficient to produce what is considered to be a competent professional psychotherapist. Further, and perhaps more important, the conditions of the urban school do not allow for the practice of traditional psychological counseling, which requires regular, uninterrupted sessions between client and therapist. Anyone familiar with urban schools will agree that the conditions accompanying the practice of traditional psychological counseling are not available in this environment.

The needed theoretical change is one in which the primary focus on psychological theory is broadened by additional social science foci, particularly theoretical derivations from sociology, anthropology, and political science. These disciplines study such matters as social class and race in relation to schooling and society; the relation of socioeconomic status and conditions to the individual and his or her attitudes; cultural values and their differences among societal groups and the dominant institutions of society; and the characteristics of bureaucracies and how they can be influenced. These are the concepts that can form a more adequate counseling theory for urban poor minority students, a good name for which would be *activist counseling and guidance*.

The premises of activist theory can best be illustrated by

comparison with traditional theory. Traditional theory places the counselor in a passive verbal role, with client activity as the key to beneficial change. Activist counseling has the opposite emphasis. It is the counselor who is active, who is doing. The counselor works with the client in eliminating environmental obstacles and developing new, more favorable conditions and opportunities. This leads to an equally important related issue, that of professional focus. Traditional theory concentrates on the client as the sole professional focus. The client's environment is not considered or at best is relegated to secondary importance. Attention is primarily aimed at what is going on "in the client's head." Activist counseling has the opposite focus. The conditions of the client's environment, both human and inanimate, and how they can be maximized to the client's advantage, are the primary considerations. This does not diminish the importance of the client. Rather, it assumes that one's maximum development can best be realized by recognizing and actively combatting negative environmental elements and capitalizing on the positive elements.

A social science theoretical base allows activist counseling to develop into a helping specialty for urban poor minority students. Techniques of working with community conditions, parents, employers, landlords, the client's peers, other school professionals, and other social service agencies are best developed through the understandings and skills of sociology, anthropology, and political science. They provide a global student-school-family-community perspective that allows the counselor to assume a professional role that conforms to the following principles of activist guidance, which:

1. Recognizes the distinction between client goals and values and those of the educational institution. It considers the probability that the client's values and goals may be more appropriate than those of the institutions with which they conflict.
2. Supports student advocacy and active involvement related to both within school and out-of-school concerns.
3. Supports direct counselor activity focused on concrete action that objectively helps students.

4. Is based on mutual counselor-client identification of environmental obstacles and assets to education and self-development. Strategies designed to combat the obstacles and capitalize on the assets are then mutually devised.

These principles have been developed to provide a foundation for models of urban school counseling of poor minority students that offer viable alternatives to the failure of traditional school counseling practices for this group. The balance of this chapter describes four models that put this theory into practice. These are the student advocate, ombudsman, community resource specialist, and educateur-counselor models.

### The Student Advocate

The conditions that must attend a productive counselor relationship with the urban poor minority student are contained in these statements made by Banks and Martens (1973, p. 461): "The counselor must have a clear concept of what issues or institutional practices are causing problems for the clients and others" and "Helpees must see that the counselor can and will go beyond passive empathy and actually do something to affect change."

In order to render these concepts operative, the counselor must play a role in which he or she ceases to behave as an instrument of order, control, and adjustment. In urban schools generally, administrators have co-opted the guidance function to serve their needs of ordering, classifying, pacifying, and controlling students. The counselor has meekly accepted this role by coloring it with the ideology of "adjustment." Little thought has been given to whether or not this constituted adjusting the student to a pathological or otherwise destructive school milieu. There has simply been blind forcing of the student into the mold preordained by the school. This stance and the professional role of treatment through passive rhetoric have prevented counselors from meeting Banks and Martens' conditions. This traditional counselor is generally viewed by the urban student "as a member of the establishment who represents an alien ideal" (Walz and Miller, 1969, p. 864).

The student advocate model represents a remedy to this malaise. The counselor as advocate is most closely related to the concept of an attorney as the advocate of his client. The attorney must know and respect the law, and is bound to conduct himself as an officer of the court. This is one side of the attorney's role. The other side is the attorney's duty to the client. The attorney must strive to develop evidence and interpret the law to the client's advantage. This places him in an adversary role to the other attorney and at times even to the judge and traditional interpretations of the law. It may even cause him to challenge a law on the grounds that it is unconstitutional. This is not interpreted as a betrayal of his colleagues (judge or prosecutor) or of his profession. Rather, it is seen as his or her obligation. It is this adversary role that protects jurisprudence from mindless application of law, forcing all defendants into a preconceived mold when they appear at the bar.

Another concept appropriate to the student advocate role is what Gordon (1971, p. 480) calls "the guidance counselor as resident sociologist in the school . . . constantly turning his attention to how the system is functioning and in what ways it is helping and what ways it is hindering the accomplishment of its legitimate purpose." The advocate is continually analyzing and evaluating information he develops on behalf of his clients or for all of the school's clientele. He is a systems analyst in the sociological sense, seeking to discover the malfunctions of the school that impede or retard wholesome educational and personal development of students. He is, according to Gordon (1971), "a kind of quality control person," ensuring that the student does not get lost or trampled on as the urban school moves on its bureaucratized course, following highly specialized personnel procedures and rules and regulations standardized for uniform application to all students. The advocate role, as Amos and Grambs (1968, p. 3) indicate, is one of "making sure that the disadvantaged student is not lost in the shuffle and that he is understood and treated as an individual . . . keeping him off the impersonal conveyor belt of referral procedures. . . . They need some familiar figure to personalize their relations."

If there is any doubt of the need for counselors performing the student advocate function, consider the situation un-

covered by Chandler and Plakos (1969) in a California public
school. They investigated the practice by which Mexican-American children were classified as educable mentally retarded
(EMR) and found that the EMR classification was based on performance of students on the Wechsler Intelligence Scale for
Children (WISC). Students scoring below 75 were classified
EMR. Chandler and Plakos checked the validity of this practice
by retesting these students. They used the same test, the WISC,
except that they used the Spanish-language version. The results
for the forty-seven students who were retested were: (1) a
median score improvement of thirteen points (from 70 to 83);
(2) thirty-seven students scored 75 or over; (3) twenty-seven
students scored 80 or higher. We see that over three quarters of
the students were incorrectly assessed as to their intelligence
level. The English-language version of the WISC did not account
for the language handicap under which the Mexican-American
children suffered in this classification procedure. Yet, if it had
not been for the intervention of these two researchers, these
thirty-seven students would most probably have remained in the
EMR category. They would have carried this stigma, with its
attendant psychological and social injuries, throughout their
years of schooling and probably throughout their lives.

There are countless similar situations occurring continually to individuals and groups of urban poor minority students
in the public schools of the large cities. These miscarriages of
education do not occur because urban educators are cruel or
stupid. They occur because large-city schools operate under
great pressures with limited resources and because the system
does not allow for the kind of feedback and checks that would
prevent such occurrences. Hence the need for a "school sociologist," an advocate concerned with uncovering such conditions
and forcing their redress.

Chandler and Plakos operated as independent researchers,
from a base outside the school system. They were not con-
strained by their employment from exposing the situation. The
school counselor, acting as student advocate from within the
system, would find his task more sensitive and complicated.
There are several conditions that must obtain for the successful

use of the student advocate model. First, the faculty and administration must accept this role as one beneficial to students, to the school generally, and to their own professional roles and development. This can best be accomplished by offering examples of the need for an advocate and then developing working relationships based on trust and common commitment to student welfare. The main ingredient for gaining faculty acceptance and support for the student advocate role is the same as is needed to gain student support and rapport. The student advocate gains acceptance from both student and staff by showing that he can *do* something, that he can achieve concrete results. This is the unique professional characteristic that gives professional status and success to the student advocate.

Yet this may not seem to be a valid distinction, for do not all helping professions act with the end of gaining concrete results? The point I am making can best be illustrated by contrasting the student advocate approach with that of the standard model of psychological counseling. The psychotherapist works on getting something done inside of the client's head. The results achieved are not easily discernible at any precise moment or point. It is mainly a gradual, developmental process, with the therapist's work tailing off as the client demonstrates increasing ability to cope and/or to develop a more positive self-image. The success of the therapist is seen in the client's improved psychological state. But the emotions are hard to measure, and while client improvement may be discernible it is also a rather vague condition to objectify.

In contrast, the work of the student advocate is entirely with conditions outside of the student's head. It is with the manner in which school personnel or others involved with the student may impede or retard the client's academic progress. The advocate's role also includes the "things" of the student's school-related environment—classrooms, books, money, a quiet place to study at home, eyeglasses, and whatever else is needed to sustain the student. Once a goal has been agreed on by advocate and client, success is easily objectified. Either a part-time job was secured, or it was not. Either a tutor was secured to help the student with a difficult subject, or a tutor was not secured. These clearly objective factors are the elements in what a student advocate does. The rate of accomplishing these changes is the most important measure of the advocate's success.

While acceptance of the advocate's role by students, staff, and parents is primarily related to what he can accomplish, it is also important to note that the style he employs in his work is an important secondary condition to acceptance. If the change from one teacher to another for the student is accomplished with embarrassment to the original teacher or in a manner that allows the student to brag about it to his friends or to "rub it in" to the original teacher, the advocate's success will be transitory. The advocate must be as sensitive and skillful in human relations as his counterpart who deals in sensitivity training or human awareness work.

The advocate must not allow himself to be seen as the thorn in the side of the "establishment." He cannot afford the luxury of being the good guy who helps the students against the bad guy. One reason for this admonition is that life is usually far too complicated for clear definitions of who or what is good or bad in any given educational situation, and the complications increase exponentially when one enters the realm of human motivations. A more practical reason for avoiding the "white knight" role is that one's ability to positively influence student welfare will be inexorably decreased in proportion to the alienation and resentment of the student's significant others to the advocate.

Therefore, the student advocate must focus on the client's needs as the two of them see these needs, not on the personalities or motivations of those involved with the client. Fixing blame, recriminations, and other personal attacks must be outside of the advocate's purview. Attention must simply be on removing the impediments and capitalizing on the advantages found in the student's educational environment.

The student advocate's relationship to the principal might be compared to that of a lawyer to a judge. The judge may have the final word, but the attorney suggests, argues, objects. He does all he can to influence the judge on behalf of his client.

The advocate's relationship to teachers is a peer relationship. They are equals, each with their own areas of expertise and responsibility.

If there is one element of traditional counseling theory that most clearly supports the student advocate role, it is the following ethical standard of the American Personnel and Guidance Association (APGA) (1971, p. 207): "The APGA member's *primary* obligation is to respect the integrity and promote the welfare of the counselee or client with whom he is working."

We now turn to an incident that occurred in a Chicago public elementary school (Royko, 1972). The sixth-grade classroom was overcrowded. The number of students exceeded the specified limit, so two new sixth-graders were simply put in an undersubscribed fifth-grade class, where they would presumably get some work appropriate to the sixth grade. In any event, they were assured that they would advance to the seventh grade the next year. Both sets of parents were too confused or unsure of how school procedure worked to have any influence on the situation.

The story came to light because an outraged teacher informed a newspaper columnist about it. His or her identity was not revealed. As with the California EMR placement, exposure and consequent remediation occurred by taking the matter beyond the school and into the public arena. The student advocate must deal with similar problems, most of which are as unfair or as educationally unsound as these two examples, but not as flagrant or dramatic. However, these examples serve as a basis for discussing how a student advocate might have dealt with them.

Consider the plight of the "EMR" students. They were even worse off than the "fifth-grade sixth-graders," in that they did not even realize they were misplaced. In order to even uncover this situation, let alone correct it, the advocate would have to be an aggressive, seeking person who spent more time in the halls, classes, and offices of the school and in neighborhood stores and social agencies than in his own office. It might be uncovered by chance conversations with one of the affected stu-

dent's teachers or perhaps with a boy's community center coach
or girl's employer. Just a couple of perspectives on the student
from such people that contradict the EMR judgment would be
sufficient to initiate a check.

The advocate would then assess the positives and nega-
tives and possibly view being tested in a secondary language as a
negative and the option of intelligence testing in the student's
primary language as a positive that ought to be introduced. Concentrating on the issues related to the client's welfare rather
than attempting to fix blame might then lead to the necessary
retesting. The subsequent changes in placement would be
handled quietly and expeditiously. The advocate is not there to
prosecute. He has accomplished his task and, until proven
wrong, assumes all school professionals are interested in doing
the best job they can. When he or she has evidence of malice or
bias, that would be the only time to "go after" another professional. Among the many reasons for exercising caution in this
regard is that there is no reason to assume that the advocate has
all the answers or is always "in the right." Another is that the
people alienated by the advocate may be critical to success in
future cases.

The case of the misplaced sixth-graders could more easily
have come to the attention of the advocate before it reached
the point of public exposure. The probability of this occurring
would be in proportion to the rapport existing between the advocate on the one hand, and students, parents, and even teachers on the other. Good rapport will allow the advocate into the
formal and informal communications systems of school and
community. Hence, it would be difficult for two sixth-graders
to be placed in a fifth-grade room without the advocate's
knowledge.

The advocate's relationship with the students involved
would not be, as is most typical, one in which he tries to get
them to adjust to the situation. Nor would he or she insist that
the clients take the initiative in resolving "their" problem.
Rather, the problem would be viewed as one mutually shared
by advocate and clients. Once a course of action is agreed on,
both client and counselor-advocate share responsibility and
efforts in accomplishing the mutual goal.

The advocate would work with the principal, not against, in resolving the situation. This might require the advocate to discuss the matter with officials of the teacher's union or to devise some alternate plan with the principal. Perhaps, with the union's concurrence, the sixth-grade teacher would accept a larger number of students this year, in exchange for release from a duty period or some record-keeping chores, which the advocate would handle or get a community paraprofessional to handle. There are numerous alternatives. The advocate would continue to combat this negative situation by striving to uncover the proper combination of positives to facilitate his clients' educational and social development.

The skills and understanding needed in these tasks span the gamut of the social sciences. Consider the political science understanding needed in dealing with the union or the sociological awareness implicit in deciding to check the intelligence test scores of the Spanish-speaking "EMR" students. The same is true for the other counselor roles for poor urban minorities based on the social sciences and grounded in activist techniques.

## The Ombudsman

Although the concept of the ombudsman is new to American society, it has existed in Sweden since 1809. The ombudsman is an official who investigates citizen complaints and problems relating to government officials and agencies. Literally, the word means "one who represents someone." Koltveit (1973, p. 198) explains that "The original ombudsman was expected to investigate a complaint and take one of several courses of action: either dismiss the complaint with an appropriate explanation or correct the situation by use of persuasion, by making it public knowledge, or by suggesting prosecution of the offender."

The basic purpose of the ombudsman is to make government more responsive and controllable in an age of increasing impersonality and organizational complexity. This need has already been recognized in America by bills introduced in over sixteen states, as well as by actions of higher education institutions and school districts. The impetus for this movement is captured by Pennsylvania State Representative Butera, who supported a state ombudsman bill by stating that "What we need is a champion of the Little Guy—to attack the red tape and rescue the people from the sometimes insolent attitude of government bureaus and bureaucracies" (Grossman, 1971, p. 11).

The school counselor cannot precisely mirror this role. Exposing the error of a staff member to public knowledge may be fine for newspaper columnist Royko or for outside researchers, such as Chandler and Plakos, but not for the staff member's colleague. The ombudsman must work with these people. For the same reason, the educational equivalents of suggesting prosecution—that is, working for a teacher's dismissal or disgrace or perhaps even working for actual criminal prosecution—must be the rare exception, rather than common practice. Not only is the educational ombudsman limited in his power in this way, but he is also limited by the need for impartiality. Here is the difference between the student advocate and the student ombudsman. The advocate works in the interest of his client; the ombudsman works in the interest of equity. While the advocate seeks to use the law to his clients' best advantage, the ombudsman is simply interested in preserving fairness and balance within law, regardless of whose interests are served. This is not to imply that the ombudsman is not interested in helping clients. It is more a matter of the role assigned to the ombudsman as an arbiter, an impartial agent seeking to personalize the bureaucratic process for students.

This role is particularly important in large, inner-city schools, which generally are highly bureaucratized. Bureaucracy has certain goals and characteristics particularly important to schooling in urban poor areas. These goals and characteristics are (Menacker, 1974, pp. 33-34):

1. Legitimizing and justifying the existence of the organization.
2. Promoting maximum organizational efficiency.
3. Predetermined organizational and individual objectives.
4. Stress on group integration and function.
5. Division of function, authority, and responsibility.
6. Unemotional, impersonal relationships.

7. Submergence of individual needs and desires in favor of organizational goals.
8. Rigid adherence to organizational rules and regulations, often for their own sake.
9. Rigidly enforced rules of normative behavior.

These characteristics help make the typical inner-city school the depersonalized, insensitive, unresponsive institution it is so well known to be. Barring a total organizational and attitudinal change in urban school systems, these conditions make the ombudsman role critical to student well-being. This is particularly so for urban poor minorities, given their characteristics of passivity and defeatism in the face of dominant social agencies such as the school. These students need some recourse, some mediating, helping force within the bureaucratic ambience that can serve to personalize the elements of the school for the student and give the student a feeling of some influence over his destiny as he interacts with the school. The ombudsman serves to even the balance between the student and the bureaucratic agents and agencies of the school, by serving as a counterweight on the student's side. The professionals have adequate resources for protest, redress, and hearing in relation to students. They can demand a conference with the parents, initiate the process of suspension, send the student to the disciplinarian, fail the student in a course, give the student penalties, such as serving "makeup" or "detention" periods, and more. The school authorities are at no loss to devise numerous effective means of student control. But what of the complementary need of students to effect some countercontrol against the school professionals?

B. F. Skinner discusses the concept of countercontrol in a film titled *Token Economy: Behaviorism Applied*. He makes the point that the most insensitive, cruel treatment of wards by their caretakers occurs in these four institutional settings: prisons, institutions for the mentally defective, institutions for the very young, and institutions for the very old. The reason for this is not that the caretakers working in these four types of institutions are any less humane than workers in other human service settings. The reason is that these people gradually become less sensitive and careful of their clients because their clients (the very old, the very young, convicts, and the insane) lack the ability to exert any effective countercontrol on their caretakers. Skinner believes that all caretakers need some countercontrol to keep them from simply abandoning the human needs of their clients in favor of the bureaucratic needs of the organization that employs them. These are also the reasons why an ombudsman is needed in schools serving urban poor minorities. Students who lack the verbal skills and institutional attitudes needed to exert countercontrol fall prey to bureaucratic demands that are allowed to take precedence over student needs.

According to Drew (1973, p. 317) the ombudsman's role is to redress grievances and prevent infringements on freedom. "He should, in a word, *effectuate* justice." Drew believes that in order for the ombudsman to be effective in his role, he must, above all else, be *credible* to people, which can only be accomplished by *producing results*. Here again is the activist emphasis on the guidance specialist getting something accomplished in the objective, tangible realm rather than in a subjective, psychological sense.

Since the ombudsman is the advocate of justice, rather than of any particular student or group of students, the power of his office rests on the moral force of the society he is serving. It must believe he is exercising integrity in his work (Drew, 1973). Therefore, the ombudsman must be prepared to deny the legitimacy of a complaint if on investigation it appears to be without merit. Indeed, many of the complaints lodged would be of this type, and the ombudsman's credibility with the faculty and administration would rest on the ombudsman's ability to deny inappropriate grievances. His role is not related to gaining popularity with students by always championing their causes. Indeed, if he does this, his role will rapidly degenerate into what Koltveit (1973) calls "a wailing wall," one who is not seen as an impartial instrument of redress, but simply as someone to complain to, on the possibility that some advantage can be secured, whether justified or not.

Koltveit (1973) suggests two appropriate techniques for the ombudsman in dealing with just student grievances: arrange a conference between the student and the alleged offender, with the ombudsman serving as an arbiter or, if this is unwise or fails to resolve the problem, refer the student to the appropriate school official—dean, principal, superintendent, and so on. In either situation the ombudsman serves not as an advocate but as an agent, clarifying the issues and facts, seeking maximum exposure and even-handed resolution.

The ombudsman not only should respond to individual student problems but also should act as a general force offering effective counterbalancing between the power of the school bureaucracy and the relative powerlessness of the student body. A very effective method for doing this is found in the process of simple exposure and dissemination to staff, students, and parents of current judicial decisions on the civil rights of students. Consider the impact of a decision such as the 1975 U.S. Supreme Court decision in *Goss* v. *Lopez*. In that case, the Court established the requirement of "due process" procedures by school authorities when suspending or expelling students. The earlier case of *Tinker* v. *Des Moines School District,* in which the Supreme Court established that students carry the right of "symbolic speech" as well as other civil rights into the school with them, would have a similar impact on policies and procedures of student control that affect the psychosocial development of students. School authorities who were unfamiliar with these decisions or were seeking to ignore them as a matter of administrative convenience would then have no alternative but to accept these concepts, which help to equalize the power balance between the school and its client groups. In this area, as well as other areas of general information, the ombudsman can exert a powerful influence over the psychosocial climate and responsiveness of the urban school. Still, the credibility of the ombudsman will be mainly established through his or her work with individual students.

Let us consider how the ombudsman might have operated in our two previous examples with which the student advocate dealt—the mislabeled "EMR" students and the misplaced sixth-graders. In the testing case, the ombudsman would have had to discover the error himself. The kind of snooping and checking behavior implied in this is quite appropriate for an ombudsman. He does not have to wait for someone to complain if he notices the bureaucratic machinery trammeling individual rights or needs. Consider the case of Ernest Whittum, who served forty-four extra years of involuntary confinement in a Maine state mental hospital simply because his case had been ignored by hospital officials. Whittum did not realize this, and there was no one around to protect his interests, so he just stayed on, decade after decade. The case was finally corrected when the hospital established a position of patient ombudsman. The ombudsman discovered the error while making a routine check of patient records ("Prepare to Free Forgotten Patient . . . , 1971). After that, he simply called it to the attention of the hospital administration, and Whittum was released.

In much the same way, the school ombudsman might notice the inordinate number of Latinos classified as EMR and, as a trained counselor, conclude that there may be a language barrier preventing Latinos from demonstrating their true intellectual ability, insofar as tests can measure it. Here is an example of how the ombudsman would use the moral force of his office, as well as his guidance knowledge. He would present his theory to the guidance staff and/or administration and request retesting in the client's native language. If no satisfaction were forthcoming, the ombudsman's next step would be to contact the school superintendent. If the credibility and moral force of the ombudsman has been established, a retest procedure would certainly be approved at some point within the school hierarchy. If not, then the ombudsman would have to decide whether he wishes to expand the scope of conflict to the public arena—first the school board, then the newspapers, community organizations, and so on.

The idea of an ombudsman publicly opposing the organization employing him is not as farfetched as it may seem. This has happened at some universities and is most strikingly seen by the role of the *Washington Post* ombudsman, whose public opposition to some of the policies and activities of that newspaper have been to the credit of both the newspaper's management and the ombudsman.

In the case of the misplaced sixth-graders, we can assume that the ombudsman would have been contacted by the students, their parents, or even a teacher who might have known of the situation. The ombudsman's task would then be to investigate the situation and determine if the students were being educationally deprived by the arrangement that placed them in a fifth-grade class for a second year, presumably with some additional attention to sixth-grade material. Perhaps a meeting that included the principal, a union representative, students, parents, and fifth- and sixth-grade teachers could be arranged in which the views and needs of all concerned parties were aired. With the ombudsman acting as moderator, it seems reasonable to hope that an adequate solution to the problem would be found.

In contrast to the student advocate, the ombudsman would not necessarily push for a solution previously agreed on by him and the client. His interest is equity, rather than securing predetermined ends for his client. He may sacrifice rapport with his client, but he gains in his stature as an impartial force for balancing the odds between the clients of the school and the professionals who run the school system.

## The Community Resource Specialist

The two previous models of activist counseling specialists both have their focus primarily within the confines of the school building. We now turn to two models that have a primary emphasis on the total life space of the student, as it affects his or her education. It was stated earlier that a major distinction between traditional and activist counseling models is that activists take more account of the client's environment than do traditionalists. However, even activists may tend to have a narrow concept of the environment that influences the client's education. The information supplied by Coleman (1966), Jencks and others (1972), and other sociologists, anthropologists, and practitioners of related social science suggests that a broad interpretation of environmental influences on schooling is needed. For example, Coleman concluded that the influence on schooling of the parents' socioeconomic status and even of the parental socioeconomic status of the student's classmates was far greater than teachers, books, school buildings, or anything else.

Too often, such information is taken to reinforce the notion that this simply serves to show how little the school can do. The school cannot influence the client's environment, nor can it overcome or remediate the overwhelming deficits to adequate education caused by an inadequate environment. Gordon and Smith (1971, p. 371) challenge this position: "Surely, it must be inferred from what we already know about the wide range of adaptability in humans that with determined effort in the area of environmental manipulation we can effect significant improvement in the educational product."

Given the new information we have about the pervasive influence of the student's out-of-school environment on his or her education, it is necessary for counselors to accept the challenge of Gordon and Smith. The way to do this is to develop a counseling model, with a primary focus outside of the school, on the environmental determinants of school performance. In an earlier paper, Gordon (1968) pointed out the direction that these efforts must take: "I feel that guidance must be chiefly concerned with the motivation and facilitation of development and learning. I am not at all certain that this objective is best accomplished through the person-to-person interview of the counseling relationship. . . . It is far more important in the development or redevelopment of children who are greatly handicapped by poverty, by prejudicial attitudes directed toward them, by limited opportunities, and by limited experiences that we attempt to make significant changes in their conditions of life, modifying and removing the things standing in their way, rather than emphasizing a change in the individual's attitude toward these obstructions." The direction indicated conforms to activist theory and implies attending to such characteristics of the urban poor minority student as the primacy of concrete, immediate reinforcement and changes, active personal assistance in helping to combat the negative elements in the environment, and an emphasis on action rather than conversation.

In this role, the guidance specialist must not only be as familiar with the community as with the school but he must also be based in the community. He must have an office there, as well as in the school, for the majority of his time must be spent out in the community. Consider the case of Alice Wilson. She was not a behavior problem, and although she was often tardy or absent this was not the major cause of the exasperation she inspired in her teachers. Many of them found her harder to cope with than the worst behavior problem or chronic truant. The problem was that "she just sat there." She would calmly and passively stare in one direction throughout class, and when the teacher would jolt her out of her apparent stupor she would try to oblige the teacher as best she could, which was rarely at an acceptable level of classroom performance. She took her failing grades with unruffled good grace, expressed the desire to do better, and listened carefully to the teacher's instructions about how that could be accomplished. However, she rarely showed any improvement.

This is a case that might well be referred to the community resource specialist. Operating from his community base, the resource specialist would gather information about Alice's home and community situation. In this case, the resource specialist found out that Alice was being raised by her aged grandmother, a deeply religious, illiterate woman raised in the South, who had come to New York with her daughter and three young granddaughters. A couple of years afterward, the daughter left the family, leaving the grandmother in charge of raising the three young girls, of whom Alice was the oldest.

The resource specialist prevailed on the grandmother's pastor to arrange a conference between the two of them following a meeting of the church's senior citizen group. The pastor knew the resource specialist from mutual participation in community organizations and activities. Therefore, he gladly introduced the grandmother to the resource specialist. With the pastor helping to establish a harmonious atmosphere, the grandmother and counselor developed an easy and comfortable rapport. The main point made was the need to spend more time together to discuss Alice's school problems in detail.

Their next meeting was held at the Wilson home, while

Alice was at school. The resource specialist discussed Alice's poor school situation, and the grandmother was both surprised and concerned. It seemed that she did not understand the grading procedure and that Alice usually signed the grade reports. The most critical information gathered was about the family diet. On cold days, grandmother gave Alice a shot of whiskey before she left for school, and on almost every day of the year she was sent off with a breakfast of sorghum (a molasses-based spread) on white bread and black coffee. There was rarely enough money for Alice to buy lunch, and the grandmother never had the time or energy to consider making one for her to take along to school. Suppers were almost always variations on a theme dominated by potatoes, rice, beans, greens, and small amounts of cheap, fatty meats.

With grandmother's consent, the resource specialist contacted the local public health facility, which arranged for Alice to have a complete physical examination. The result was a diagnosis of malnutrition. Working with the public health authorities and the family's caseworker (they had been public aid recipients shortly after arriving in New York), a plan was devised to help Alice and the rest of the family. A dietician was brought in to work on planning meals, Alice was given a serving job in the school cafeteria that earned her lunch and some spending money, and the pastor started a new church group consisting of parents and their children devoted to increasing communication and understanding between them. These developments did not work a miraculous conversion to superstudent status for Alice. It did, however, stop her precipitous slide toward dropping out of school. She survived well as an average student, developed confidence in her ability, and developed a much improved self-concept. Part of the reason for this improvement was Alice's realization of her grandmother's limitations and, consequently, the need for Alice to accept more responsibility and control over her own welfare. The grandmother also grew in awareness of Alice's needs and her ability to meet them.

This was a case of environmental factors overwhelming the Wilson family. Alice and her grandmother were unable to cope with the demands placed on them by society. Therefore, perhaps the most significant factors leading to improvement were the concrete alterations made in their basically alien, hostile environment. Deficits such as inadequate diet and a lack of adequate funds were combatted and mostly removed. Positives such as the pastor's influence on the family were capitalized on. Without first solving the immediate, objective problem of Alice's malnutrition, none of the other changes would have been maximally effective.

Finally, this case illustrates another important principle of activist guidance, regardless of the particular model being used. That is the principle of parsimony. The activist counselor considers the most basic, necessary and immediate elements of human function first, in diagnosing needs. In this case, for example, it would have been worse than foolish to treat Alice by psychotherapy, under the assumption that all she needed was to be better motivated or inspired. Diagnosis properly started with physical health, and the root problem was found and treated. Only then could higher-order needs be meaningfully attended to.

A good theoretical base for this principle of parsimony is found in Maslow's (1954) theory of human motivation. It states that lower-order needs must be satisfied before a person can fill more elaborated, refined higher-order needs. The theory conforms to the parsimony principle by stating that the first order of needs that must be satisfied is physiological. Only then is the person motivated to satisfy the next highest order of needs—the safety needs. After these are satisfied, the person can move on to the affective areas, such as belonging and love, esteem, and self-actualization. In the urban poor milieu, the counselor is well advised to consider the effects of the client's environment on satisfaction of basic physiological and safety needs. These needs can best be satisfied through direct, concrete interventions. Only then can the counselor turn to the psychoemotional problems with which his or her work is presently most closely associated.

### The Educateur-Counselor

This final model, like the preceding one, has a broad focus on the total life space of the client. The educateur-counselor model differs from all three preceding models in that it is designed specifically to help the emotionally disturbed youngster. It has its theoretical base in a European approach to helping disturbed and maladjusted children through reeducation within a total milieu programming concept (Linton, 1971). Of the models presented, it is most closely related to the community resource specialist and has activist counseling theory as a prominent feature, as indicated by this passage from Linton (1969, p. 321): "One of the central purposes of the educateur's work is the social reintegration of the maladjusted child. This does not imply efforts at personality reorganization, but rather attempts to alter the environmental forces in the child's life to the extent that they become supportive rather than destructive."

The educateur model originated in France at the close of World War II, as a stopgap measure, given the inadequate supply of psychotherapists needed to treat disturbed children. Minimally trained people who seemed concerned about the children and who seemed able to relate to these clients were employed to help them, with remarkable success. The elements that were found to be most related to successful repair of these children were incorporated into a training program for this new specialty. The program emphasizes practitioner skills in vocational training, physical education, and arts and crafts as vehicles allowing the educateur to relate to the client and help him reintegrate with the dominant social system. The educateur is trained to identify and appreciate the importance of the total life space of the client and the behaviors that need to be modified to make him more acceptable in his environment. Attention is also directed toward developing educateur skills for concurrently changing the attitudes toward the client of his family, friends, teachers, and other associates.

The educateur becomes totally involved with his clients, in all aspects of their behavior and environment. He participates in a variety of helping vocational, recreational, and academic activities with them. He also supports them through participation in relations with their significant others. No psychotherapy is applied. Rather, there is role modeling, objective, concrete helping, and mutual participatory activities that emphasize doing rather than talking. It is an in-depth, total milieu relationship.

The educateur model, since its beginnings in France, has spread throughout Europe and even to Africa and, most recently, to Canada (Menacker and Linton, 1974). Educateurs have worked in either live-in institutions for disturbed youngsters or *en milieu ouvert,* the child's natural setting. Given the growing interest in directing the attention of school counselors toward the total environment of their clients, the educateur model represents a tested theoretical technique for adaptation to school counseling.

The educateur-counselor, like his community resource specialist counterpart, would focus more on the total environment, the school being considered as only one part of it. Unlike the community resource specialist, the educateur-counselor would emphasize direct work with the client in a reeducation program. Another difference is that the educateur model was designed as a milieu therapy for emotionally disturbed and maladjusted youngsters, rather than for the general run of students. This marks the distinctive role of the educateur-counselor: a guidance specialist for the emotionally disturbed, a counterpart to the special-education teacher.

In this role, the educateur-counselor would bridge the gap between the two traditional educateur environments and would work both in the institutional and natural environments of the child. His task would be to facilitate reeducation of his client in both settings. Linton and Menacker (1975, p. 3) describe the school educateur-counselor's role as follows: "This new role for the counselor would involve an action-oriented, personally committed approach to . . . counseling. The counselor would utilize a reeducation model in attempts to provide the child or adolescent with alternative and more appropriate behavioral goals. . . . It would involve . . . direct engagement by the counselor with the child or adolescent in high-interest activities . . . which young people enjoy, and during these activities they are more inclined to accept behavioral suggestions and model the behavior of someone they like and see as a friend." Such activities would include helping students study for tests, playing pool with them, playing Monopoly or basketball, teaching them to drive a car, helping them get a job, teaching them how to weave, exploring careers, or whatever else seems appropriate. Through these mutual activities, the educateur-counselor presents the behavioral cues that the client models, gaining the self-esteem to reeducate himself to cope with his environment. Concurrently, the educateur-counselor works with the client to alter the conditions of the environment so that it becomes more hospitable and less conducive to producing social and emotional disturbance in the client. This is done by convincing an employer to hire a client, teaching parents to be more accepting, helping the family dress up their home, getting the client involved in a social or athletic activity, and so on.

The most essential skills needed for this task are the most highly prized in the European educateur-training programs. First is possession of a natural personality acceptable and agreeable to typical clients. Part of the process of candidacy for educateur training is living with typical clients and being judged by them as acceptable or not. After that, the educateur must be proficient in several crafts and sports. While psychological theory and technique are part of the training program, these nontechnical elements are the most highly prized.

The school educateur-counselor in the U.S. context should be prepared both as a traditional school counselor and as an educateur. The latter is generally a three-year program, but certainly could be reduced to between one and two years for trained counselors. Emergence of this specialty would fill the present void for specialized counseling treatments for the large number of socially and emotionally handicapped students in America's urban schools.

## Summary and Conclusion

Traditional psychotherapeutic models of counseling have failed in urban schools serving poor minorities. This failure is the result of three factors: (1) urban school conditions make regular extended, uninterrupted psychotherapy impossible; (2)

school counselors are not well trained in psychotherapeutic technique; and (3), most important, the characteristics of urban school clientele mitigate against the effectiveness of verbal, passive helping techniques.

The alternatives for greater counseling help for urban poor students I have proposed are based on activist theory, which emphasizes direct, concrete helping activities in such specialized roles as student advocate, ombudsman, community resource manipulator, and educateur. Each of these models is rooted in activist theory and emphasizes active participation with the student in the objective features of the school and community environment. They are designed to provide helping techniques that are congruent with the characteristics of urban poor minority students. They all allow for opportunities to capitalize on the positive features of the client and his environment and to combat the abrasive, negative features.

The professional techniques employed have their theoretical basis in such social sciences as sociology, anthropology, and political science. Psychological theory is not abandoned. Rather, it is combined with these other disciplines in developing action-oriented approaches to student service and environmental alteration.

These approaches require significant changes in the job descriptions, professional relationships, and professional activities of school counselors practicing them. They must have a power base relatively independent of the usual, bureaucratically organized hierarchical relationships that exist within urban school systems. This is particularly necessary for the student advocate and ombudsman roles, where there is abundant potential for conflict with school authority, regulations, and accepted practice. School authorities must also recognize the needs for radical departures from traditional concepts of on-the-job requirements and behavior. The student advocate or the community resource specialist may need to put in a ten- or twelve-hour day on a particularly urgent problem, and this may quite likely occur on a Saturday, on a Sunday, or both days. The same is true to a lesser extent of the ombudsman and educateur-counselor. Therefore, activist counseling roles must be accompanied by flexible time schedules and attendance requirements. These professionals cannot be asked to rigidly adhere to a nine-to-five schedule, when they must sometimes work evenings or weekends to do their jobs successfully. Certainly they must be required to average thirty-five or forty hours per week or whatever the system requires, but there should not be the day-to-day monitoring that is the case with teachers or traditional counselors.

There is one final point to address in closing. There would be no need for these activist counseling models if urban poor students were adequately served by traditional counseling models. By the same token, these models are less appropriate to middle-class and affluent members of the dominant race and culture. Social, economic, political, cultural, and moral developments in the total society will determine the length and degree to which such special adaptations must be employed. If the root causes that have made cultural difference a handicap in schools (particularly racism) could be eliminated, there would be little need for such special treatment models. Until that happy time, special adaptations to the special needs of urban poor minorities will continue to be the best approximation of educational justice that the counseling profession and other human service professions can provide.

# 10

# Dreams and Realities of Alternative Counseling Centers

## Chris Hatcher

America in the 1960s was exciting, frustrating, optimistic, and chaotic. It was a time of numerous contradictions and rapid social change. Economic conditions were excellent for most, but some still existed in extreme poverty. John Kennedy and the New Frontier, Lyndon Johnson and the Great Society, civil rights activism, and the Peace Corps symbolized a utopian optimism, despite several crises that almost resulted in nuclear war. A population of youth was raised with plans and dreams cut off by the draft of the Vietnam War, a war that most did not believe in but that the conventional political system seemed unable and unwilling to stop. A growing mood of experimentation and personal exploration prevailed among America's large middle class. Psychedelic drugs, encounter groups, and the pill all made new experiences readily available to large numbers. In contrast to the relatively conservative background of their par-

199

ents, many youth attempted to turn on, tune in, and drop out of the traditional culture.

Youth in particular were affected by these contradictions and changes, and large numbers became members of an active counterculture. They clustered in numerous social groups and neighborhoods in many of our larger cities, peaking with San Francisco's "Summer of Love" gathering in 1967. "Straights," "jocks," and "freaks" became the three main social membership options for high school students. Drug experimentation became a prime social and spiritual activity. Many found personal, philosophical, or political life-styles that seemed to represent a better way than that which they had left behind. Some, however, found terrifying insecurity and disorientation, severe parental rejection, and exploitation by hustlers within the movement itself. While the Indians of the Southwest and Mexico had centuries-old traditions of myth and ritual to guide their drug use, the youth of the 1960s had no signposts or supports (Holleb and Abrams, 1975). For a significant majority, the drugs that had promised new joy and experience brought lasting visions of anxiety and fear.

Traditional clinics and social services experienced tremendous difficulties in trying to deal with young people in the second group. They were frequently unfamiliar with the medical procedures for counteracting the diverse drug reactions and overdoses, and both the young person and the professional often became hostile representatives of their own life-style choices. In the midst of this came the first alternative counseling centers, created by people who straddled both cultures. They were hip and street-wise but also had organizational abilities they had learned in the traditional system. Their message to government agencies was: "We know how to work with these kids. We can speak their language—you can't, you won't solve the problem by busting them or kicking them out. Give us some space and money and we will help them get it together" (Holleb and Abrams, 1975, p. 2). Communities and government agencies listened and bought the idea. So, with little money, inadequate space, and a lot of interpersonal commitment, a new alternate network of service began for adolescent health and adjustment problems.

There are now more than 1,400 telephone hotlines and walk-in counseling centers, over 100 runaway houses, 400 "free clinics" for medical problems, and 100 residential therapeutic communities (Glasscote and others, 1975). Although the drug abuse crisis has decreased substantially, these alternate agencies have earned and retained credibility and viability as service providers. Beginning from an initial focus on bridging the gap between youth and the traditional culture, the alternative agency concept has been actively utilized by black, Chicano, Asian, geriatric, child abuse, urban-low income, single-parent, self-help, and parole-probation special-interest groups. This chapter will examine this new group of alternative counseling centers by examining the philosophical differences between alternative and traditional counseling agencies, organizational stages in alternative groups, basic services, three specific agency examples, and the implications of this new system for counseling and community psychology.

## Philosophical Positions of Alternative Centers

Alternative counseling centers are more than just another group of new private agencies in that they have evolved a rough system of values that underlies their operations. While not every center adheres to all of the following principles, these ten items do present a commonly endorsed picture.

1. Services should be free or almost free. The early street organizers had a great deal of experience seeing people go without medical or social service support because the charges were too high. They were determined that no one should be turned away because of inability to pay.
2. People should be seen immediately. Most public agencies have long hours or days of waiting, and the number of people who simply walk out without ever being seen is quite significant. The street organizers knew they had to establish a personal contact very early, or they would risk being classed as just like the other establishment agencies.
3. Staff members have a cultural and experimental background similar to that of the client, and they like the people they

are working with as clients. This does not necessarily mean that everybody has to be an ex-addict who grew up in the ghetto, but it does place personal life experience close to the top of hiring criteria.

4. There should be no unnecessary status split between staff members and clients. A premium is placed on personal involvement of staff, recognizing that almost all organizations use status as a distancing technique between groups. This effort would materialize in relating to clients on a casual, first-name basis and in constantly planning fewer meetings or activities that are limited to staff only.

5. Personal and job activities for staff are often mixed. There is a sense of community or family, with an endorsement for more direct expression of feelings between staff members. Many individuals adapt to organizational stress and job demands by putting away and carefully protecting their personal lives. While alternative agencies recognize the importance of personal space, they are trying to avoid setting up a system that may need external outlets for feelings and problems in order to continue to function.

6. There should be a minimum of formal organizational structure. Of course, this tends to be more of a goal than a reality. Almost everybody can agree that informal structure in any new organization appears rapidly and can become far more complex than comparable formal systems. Even so, alternative agencies constantly elect an informal system and indicate that they employ more democratic approaches to problem resolution. It is also possible that this goal really evolved more from a common negative experience of staff to vertical systems of management, with the intention of eliminating the layers of bureaucratic middlemen and managers who do not have direct service contact with the people.

7. A client can be seen without giving a last name or any other identifying data. Many of the first alternative agencies came into existence during the rise of the drug culture in the 1960s. Drug laws were both considerably more severe, and enforcement was very active. The majority of later alterna-

tive agencies also developed with minority groups who were uniformily fearful of the misuse of or access to any identifying information by law enforcement groups. This adherence to the right of the client to anonymity has not been without a price. A number of agencies lost funding or were forced to close because community members with significant political power felt that law enforcement took priority over social service approaches to drug-associated problems.

8. Time-limited counseling or service is primarily to encourage the development of self-supports and to avoid establishing long-term dependency. Alternative agency founders have been heavily influenced by Gestalt therapy and philosophy, which stress responsibility for one's own behavior. Such a philosophical approach was most useful in dealing with the passive, dependent, powerless life-style of many of the individuals whom alternative agencies were interested in reaching. The goal was that street drug or welfare agency dependency would not be merely replaced by a new type of institutional dependency. It should be recognized that it is possible that less-realistic motives were also involved—that alternative agencies had to offer short-term services because they did not have the fiscal stability for long-term services.

9. Staff members will actively assist the client in negotiating the social or legal bureaucracy, if necessary. Public assistance for food, shelter, jobs, or legal defense is often too difficult to negotiate and filled with a number of barely understandable time delays, so many people simply give up, returning to street-wise or extralegal ways of living. Alternative agencies hoped that if they got people over that initial barrier, then they could begin to teach them that one can make the traditional system work for oneself. Admittedly, there have been two problems with this approach. It can slip from a social learning process to another way to rip off the system. Further, this approach can often come into conflict with the self-support goals.

10. Alternative agencies are more concerned with informed choice and the idea of taking responsibility for one's own behavior than with "adjustment" to the larger society. They

are more willing to consider social and political issues as part of the therapy process. This is in sharp contrast to the more traditional therapeutic approach, which would see this as a resistance or impasse to dealing with the more important intrapsychic issues.

## Organizational Stages of Growth in Alternative Centers

In our discussion of philosophical positions, a special point was made of the importance of change as a valued process in alternative centers. Individuals who have functioned primarily in traditional settings often experience difficulty in seeing that definite developmental patterns do underlie the apparent surface anarchy.

Most alternative centers begin with a stage of consensual organization. The idealism and motivation of a relatively small group of people is very high. There is an agreement to start to do something, but there is also great ambiguity about just exactly how to go about it. While the initial series of meetings are both confusing and frustrating, a great deal of interpersonal bonding occurs, producing a common experience of community and shared ideals. Entrance requirements into this early group are very minimal, and the membership is very fluid. Everyone seems to be involved in doing the same kinds of things, as job roles are relatively undifferentiated. Group members are very protective of their own independence and of their right to do the job in their own way. Leadership is primarily by small-group consensus, but aggressive, dynamic individuals occasionally assume the function of leading.

The second stage is marked by a period of rapid growth and informal differentiation (Clark and Jaffe, 1973; Holleb and Abrams, 1975). Growth produces more duties and requirements, frequently in the form of paperwork. Informal role and membership boundaries are known to staff members but are not written down. Slowly a small core group appears for making the day-to-day decisions, although major items remain for total group decision. This small core group frequently more resembles a tribal elders system than a rulers system. The larger group seeks them out for counsel and advice and will often follow that advice but is not compelled to. A person may become a member of this core group by (1) involvement in the initial stages of the program, (2) performing a certain task that others cannot or will not, and (3) by sheer number of hours at the program over a long period of time (Kolton and others, 1973). High staff turnover becomes more evident, and the "burn-out problem" becomes a concern:

> None of us were worried about staff burn-out, although it did happen several times. I took one day off the first year I was there. I had a big trip of working twelve hours a day. It kind of went by the woman who was a supervisor; she didn't quite notice it. But then at the end of that one year, all of a sudden I wanted to be anywhere but at the program. I spent about a week in the mountain, and when I came back everything was all right. With most of our staff, we'd give them a week or two off, and they would get to go home, or they would go to San Francisco with some volunteers living up there. They could come back physically, but they never would come back mentally. I guess they were allowed to go too long without some sort of vacation. They became so involved in the program and got so wrapped up in it that once they split and were able to let their minds go, after two or three days away from the program they could never quite bring back their concentration. I was never able to figure it out, if it was just vacations were too far apart, or we demanded too much of the staff at that one time. I know at times we were open about 120 hours a week or so, with only two volunteers working twelve-hour shifts, and that probably was terrible. It didn't seem that bad when you were doing it, but when I look back on it, I shudder. You start working at eight in the morning and finish at midnight. When you're doing it it doesn't seem that bad. I guess that's how we burned out so many

people. Now it's a straight forty-hour week [Kol-
ton and others, 1973, p. 77].

A third stage occurs when some of the informal rules are
written down and formalized. Some staff are now recognized as
administrators and others as service providers. Sheer size begins
to undermine the democratic process, and both interpersonal
and subgroup communications break down. People begin to
think about rejecting strong leaders who will not release or
share power. The type of staffing also changes, moving from
self-help to skilled nonprofessionals and individuals preparing to
enter the profession. An increasing amount of attention is devoted to "quality of service." A staff member of one center
commented, "It used to be more-together street people serving
the less-together street people. But it's changed. The street people now tend to be into heavier stuff. And now it's like the students and professionals serving a pretty side population of all
kinds of people" (Holleb and Abrams, 1975, p. 47).

The staff begins to further align along generational lines:
older and newer. Newer staff usually has a different sense of
commitment and this produces sharp conflict:

The people that we started with, the people
that are here almost every day, those people like to
say they work twenty-four hours a day and are
really committed. We haven't had that happen with
other kinds of people we hire; they're not that
breed. Some of the people that we have wanted to
hire have a lot of ghetto experience. They're really
street-wise. They don't have those middle-class virtues, like we can't always count on them being
there when they said they were going to be. Not so
much as unreliable, but they have a different kind
of reliability, just different ways of operating, different things being the cultural norm. Our problem
is seeing that this is just a different way of being
and changing our requirements, instead of making
everybody do the same thing, we try to leave our

structure flexible enough so that if somebody whose regular pattern is to play music and do things of that nature half the night, it's really unrealistic to expect to schedule them regularly to be one of the people that is there in the morning. The other thing is we're all pretty verbal, pretty articulate. It hasn't been so with some of the new people that we've taken on the staff. They haven't been accustomed to the encounter thing and self-examination and verbalizing. For us to not push them, but instead let them find their own ways of getting the same thing accomplished, is a real struggle. We have no intention of giving up, because the benefits that we have found from getting totally different kinds of people on our staff who really call us on a lot of our idealistic kind of assumptions and bring a different focus to us have been good, believe it or not. When we think now about hiring a new person, we turn down a lot of people like ourselves [Kolton and others, 1973, p. 79].

The final (at least so far) stage is reached with great difficulty. Many fledging agencies have died much earlier. Here, the alternative center becomes a kind of constitutional democracy, with a written charter or operations guide. An ethic of shared and shifting leadership is accepted, and a far greater degree of independence is accorded to subprogram units. A significant number of the staff have begun to consider long-term or career employment in alternative counseling settings. Residual conflict periodically flares between the original ideals and the desire for stability and interface with other community systems.

This compromise picture develops from the pressures of both the countercommunity and traditional service demands, as presented in Table 1.

At this point, one might ask if the alternative center has not become very similar to the traditional center. I would respond that they are still very different, in that "the medium is the message." Although older alternative agencies do acquire

**Table 1. Counter Community Versus Traditional Service Demands.**

| Counter Community | Traditional Service Demands ⟶ | Alternate Service |
|---|---|---|
| Goal is development of a group supportive of *personal growth* (determined by the individual's needs); close relationships between members. | Goal is development of an organization whose purpose is to *help people* who are disturbed and to treat people defined as disturbed by someone in authority. | Organization whose purpose is to help people who ask for help, to help people in transitional phases, to create social changes in society. |
| *Respects individual's values,* confronts itself around contradictions, tries to resolve conflicts through group and individual interactions; emphasis on autonomy and individual freedom—absence of structural limits to greatest degree possible—tolerance for wide differences. | Conforms to socially acceptable *"middle class"* *values*; attempts to manifest these values through interventions; supports the status quo. Conflicts resolved by authority. | Attempts to bridge gap between certain middle-class values necessary for survival and countervalues of clients to maximize support and help to any individual undergoing change. Conflicts resolved by consensus or people involved, and finally by authority. |
| *Authority* derived from *consensus* of group; leadership emerges around felt needs of group and for group-defined tasks. | *Authority* derived from *credentials,* seniority, expertise confirmed by other authorities. | Authority derived from experience, skills, talents, within the program—affirmed by other leaders or authorities. |
| Group works *against hierarchy* since it defeats purposes and runs counter to values. | *Hierarchy is imposed* through structure, based on authority exercised through policy; hierarchy reflects class distinctions, isolates individuals from lower levels. | Hierarchy emerges out of work, structure created to conform to hierarchy; hierarchy should neither reflect class distinctions nor isolate upper levels from all phases of work. |
| Group *shares resources* on subsistence-needs basis. | *Resources concentrated* on upper levels. | Resources shared on basis of responsibility and aim at equalization. |
| *Roles* determined by *behavior.* | *Roles* determined by *credentials.* | Roles determined by tasks relevant to the purposes of organization. |
| Each individual inherently valuable. | Differences in levels. | Differences in abilities and performance. |

*Source:* Jaffe (1973, p. 212).

similarities to traditional agencies, their historical and ongoing process approach to delivering services has been, and remains, decidedly unique.

This overview of the organizational stages of alternative counseling centers has focused on intragroup development. However, as Seymour Sarason has pointed out in *The Creation of Settings and the Future Societies* (1972), such new agencies often do face immense resistance from existing agencies. The two groups compete in the area of ideas and values and for limited support resources. Most communities have a mental health or social service power structure. Like all power structures, it serves to stabilize territorial claims and to exclude new members. Frequently, the power structures are built on cooperating parallel bureaucracies (Graziano, 1969). They are parallel in the sense that, while they initially appear to be autonomous, they share similar organizational structures and methods of approaching service delivery, and they are staffed with individuals trained in a similar management process. The parallel bureaucracies contribute upper-level management personnel to the area/resource planning, interagency, and joint fund-raising boards. Especially in small communities, this means that innovators are likely to have to deal with the same individuals, who occupy multiple but different roles across several boards or interagency groups. This power system of parallel bureaucracies can respond to innovation by active rejection or by altering the idea to incorporate it into the existing structure. The more subtle and lethal approach, however, is to encourage the innovator and to support the new ideas, but to tie them to lengthy special study committees and task forces that doom any real implementation. This type of response creates innovation without change, in which conceptual abstractions are supported, but does not change any basic structure. A primary example of this occurred with the Community Mental Health Center Act of 1963. Most of the creative, high-quality community centers are located in places where few or no services existed previously. On the other hand, a number of the larger hospitals in urban areas obtained the funds and just expanded traditional in-patient and out-patient services, producing innovation without change. It becomes clear that surviving alternative counseling centers have developed expertise in more than just intragroup development.

## Basic Types of Alternative Services

Although by no means inclusive, the following groupings are very useful in understanding the range of activities of alternative centers.

Telephone services were first used systematically in the 1930s by Alcoholics Anonymous, followed in the 1950s by the American Academy of Pediatrics Poison Control Center. Their contemporary use as an outreach tool, however, was begun in the early 1960s by the hotline of the Division of Adolescent Medicine of Los Angeles Children's Hospital. The growth has been dramatic. According to the National Crisis Intervention Clearinghouse, there are over 1,400 telephone centers in the United States with each usually having one to three paid staff and twenty to sixty volunteer staff (Glasscote and others, 1975). They provide easily accessible service to large populations and an anonymous contact for those in fear of more direct methods. While the nature of their service delivery system makes evaluation difficult, telephone outreach services constitute one of the most widely utilized activities of alternative centers.

Credit for designing and implementing the first runaway house for youth usually goes to San Francisco's Huckleberry House which opened its doors in 1967 (Glasscote and others, 1975). The concept was to provide runaways with a bridge between their parents and the drug subculture. An alternative to "living on the streets" was offered in the form of short-term housing and food, together with nonpressured individual and family counseling. Variations of this design are now carried out in over 100 identified runaway houses in the United States. For the most part, runaway houses, although staffed and run in the pattern of alternative centers, have received better recognition and support from more traditional funding sources. This appears to have been partially due to their success in reuniting runaways and families and to the national publicity and political interest in the problem following a long list of murders of adolescent male runaways in Houston, Texas, in the early 1970s. Still, the 100 centers are not evenly distributed geographically, nor are their locations as closely correlated to high problem incidence as one might expect. Here again, the ability of the alternative center staff to deal with varying levels of community cultural values is the most frequently reported issue in program initiation and survival.

Although Synanon has had the greatest public visibility, it is difficult to establish which is the first such therapeutic community. These programs have been primarily directed toward narcotic and polydrug users, juvenile justice repeaters, and first-episode schizophrenic populations. In the 100 identified therapeutic community projects, most rely on strong peer demands and influence to change behavior. Staff members are very frequently treatment program graduates and tend to very actively confront dependent and manipulative behavior. The term of residence usually ranges from three months to one year. However, Synanon and a few other programs permit an ongoing residency, with jobs, social activities, and even schools for the children. There have been mixed reports of success and failure for therapeutic communities. Good follow-up research has been minimal, and there has been wide citation of some cases of individuals who functioned quite effectively while in the therapeutic community but who quickly returned to old patterns as soon as they left. Most, however, are well past the initial stages and have achieved substantial financial and political support.

The first contemporary free medical clinic, the Haight-Ashbury Free Clinic in San Francisco, was founded in 1967 by a doctor, David Smith. This was closely followed by the opening of a free clinic in Seattle, Washington. Both were in response to the numerous health- and drug-related problems of the youth subculture of the late 1960s. It is obvious that the offering of free medical services is not a new idea, but this use of the word *free* was to reflect more than no charge per patient visit (Smith and Luce, 1971). The original philosophy of the free clinic was that *free* was not intended as an economic term but more as a reflection of a way of doing things. It was felt that health care was a right, not a privilege, and that medical institutions should recognize and show more adaptation to a consumer population with diverse cultural backgrounds. In the drug crisis beginnings of the free clinic movement, a major issue was to be free from the red tape of the bureaucracy and to be free to treat people as individuals in need rather than criminals. Further, many free clinics place a great emphasis on holistic medicine, investing a large amount of time in looking at the emotional and social aspects of the patient's life. Current free clinics number over 100 and are primarily supported by medical students, medical residents, and young physicians. Organized medicine strongly and actively opposed the free clinics, presenting a mixture of concern for quality of care and of resistance to any change in the traditional health care delivery system. The young physicians in the free clinics won over their critics in 1972 when they received the endorsement of the American Medical Association. Although initially directed at meeting health needs in the young, drug-using subculture, counseling services were soon incorporated into the adjustment, legal, vocational, and housing areas. More recently, minority and ghetto political groups have been especially active at the neighborhood level in this service combination for both health needs and social issues.

Although walk-in centers, the last type of service activity in our review, are in great evidence across the country, surprisingly few research studies on them and almost no statistical data are available. As differentiated from traditional mental health walk-in services, the alternative center is usually located in an old home or storefront. "Hanging around," talking, and socializing receive far more support than is the case with traditional walk-in services. The clientele are usually from an identified special-interest group, such as the young, students, minorities, neighborhood groups, feminists, aged, or gays. In addition to intrapersonal therapy services, alternative walk-in centers are very involved in community-building activities in the political and social areas. This range of activities allows many individuals to make contact with a source of support that is not possible in the limited ways offered by traditional mental health walk-in services.

## Three Specific Examples

Now let us look at these goals and principles in action by looking at the operations of three alternative centers. Each has its unique aspects and is geographically distant from the others but share common developmental problems.

Union City, California, is a small suburban town located in the southeast San Francisco Bay area. The population is comprised primarily of the families of skilled tradesmen, small businessmen, and semiskilled workers who work in Oakland, San Jose, and adjoining areas. The majority is Caucasian, but there is a significant Mexican-American group as well. Union City has most of the advantages and some of the problems of the typical small suburban town. There is an easy friendliness among many of the citizens, a genuine concern expressed for "our city," and a relatively young, energetic local government. Problems that they struggle with include environmental quality, zoning issues, and some conflicts between parts of the Caucasian and Mexican-American groups.

Several years ago, the previous police chief became concerned with trying to reduce the number of youth who involved themselves in the criminal justice system. Together with a group of interested citizens, he obtained Law Enforcement Assistance Act (LEAA) funds to begin a program to divert first-offender youth from the traditional court system to a counseling and vocational support system. The program got off to a shaky start with one M.A.-level counselor, one B.A.-level counselor, a secretary, and a community board. The tragic shooting and death of the police chief markedly increased the difficulties of the fledgling project. The loss of the single, charismatic leader forced the staff to deal as a group with issues and decisions for which they were unprepared. Not having passed through the usual developmental stages of the alternate service agency, the staff did not have agreed-on mechanisms for solving problems. This lasted for about one year until the appointment of a master's-level director with organizational skills, "street experience," and strong support from local government. A series of anticipated changes occurred: A more active community board began to take shape, program evaluation and client accountability procedures were instituted, and personnel positions were upgraded to the Ph.D. and M.A. levels. Following the resolution of this crisis period, more participatory management emerged, and alternate service system values became more prominent.

This unlikely combination of counseling and community psychologists and police officers apparently works in many settings throughout the United States. Recidivism (the rate at which youths commit new offenses) is much lower for the diversion program than for similar offenses handled by the traditional juvenile court systems. As one police chief has put it: "The ideal thing about the youth service bureau is it's flexible to meet community needs. A bureaucratic organization is not as flexible. I like to light fires under social services agencies because they are not always dealing with immediate needs. They're not dealing with them at night, for instance, when things are hot. They want to do it during normal business hours in a sterile office. The youth service bureau will respond to us twenty-four hours a day, and believe me, we use them. We want to keep kids out of the criminal justice system. Once they're in, there's a damn good chance they're going to stay in."

The Union City Youth Service Center survives and grows today because community groups and local government feel that it works better than traditional social service agencies. It is somewhat atypical from the usual alternate agency in both group development and police agency involvement, but it is very representative in terms of its survival by a compromise combination of counterculture value systems and traditional service demands.

Milwaukee, Wisconsin, is part of America's Midwest. Most of its people are in working-class and skilled trade jobs. They come from a heavily ethnic background, primarily German and Polish, with a 10 percent black population. The youth counterculture appeared in the late 1960s, mostly on the East Side, near the University of Wisconsin-Milwaukee. The first alternate agency created to reach this population was a telephone service, the Underground Switchboard. One physician, completing his residency in psychiatry, had previously spent some time in the

Haight-Ashbury Free Medical Clinic in San Francisco. This individual, together with a psychologist, became interested and active in running rap groups for youth in the counterculture. These two first formed a free medical clinic, and then, in 1970, a counseling center (Glasscote and others, 1975). The counseling center began with a commitment to free service, to minimum paperwork and bureaucracy, and to volunteer counselors, *all* with professional degrees. Private funding was followed by an LEAA grant, and, much later, by some United Way support. Good, hard effort, combined with the professional nature of the volunteer counselors, has yielded excellent results in community acceptance. Relations with the police department have been more problematic, usually around police investigations of drug use in the East Side of Milwaukee.

The counseling center is now well established, overseeing a variety of services including walk-in, telephone, short-term legal aid, and "growth activity" counseling, plus a runaway house. It has nineteen paid staff and has sixty-five volunteers who provide service equivalent to eight full-time staff. Many different types of training are represented, a majority having their graduate training in counseling psychology, clinical psychology, and social work. The size of the budget is approximately $250,000, but the cost per client visit is low—only $9.05. Thus, while the size of the budget is quite substantial, the cost for the number of clients served is really quite low.

Although larger than most alternative agencies and somewhat more traditional in the staff training requirements, the Counseling Center of Milwaukee does provide free, anonymous service, with volunteer staff, and does so in the context of an alternative value system. It appears to have merged aspects of both the traditional and the alternative into continuing, functional viability.

El Paso, Texas, is a city of 400,000 in semiarid desert country near the Mexican border. One must travel 400 miles to reach the next major population center. Over 60 percent of the population is Mexican-American, and one is just as likely to hear Spanish as English in street and shop conversations. The living costs are relatively low. Census data show that the native population is relatively stable; people who are born there tend to stay there. The rich bicultural heritage, low cost of living, warm climate, and casual life-style contrasts with relatively well-defined and separated social classes and lowered concern with social service systems. Southwesterners have traditionally taken care of their problems by themselves and have looked to friends, not the government, if help was needed.

The city has struggled with many crises in its social service systems: national news investigation of its juvenile court system, a substantial methadone mismanagement scandal, state and National Institute of Mental Health (NIMH) investigations of its mental health delivery systems. One of these investigations told the local mental health system to begin immediately several programs required by the federal funding law. One of these programs was a telephone crisis intervention center.

Since none of the area professionals had qualifying experience in telephone crisis intervention, the position of director went to a relative newcomer with a master's in counseling and substantial clinical experience in a well-recognized East Coast mental health center and crisis service. The program was staffed by the director, a secretary-crisis worker, Ph.D. and M.D. consultants, and a large group of volunteers. Bilingual responsiveness was maintained at all times. An attitude of participatory management was established from the beginning with everyone doing clinical work, typing, clerical, and housekeeping. Compensation for paid staff was good, but everyone worked considerably beyond the required hours. Substantial time was often allocated for group and personal growth needs. The volunteers came from all age groups and had varying degrees of local residency. Each volunteer had to pass a somewhat lengthy and heavily performance-oriented training program, with sections devoted to homicide, suicide, psychosis, bicultural conflict, and issues in normal developmental adjustment. Because of the traditional social service sensitivity of the community, extremely careful attention was paid to follow-up, to relationships with other agencies, and to talking to all socioeconomic and cultural groups.

The program grew rapidly, serving 400 callers per month,

establishing an active five-month master's-level internship with the local state university, and becoming a nationally recognized research group on Mexican-American suicides. The first director left after about a year and a half, when her husband moved to another area. The second director had a master's in counseling psychology, had interned at the crisis center, and was bilingual. Approximately one year later, a new director was appointed to the mental health center by the local funding agency. The new director cut off the funds for the center, rejecting the praise accorded it by NIMH, the state mental health administration, and research groups. Staff and volunteers left, and the program dwindled to nonfunctional status.

What happened? In our first two examples, the program achieved alternate service compromise status and survived. In this last example, the program did not. Many factors could have been responsible, but one appears to have been the major one: basic politics. Each alternatively organized and value-oriented service agency is likely to face marked external resistance, despite the quality of its service. To survive, then, each alternative agency must carefully balance external demands, versus the importance of the maintenance of its own value system. This will be even more difficult in the late 1970s. Most alternative agencies got started during a more positive economic period, when money was more readily available. Their competition with traditional agencies was made for survival and community position. Today, even well-established traditional agencies must struggle to maintain their level of funding. Federal support for social programs has all but disappeared, and the private foundations have tired of exciting new ideas that die as soon as the private money is gone. If alternative agencies can continue to build their new ideas in the face of this significant new challenge, they will have attained a significant position in the development of human service systems.

## Implications

In summary, this chapter has sought to examine the new group of alternative counseling centers by overviewing the phil-

osophical differences between alternative and traditional counseling agencies, organizational stages in alternative groups, basic
services, and then three specific agency illustrations.

The implications of this new group for counseling and
community psychology and others are basically threefold: (1)
alternative systems have survived, and have obtained ongoing
viability as service settings because other, more traditional systems did not respond to populations in need; (2) in alternative
systems, organizational changes and periodic upheavals are expected, and may indicate a healthy, growing process, rather
than ineffectual, dying process; and (3) normal adjustment,
psychological pathology, and social issues are frequently too
overlapping to be separated. The functional staff member must
be sensitive to each factor, not just trained in a narrow discipline. Counseling and community psychologists need a clearer
experience with clinical issues, and the more clinically trained
individuals need greater experience with the social issues across
the full socioeconomic range. Finally, all of the professionally
trained groups need to maintain a sensitivity to the usefulness
of people who are functionally effective but who have nontraditional background experience.

If we can learn from the alternative system experience,
both new and traditional systems will benefit. If we cannot,
new populations in need will emerge and find limited responsiveness from professionals, and the two groups will become
more and more separated.

# 11

# New Horizons in Working with the Elderly

Theodore H. Koff
Betty Koff

The majority of persons arrive at the threshold of older adulthood (commonly associated with age sixty-five) with intact personalities. The individual does not wake up on the morning of his sixty-fifth birthday and accept the premise that "Today I am aged," any more than the seventeen-year-old miraculously becomes adult at eighteen. Americans have always thought of themselves as youthful, and as recently as 1970 their median age was twenty-eight. The median age will be over thirty in 1981 and forty by the year 2030, when the number of persons over sixty-five will reach fifty-six million; that is, one out of six Americans by the year 2030 ("The Graying of America," 1977).

Despite this rapid and accelerating increase in the numbers of older people, community mental health centers largely underserve this group. Too often counseling services are not adequately extended to older people because of their proximity to death and because of our own feelings of helplessness in dealing with the end of life. This denies needed services to older persons and denies needed experience in relating to this group to the staffs of community mental health agencies. The excitement of working with youth is connected to the promise of the future—but there can be equal rewards in helping the aged, whose future may not be as long. The very fact of the limited future produces greater urgency to assist the older client and greater satisfaction in the successful resolution of problem situations. The bumper sticker that proclaims, "Gerontology is a sexy business" really means that there are major professional and personal rewards in store for those who commit themselves to work with the elderly.

Society as a whole does not view the older person (age sixty-five and over) as "very good at getting things done" or "very bright and alert" or "very open-minded and adaptable," according to the 1975 Harris survey for the National Council on the Aging (NCOA, p. 13). The young respondents in the Harris survey associate the years from sixty to seventy with poor health, physical deterioration, illness, financial problems, virtual absence of sexual activity, and limited mobility and activity. Studies show that the median income in older families headed by a person sixty-five and younger was $14,698, while the median for older families was $7,505 (Brotman, 1977). Clearly, lack of money is a fact of life for the older person. Being old can mean not only reduced income but also fewer close contacts as contemporaries move away or die. Illness and infirmity often increase, and most people eventually need some kind of help. This may range from informal assistance from friends and neighbors to organized programs of health and social services (Kahl, 1976).

The delivery of social services to the aged is difficult at best. The outlook is particularly dismal for elderly members of ethnic and cultural minority groups. For many of these people, the factors that contributed to a lifetime of economic and

psychological struggle are exacerbated in old age (Bell, Kasschau, and Zellman, 1976). The factors that most affect the use
of services by elderly minority group members are cultural:
communication and language barriers, low socioeconomic
status, and restricted physical and financial access to health and
social services (Bell, Kasschau, and Zellman, 1976).

How do older persons view themselves? The typical older
person appears to evaluate certain aspects of self quite positively; for example, moral virtues and adequacy of performance
in occupational and familiar roles. At the same time, he or she
minimizes in self-image many negative aspects; for example, failing health, personal appearance, and relative lack of education.
Moreover, there is a tendency for older people, at least as long
as they maintain their health and major life roles, not to regard
themselves as old (Riley and Foner, 1968). People sixty-five
years of age and over identified the following serious problems
for themselves: poor health; fear of crime; loneliness; not
enough money to live on; feeling neglected, dependent, or bur-
densome; boredom; lack of adequate medical care; too little
education; not enough to do to keep busy; too few friends;
poor housing; not enough job opportunities; lack of transportation; and inadequate clothing. For the most part, these are
societal problems inflicted on the older person at a time when
the personal resources of the "victim" are not of sufficient
strength to counteract them or to substitute new life patterns.
Except for poor health, fear of crime, and forced retirement,
the problems of older people turn out to be very comparable to
those of younger people. "Problems do exist for older people.
But the same problems do not exist for all older persons, sub-
stantiating the fact that the aged are a mixed group. Nor should
*having* a problem be confused with *being* a problem" (National
Council on Aging, 1975).

The goal of counseling older people is to assist them to
assume a self-advocacy role with family, peers, neighbors,
tradespeople, health practitioners, and service deliverers they
encounter. This self-advocacy can lead to collective advocacy in
which older persons can join ranks to help solve some of the
problems in the community and to have others in their environ-

ment become more responsive to their needs and concerns. Power, mastery over one's fate, is a positive force in any human life, regardless of the age of the individual involved. Personal freedom in decision making, the availability of alternatives, and opportunities for independence should be considered innate human rights.

A crucial component of the older person's problem solving should be rejection of the negative attitudes of aging and the aged self and to project, where appropriate, the responsibility to the larger society. The counselor's skills should include the capacity to separate the individual from the myths and stereotypes with which society has associated the aging person and to view each client as unique.

Each individual is unique, has a value system, belongs to a particular group that may have great significance in his or her life, and has a style of living that is also important. The counselor, despite training in human growth and development, often cannot understand all the uniqueness and peculiarity that come from living a long life. Groups based on retirement age or other patterns of older persons can create a form of group segregation for which older people may have been forewarned, but not prepared. The counselor who approaches the older client with a commitment to breaking down stereotypes and reinforcing the innate human worth and value of his or her client will support and nurture that older person's own self-advocacy.

The counselor also can be an advocate for effective institutional response, for appropriate institutional design, and for avoidance of architectural barriers. He may work for "Senior Power," the "Gray Panthers," and other movements that enable the aging person to age with dignity and power and to die in a manner of his or her own choosing, with his or her own decisions respected. Counseling for the aging person should be based on the premise that all persons should be treated in the most respectful manner. This includes working to assure that the aging person will not be omitted from the mainstream of our society. Ultimately the most effective counselor role would encompass a successful advocacy position ultimately directed toward full acceptance of the aging person and the absence of need for any special advocacy.

In fulfilling this role, the counselor deals with the following major variables:

1. The individual client—strengths, weaknesses, goals, potentials, and limits.
2. The setting in which the older person is located at the time—the potential for continuity of that setting or the attractiveness of a new setting or role. The person living at home about to move to a congregate care housing project must consider the loss as well as the gain in the new setting.
3. The human resources and community support structure available to assist the older person—the combination of counseling with and for the aging. Realistically, counseling for the aging may be more effective than counseling for the aged, but it is in the latter setting that services to the elderly are expected to be provided.

Many of these major issues can most effectively be confronted in groups, where participants can benefit from the support and shared experiences of their peers in discussions guided by a counselor. Elderly persons can be helped by group interaction to gain the acceptance, status, and purpose needed by all individuals. Depending on the setting and purpose of the group, Shore (1964) identifies some of the following important objectives in group work and recommends that, whenever possible, counselors (1) work with small homogeneous groups, emphasizing human dimensions rather than mass activities; (2) involve the isolated individual who may lack the skills for group relationships; (3) be cognizant of individuals' histories, habits, work patterns, and cultural interests, to create opportunities where commonalities can be identified and supported; (4) provide socializing experiences in which interpersonal relationships are stressed; (5) involve participants in activities consistent with their own needs and interests; (6) assist in developing indigenous leadership in self-governing activities that encourage self-direction and individual choice; and (7) strengthen linkages to family members and community members by encouraging their active involvement.

Within the institutional setting, groups designed around

function by resident governments can be especially useful. Elderly members may be participating in an applicants group, new residents group, family group, or division (dietary group, social committee, service committee, and so on) of the resident government itself. Availability of adult study groups in an institution "increases interaction and creativity, and provides not only enjoyment but opportunities for group process and adult education" (Shore, 1964, p. 167). A tenants' council in Parkview Towers, St. Louis, created a self-governing group "that stressed full participation of the elderly in defining their needs and carrying out their services" (Blonsky, 1973, p. 78). Group activities at Swope Ridge develop a feeling of belonging within the home and within the community. "Every resident at Swope Ridge is given a voice in his affairs and also is urged to perform voluntarily some function, no matter how small, that is useful to others" (Swope Ridge, p. 1). Resident government groups "offer the aged persons living in the institution a much-needed opportunity to become, once again, a decision maker, a contributor to his own and to others' welfare and an active citizen in an all too quickly shrinking personal world" (Brody, 1974, p. 130).

This chapter identifies eight areas that provide the greatest risks for the older person, and the greatest opportunities for the counselor's intervention. These are retirement, poverty, relocation, protective resources, institutionalization, death and dying, grief and depression, and drug misuse and abuse. Subsequent sections will discuss each problem, suggest opportunities for the counselor, and present illustrations from current practice.

### Retirement

One of the most important changes that may take place in the life of an older person is retirement. Some view this change as a loss: loss of status, income, or life-style. Others welcome it. Retirement preparation has most frequently been urged on the basis that retirement precipitates a radical transition in the individual's life and that advance programs can help the individual adjust to this transition. This crisis rationale postulates that America is a work-oriented society, with occupational identity pervading all other areas of an individual's life. When an individual moves into retirement and relinquishes the work role, the subsequent role loss constitutes a personal crisis. Sometimes the self cannot be perceived outside the work role; the unemployed self has a moribund quality. So intuitively appealing is the personal crisis explanation that researchers, as well as laypersons, refuse to abandon it in the face of mounting contradictory evidence.

Some studies found that, while retirees in two quite different occupational settings carried over their work role identity, the problem of *continuity* was a more appropriate characterization of the retirement transition than was *identity crisis.* Considering that retirement per se has no negative impact on individual health or psychological well-being, the true crisis is not the implementation of retirement, but rather the fact that society perceives retirement as an end in itself rather than as the culmination of one phase of life, which forces the individual's confrontation with his or her own obsolescence. Only recently social planners have begun to realize that retirement actually constitutes a "career" of its own, requiring provisions for interpretation, planning, and training. Resources to accomplish all three of these components must be devised, accepted, implemented, and evaluated (Taylor, 1972; Sussman, 1972; Hunter, 1968).

Studies of national retirement trends document the need for anticipatory socialization in the form of preretirement counseling. Training can minimize the shock and subsequent demoralization that follow an abrupt termination of major roles associated with membership in the work force. Goals of past retirement preparation programs have varied. Counseling has been seen as a program to develop favorable attitudes toward retirement, thereby promoting healthful adjustment to a new life role by the retiree. Information dissemination and stimulant-to-planning devices properly fall into another category, which emphasizes planning. Typically, these programs have been conceived as including the counseling function.

Preparation for retirement should be focused on successful living in a new milieu that has its own definitions, modalities, and delineations. As retirement years expand because of earlier job leaving and extended life span, the retirement career is achieving great personal and societal importance. Effective financial planning, development of nonwork activity patterns, and adoption of appropriate health care habits can be most effectively initiated during the middle years, when there is time to conserve or even expand resources for the later years. Preretirement programs have been offered by community colleges, universities, and social agencies, as well as by industries for their own employees (Streib and Schneider, 1971).

Counseling services can be most effectively accomplished in preretirement planning when they utilize group sessions. Counseling staff should enlist the assistance of appropriate guest lecturers recruited from the community. Gerontologists, lawyers, physicians, representatives of insurance companies and state agencies, administrators of health and long-term care facilities, and others can be recruited and utilized. It is crucial that a majority of resource persons be the retiree's contemporaries, so as not to isolate, but rather to strengthen self-image at this critical time. Beyond easing the termination of the long-term work role, one of the goals of any preretirement program should be to develop new roles in the community for people to assume in retirement. Involving retirees who have adjusted and become reintegrated in the community provides positive identification with retirement. Preretirees welcome the opportunity to discuss viewpoints and concerns about retirement with their peers in a supportive learning situation. Programming should actively involve preretirees and spouses in discussion of a great many aspects of the retirement process. In addition to receiving basic factual materials concerning retirement, individuals must be able to consider the future in an atmosphere that encourages and supports examination of individual needs, attitudes, values, feelings, and fears about the forthcoming change in their lives. As group members explore their fears and aspirations about retirement, there is observable movement toward individual problem identification and a commitment to retirement planning, problem solving, and self-actualizing behavior.

Workshops can be provided to consider such key issues as personal money management, social security, insurance, property, and wills; changes in living environments, changing health needs; leisure and recreation; education; and any other areas of interest or concern expressed by members of the group. The latter might range from travelogues through consumer protection, human sexuality, community social services, and planning and making provisions related to death (Ash, 1966).

*Case Illustration.* Audiovisual aids can be most helpful to counselors in preretirement programs. For example, the Ethel Percy Andrus Gerontology Center has published a series of booklets on retirement that direct the reader to an examination of the major issues and raise questions about the reader's participation through a checklist. The series titles are "Getting Ready for Retirement" (1975a), "Is My Mind Slipping?" (1974b), "Nutrition for Health and Enjoyment in Retirement" (1974c), "What About the Generation Gap?" (1975c), "Health and Physical Fitness in Retirement" (1974a), and "Sex, Romance, and Marriage" (1975b). These booklets may be ordered from the Andrus Gerontology Center, University of Southern California, University Park, Los Angeles, Calif. 90007.

Also available is a series of twenty half-hour television programs, titled "New Wrinkles on Retirement," designed to assist persons who have retired or who are planning retirement. The series topics include "Facing Inflation," "Vigor Regained," "A Time to Learn and a Time to Play," "Marriage and Love in the Middle Years," "Confronting Loss," "Your Heritage," "Avoiding Quacks and Frauds," "Maintaining Happiness." These may be ordered from the Georgia Center for Continuing Education, University of Georgia, Athens, Ga. 30602.

### Poverty and the Older Client

Lack of money is a problem many elderly persons experience. Statistical information points to diminished income levels for families or single individuals over sixty-five. While not every older person is financially in need, a greater proportion of persons over sixty-five are poor than are their younger counterparts. For some older people, poverty comes with retirement and can be viewed as an acute problem of their increasing years. Elderly persons who experience diminished financial resources and become poor as a result of loss of income, increased medical expenses, inflation, and so on, have a somewhat different outlook from that of their peers who have lived through a lifetime of poverty. Loss of acquisitive means, which in many cases amounts to "reduced means" (Kosa, 1975), is in sharp contrast to the chronic poverty of those who have been unemployed and underemployed throughout their lifetime. The latter have usually experienced a series of formal relationships with bureaucracy that may have become a way of life (Cohen, 1969).

The poor feel powerless. Convinced that they are unable to control their own destiny or to make choices, the feeling of powerlessness they develop may be one of the most important factors in their reaching a state of chronic dependency. From a health standpoint, the poor experience worse nutrition, higher disease rates, a lower life expectancy, and higher death rate than the rest of the population. Even though many services are offered, these services are often inaccessible because of location or method of delivery.

Cohen (1969, p. 41) in his description of the chronically poor, states, "The implications of the differences one finds in value orientation between the poor and general American society are that the poor share a common life style or culture which is internally consistent and distinctive from that which is dominant in the general community." This description suggests that a counselor who serves the impoverished is engaged in an intercultural enterprise. Some authors describe this life-style of the poor as "the culture of poverty," involving people who are the most deprived, who have been poor generationally, and who have developed certain characteristics because they lacked opportunity and resources. Their behavior is part of their value orientation and considered normal. It has helped them survive. (A word of caution seems appropriate here. One can generalize about a group of persons, but not about specific individuals. No one individual will have all the characteristics of the group.)

Armed with this knowledge, how can the counselor assist

the older client who has experienced a lifetime of poverty? Because the pervasive theme of powerlessness equated with dependency has been a lifetime experience, can power and a measure of independence be introduced or achieved in the later life of such an individual? The counselor can provide opportunities for the client to look at alternative solutions to the problems, to make choices, and to participate in groups whose members make decisions about their destinies. Participation of poor persons is favored and promoted in many of the newer federal programs and in the self-help programs of ethnic minorities. By providing opportunities for the elderly client to gain power, the counselor can fulfill the goal of assisting the client to assume self-advocacy. Additionally, the counselor may sometimes find it necessary to help the older client get assistance from a public or private agency.

Many programs have been developed in recent years. Both voluntary and public agencies now constitute a fairly comprehensive network of services, although gaps continue to exist. Services present in some communities may be unavailable in others, however.

The following are examples of federal or national programs for the elderly: RSVP (Retired Senior Volunteer Program), VISTA (Volunteers in Service to America), Foster Grandparents (Sponsor: ACTION), SOS (Senior Opportunity for Service; Sponsor: Office of Economic Opportunity), and Senior Community Service Programs (Sponsor: National Council on Aging).

Local resources are information and referral services, Health Planning Councils, Area Agencies on Aging, the Social Security Administration, the Consumer Protection Agency, Medicare/Medicaid Agency, Senior Citizens Legal Aid groups, and local welfare departments.

## Relocation

Throughout the life cycle, most individuals develop such basic psychological anchor points as a positive body image, an acceptable home, socioeconomic security, patterns of satisfying activities, and a meaningful purpose in life. Medical or financial setbacks, termination of significant life roles, and other age-imposed changes may make maintenance of such anchorages difficult for the older person. Depression in later life may be precipitated by disruption of life patterns. Forced relocation in old age represents a complex sequence of experiences and emotional responses; it disrupts past relationships, established routines, and special orientation. The ability of an individual to cope with the stress resulting from a move depends on personal resources, especially the individual's prior mastery of new situations. In youth, a move often signifies upward mobility and positive accomplishment, but the older person often relocates out of need, rather than desire.

Moves from one independent living situation to another may be made at the time of retirement, when children leave home, on the death of a spouse, with the recognition of perceptual or motor difficulties, or when altered economic status suggests a move to smaller quarters. Many elderly people choose to remain within a familiar locale; others prefer to move to milder climates and/or retirement communities where they hope to find the companionship of others their own age.

The move into an institutional setting often is by an individual unable to choose his or her own options. When emotional problems or medical emergencies prompt an involuntary move into an institution, other stress factors combine with the precipitating situation, with results that are often traumatic. Discharge from an acute care facility and a return home may not always be possible, and the individual may be transferred to an extended care facility—a nursing home or sheltered care facility. In some cases, this is a permanent placement. In others, the individual may in time be sufficiently improved to return to the community, where there may be few or no supportive services.

The situational demands of relocation are often so disruptive that sharp declines in morale and increases in disorientation and mortality or morbidity rates result from one or a series of moves. A sense of helplessness and powerlessness combined with anxiety has been observed to mount as older persons await institutionalization; this often assumes behavioral expression in depression, withdrawal, and lowered self-esteem.

A definite relationship has been found between social class and the depth of grief experienced during relocation: the higher the status, the less the likelihood of severe grief. It is primarily because external stability is so important to lower socioeconomic groups that dislocation from a familiar residential area has a particularly disruptive effect on their spatial identity (Yawney and Slover, 1973).

Older people living by themselves in the community may actually function within a supportive environment created by dependency on family members, neighbors, local merchants, and landlords. The impact of relocation is the destruction of these life-supportive ties. The relocated individual must not only adjust to a new environment but must also develop a new network of social supportive relationships within that possibly threatening environment. However, the effects of moving are not always negative—in many cases, a changing urban pattern breaks an older person's supportive ties, and relocation may enable him to reestablish those vital relationships more easily.

The counselor's role in relocation should begin with a thorough assessment of the psychosocial functioning of each individual who plans to move in order to determine the individual's capacity to withstand stress, his or her readiness to cope with the event, and the unique constellation of his or her needs and suitability to the new environment. Poor health or severe disorientation often precipitate a decision to relocate; they also may minimize the person's ability to survive the relocation. In such cases, alternatives to relocation should be explored. If possible, the move might be delayed while the person's readiness is strengthened through therapeutic intervention. The reaction and subsequent adjustment of each person to the event are unique. The counselor must be sensitive to the wide individual differences among the elderly.

The counselor can ensure some measure of adaptive success through maintaining frequent contact to monitor orientation, mood, activity patterns, and behavior; to offer support; and to provide psychological security. Open discussion of limitations and strategies to achieve successful adaptation can be initiated and carried through during the first several months in the new environment. Ongoing personal involvement in decision

making should include discussion of choices as to the new setting and disposal of familiar articles and possessions, as well as
of adaptations in life patterns. The counselor can introduce the
older person to the new environment prior to the move, so that
a progression of adjustments can be achieved. Frequent visits to
the new environment enable the elderly person to become
familiar with the resources offered there and can smooth the
transition as well as provide an opportunity to work through
any fear about the move. Assurances about the availability of
transportation, health services, shopping, and other services contribute to a more successful adaptation. The older person's
family can play a role at this time, and the counselor should
actively work with its members when possible, particularly
when the relocation is into an institutional setting.

The counselor should support the older person's participation in all decisions in an effort to maintain the client's identity during a period of disruption. Strength can come to the
client when sufficient time is offered to arrive at a decision to
relocate and to muster inner resources to deal with the move.
The counselor can, additionally, advocate patience, kindness,
and respect on the parts of all participants in a relocation action, thereby minimizing or preventing the severity of stress.

## Protective Services

The problem of the aged person who needs protective
services becomes evident when his or her way of living and incapacities arouse concern or revulsion in others (Wasser, 1971).
Examples of persons requiring protective services are those who
are discovered in a state of malnutrition despite sufficient
income and the ability to purchase food; those living in an unsafe, dirty environment; and those who refuse help in moving to
more acceptable quarters. Also included are persons who are
demanding, suspicious, and unable to relate to others; who are
unable to live alone because of severe incapacities; or who are
victimized and/or physically or mentally abused by a relative or
other persons. Many older persons in need of protective services
are not capable of being cured, in the sense that their prime

levels of physical and mental functioning cannot be restored. Certain aspects of the life course are irreversible, and the professional would be overwhelmed with the futility of any service effort designed to "cure" them.

Unfortunately, people who need protective services are frequently unwilling or unable to accept the assistance offered. The aged person's failure to seek help or refusal of help offered does not represent a measure of need but may cover up his or her underlying desperation. Judgment and perception, as well as physical strength, may be so diminished that his or her response is mistrust. The aged person may mistrust others because of previous attempts of others to direct and control him or her or because of his or her own decreased abilities to cope with his or her life situation (Wasser, 1971).

The older person in need of protective services may be an involuntary client, one who did not seek counseling assistance. Ordinarily, a person asks for help and in so doing gives consent for the process. Agencies customarily are organized to give emphasis to the client, who voluntarily agrees to work with the counselor. In a protective service situation, the counselor may be dealing with an unmotivated and involuntary client. The counselor's first step is to help the aged person to become a voluntary client by helping him or her accept the services offered, even though the client did not ask for help originally. It then becomes possible to work on a voluntary basis with most clients having problems requiring protective care (Wasser, 1971).

Some clients may continue to refuse help, such as lifesaving medical attention or relocation to a safe, clean environment. In such circumstances, the counselor must learn first to understand and evaluate the basis for the refusal. It may then be possible to offer assistance in a way that will be acceptable to the client by adapting the delivery method or the manner in which the help is given.

Older persons who are experiencing difficulties in maintaining independent lives or who are increasingly unable to cope effectively with their environments often are institutionalized and congregate in facilities where "their needs can be met most effectively." Although custodial institutionalization may seem to represent the most positive solution to the problems of the aged in the need of protective care, it should be considered only after thorough exploration of other available community resources. A better alternative often would be to allow such individuals to remain in their homes, introducing support systems or prosthetic measures to keep them functioning. The latter approach promotes the individual's healthful return to independent living, in contrast with the former approach, which supports a whole range of highly maladjustive behavior and morbidity.

Multipurpose senior centers, senior citizens clubs, nutrition and socialization programs, special needs transportation, daycare centers, walk-in clinics, home health services, homemaker services, and a variety of other social services, singly or in combination, can enable the older person to extend the period of independence and residence in the community.

*Case Illustrations.* The two programs described here illustrate the type of service that is being offered to aged people. First, Supportive Services for the Aged is financed through Title XX of the Social Security Act and is administered by the Pima County (Arizona) Health Department. The program addresses the plight of those elderly who because of a lack of available community supportive services face institutionalization before they desire that environment or need that level of care. The Pima County program serves individuals fifty-five years of age and over and considered at risk of inappropriate institutionalization. Information on the program may be obtained from Pima County Health Department, Supportive Services for the Aged, 151 West Congress, Tucson, Ariz. 85701.

The program provides a coordinated delivery system of services that are considered critical if an elderly person experiencing functional decline is to be able to continue independent living. The service components are home health and homemaker, transportation, adult daycare, home-delivered meals, and socialization and nutrition opportunities. Social workers called *facilitators* provide a single point of entry to the entire package of services. They are responsible for intake, assessing individual needs, and assuring delivery of the appropriate service, and, in their client tracking, assume an advocate role, monitoring any change in the client's situation and tailoring services to meet the changing needs.

The second program that illustrates current support services is in Los Angeles. Jewish Family Service developed a program to enable elderly persons to cope more effectively with their day-to-day problems. Since older individuals experience problems that may affect their capacity to live independently, the program seeks to effect changes in the community that will enhance living for all residents as well as assist elderly persons to deal with their life situation. The program is designed to convey a sense of entitlement and accessibility, not charity, with consideration for the cultural context of the community. Information may be requested from Jewish Family Service, 6505 Wilshire Boulevard, Los Angeles, Calif. 90048.

The service model selected was intended to encourage, enable, and aid older people to use social services as early as possible. Locations were selected within shopping centers and in storefront offices to provide visibility and easy access to service. Service is on a walk-in basis, with no appointment necessary. Services offered are individual counseling or group experiences and include information and referral, marital and intergenerational relationships, case or class action advocacy, medical or mental health referrals or interpretations, home help, employment and housing services, burial information, financial aid, help with forms and letters, help with shopping and transportation, home helpers, and home-delivered meals.

## The Aged in Institutions

Approximately 5 percent of persons over sixty-five in the United States are currently living in institutions, about 15 percent will ultimately live in institutions, and about 20 percent of all deaths will occur within long-term care facilities. Elderly persons who will experience institutionalization are in need of special attention; many will need counseling if they are to cope with a new environment that is comprised of both the physical setting and the people in it—residents, staff, and people in the community. Counselors therefore should direct their skills to each of these three groups of persons.

Not all institutional residents need or choose to avail themselves of counseling services, yet all need an opportunity to have warm personal relationships and to experience a sense of belonging, a feeling of being loved and cared for, of being worthwhile and useful. The counselor must be sensitive to opportunities to further these positive, human goals.

Of special concern in institutional counseling, and one of the most difficult problems encountered by those caring for residents in long-term care facilities, is the older person with severe mental impairment. "Since the great majority of the elderly persons residing in these institutions display a significant degree of such impairment, their care is of the greatest importance, both for the residents themselves and for the staff who must deal with them on a daily basis" (Goldfarb, 1973, p. 39).

The term *mental impairment,* as it is used here, means that type of organic brain disorder characterized by a relatively permanent deficit in the capacity for intellectual functioning. Symptoms may be confusion and impairment of orientation, memory, perception, knowledge, and judgment. Chronic brain syndrome may result from permanent organic changes of cerebral tissue. There is evidence to suggest that the problem is linked to age, since it occurs most often in persons over eighty-five. Because the group over eighty-five is the most rapidly increasing segment of the population, increased problems related to institutionalization and mental functioning can be anticipated. It should be noted that the concept of "brain syndrome" is challenged, because of the uncertainty of symptoms, causes, and manifestations involved. In too many situations, "chronic brain syndrome" is a wastebasket diagnosis comparable to "senility" and is selected because of the absence of any clearly definable diagnosis. In fact, the diagnosis is not definitive, because it is impossible to examine brain tissue in vivo, and some postmortem studies of brain tissue do not support the diagnosis of chronic brain syndrome (Jarvick and Cohen, 1973). Some researchers (for example, Snyder, 1977) suggest that mental functioning needs to be studied using as many as twenty-seven different functional characteristics and that only then will we have an understanding of the capacities of the individual.

Impaired mental functioning among the elderly is often a temporary, reversible symptom. It can be caused by depression, malnutrition, electrolyte imbalance, drug interaction, and/or dehydration. It is therefore extremely important that people suspected of suffering from impaired mental functioning be subjected to a thorough medical examination to diagnose and treat reversible conditions or rule out their presence.

Goldfarb (1973) provided a tool designed to examine the presence and severity of mental impairment. The test, known as the Mental Status Questionnaire, consists of ten questions posed to the older person by the examiner as part of an interview or conversation. Questions posed relate to orientation and recall of present and past events. Recently, Lawson, Rodenburg, and Dykes (1977) developed a similar scale for evaluation of persons with organic cerebral disease which reflects impairment of orientation, emotional control, motor ability and communication. Both the Goldfarb questionnaire and the Dementia Rating Scale developed by Lawson and his associates tend to focus on limitations of ability rather than strengths. Any assessment of limitations and strengths in the elderly must be sensitive to language barriers, hearing deficits, and sight distortions that are not part of organic brain damage. Newer approaches suggest the desirability of focusing on strengths, on functional capacity, and especially on identifying areas of mental functioning that can be strengthened. This provides an opportunity for constructive participation in the life of the elderly persons.

An understanding of the presence and severity of mental impairment is important for the counselor assessing the capacity of the client to participate in a counseling dialogue or in group encounters. When severe mental impairment is present, it is still important to provide a warm, supporting, stimulating environment, but it becomes especially important that the staff be aware of the client's limitations. Staff involved in daily contact and care of persons with severe mental impairment need special support techniques to enhance their capacity to provide an accepting environment for the clients. Staff understanding and staff morale and satisfaction will determine the quality of life for the institutionalized older person. For this reason, counseling for the person with severe mental impairment also becomes counseling for the personnel and the person's family. Staff must accept erratic behavior and the absence of overt rewards from the client group, which may make them question the value of their personal contribution to the residents. Again, the counselor is called on to be an advocate, interpreting client behavior to staff and family so that reaction to the client will be understanding and supportive despite disturbing behavior.

Several treatment approaches are especially effective with institutionalized persons with severe mental impairment. The counselor acts as a manipulator of the institutional environment in order to support and meet the needs of the individuals residing there. The treatment modality is effective because it communicates to staff a legitimate, institutionally supported treatment approach, reinforcing the adage that where there is life there is hope. It also enables staff to assume a role that is more than custodian of a body and its physiological functions.

Counselors should familiarize themselves with "Guidelines to Treatment Approaches" by Barnes, Sack, and Shore (1973) for an overview of a broad range of mental health treatment modalities and should be prepared to be advocates for the development of appropriate treatment modalities and instruct staff in their use. They should also participate in staff review of the needs of residents, referring residents to specific institutional treatment programs. Staff should be encouraged to turn to the counselor for direction and guidance in responding to the social and personal needs of the institutional residents. The counselor's response will be helpful to the resident if it triggers the appropriate treatment plan, motivates the staff with new insights into the needs of the resident, or enables the staff to derive a sense of creativity and accomplishment in working with the institutionalized person.

Of special usefulness with mentally impaired institutionalized persons is the reality orientation program initiated in 1958 at Winter Veterans Hospital in Topeka, Kansas, by James Folsom and further developed in 1965 at the Veteran's Administration Hospital in Tuscaloosa, Alabama. "The backbone of reality orientation is the repetition and learning of basic information such as the patient's name, the place, the time of day, day of week and date, the next meal, time of bath. This essential repetition and relearning is conducted both formally and informally" (Barnes, Sack, and Shore, 1973, p. 55). The informal activities are carried out by all staff twenty-four hours a day, supporting the older persons' orientation throughout the day. This is especially important, because institutional living may confuse the residents' orientation. Formal classes should be conducted on a daily basis in the same setting by familiar persons in small homogeneous groups, according to the participants' abilities. Classes should repeat the reality orientation characteristics of name, place, and time. (More information regarding utilization of Reality Orientation programs can be requested from: Mrs. Dorothy Scarborough, Reality Orientation Program, Veteran's Administration Hospital, Tuscaloosa, Ala.)

The prosthetic environment, physical therapy, regular diet, and announcements to jog the memory will help persons with cerebral damage to use their remaining capacities in a more efficient fashion than they otherwise could. In addition to problems of mental impairment, counselors should be aware of sensory loss among older persons and of the fact that sensory deprivation caused by loss of hearing and sight reduces the ability of an individual to deal with his or her environment. Counselors should seek medical evaluation of hearing and vision as part of a total physical examination and review of medication regime to understand both the capacities and the limitations of each client.

Another problem often encountered is depression, frequently manifested by physical complaints that may be mistakenly dismissed as resulting from old age. Help for the depressed person is possible if helpers recognize that such behavior is not random or accidental but is an expression of the person's search for relief from suffering. Support provided by staff members can decrease feelings of helplessness, unworthiness, and futility. Response to the depressed person should include a complete physical examination to determine whether physiological decline and/or illness are contributing to the depression.

Gelwicks and Newcomer (1974), by clearly identifying

the behavioral responses to institutional design, suggest yet another role for counselors in long-term care settings. Design characteristics that support independence, privacy, security, socialization, and dignity should be identified and utilized in a total therapeutic environment. Efforts to influence the nature of design may reduce the need to help the older person adjust to the institutional environment. Environmental counseling, more commonly called *advocacy,* is an important counseling function directed toward enabling the older person to enjoy as many opportunities as possible in an institutional environment. Architects, administrators, boards of directors, and county and city governments thus become clients who need the counselor's interpretation and advocacy so that individual needs can be met in an environment supportive of older persons.

*Case Illustrations.* The following examples describe programs of institutionalization for the aged.

First, Hillhaven, Inc., a national organization operating nursing homes throughout the United States, has provided reality orientation and therapeutic community opportunities for the residents of its institutional care settings. Hillhaven employees are provided ongoing training in the use of these therapeutic modalities, and administrators are held responsible for the functioning of these programs. Information is available from Hillhaven, Inc., National Office, P.O. Box 11222, Tacoma, Wash. 98411.

Counselors at Hillhaven homes are expected to assist in program development and to provide in-service training for staff members, enabling them to better understand the confused and disoriented resident. Counselors are charged with orientation of members of patients' families as well as of the medical and nonmedical communities.

The second example is Golden Acres (The Dallas Home for Jewish Aged). Here, staff members modified the reality orientation program in their own style and evolved the LIFE program, representing *love, interest, fulfillment,* and *enrichment.* Underlying the LIFE program is a credo that says: "Aging is a normal process of living and need not be a period of mental and physical deterioration. The resident of the home is an individual to be treated with respect and dignity due one of his years. The resident of the home should be provided such support by the staff that he perceives its members as hopeful, dedicated, and interested in restoring him to the best life he can live. The LIFE program should be planned with the resident and his family and a rehabilitation-resocialization program should be established, emphasizing the resident's abilities, not disabilities" (Shore and others, 1971, pp. 12-13). (More information may be requested from Dallas Home for Jewish Aged, 2525 Centerville Road, Dallas, Tex. 75228.)

## Death and Dying

Death is a universal experience, one that each person will experience, both in the loss of loved ones as well as in one's own dying. An older person is closer to that eventuality than his or her younger counterpart. This stage of development involves "acceptance of one's one and only life cycle" and nonacceptance is signified by fear of death. This implies that acceptance of death may be related to the extent of satisfaction with the way the individual's life has been lived (Brody, 1974). Many persons, old and young, are dissatisfied and feel unfulfilled in their lives. The older person has comparatively little time left to make changes, to undo, or to change course. The counselor can help the older individual to accept or tolerate his or her one and only life experience. One useful natural tool that has been suggested by Butler and Lewis (1973) is the use of reminiscences or life review. Life review is very similar to psychotherapy, in which reviewing one's life leads to understanding of the present situation. Some individuals experience painful regret, anxiety, guilt, despair, or depression. "The most tragic life review is that in which a person decides life was a total waste" (Butler and Lewis, 1973, p. 44).

Examples of some positive results of reviewing one's life can be righting old wrongs, making up with enemies, coming to an acceptance of mortal life, and feeling pride in one's accomplishments and of having done one's best. The review can become an opportunity to decide what to do in the remaining time, to work out material and emotional legacies. Some people may trace their family backgrounds; others may create works of art or write memoirs.

The actual dying phase of life is usually managed as a medical problem, but personal, social, cultural, and religious considerations are important factors in reactions to death, and the counselor can help individuals or groups learn to deal with these (Koff, 1975). The care of the terminally ill is incomplete without counseling—both for the patient and the family. Often the focus has been only on the patient, but Elisabeth Kubler-Ross (1969) points out that the acceptance of death is often more difficult for the patient's family than it is for the patient himself. Help must be available to both.

Clergy have long filled the role of friend of the family, but counseling other than spiritual—namely, financial, practical, and emotional counseling—is often unavailable, especially on an ongoing basis. Death involves more than prayers and tears—it is a web of insurance policies, bills, attorneys, physicians, guilt, loss of income, and funeral preparations. To help the dying person and his or her family cope with the reality of impending death, supportive relationships during illness are necessary. The counselor can provide assistance with the practical aspects of life and dying and ease the emotional trauma of separation and grief. Care must continue during the family's time of bereavement (Hillhaven Hospice).

Because many older persons die in institutions, those that reside there have opportunities to observe the way dying is treated. Each resident thus learns of his or her own eventual fate, and each death becomes an anticipation or rehearsal of his or her own dying. Individuals prepare for anticipated trauma by rehearsing, in the mind, the sequence of events and consequences and the responses of others related to them. By reviewing and sorting out the situation, the "worry work" becomes productive, because it provides a rehearsal for coming events. Counselors must recognize the value of this social rehearsal for dying as a process in which the institutionalized older person is an active participant (Koff, 1975).

In many long-term care facilities, attempts are made to

disguise or hide the death of a resident. The message is clearly given to surviving residents that the life of the deceased is insignificant, because his or her death is not commemorated in any way. The surviving resident then learns that his or her own death will be treated in a similar fashion. Instead of being hidden or disguised, there should be an openness about death and dying, scrutiny of institutional practices and counseling assistance for each resident to determine how his or her death will be handled. The counselor has still another responsibility related to assisting the individual resident—to assist others who care for the resident to recognize his or her needs and wishes in regard to death and dying (Koff, 1975). Even though an effort is made to involve the resident in planning, some individuals may wish to avoid discussion of death and dying. This wish must be respected, but it should be realized that the wish does not necessarily mean the person is not observing nor rehearsing his own anticipated death. Counseling individuals at the end of life is of equal importance as providing help for those individuals with a future. Each situation is one of uncertainty with the stress being that of fear of the unknown.

*Case Illustration.* Hospice is a health care program designed to meet the special needs of terminally ill patients and their families. This program offers the kind of care that will enable patients to live out their lives as fully and comfortably as possible.

The hospice program, based on sophisticated medical and nursing care, employs new pharmaceutical and other treatment methods to control pain, nausea, and loss of appetite—conditions that deprive patients of strength, will, and sometimes even their human dignity.

Hospice considers the basic unit of care to be the patient and family and offers its services to both in administering to medical, emotional, social, and spiritual needs. Teams of professionals and volunteers help the family unit mobilize its own resources to cope with the difficulties of every member. Most importantly, the team listens to the patient and the family and offers constructive help with whatever problems must be confronted. Additional information may be requested from Hillhaven Hospice, 5504 East Pima Street, Tucson, Ariz. 85712, or New Haven Hospice, 765 Prospect Street, New Haven, Conn. 06511.

## Grief and Depression

Grief and depression are emotional reactions to loss of function, a person, or of a body part. Persons of any age may experience loss with the subsequent feelings of grief; older persons are more frequently confronted with multiple losses. Death of a spouse, friends, colleagues, and relatives; loss of income and participation in community; and loss of physical health and mobility exemplify the kinds of loss that more commonly occur in aging. Grief and mourning have purpose. They provide a beginning of acceptance of the reality of loss and discovery of ways to fill the emptiness it causes (Butler and Lewis, 1973). During the height of the bereavement period, many grieving persons experience insomnia, anorexia, and other somatic complaints.

The management of grief must be preceded by recognition and understanding of the necessity of the underlying process. It consists of remembering the lost individual (or function) and of working through the pain, guilt, and anger that go with the memories (Gramlich, 1968). Often it is possible to anticipate loss before it actually occurs. An individual may then begin to grieve before the actual bereavement and, in rehearsal for the event, find strength to withstand the dreaded occurrence when it comes (Arkin, 1974). The longer the bereaved-to-be "knows" in advance, the greater the opportunity to reduce the intensity and duration of the acute grief reaction (Blank, 1974). The bereaved person usually experiences such physical symptoms as sleeplessness, an empty feeling in the pit of the stomach, weak knees, and a tendency to deep sighing. Emotionally, the person experiences great distress. Guilt feelings and anger are frequently present, along with a disorganization of normal response patterns. The bereaved person may wander about aimlessly, pace the floor, and be unable to work.

The absence of depression after a loss is considered abnormal. Successful grieving includes anger, guilt, sadness, and much pain for the bereaved person. Persons who remain stoic, show no signs of grief, or who have not experienced the painful process tend to experience varying degrees of difficulty or prolongation of the grieving process, which may result in prolonged depression, suicide, and troublesome somatic symptoms (Parks, 1973).

The counselor's role in helping the older person to grieve successfully, whether the grief precedes the actual loss or follows it, is primarily to listen to and offer support and concern while the individual expresses feelings that may be difficult or even unacceptable to him or her.

*Case Illustration.* The Southeast Community Mental Health Center in San Francisco provides a continuum of mental health services for the elderly. The focus is on maintaining the older person in the community by providing (1) a responsive service easily initiated by a call from the older person, a friend or family member, or a social agency; (2) assessment of needs and services delivered to the older person in his or her own home; and (3) simplifying the process for initiating the service and accessibility to the other services in the continuum.

The initial home visit and assessment of the needs of the client is made by a psychiatrist and social worker. The client's family is included wherever possible. A care plan is developed and may include home care or care in an acute or psychiatric hospital or long-term care facility until the client is no longer in need of the mental health services. Support services may be needed by the client, examples of which are legal aid, transportation, homemakers, and visiting nurses.

More information may be obtained from: Southeast Community Mental Health Center, Geriatric Service, 800 Potrero Avenue, San Francisco, Calif. 94110.

## Drugs and the Elderly

The counselor should be aware of some physiological changes that take place as the human organism ages and that affect the way in which the body responds to drugs. Generally, the liver metabolizes most medications, and the kidneys excrete drugs from the body. Filtration through the kidney decreases with increasing age, as does the renal blood flow. Metabolic activities of the liver slow down with age. What this means for the counselor is that the same dose of a drug given an older person will affect an older person differently from a younger individual. The older person will generally experience longer-lasting effects and, if a drug is given repeatedly, may feel cumulative effects. The situation may occur as a result of self-medication, including abuse, as well as of prescribed drugs. Acute and reversible mental changes can occur and are identifiable by the following symptoms: fluctuation in the level of awareness, visual rather than auditory hallucinations, misidentification of persons, and restlessness (Burnside, 1976). A complete and comprehensive physical examination is in order if some or all of these symptoms are present, because problems other than drug reactions may cause these symptoms, including dehydration, malnutrition, or electrolyte imbalance. Drugs frequently prescribed for the sedative or tranquilizing effect as well as those for cardiac disease are among those that may cause problems. The chance of adverse reaction to medication increases with the number of drugs taken. An additional problem comes from the tendency of elderly persons to mix prescribed drugs with over-the-counter medications or with alcohol.

Abuse of drugs, including alcohol and opiates, among the elderly is a common problem that is frequently overlooked (Schuckit, 1977). The older person who abuses opiates is frequently the drug abuser who has grown old. These individuals differ from their younger counterparts in that they are less likely to use heroin, choosing synthetic opiates instead. Their use of drugs is generally less frequent. The older drug abuser tends to be medically sicker and will need medical care and housing supports (Schuckit, 1977). Methadone maintenance may not be the treatment of choice, according to various authors cited by Schuckit (1977). Elderly addicts do not appear to present a threat to society, as do their younger counterparts, because of their decreased ability to "hustle" or steal. The most frequent deliberately abused nonopiate drugs are laxatives, aspirin compounds, and sleeping pills such as barbiturates. The extent to which alcoholism is a problem in the elderly is not known. What is known is that the majority of actively drinking older alcoholics began having a problem in their late forties or fifties. They are frequently seen in detoxification centers and tend to respond favorably to treatment (Schuckit, 1977).

Drug abuse and misuse in the elderly is a definite problem that may relate to feelings of uselessness and helplessness, reactions to alienation, and feelings of low status in society. But elderly individuals who do not abuse drugs may also experience the same feelings. In other words, there may be an association between growing old and abusing drugs, but no evidence exists that these factors contribute to abuse of drugs (Schuckit, 1977). The role of the counselor is to be aware of the changes that can occur as a result of drug misuse or abuse, to suspect its occurrence, and to refer the client for appropriate medical care.

## Summary

Counselors are needed to provide warmth, acceptance, and human concern to older persons, both individually and in groups. The phrase "counseling *with* the aged" is used to describe this role. A second role in counseling the aged is to assist them in becoming self-advocates. Self-advocacy can lead to collective advocacy, in which older persons can join together in order to promote others in society to become more responsive to their needs and concerns. This role is called "counseling *for* the aged."

Much of the counseling needed by older persons is preparation for adapting to change. This presents unique opportunities for the counselor because of the stresses that often accompany aging. Such stresses may include illness and loss of various kinds. Eight areas of greatest risk for the older person and of greatest opportunity for intervention are retirement, poverty, relocation, protective services, institutionalization, death and dying, grief and depression, and drug misuse and abuse.

The greatest contribution the counselor can make in working with older persons is to separate the individual from the stereotype with which society has associated the aging person and to view each client as a unique human being.

# 12

# Computer Technology in Counseling

G. Brian Jones
Jo Ann Harris-Bowlsbey
David V. Tiedeman

In the 1950s, business revolutionized its procedures with the help of computers, but education has been more resistant to a similar revolution. By 1960, education had involved computers in administrative and clerical tasks such as scheduling, payroll accounting, and producing report cards. However, the use of computers by the students, either for computer-involved instruction or for assistance in career decision making, was a later development, beginning about the mid 1960s and maintaining only a precarious foothold even today.

Stiller (1970) points out that it is in the field of fact dispensing that computers and other media have their most immediate impact. At the same time, he identifies applications in student appraisal and orientation, all of which can be used to assist counselors to perform their functions better by shifting to such media those tasks that they can perform more efficiently. Stiller seems to agree with the estimate made by Tondow and Betts (1967) that counselors spend 85 percent of their time dispensing information that could be handled by a multimedia support system.

Despite present uncertainty about continuing computer involvement in counseling, we believe strongly in its value. This chapter discusses current applications of computers to counseling in the United States, some of the problems that seem to limit more extensive applications, and some forecasts about future usage. It is designed to give the counselor a practical introduction to the uses of computers in everyday settings. At the same time, this chapter orients the practitioner to some of the issues facing the developers of computer technology in counseling, in the hope that counselors will share a commitment to the resolution of such issues. Throughout this chapter an attempt is made to keep technical language to a minimum. Even so, the reader may find that this is a new learning area. However, the rewards of learning some of the terminology should become evident when the reader approaches a computer expert to discuss a program for his or her school or agency.

## Computer Capacities for Counseling

Computers have several capacities of high potential value in career decision making. These include:

1. Storing, instantaneously retrieving, and updating masses of data. This capacity is particularly significant in a nation that has more than 2,500 two- and four-year institutions of higher learning, thousands of proprietary schools, and 21,741 occupations, as identified in the 1965 edition of the *Dictionary of Occupational Titles*.
2. Interrelating data about the person and the environment so that both are personally relevant to the user at critical decision-making points.
3. Sorting through masses of data using the matches described in Item 2 to provide on command personally tailored lists of educational or vocational options.
4. Simulating conversations or structured interviews using

phone lines and interactive terminal devices, such as type-writer terminals or cathode ray tubes.

5. Monitoring the use of a computerized system to provide feed-back, review, and personalized assistance to counselors or clients.
6. Controlling and coordinating audio and visual material with text provided in printout format.
7. Providing an individualized package of services to many users simultaneously, for many hours each day, and in a wide variety of settings. More specifically, for student users a comprehensive information system could include facts and information on:
   a. Each individual's personal assessment characteristics (abilities, interests, values, physical features, and personal and social behaviors).
   b. The status of an individual's problem-solving and self-management skills.
   c. A person's past and current short- and long-range goals and plans.
   d. An individual's academic history.
   e. The assessments that others (for example, school staff) in an individual's life have made of various aspects of her or his career skills and functioning.
   f. The range of career (occupational, educational, and training) options available.
   g. Relationships among different patterns of personal characteristics and actual membership, satisfaction, and success in different career options (occupational clusters or families).
   h. State and local legal requirements that must be considered when career decisions are made.
   i. Resources available within the instructional system to help each individual achieve her or his career goals.

It is assumed in this chapter that such a system must be available if young people are to receive assistance with all aspects of their career planning and development in each career area.

The value of such capacities seems almost self-evident,

considering the inadequate number of counseling personnel and the kinds of noncareer duties currently performed by many employed counselors. There is a wide variation in the counselor-student ratio in the United States. A desirable ratio is considered to be 1:300, but the one that is reality for many of our large-city schools is 1:1000. Clearly, with either ratio, it is difficult for a counselor to provide appropriate, sufficient, updated information to counselees about the thousands of options open to them in the processes of career choice and development.

As a further example, the role of secondary school counselors suffers from lack of clear formulation and acceptance. The result is that many administrators view counselors as quasi-administrators and delegate to them such functions as course registration, schedule changing, attendance keeping, discipline, and record maintenance. Therefore, deliberate assistance for the career decision making of students largely loses by default.

## Computerized Counseling Systems

Computerized automated systems in counseling have primarily dealt with providing facts and information in the educational and vocational areas of careers and have comprehensively covered most aspects of career planning and development in these two areas. This chapter does not list and assess all such approaches; that has been done effectively in the literature—for example, see Rosser (1969), Bohn and Super (1969), Moorhouse (1969), Perrone and Thrush (1969), Scates (1969), Loughary (1970), Super (1970, 1973), Harris (1972a, 1972b), Herr and Cramer (1972), Willingham, Begle, and Ferrin (1972), and Miller and Tiedeman (1973). One major problem in studying this array requires understanding important variables that distinguish one approach from another. The most useful scheme for organizing and comprehending computer systems is that presented by Miller and Tiedeman (1973). The scheme categorizes computerized systems into the following four groups: indirect inquiry; direct inquiry without system monitoring; direct inquiry with system monitoring; and direct inquiry with system and personal monitoring.

In an *indirect inquiry system,* users complete a question-

naire in which they enter data about themselves and indicate
the characteristics of educational institutions, financial aids, or
occupations they are seeking. Such systems are normally characterized by the following:

1. Each request is held at a central location until receipt of a
   sufficient number of such requests to warrant processing.
   This procedure, normally called "batch processing," may
   cause a user to wait hours, days, or weeks before receiving
   feedback.
2. Each user, due to time and cost considerations, normally
   only submits a query once.
3. Users do not know which of their chosen characteristics affect their options and therefore do not have studied opportunity to receive different or increased options.
4. Users do not receive counseling or assistance with their decision making other than that contained in printed instructions.

In a *direct inquiry system without system monitoring,*
inquirers have direct access to the data file because they make
use of a terminal device connected directly to the computer.
They gain access to the data file with the help of instructions
and code words available at the terminal or in complementary
manuals. These systems are ordinarily programmed so that a list
of schools or occupations cannot be called until each user reduces the possible number of items in the list to a predetermined somewhat smaller number by specifying the characteristics that her or his items must have. To let the user know what
each selection does to the available possibilities, such systems
ordinarily report the number of items or options still remaining
after he or she makes each selection of an additional characteristic. Characteristics of direct inquiry systems without monitoring
are that:

1. The inquirer's request for data receives almost instantaneous
   attention.
2. The inquirer's use of the system may be multiple or sequen-

tial, with immediate or later alteration of specified characteristics producing different sets of options.
3. The inquirer is constantly aware of how his or her chosen
characteristics are altering or diminishing the open options.
4. There is no "within system" counseling for the user, but such
systems are normally designed to promote counselor participation and collaboration.

A monitoring function entails the overseeing capability of
a computer system that enables it to keep a record of alternatives the user chooses and pertinent data about the user, to relate these data to the chosen alternative, to comment on the
consistency of these two in accordance with a decision table
determined by the system's designer, to state the probability of
success in appropriate alternatives, and/or to review a path of
decision making. Such activities simulate a formalized type of
counseling. In *direct inquiry with monitoring,* systems incorporate these kinds of capabilities and are more likely to make use
of a visual display device, such as a cathode ray tube or filmstrip
projection, than of a teletype or printer device. These systems
have the characteristics of systems involving direct inquiry without monitoring, as well as the following:

1. Users have at their command a variety of scripts, approaches,
modes, and branching opportunities that allow them experiences in addition to data file retrieval and successive possibility definition.
2. The data files generally can be accessed by various means and
search strategies.
3. These systems typically store data about each user that can
be meshed with data about educational and vocational options to generate personalized or new data.
4. These systems provide some formalized counseling through
monitoring.
5. These systems monitor the decision-making path of inquirers
and display it for them and sometimes for counselors as well.

The fourth type of system, *direct inquiry with system*

*and personal monitoring,* in addition to these characteristics, contains instruction in deliberate career decision making; permits users to store data about themselves to use in their later career decision making; and permits users first to personalize and later to use its original monitoring procedures to supervise their own decision making.

These four categories of computerized systems help the computer-counseling novice to resolve some of the confusion problems experienced by any person making initial contact with this field. However, the generality of some of these categories should be recognized. This is especially true of the first type, which should also include innovative computerized alternatives such as local and regional job data services and services that provide test interpretations and synthesis of psychometric data in the area of personal assessment—for example, Weiss's (1968) computer-assisted interpretation systems and Prediger's (1970) Test Validation and Information Feedback System. The first category probably also covers automated progress-monitoring services for youth career development. Smith (1969) provides one example of such an approach. He describes the ALERT program, which uses data derived from follow-up studies of four successive classes of graduates to monitor current students' plans, activities, and characteristics. The computer apprises counselors of "alert" conditions for specific students, such as those who select courses considered inappropriate for their post-high school plans or those who are not enrolled in classes required of all graduates with similar plans.

Another such computer monitoring example is presented by Flanagan (1970) in one of his descriptions of Project PLAN, a nationwide attempt to provide individualized education. PLAN illustrates the diverse ways in which a computer can be used in an educational context when direct inquiry is not available or desired. In PLAN, the computer was designed to enable career planning to integrate with student learning activities in subject-matter disciplines and to provide a wide variety of indirect interventions that facilitate student career planning, particularly through helping each student and her or his parents develop a program of studies of specific instructional modules and teaching-learning units related to the student's long-range educational and vocational goals. According to Flanagan (1970, p. 9), "The major strategy of the PLAN educational system is related to the guidance and individual planning functions, the program of studies, and the analysis of students' results on module and achievement tests. These aspects are also heavily dependent on the computer, primarily for doing scoring, keeping records, matching, and making predictions and indicating probabilities. The computer thus becomes a very valuable resource for the teacher and student in planning and guiding the student's educational program."

## Current Status

At this time only one indirect inquiry system is in operation in the United States. Approximately fifteen other commercial indirect inquiry systems have gone out of business. Seven direct inquiry systems are in operation, three with a monitoring function and four without. Five of these seven systems are briefly described in the appendix at the end of the chapter. Detailed information can be obtained from the persons cited there for each system. The Information System for Vocational Decisions (ISVD), which Tiedeman directed, was the only example of a direct inquiry system having both system and personal monitoring available. ISVD existed in prototype form in 1969, but its operation has so far not proved financially feasible. Careful review of Appendix 1 will give the counselor enough basic information to begin discussing computer applications with specialists in this field.

## Media, Methods, and Materials

Computers are not the only support systems that can help counselors and provide direct counseling functions. One of the most analytical and comprehensive surveys of media, methods, and materials is that published by Willingham, Begle, and Ferrin (1972). As illustrated by their tables (reproduced as Table 1), they divided media into two categories: computer-based and

**Table 1. Role of Technology in Guidance.**

| Functions of Technology in Guidance | Goals | Services | Current Status | Likely Developments | Examples |
|---|---|---|---|---|---|
| **Computer Based** | | | | | |
| Vocational Information | Provide up-to-date information on general and specific career opportunities and on student career interests | • Help counselor know students' career interests<br>• Provide instant access to job description information<br>• Provide information on specific job openings<br>• Match occupations with interests and abilities<br>• Provide supply-and-demand data<br>• Suggest new occupational areas for exploration | Considerable experimentation done, but school districts slow to pick up workable models despite widespread acknowledgment of utility | County/state manpower agencies will move toward integrated listings of job openings; school districts will begin to develop, albeit slowly, interactive systems for usage of both counselors and students | CVIS<br><br>VGIS<br><br>OTIS |
| Educational Information | Provide information on a range of postsecondary education alternatives, seeking to match individual interests and abilities with institutional offerings and environment | • Information on institutional programs and characteristics<br>• Allow student to weigh characteristics according to importance to him<br>• Give student list of institutions that match his indicated abilities and interests<br>• Provide probability statements on chances for admission | Although a large number of national college locater services were established in the 1960s, very few exist now. A few interactive systems are in operation around the country, but they touch very few students so far | Students increasingly will seek information on a variety of postsecondary education options, not just colleges. Further, they will seek them in conjunction with information about specific careers | CLS<br><br>CVIS<br><br>ECES |

| | | | | | |
|---|---|---|---|---|---|
| ...raining in Planning Skills | To increase competence in the process of making informed and rational career decisions | • Cause students to examine their values<br>• Enable them to interpret relevant data accurately<br>• Lead them to explore options systematically<br>• Help them formulate and test tentative plans | Largely in the experimental stage, but some projects that did produce operational systems are currently shelved | By and large secondary school systems will probably utilize written materials and gaming techniques rather than computerized systems | SIGI is probably the best example, even though it is geared primarily for community college students |
| Academic Advising | To help students plan their academic programs in line with expressed interests, abilities, and career goals | • On-line course registration<br>• Long-range courseplanning<br>• Interpretation of past achievement and test scores in light of expressed interests and goals<br>• Predict chances for admission and likelihood of success at selected postsecondary institutions | There has been considerable experimentation in each of these service areas over the past 5 years, but currently most operations are located within postsecondary institutions | Secondary schools will tie into and profit from current university experimentation, particularly with respect to course registration and planning | Broward Junior College (Florida)<br><br>CVIS |
| Counseling | To provide a system that would sensitively listen to counselee, analyze communications, and respond appropriately | • Privileged communication to facilitate openness<br>• Bring objective information about the student to bear on the problem or issue<br>• Take student through systematic, analytical process | Not much going on | Not much in the near future | AUTOCOUN was one of the best examples, but it was an experimental project; funding ended in 1968 |

*(continued on next page)*

**Table 1 (Continued)**

| Functions of Technology in Guidance | Goals | Services | Current Status | Likely Developments | Examples |
|---|---|---|---|---|---|
| Educational Monitoring | To keep an up-to-date record of progress of students toward personalized, stated goals | • Provide information on a student's background, academic progress, test results, nature and frequency of contacts with professional staff, and other variables<br><br>• Aid student in career planning through use of above information<br><br>• Enable professional staff to monitor individual and group progress and spot problem areas | Early in developmental stage; most interesting projects are part of total individualized instruction systems; staff rather than students are primary users of information currently | Although total individualized educational systems will probably be several years in coming, various elements of students' records will increasingly be stored in a computer in easily retrievable form | PLAN is a total individualized educational development system, one of the very few in operation<br><br>See also Hughson (California) School District |
| *Other Media (e.g., film, microfilm, videotapes, telephone systems, simulations, aperture cards)* | | | | | |
| Vocational Information | To provide students with concise but thorough information about the nature of local job opportunities and the necessary access procedures | • Give detailed information on job openings, earnings, requirements, employer addresses, the nature of the actual work performed, etc.<br><br>• Provide taped interviews with those in fields of interest<br><br>• Make available data on supply and demand<br><br>• Students investigate job areas by making their own films or videotapes | The VIEW system using IBM-type aperture cards and written reports is being adopted throughout California and within other states. Also, a variety of other local and county systems are underway throughout the nation | • The need for localized specific career information is widely recognized; usage of programs and materials that meet this need will spread rapidly<br><br>• Commercially prepared material will expand, but student prepared materials probably will come about very slowly | San Diego Career Guidance Centers provide several services including VIEW and Dial-a-Career |

| Educational Information | Identify and describe those institutions that have programs and characteristics suited to a student's interests, abilities, and career goals | • Information on institutional programs and characteristics<br>• Provide "humane" descriptions of institutional environments | Although many institutions have produced films about themselves, they are intended for large presentations or for general audiences, and therefore are used infrequently as a source of educational information by potential applicants. Most information continues to come to students from books and pamphlets | Insofar as educational information is related to career-information programs, the primary development will be describing career-training programs and local institutional offerings |

*Source:* Willingham, Begle, and Ferrin (1972 pp. 18-19).

others (for example, films, microfilms, videotapes, telephone systems, simulations, and aperture cards). For each category, they identified the major functions of such technology, and for each function they listed what they perceived to be its goals, services to students, current status of research and development, likely future developments, and examples of approaches. Study of this table will provide the counselor with an excellent practical framework for examining this type of technology.

This table indicates that the domain of media, methods, and materials focusing on career facts and information is extensive and creative. Recent years have seen exciting innovations in the use of multimedia support systems (Burnham, Johnson, and Youst, 1970; Martin, 1967), films (the Denver Public Schools in 1972 produced ten career guidance films that are used in a series of twenty-four thirty-minute television career guidance programs; and Doubleday Multimedia's "Careers in the '70's" series of thirteen career guidance films that received supportive evaluations in a study reported by Mitchell, 1972), microfilm aperture readers and cards (Stewart, 1969), comic books, audiotaped and videotaped interviews with workers, and learning activity packages dealing with all necessary elements for the individualization of a single career guidance activity or a set of related activities. It appears that the development of innovative approaches (computerized and nonautomated) to media, methods, or materials is *not* an urgent need in this domain. Instead, a strong case can be made for the need to improve the adaptation, dissemination, utilization, and evaluation of available resources.

## Factors Influencing System Survival

It is alarming to realize that of the twenty-five to thirty computer-involved counseling systems that underwent development in the United States during the 1960s and early 1970s, not many more than the five described in the appendix remain in the field at this time. These hard financial lessons have taught that systems that survive: (1) are direct inquiry systems; (2) are directed to school populations at the secondary level, with the exception of the System for Interactive Guidance and Information (SIGI); (3) are cost feasible; (4) make use of standard terminal equipment; and (5) specialize in providing information retrieval, sorting, and synthesis for the purpose of career decision making, although SIGI goes beyond this. Direct inquiry computer-involved counseling systems are bought if they cost no more than approximately $2 to $6 per student hour of use. (These cost estimates were made in 1976. Inflation rates since then should be used to update these figures.) The inclusion of a variety of counselor-support and administrative-support functions to form an integrated educational package, such as was done in the Computerized Vocational Information System (CVIS), holds high potential for minimizing the cost of student use by maximizing the cost savings and efficiency inherent in such functions as scheduling, schedule changing, and attendance keeping. The use of computer-involved counseling systems is not widespread at this time. Interest, however, seems to be increasing. The distribution of the CVIS package has doubled in the past year. Evaluation studies that have been conducted have concluded that (1) students like to use computer-based systems, learn to operate them easily, and do not feel dehumanized or depersonalized by them (Harris, 1972a); (2) parents accept computer-based systems with enthusiasm (Myers and others, 1972); (3) students who use computer-based systems show an increase in vocational maturity, as measured by instruments of vocational maturity, specifically Super's Career Development Inventory (Harris, 1972a; Myers and others, 1972); (4) students who use computer-based systems indicate that they gain greater specificity of information about options, increase their alternatives, crystallize vocational planning, and engage in a variety of exploratory behaviors to gain further information about career options (Harris, 1972a); and (5) some counseling-related functions (selection of high school courses and occupational exploration) can be as effectively done by a computer system as by counselors (Melhus, 1971; Price, 1971). The results of these studies notwithstanding, we still conclude that there is limited rigorous evidence on the costs and impact of computerized counseling systems. However, there is also a similar lack of such data on computerized approaches to educating (let alone guiding, counseling, or placing) students. For example, many articles on cost effectiveness and its relationship to computer-based instruction have been written, but most of these are theoretical treatises (such as Singh and Morgan, 1971). Few studies have been conducted along the lines of that by Lenn and Maser (1971), who found that the presentation of programmed lessons at a computer terminal was equally as effective as was printed material but that the computer required more student time and was more costly than the workbook format.

## Need for More Data on Costs and Impact

We believe a key factor that could facilitate the survival of computer-involved systems is the collection of more extensive data on their costs and impact than are currently available. In education, there is much talk about the need for such evidence on key instructional and counseling strategies. Frequently demanded are studies that incorporate cost-effectiveness, cost-efficiency, or cost-benefit analyses. However, clear definitions of these terms usually are not provided. We use these three concepts as follows: *Cost-effective analysis* entails a comparison of the degree to which a single strategy or approach (such as a computer-involved system) meets its predetermined objectives using specified resources required to produce those outcomes; *cost-efficiency analysis* includes a comparison of multiple strategies as related to their separate input resources. Such studies of alternative approaches must evaluate those approaches primarily on the basis of objectives they have in common; and *cost-benefit analysis* entails not only looking at the achievement of desired outcomes (as specified in predetermined objectives) but also the desirability of each objective in the light of long-range time and social considerations, as well as in the light of the occurrence of unexpected side effects (positive and negative) of each approach.

A sequential relationship is apparent for at least two of these three concepts. It must first be possible to conduct a cost-effectiveness analysis of an approach, in order to compare it with other approaches in a cost-efficiency study. At the same time, different levels of cost-benefit analyses could precede or follow either single-strategy or multiple-strategy analyses. However, implementation, not definition, of these three concepts is the critical problem.

One concern that has inhibited the implementation of such analyses of computer counseling systems is the belief that most of these computer systems are in their early developmental states and should not be subjected to cost or impact surveillance until they are more fully developed. Grayson (1972) stated this point of view succinctly for instructional approaches in general when he concluded that, for all applications of technology in education, cost effectiveness should *not* be an issue in the research and development stage, since it is a valid measure only in terms of operational systems.

A second reason for this reluctance stems from recognition of measurement problems entailed in designing, conducting, analyzing data, and reporting even the most basic cost-effectiveness analyses. Although the designers of computer-involved counseling systems have not devoted extensive attention to this issue, much of the discussion addressed to educational technology in general applies here.

Grayson (1972) reviewed the problems of assessing benefits (including specification of goals and objectives and selection of appropriate instruments to measure the degree of attainment of these goals and objectives), analyzing costs, and determining the relative efficiency of comparable strategies. Wilkinson (1972) focused on the problem of analyzing costs and concluded that "Most data on the costs of instructional technology lack the necessary scope and depth to help education's managers make policy decisions" (p. 34), and "This article has pointed out only a few of the many areas where information is needed for the cost analysis of instructional television. The same type of questions need to be answered for *all* technological instructional strategies if the needed cost-effectiveness and cost-benefit studies are to be produced. Most of these questions focus on the accurate description of actual costs, which is the essential data base from which the predictive and comparative studies must be constructed—the MISSING data base" (p. 38).

This problem of cost estimates was also identified by Tickton and Kohn (1971). From their survey, they concluded that the data usually available for computation of costs are not satisfactory (since accounting procedures are not uniform among districts; cost data are not comparable; and classifications of costs, calculations of unit costs, and estimates of savings are usually made in arbitrary ways). Lewis (1970) listed three major obstacles to conducting comparative evaluations: the number of variables existing in classrooms where media studies usually are conducted; the vagueness of most educational objectives; and the versatility of media (in that each medium can be used for a wide range of purposes, therefore making it difficult to separate out for evaluation a single use in any one instance).

Anastasio and Morgan (1972) concluded that "judgments as to cost effectiveness are usually ill formed or unreliable. Consequently, schools do not have sufficient incentive to increase effectiveness, because there is no systematic feedback indicating the school's performance in achieving instructional goals" (p. 42), and "Clearly, since cost effectiveness is a significant issue in the acceptance of computers in instruction, there will have to be careful analyses of existing costs, at all levels for comparison. . . . These problems in comparing instructional methods are exacerbated by the inability of most schools and colleges to measure the cost or effectiveness of conventional instruction" (p. 43). With a more positive conclusion, Molnar (1970, p. 297) outlined at least seven impediments to valid cost-impact studies, but still decided that there is a future for cost effectiveness: "Sesame Street and the work in CAI [Computer Assisted Instruction] have demonstrated that it is possible to engineer materials that will achieve learning effectiveness. Given a 'critical mass' necessary to produce quality materials and regional networks, to deliver the program to large audiences, the cost effectiveness of media systems can also be demonstrated" (p. 297).

The critical issue highlighted by this brief literature review is how to initiate and conduct such demonstrations in the field of computerized counseling systems. We are convinced that such analyses are not only highly desirable but are also feasible.

Godwin (1969), who has been involved in many of Educational Testing Service's research and development efforts in this field, seems to agree that at least the cost issue should be faced much more directly: "These comments are not intended to suggest that the simplest and least expensive way is the best, or that all new-fangled devices are to be avoided. . . . However . . . the complexity and expense are very real factors in this area and they ought to be weighed heavily in considering alternatives. Schools often operate with limited budgets, budgets which will not support excessively expensive systems. Nor is the financial picture likely to improve in the near future. To produce an automated guidance system, however magnificent, which is beyond the reach of most schools is surely no help to the average guidance counselor. To produce a system which schools can barely afford by draining funds and manpower from other critical areas imposes on us the obligation to be certain that their funds are as well spent as possible and that the system carries no unnecessary luxuries" (Godwin, 1969, p. 76). The extent of available cost and impact evidence will be briefly summarized in the following section.

## Evidence on Costs and Impact

Our search revealed that most computerized counseling systems that were developed in the United States over the last ten to fifteen years either were not analyzed to provide costs or impact evidence or were considered to be in such early stages of basic research that they were inappropriate for premature evaluations.

Ross (1971) discussed the only example we found of a multiple-approach study aimed at cost-efficiency analyses. He conducted a comparison of two approaches for delivering occupational information in an Oregon community college: the computerized Occupational Information Access System (OIAS), referenced in the appendix, and the regular counseling staff. On the basis of student reactions, he found they were equally satisfied with both approaches but that counselors were perceived as having more impact on students' career plans and certainty. However, Ross speculated that a 50 percent decrease in student search time and a similar decrease in counselor time is gained through OIAS. Further, he estimated that OIAS costs $3.51 per user for full-time use, while counselors cost $44.65 per user on a similar pattern. (These are 1971 costs that must be adjusted in terms of inflation rates since that time.) He concluded that the cost models be outlined for each approval "indicate that the OIAS delivers occupational information at less than 10 percent of the corresponding cost per user of the Counseling Center. OIAS is, in fact, much less expensive than counselors as a system for delivering occupational information" (Ross, 1971, p. 12). Although this conclusion seems rather strong, this was truly a pioneering study, perhaps lacking in research rigor but headed in a direction that attempted to provide empirical data of critical relevance to this chapter's concerns.

No other studies attempting cost-efficiency analyses were identified. Two computerized systems, the Computerized Vocational Information System (CVIS) and the Education and Career Exploration System (ECES), have been subjected to preliminary evaluations entailing comparative designs. In addition, CVIS seems to have more specific and valid data on costs than are available on any other sophisticated computer-involved counseling system. No system is supported by cost-effectiveness, cost-efficiency, or cost-benefit studies (as defined in this chapter), even at the elementary level conducted by Ross (1971).

Harris (1973, p. 13), the creator of CVIS, conducted calculations of CVIS costs and produced the following conclusion: "CVIS costs $18,000 per year for a six-terminal, two-printer installation which serves 3,450 students. Total cost divided by student enrollment yields a per-student cost of $5.30. Having a human counselor in the building for each student costs $60.00 per year per student. Total cost of the system per year divided by student users yields a cost of about $2.00 per student hour, and this calculation gives the administration a host of on-line functions at no extra cost" (once again, note that these are 1973, not current cost estimates).

These calculations indicate that computer costs per student are approximately 10 percent of counselor costs, which is consistent with the conclusion noted earlier from Ross (1971). However, Harris' caution about not drawing any conclusions from this comparison seems appropriate. Such comparisons should be made only if the approaches being compared relate to the same objectives. Both Ross and Harris believe that the computers and counselors mentioned in their calculations did not have common objectives. Harris (1973, p. 9) illustrated this noncomparability when she stated that "computer systems are doing a job with vocational information which counselors have simply not done. Thus, computer-based systems have been largely an addition of services to the guidance department, not a replacement of services already being done by counselors."

Three evaluations have been made of CVIS. All were doctoral dissertation studies, the most recent of which was Harris' own investigation. Melhus (1971) found that CVIS and counselors did not produce differential effects on the occupational plans of sophomores with high levels of problem-solving ability, but that counselors influenced sophomores with low levels of ability to make significantly more changes in their plans than did CVIS. Price (1971) compared the course registration effects of counselors and CVIS. He found no significant differences between counselor and computer-scheduled students on four dependent variables: students' understanding of information relevant to course selection, students' reactions to their course selection experiences, evaluations of student course selections by a panel of five counselors, and subsequent course changes made by students.

Harris (1972a) compared CVIS with a no-treatment (or regular counseling only) approach on four dependent variables, all derived from students' responses to a Vocational Plans Questionnaire and a Career Development Inventory (CDI), which is described hereafter. These variables are number of occupations that students report as options for them; students' perceptions of the degree of congruence between their educational-vocational plans and their abilities and achievements; the range and accuracy of students' occupational information; and students' vocational maturity, operationally defined by composite scores on three scales of the CDI (awareness of the need to plan, knowledge and self-reported use of career-planning resources, and information on career decision making). When both instruments were administered on a pretest and posttest basis, Harris found no significant differences between the effects of CVIS and no-treatment (or regular) conditions on the first two variables. However, she concluded that the use of CVIS did appear to effect an increase in students' knowledge about occupations they explored at the computer terminal and in their vocational maturity as measured by the CDI. The most recent evaluation of ECES (Myers and others, 1972) produced similar results on the CDI. In fact, this led Harris (1973, p. 13) to conclude that "Use of present computer-based systems results in increase in awareness of need to plan and knowledge and use of resources, but not in decision-making skills."

The CDI was not the only instrument used in recent evaluations of the ECES (Minor, Myers, and Super, 1972). Myers and others (1972) summarized the results of two years of field trials of this computer-based system in Flint, Michigan, as well as the findings of an earlier one-year, preliminary field test in Montclair, New Jersey. In the most recent year of testing, the effects of the ECES were compared with those produced by the ECES plus a counselor-led set of units preparing youth for career exploration and use of the ECES and those produced by the regular guidance programs that tenth-graders received in the participating high schools. The investigators administered the CDI to 10,000 students on a pretreatment basis to obtain 2,234 usable tests for the posttreatment comparison. They reported significant differences between ECES users and nonusers on two of four CDI variables: orientation to vocational planning, and choice and use of resources for vocational exploration. These are the same two variables that produced differential effects in the Harris (1972a) study of CVIS. Similar differences were found between students who used only ECES and students who used counselor units plus ECES. These results favored the latter group of subjects. Both groups of ECES users were "highly positive" about ECES.

From their three field trials, the ECES investigators (Myers, Minor, and Super, 1972, pp. 65-66) concluded that:

- Students who use ECES "enjoy using it, find it easy to use, and feel that they benefit from it."
- These students "show small but clearly real gains in two important aspects of vocational maturity: planning orientation and choice and use of resources for exploration. ECES alone does not lead to gains in decision making or occupational information possessed."
- Their parents are "pleased with it, want it to be available to the children, and—most important—become more involved in the planning efforts of their children."
- Their counselors "value it highly, estimate that it has a positive effect on students, and think it ought to be available to more students."
- "The more time a student uses ECES, the more gain the student shows in planning orientation and choice of resources for exploration."
- "When combined with a carefully planned program for developing decision-making skills, the use of ECES contributes to meaningful gains in planning orientation, choice of resources for exploration, and in the decision-making skills."

Evaluative data (Impellitteri, 1969) are available on one other computerized approach, the Computer-Assisted Career Exploration System (CACE), but these data are not summarized here, because the system has not been operational for a long time.

Although empirical data are lacking, there are consistent theoretical papers suggesting that automated counseling systems require further research and development as well as more concerted cost-effectiveness, cost-efficiency, and cost-benefit analyses. Not all of the literature agrees with the final part of this statement: Some authors believe that such analyses must be postponed until computer alternatives reach much more sophisticated stages of development.

The Commission on Computer-Assisted Guidance Systems of the National Vocational Guidance Association (1971) presented guidelines so that a decision maker exploring computer-based approaches could make informed decisions about the quality of each approach. Even though the commission stated its recommendations tentatively when it noted that it was early to develop rigid standards for the use of such systems, it omitted entirely any introduction of future issues related to costs, benefits, and the relationships of these two factors. The commission attended primarily to ethical issues.

Super (1973, p. 304), in one of the most recent publications on computers in career guidance, concluded that no computer-supported system had a price tag and that "Perhaps only one generalization concerning costs is possible at this time: multiple sessions at a computer terminal to carry on a personalized dialogue concerning educational and occupational decisions will in due course cost little if any more per pupil than the price of a good book." Super also reviewed instruments and criteria used to evaluate computerized approaches, while pointing out that refinements in both areas are needed before more intensive evaluations can be conducted. Super's document, along with that of Harris (1973), represent the most detailed discussions of the cost and impact of automated systems available to our literature review. Apparently interest in these concerns is increasing, but they will not be easily resolved. As noted later in this chapter, the counseling profession will have to place more emphasis on the collection of impact and cost evidence in future if this rather glaring gap is to be filled.

## An Example of Future Systems: Project DISCOVER

Future trends in this field can be illustrated by a computer-based guidance system called DISCOVER. This system was conceptualized by one of the authors of this chapter, JoAnn Harris-Bowlsbey, and members of her former CVIS team. DISCOVER therefore represents a second-generation system that may predict something about the direction of future computer-based guidance. DISCOVER, although having some of the same objectives as CVIS, has some differences. It attempts to provide long-term support to career development, as well as to provide the sophisticated information retrieval and search functions so typical of present systems. In content, this means that the system includes the presentation and clarification of occupational

values, the presentation and practice of occupational classification systems, the presentation and practice of decision-making
skills, and assessment of interests and competencies. Further,
DISCOVER was conceptualized at three levels: grades 4-6,
grades 7-12, and adult. To date, funds have been available for
development of the grades 7-12 version and the college-adult
version. It is also designed to have a higher degree of transporta-
bility than CVIS has. This aim is being achieved by a combination of better documentation, a concerted effort not to impose
rigid conditions on the user site, and use of a programming language that has maximum compatibility from machine to machine.

   Characteristics of CVIS that have contributed to its cost
feasibility and good acceptance have been maintained. These
are:

1. Provision of counselor and administrative-support functions,
   as well as career guidance functions.
2. Use of standard terminal equipment.
3. Author language capabilities that allow local sites to modify
   existing material or add new developments.
4. Construction of a direct-inquiry system, with a high degree of
   use of personal data and monitoring.

   DISCOVER makes use of an IBM 370 central processing
unit and of cathode ray tube terminals with light pen capability.
Figure 1 provides a graphic illustration of the system's content.
The users' progress through the system, however, is much more
flexible than the arrow in this exhibit implies. They may choose
to enter the system at any point, may follow the sequence as
depicted here, or may follow a sequence recommended by the
taking of an on-line assessment of career development, contained in the entry module. Here is the content of each of these
modules:

   00. Entry. The entry module introduces the user to the
system, explains its many special features, and teaches him or
her how to use the terminal. It monitors each person's use of
the system, recording each entry and exit point. Each user has

**Figure 1. The Discover System.**

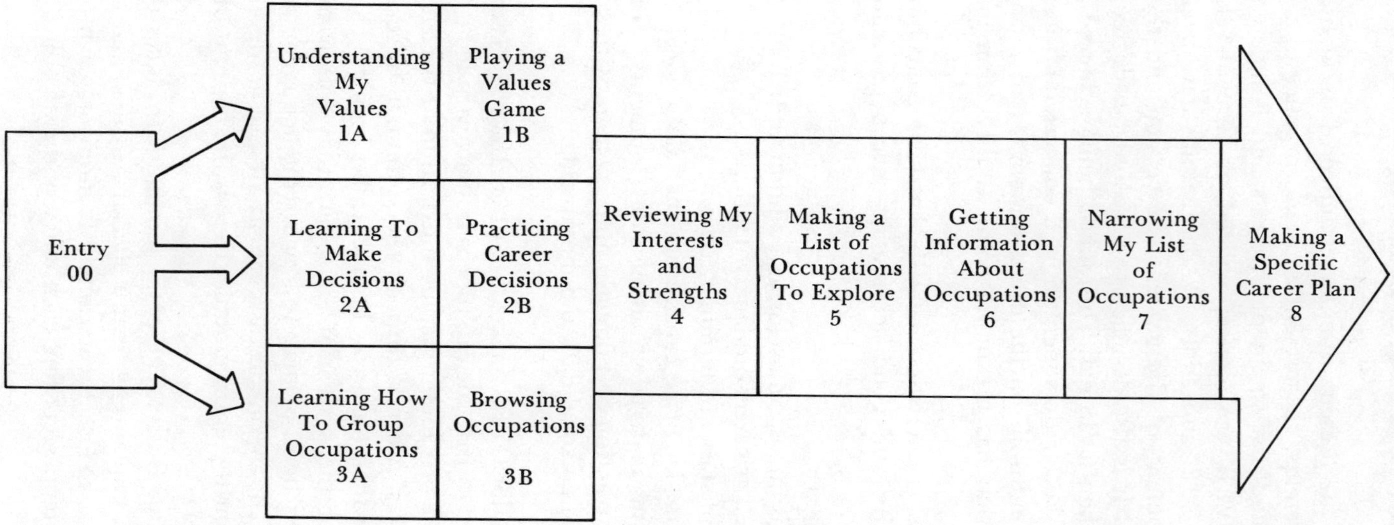

the opportunity to complete an on-line career development inventory. The results serve as the computer's guide in suggesting which modules of the system will be most appropriate.

1A. Understanding My Values. This module contains a number of experiences that lead the user to think about what a value is, to analyze personal values, and to decide on actions to implement those values. The last part of the module proposes nine values related to occupations. The user rates the personal importance of each and then may ask the computer to search its data file for occupations that can provide the combination and weighting of the values assigned by the user.

1B. Playing a Values Game. This module is a Monopoly-type game that may be played by one or two players. In the beginning of the game, each player is invited to place relative weight on three possible goals: income, recognition, and happiness. Winning the game consists of reaching the goals selected while having to make decisions about choice of occupation, educational options, use of leisure time, or life-style at the same time as being subjected to some of life's events (such as unexpected setbacks, unexpected opportunities, and payment for necessities such as housing, clothing, and transportation). The user also acquires "plan cards" that allow more control over life than the computer's rolling of the die affords.

2A. Learning to Make Decisions. This module presents a planful decision-making process in flowchart form and provides a number of exercises designed to illustrate and provide practice in the decision-making steps. Also illustrated are other nonplanful decision-making strategies (intuitive, impulsive, delaying, agonizing, and so forth). The user is assisted to identify his or her present style of decision making.

2B. Practicing Career Decisions. This module uses a career decision tree developed by Super to (1) show the key decisions that lead to entry into a given occupation, (2) plot a given user's course up the twenty branches of the tree, (3) simulate the career paths of others, and (4) allow the user the opportunity to "play" his or her own life in a variety of ways by making decisions in this low-risk, simulated way.

3A. Learning How to Group Occupations. This module presents the world of work by way of two organizing principles:

the data-people-things-ideas division that is the American College Testing Program's (ACT) refinement of the 1965 *Dictionary of Occupational Titles* classification system and Holland's (1973) six groups. A number of exercises are presented to give practice in using these classification systems; the user's responses are monitored for the purpose of providing more instruction if needed.

3B. Browsing Occupations. This module makes use of the Holland classification system as an organizational structure by which the user can browse through approximately 450 occupations in the system.

4. Reviewing My Interests and Strengths. This module entails an on-line administration and interpretation of Holland's *Making Vocational Choices* (1973). This instrument collects self-reports of career-related interests, experiences, and competencies.

5. Making a List of Occupations to Explore. This module provides the user with alternate ways to generate a list of personal occupational options by (1) relating occupations to personal work values, (2) using the results of the self-directed search, (3) selecting titles from a list of occupations, (4) combining selected occupational characteristics (such as salary level, place of work, level of training, and degree of independence), and/or (5) relating preferred courses to occupations.

6. Getting Information About Occupations. This module uses a series of displays to give the user information about a job, its duties, benefits and limitations, educational requirements, future outlook, and additional sources of information. The user concludes with a list of occupations in which he or she has high interest.

7. Narrowing My List of Occupations. This module assists the user to narrow his or her personal occupational list by applying the decision-making principles learned in Module 2A to this decision. Each user attains this narrowing to a first-choice occupation and high-priority alternates by (1) asking for additional information about any occupations listed; (2) comparing information about two occupations; and (3) analyzing the remaining occupations in light of identified work values, desired level of training, and interests and competencies.

8. Making a Specific Career Plan. In this module, the user maps out a career plan for one specific occupation at a time. The first step entails learning the available paths of entry into the occupation. As a second step, the user chooses a specific place or institution in which to implement the occupational choice or to get the training for it. Planning may also involve finding appropriate loan funds, grants, or scholarships. This second step involves sophisticated searches and interaction with eight large data files: all four-year colleges in the nation, two-year colleges, technical and specialized schools, local jobs, apprenticeships, continuing education opportunities, military programs, and financial aids.

## Recommendations for the Future

We conclude this chapter with a series of suggestions that we believe can facilitate future developments and school applications in the field of computer-involved counseling systems. These recommendations are primarily addressed first to system developers and then to practicing counselors considering use of such systems with their clients. But representatives of each of these two groups must be knowledgeable about the needs and constraints of the other because that which is primary for one is still of secondary importance to the other.

*Recommendations to System Developers.* Efforts must be directed to providing evidence on at least the following variables for key approaches (these variables are listed in the order in which data probably should be collected): construction of operating systems, impact on inquirers and the institutions serving them, costs, cost-effectiveness analyses, cost-efficiency analyses, and cost-benefit analyses. We cannot completely agree with Tickton and Kohn (1971, p. 9) when they state that project directors have not collected evidence on some of these variables because "they did not want to know too much about costs or cost-effectiveness. The knowledge might be embarrassing." Some developers do not seem to have been concerned about such information. Others have wanted the evidence but have not had the resources to conduct the necessary studies. Harris (1973, p. 14) also seems correct in her conclusion that it "appears that CVIS, SIGI, and ILS are approaching cost feasibility." But such systems still need detailed cost-effectiveness evidence to accompany such cost-estimate information.

From the early stages of their research and development activities, the developers of computer-involved systems should give attention to impact and cost factors. These factors relate to high-priority decision-making data needs for most persons, including student inquirers, who will make decisions on the utility of an approach. Funding sources should require that these developers outline a plan of action for handling such concerns and monitor its implementation. This recommendation is not expected to be received enthusiastically. Some developers believe that such considerations should not receive attention until their products reach the marketing stage. Others probably will counter by stating that they have considered these factors throughout their research and development activities. However, the literature does not reflect such considerations. The timing of moving these impact and cost considerations out of the discussion phase and into the phase of empirical data collection is the critical issue. It is difficult to conjecture about specific times or instances, since these probably will vary greatly from system to system. However, a rule of thumb would be that preliminary evidence should be collected when users are exposed to a system after the first debugging and revision cycle. Such field trials should be scheduled as early as possible, even if it necessitates assessment of a prototype of the fully developed approach. This recommendation recognizes the problems entailed in conducting cost and impact studies. By reviewing the apparent frustrations of authors such as Molnar (1970), Anastasio and Morgan (1972), and Wilkinson (1972), this chapter has summarized some of the problems related to the specification and collection of cost data. Experimentation with some of these authors' suggested solutions, such as improved accounting methods, is necessary.

The weight of the evidence considered in this chapter suggests that cost and impact studies are possible. However, the "how to do it" details must be made available to the system developer and the practitioner who must validate such studies under specific conditions of use. There is an urgent need for some highly visible feasibility studies, particularly ones that investigate procedures for conducting cost-effectiveness analyses on automated counseling approaches. The desired outcomes of such prototype efforts would be at least to demonstrate that such analyses can be conducted, to illustrate that they can provide critical decision-making information in a timely manner, and to document example procedures and instruments needed to implement such studies. If such outcomes occur, specific guidelines and related training procedures could be made available to help developers and practitioners conduct such studies at different levels of effort and sophistication.

Consistent efforts must be made to conduct these evaluation activities in the context of a comprehensive and systematic planning process. This kind of process covering the cycle of program design, implementation, evaluation, feedback, and revision is well documented by Jones and others (1974) and Campbell (1972). Beyond these references, this process is generally missing in the counseling and guidance literature. Far too often developers use what they think are priority career planning and development needs of their users and also automate the administrative tasks that they believe their institutions need. On this questionable foundation, these developers work with abstract global goals for their approaches, goals that lack the preciseness that results from basing desired outcome statements on empirically derived data related to high-priority needs. Both system designers and practitioners must have precise knowledge of specific behavior outcomes expected; the variety of media, methods, and materials with high potential for helping inquirers achieve such outcomes; and relevant criteria for determining when these outcomes occur.

Another hard problem for systems developers in the current state of the art is the establishment of facts and information. There is the possibility that regionalized or nationalized rather than localized approaches to provision of facts and information should be established. This recommendation is a novel one. Venn (1970, p. 24) mentioned one aspect of it when he proposed that a "national center for occupational and educational-technical programs should be established with federal funds through the Department of Labor and the Office of Education. Such a center should have a computer data bank available through a telephone tie-line, with printouts, to all state and regional centers. Regional centers with data banks containing local and regional information should be established with tie-lines to every high school and two-year postsecondary institution. Guidance and placement personnel would then have specific data for student use during guidance counseling and placement functions in the schools. Such programs are already in use, and a national effort in this direction would make the cost of individual terminals entirely feasible." Winick (1970) described a job-bank data approach used in the New York State Employment Service, while Huber and Ullman (1970) suggested the need for a "nationwide computer-aided job-matching network" (which tends to sound more oriented toward employment service-oriented than toward individual-career planning and development). The National Vocational Guidance Association (1971, p. 6) made the following recommendations on the topic of improved provision of educational-vocational facts and information:

1. Certain information should be collected and stored on a national level, for example, the structure of occupations, occupational requirements, and general salary schedules for occupations.
2. A state or region may have educational or occupational characteristics that clearly set it apart from other geographic areas. In such cases it may be desirable to have centers in which statewide or regional data are collected, stored, and dispensed. Such a data base may also be a viable alternative for areas in which local handling of such processes is not financially feasible.
3. The groups were unanimous in recommending that information appropriate to a given community or metropolitan area be computerized. Communities or local organizations responsible for such data bases would then provide and update information of local relevance, such as opportunities for employment in specific occupations in a given locale.

*Recommendations for Counselor Adaptation and Adoption.* The systematic and comprehensive planning process recommended here is partially reflected in the following series of questions listed in a National Vocational Guidance Association monograph edited by Harris (1972b, pp. 14-15). This monograph discussed the role of computers in counseling and guidance, issues and questions related to computer applications, and solutions to key concerns. It is a document with which all practitioners considering future work in this field should be well versed.

1. What are the guidance needs in the school setting?
2. What problems must be solved and what approaches must be used in order to meet these needs?
3. Can some of these needs be better met by utilization of computer time than by utilization of other media or counselor time?
4. What are the specific goals and measurable objectives of the guidance program?
5. If yes to No. 3, which of these objectives (question No. 4) should be assigned to the computer?
6. What systems design is necessary to ensure that the functions performed by counselors and those performed by computer are complementary and supportive to each other?
7. Is there sufficient administrative and financial support to warrant continued planning?
8. If the answer is yes to question No. 7, will the computer system serve only the guidance department, or will it also be used for administrative tasks and/or computer-aided instruction?
9. Should the school design its own computer-based guidance system or make use of one of those already designed and programmed?
10. What will be required in money, personnel, facilities, inservice training, computer equipment, time, and expenditure of energy to implement a computer-based guidance system?
11. Is there sufficient financial and personal commitment from the local school and/or public funding to continue planning?

12. Should the school install computer equipment of its own, hook up to a large regional data-processing center, buy time from a commercial firm, or find a nearby computer with time to spare?

13. What is the plan for implementation, including time schedule, assignment of personnel, orientation to and training of counselors in the computer system as one component of the total guidance systems, ordering of necessary phone and computer equipment, and so on?

14. How will the computer-based system be evaluated in the light of the objectives previously set? To what extent are suitable evaluation instruments available and practical? To what extent will these need to be developed? Is the school's commitment to the project and to the evaluation such that adequate evaluation will be feasible?

15. How will the system be updated and continuously changed in light of evaluation feedback?

16. How can the system be eliminated if it proves ineffective, and what are alternate plans for reaching the same goals?

Another National Vocational Guidance Association publication (1971, p. 6) on the role of computers in guidance developed specific recommendations in the light of these issues: the need for lower computer costs and the need for comprehensive, accurate, and readily available data and information for student educational-vocational decision making. Recommendations related to the issue of costs included:

1. Smaller schools or school systems could collaborate and share the cost of a computer.

2. A computer terminal could be placed in each school building, with a centrally located computer serving many schools or school systems.

3. Computers should be financed and utilized on a statewide basis, or perhaps on a county-wide or Board of Cooperative Education Services level.

4. Computers could be located in technical or vocational schools, with elementary and secondary schools having individual terminals.

5. Where cooperative programs exist between schools and the employment service, occupational and labor market information could be made available to schools from the computerized job bank system of the public employment service.
6. Schools could explore the possibility of contracting with industry for computer usage on a part-time basis. Some industries or service organizations with extra computer time available might be willing to provide free computer service in the public interest.

Along with developers of computer-involved systems, practitioners who adapt such systems in applied school settings must explore alternatives for making their approaches feasible in terms of costs while establishing their approaches on comprehensive and accurate data and information bases. Three possibilities are relevant here. The first, dealing with support of efforts to secure regionalized and nationalized data files, has been presented in the prior subsection. Second, there is the possibility of integrating one or more of the four kinds of computerized counseling systems listed earlier in this chapter with either computer-assisted or computer-monitored operations or both. It appears that such combinations would facilitate each school district's greater use of available computer facilities. This extension should bring computer costs into a more acceptable financial perspective. Darby, Korotkin, and Romashko (1970) conducted a mail survey of 23,033 public schools and follow-up interviews with 90 selected schools in regard to their computer activities. One of their conclusions seems particularly relevant to this proposed expansion and integration of computer operations. These investigators found (p. 1) that "the use of computers, especially in instruction in secondary schools, has grown rapidly. However, the diversity of use is still limited. The most prevalent applications are problem solving and Electronic Data Processing (EDP) skills training. The major emphasis of computer applications is on teaching students to use a computer as a tool in learning more about the subject area in which the computer is being applied. . . local sources provide the majority of funds for instructional computer use. Plans for future use generally call for expansion of present applications." Third, there is the plan, best summarized by Harris (1973, pp. 15-16), that recommends combining career guidance and administrative uses of school computer facilities. "The addition of a variety of on-line administrative functions, such as scheduling, schedule changing, and attendance keeping, to a system makes it much more appealing to the administrators who hold the power over appropriation of money. I have come to believe that computer-based guidance systems will not survive if they only perform a guidance function. There must be included in that system enough programs that oil the administrative gears of the school to capture the attention of the administrators. There is a real possibility that these administrative programs will save enough on highly accurate reporting of attendance or vocationally handicapped student enrollment to pay for the guidance part of the system, and therefore make it 'free' for student use."

## A Concluding Plea

McLuhan and Fiore (1967) clearly point out that humans and their media are interdependent. Humans make machines. Machines in their turn somewhat fashion human behavior. But in involving computers in counseling, we can look forward to an era in which humans make counseling machines while counseling machines in turn guide humans toward full comprehension of how much a machine a human really is. We urge continued humanistic development of computer-involved counseling systems, so that we may further mature to live as people existing in systems, but to live by transcending those systems.

## Appendix. Brief Descriptions of Currently Existing Computer-Involved Counseling Systems in the United States

I.  *Direct Inquiry Systems Without Monitoring*

    A.  The *Guidance Information System* (GIS) is a commercial system which made use of some of the ideas employed in the Information System for Vocational Decisions. This system, currently marketed by Time Share Corporation and Houghton Mifflin, is a direct inquiry system without monitoring. It offers the user an interactive search of four data files by entering coded characteristics which are explained in the user manual. These files are all two- and four-year colleges in the United States, specialized schools in some regions, occupations, and financial aids. The user receives both a list of options and descriptive information about each. Current cost of the system is 75 cents per fifteen-minute use, or $3.00 per hour. For further information, write to Herbert Cornell, Time Share Corporation, 3 Lebanon Street, Hanover, N.H. 03755.

B. The *Occupational Information Access System* (OIAS) is a statewide system in Oregon. It is an interactive direct inquiry system without monitoring, operating on IBM and Hewlett Packard computers with typewriter terminals. The system has six components: (a) QUEST, an on-line questionnaire that assists users to assess interests and abilities, leading to the identification of occupations in the data file which have the characteristics desired by the user, (b) information about occupations selected by the user, including local manpower data, (c) information about training opportunities within the state, (d) bibliography of reference materials for further information, (e) taped interviews with workers in each of the 230 occupations in the data file, and (f) local persons who are willing to discuss their occupations with students. The system is costing approximately $2.00 per student hour of use.

II. *Direct Inquiry Systems with System Monitoring*

A. The *Computerized Vocational Information System* (CVIS), developed by J. Harris-Bowlsbey and colleagues, Willowbrook High School, Villa Park, Illinois, makes use of an IBM 360 or 370 computer and cathode ray tubes. CVIS is a direct inquiry with monitoring system. The system has three distinct parts: the guidance system, the computer-assisted instruction system, and the administrative system. The guidance system has ten subsystems: vocational exploration at junior high level with associated visual materials; vocational exploration at secondary school level; four-year college information and search; community college information and search; technical school information and search; apprenticeship information; military information; local job search; financial aids search; and student registration. The CVIS system is in public domain and has been broadly distributed; it is currently operational in 122 sites in the United States. Current cost per student hour at the terminal is $1.92. An active consortium of CVIS users maintains its data files and shares in new developments. Further information about the CVIS system can be obtained from Jo Ann Harris-Bowlsbey, CVIS Distribution Center, Western Maryland College, Westminister, Md. 21157.

B.   The *Education and Career Exploration System* (ECES), a direct inquiry system with monitoring, was originally developed by the IBM Corporation. It has been given to the State of Michigan and is operational in Genesee Intermediate School District in Flint, Michigan. New developments and modifications of the system are underway at the site of operation. ECES III, the latest version, makes use of a cathode ray tube terminal, a microfiche reader, and an IBM 360-50 machine. ECES provides four on-line components and one off-line component. The on-line ones are exploration of 400 occupations with job duty samples, exploration of 400 postsecondary majors, and teaching and practice of decision making. The off-line component is a batch-process search of educational institutions, including four-year colleges, two-year colleges, and technical-specialized schools. Further detailed information can be obtained from Alva Mallory, Genesee Intermediate School District, 2413 West Maple Avenue, Flint, Mich. 48507.

C. The *System for Interactive Guidance and Information* (SIGI) is under development and field test at Educational Testing Service in Princeton, New Jersey. This system, unlike the others described here, is specifically designed for community college students. The system offers four subsystems: (a) values, (b) information, (c) prediction, and (d) planning. The first describes ten occupational values, assists the user to weight them, and identifies occupations that may fulfill the user's combination of them. The second subsystem provides information about occupations selected by the user; the third allows the user to receive predictive statements about probability of success in given courses or curricula related to his occupational choice. The fourth assists the user with specific step-by-step planning toward implementation of career choice. The system is designed to operate on a stand-alone PDP-11 minicomputer with multiple cathode ray tube terminals. Further detailed information can be obtained from Martin R. Katz, Educational Testing Service, Princeton, N.J. 05840.

# 13

# Innovation in Competency-Based Staff Development

Charles W. Dayton
G. Brian Jones

A particular scene is occurring more and more often in American schools these days. It happens during the spring, and involves several figures: a school or district principal, one or two members of the board of education, a director of guidance, and maybe a counselor or two. The atmosphere is friendly, but strained. The principal begins by alluding to the pressing budget strains and difficulty in obtaining new funding. The members of

*Note:* The work described in the document has been carried out under support by the United States Office of Education (USOE), Department of Health, Education, and Welfare, under Part C of the Vocational Education Act of 1963. Points of view or opinions stated do not necessarily represent the USOE position or policy.

the board cite a statistic or two in support or mention the growing intransigency of the local citizens. There is some awkward shifting and harrumphing, and finally the principal comes to the point. "Bill [or Alice, if you prefer], I have every confidence in you and what you're doing. But tell me: How can I justify spending $80,000 on a guidance budget when I can't pay for basic instruction?"

The response, when any is forthcoming, usually involves a recitation of all the activities carried on by counselors in their typical day. Each met with eleven students about personal problems, had two teacher conferences, changed registration cards for seven other students, talked to one truant, referred three others to agencies, and wrote up five reports. In this description of superhuman effort, only one thing is lacking: a clear picture of what was accomplished, as opposed to what the counselors spent their time doing. The principal nods and says thanks. The meeting adjourns. Lacking the ammunition needed to continue the guidance program intact, the principal faces the difficult decision of what to do.

Counselors are not generally prepared to cope with this problem. They go through training programs that steep them in the most advanced theories of human behavior and counseling techniques, but when it comes to demonstrating to someone what they accomplish, they are hard put to respond meaningfully. It is an "in" joke of the profession that nobody *really* knows what a counselor *does* (accomplishes).

Many factors contribute to this situation. One of them is reflected in the very description just given of a staff member's typical day. Going from one task to the next, constantly under pressure, constantly responding to the immediate crisis, he or she rarely has (or takes) the time to sit down and carefully figure out the purpose of all the frenetic activity. This might be called the *survival syndrome.* The struggle is simply to keep one's head above water, to respond to the immediate pressure. It leads to a guidance program top-heavy in crisis counseling, one that reacts to the needs of those who have reached the crisis stage, but fails to act on its own to prevent such crises from occurring. Opposed to this, a developmental program relies on a well-thought-out plan of what should happen to each student: It acts rather than reacts. It reaches out to all students, not just those who have reached the crisis stage, and tries to provide the kind of help that will prevent problems and let students who simply are ready and able to grow benefit from the program.

Closely related to the survival syndrome and the crisis counseling approach is the "counselor's counsel" syndrome. This refers to counselors' widespread feeling that they were trained to counsel and, come hell or high water, this is what they are going to do. It matters little whether this is the most effective way they can spend their time. Providing instruction to a whole class at a time, organizing and working with groups of students with similar problems, relying on written or audio-visual materials where they can provide needed information, setting up peer situations where students can help each other—all these may be far more effective in helping large numbers of students. But they are not as "personally rewarding." They do not lead to a student leaving one's office with an overwhelming sense of gratitude at a crisis resolved, or to that adoring glance or look of awe in the hall. Counselors are well rewarded for "counseling"—but when it dominates their schedule, are they helping the most clients in the most effective way possible?

A third syndrome contributing to the problem is an equally human and understandable one: a simple reluctance to change. If it has worked all right in the past, why change now? Most of these ideas that come along are fads that will pass soon anyway. Ride out the storm, and things will be fine. What this ignores is that while things remain the same in some ways they also change in some ways. It is probably not exaggerating to say that if guidance programs do not develop the means to measure their effectiveness and display it to others, they will be less of a presence in American schools in the future.

This fact, admittedly, is a threatening one to counselors. The growing demand for accountability overwhelms many. It leads to an "Am I not doing anything right?" response. The answer, of course, is that many things are being done well. What is required is not a tearing down of the whole structure, but building on the successful aspects. Fundamental to such improvement is the development of a way to measure what is being done.

Thus the survival syndrome and crisis counseling, the counselor's counsel syndrome, the general reluctance to face growing pressures to demonstrate effectiveness, and counselors' bewilderment in the face of such pressure, all combine to create serious problems for guidance programs. A way out of the woods is needed. If counselors could measure what they are accomplishing; if they could then use this information to plan a developmental program that reached all students; if within this program they could increase those actions that are particularly effective and decrease those that are ineffective, be they counseling activities or otherwise; if they could then demonstrate the results of such a program to those around them—then the solution might be at hand. "But who knows how to do that?" The only honest answer is "No one, very well." Certainly not the typical counselor. Such skills simply are not a part of traditional counselor education programs.

## An Evolving Approach to Staff Development

Many possible solutions to these problems have been considered, from using dramatic new therapy techniques to turning to technology for answers. One that seems to be raising hopes in particular is that of additional staff development (education) for those working in guidance. *A Plan for the Improvement of Guidance Services in California* (Guidance and Counseling Task Force, 1973, p. 39), based on information gathered from a sizable share of counselors working in California, concluded, "Upgrading training for on-the-job guidance specialists is a necessity for improving present guidance services. The majority of those doing the job are now on the job and will be for some years. Improving the preservice training is important, but equally . . . important is the upgrading of those holding the guidance positions currently in the schools."

A similar conclusion has been reached by researchers working nationally. Ganschow and others (1973, pp. 24-25), in trying to determine the quality of guidance programs for those students not going to college, and how such programs could be improved, concluded, "Comprehensive, well-planned programs of in-service education that focus on professional skills should be developed, and all school counselors should participate in them. These programs should help each counselor develop the skills she or he needs to meet revised certification requirements and to grow in competence so that she or he can advance professionally. These programs should be structured in close coordination with preservice counselor education programs that will result from concentrating on training in competencies to bring about student outcomes." This study thus not only points in the direction of better counselor preparation but also suggests the importance of developing actual competencies in counselors, skills they can put directly to use, as opposed to traditional programs that rely primarily on course requirements and cognitive qualifications.

It is to respond to such conclusions that in-service staff development is being developed and field-tested currently at the American Institutes for Research (AIR). Its aim is to provide counselors, as well as others working in guidance, with the skills necessary to effectively plan, develop, implement, and evaluate a school guidance program. It would eliminate the survival syndrome and overemphasis on crisis counseling by requiring, as the first step in designing such a program, the mapping out of a set of goals based on measured student needs (for all students). It would allow for appraisal of program effectiveness by having those goals translated into measurable student behavioral objectives and having information collected periodically to determine achievement of the objectives. It would counteract the counselor's counsel syndrome by having counselors determine exactly what methods work most effectively for high-priority student needs and by motivating counselors to spend their time accordingly. In short, the staff development program could provide counselors with possible solutions for many of their problems.

*Assumptions.* There are a number of assumptions made in the design of this staff development program. Often such assumptions are taken for granted. This can lead to problems, as not everyone takes the same things for granted. Let us state a few of our assumptions explicitly. First, guidance programs (this term is intended to include counseling, placement, and follow-through) are in serious need of improvement. Second, many persons working in guidance currently lack the planning and evaluation competencies needed for effective program improvement. Third, coordinated pre- and in-service staff development should be available to develop such competencies; such learning experiences should go beyond knowledge and attitude levels. Fourth, guidance programs must be able to state what they are attempting to do, measure their accomplishments, and display this information to others. Fifth, guidance programs should be strongly developmental, not primarily prescriptive. Sixth, guidance programs should focus on the career development of students, *career* being defined in a broad sense to include many aspects of life beside those related to school and work decisions. Finally, for program improvement to occur, there must be institutional and individual commitment to it.

The first five of these beliefs have already been touched on. The last two perhaps need some illumination. A growing consensus has emerged in the past several years concerning the importance of career development in young people. But career development is defined in many different ways, to mean everything from getting a job on leaving high school to developing oneself in a broad variety of ways. We prefer the latter emphasis, which stresses the total development of the individual. Occupational development then is seen to occur within the context of a whole being, not independently.

Assumption Number 7 may seem obvious. It is in fact often the most difficult ingredient to assure. Much lip service is paid to improving programs. But when it comes down to challenging entrenched authority or ingrained behavior, many reforms go a-glimmering. There must be the freedom for change in both institutions and individuals, and a genuine commitment to it, for real improvement to occur.

*Focus of Approach.* The staff development approach described here aims to be flexible and relatively inexpensive. It is structured around a series of twelve modules. A coordinator is required for each, to lead discussions, provide feedback on activities, and evaluate participants' responses to tests. A written guide is provided to help with these tasks. Module lengths vary, averaging six hours or the equivalent of a one-day workshop. Thus, the approach can take anywhere from one day to two and a half weeks, and a school can concentrate on those topics and skills it wishes. It can be used with current counselors, directors of guidance, paraprofessionals, other educators working in guidance (administrators, teachers, and consultants), and, with slight adaptation, those training to become counselors.

Very simply, this staff development approach tries to get those working in guidance to take a hard look at what they are doing, decide whether that is what they should be doing, and map out a plan for accomplishing any improvements they identify. The best first step in such a self-examination and program planning process is the definition of an explicit philosophy and set of assumptions from which to work. This is the topic of the first module. It presents the leading theories of career and vocational selection and development, including the results of a 1975 study focused on this issue. It asks staff members at a particular setting to analyze their own programs in the light of these and to choose what they regard as the best from each to serve as a foundation for what they will do in the future. Such a definition of theory and philosophy can then provide a firm foundation that will allow a program to set meaningful goals and work within a theoretically consistent framework.

The modules that follow, then, focus on the various tasks required to design and implement a program, and the skills or competencies guidance personnel need in order to perform those tasks. The tasks begin with the definition of a set of goals and behaviorally stated student objectives based on the assessed needs of students. The kinds of methods and strategies available to accomplish such goals and objectives are treated, along with program management techniques. Finally, the means of evaluating a program both over the short and long run are examined, and ways of communicating the results of such evaluations to those outside the program are treated. A diagrammatic summary of the modules and the relationship among them is contained in Figure 1.

Figure 1. A Preliminary Set of Modules for Improving
Comprehensive Career Guidance Programs.

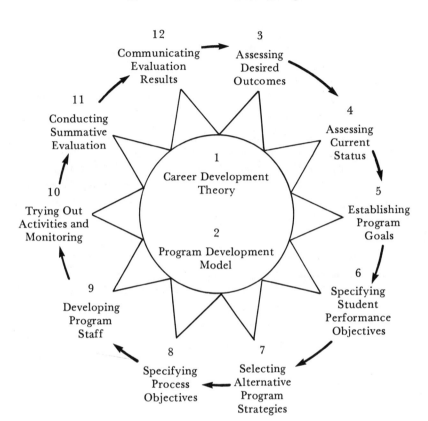

12
Communicating
Evaluation
Results

3
Assessing
Desired
Outcomes

11
Conducting
Summative
Evaluation

4
Assessing
Current
Status

1
Career Development
Theory

10
Trying Out
Activities and
Monitoring

5
Establishing
Program
Goals

2
Program Development
Model

9
Developing
Program
Staff

6
Specifying
Student
Performance
Objectives

8
Specifying
Process
Objectives

7
Selecting
Alternative
Program
Strategies

## Description of Program

The current state of our staff development approach is
summarized in Figure 1. For each of the twelve modules, a central element is the statement of measurable objectives. In this
same way, objectives describing desirable student outcomes are
central to the student guidance programs just discussed.

*Module Objectives and Purposes.* Each module has a set
of objectives that serve at least three purposes. One, they direct
the module design and writing activities. The module developers
do not begin their detailed work on module content until its

objectives have been agreed on and stated in the most measurable form possible at that point in the production schedule. Two, they serve as guidelines for the learning experiences of the staff development participants. Each module's set is presented in simplified form early in the module.

Participants are encouraged to study them closely at that point, to determine what they expected to accomplish in that module. More detailed statements also are available if participants wish to review them. Three, they shape the content of each module's performance test to help participants, and their coordinators determine which objectives have been achieved as well as which ones require additional attention. The objectives can also help the designers of the staff development materials and procedures determine which parts are working and which ones need further modification.

*Module Objectives Examples.* Two types of objectives and their component outcomes are used in our current modules. The first, knowledge objectives, are the ones on which conventional in-service approaches generally focus, if efforts are made to state explicit predetermined objectives for them at all. It is the second type, skill objectives, that is the distinctive feature of our staff development. We identified critical tasks that experts felt educators needed to perform in order to effectively plan, develop, implement, and evaluate school guidance programs. Then, the competencies educators required for successfully conducting these tasks were specified. Next, related competencies were grouped so that a module could be designed for at least two or three of the most fundamental skills in each group. Finally, these skills were expressed as competency-based objectives for each module.

This type of objective outlines the most important participant outcomes on which each module attempts to deliver. The knowledge objectives summarize selected cognitive outcomes that are prerequisites to the performance of these competencies. Two examples of such knowledge objectives and the modules in which they are found are presented as follows. Note that assessing participants' achievements of these objectives demands coordinator discretion and judgment. The stated cri-

teria provide guidelines for such assessments, but their implementation requires a skilled, active, coordinator who is not a
peer.

Module 5. Define the phrase "program goal"
and give an example of one.

Criteria: The definition should state that
goals are general statements of program outcomes.
They are not specific and behavioral.

A feasible goal should be presented. It
should meet the six criteria defined in the module:

- Be at an appropriate level of generality.
- Focus on students.
- Be written in clear, direct language.
- Be directed to an outcome, not a process.
- Suggest the types of outcomes it will lead
  to.
- Reflect the underlying philosophy and
  theory intended.

Use your judgment in evaluating the example. The last criteria, for example, may be hard to
satisfy in a given objective.

Module 8. List the advantages of writing process objectives.

Criteria: Advantages listed should include
the fact that they help program organizers to clarify their thinking, replicate their program, report
on it, and manage it.

In the twelve-module series on which this chapter focuses, competency objectives are either an enabler or a terminal
type. All of them entail skills that can be operationalized by
observable performances, preferably ones indicated by the successful development of a product having measurable relevance
for practical settings. We have attempted to concentrate on
helping participants internalize skills that are generalizable, ones
they can use in practical settings outside the instructional and
testing settings provided by the modules. Using Module 6 as an
example, it contains three competency-based objectives that

serve as enablers for the more important fourth and final skill.
One of these three is as follows. Once again coordinator judgment is required to implement the criteria guidelines provided.

> Write an outcome stating an identifiable per-
> formance for a goal statement.
>
> Criteria: The examples provided by the par-
> ticipant must meet the four criteria listed in Activ-
> ity 1, as follows:
>
> - Are the outcomes observable perform-
>   ances or behaviors?
> - Are the verbs primarily action verbs? Are
>   the outcomes subject to few interpreta-
>   tions?
> - Do the outcomes actually give evidence
>   that the participant has reached the goal?
> - Is the behavior in the outcome an impor-
>   tant or significant one? Is it worth know-
>   ing about?
> - Do the outcomes describe what students
>   will be able to do, not what will be done
>   for the students?
>
> If any participants fail to meet these criteria,
> point this out and have them keep working until
> they *can* do it right. Each participant must write
> three correct outcomes in each case.

The skills involved in statements such as this are crucial
to the construction of measurable objectives that are developmentally sequenced. However, the module attempts to help participants go further, to state such objectives for their own programs. Since participants will not conduct needs activities in
their educational settings until after the workshop, they do not
have the input data they need to write their program's objectives when they study this module. Therefore, they check their
terminal competence with their workshop coordinator after
producing a detailed plan for exactly how they will state their
objectives later. The following is the terminal objective related
to this competency in Module 6. Coordinators have to understand and be able to judge a product using the standards men-

tioned in this objective. These guidelines are discussed and illustrated in the text of the module.

> Produce a plan for developing student performance objectives for your program.
> Criteria: The time and task analysis produced should line out the tasks under each of the major headings listed, assign responsibility for each task to someone, and set a completion date for each task. In addition, the plan should be reasonably
>> • *Logical*—Do the tasks flow in logical sequence?
>> • *Thorough*—Is it detailed enough to be helpful?
>> • *Feasible*—Is it not too detailed to be burdensome; are the times allowed for the tasks reasonable?
>> • *Fair*—Are the responsibilities assigned equitably and fairly?

*Module Format.* The design specifications of our modules have evolved through pilot (preliminary, small group) and field (more intensive, large group) tests in which we have been involved over the last two years. Each module is composed of a package of materials that includes a consumable module booklet for the participant, a reusable guidebook for each workshop coordinator working with participants on that module, and support materials (for example, filmstrips, textbooks, journal articles, sample tests, and assessment instruments) referenced to various sections and objectives in the module. Each coordinator's guide contains definitions of the workshop leader's roles and functions and provides information helpful to the performance of those roles.

Each participant's booklet begins with a section that introduces the general goal and specific participant outcomes of that module; outlines the activities covered by the module, the approximate time each activity should take the typical participant, and the outcomes keyed to each activity; illustrates how the content of this module fits into the comprehensive program-planning and evaluation model that serves as the foundation for this staff development series; and provides a glossary defining important terms used in that module.

The four remaining sections include: the main text for in-depth reading, interspersed with both questions for group discussion sessions and practice activities; a postassessment, criterion test for performance feedback to each participant; the aforementioned personal application that encourages participants to apply their acquired knowledge and skills to problems in their local settings; and an appendix of materials helpful throughout the module, including an optional simulation description for discussions of real-life application of the skills, additional readings and materials related to the module's topic, and bibliographic descriptions of key references related to the module's content. Participants' booklets range in length from 40 to 80 pages, with an overall total of approximately 800 pages for the twelve modules.

*Expected Staff Development Outcomes.* The content of this twelve-module set on program planning, development, implementation, and evaluation is suggested by the module titles provided in Figure 1. However, more detailed information can be derived from the list of outcomes participants are expected to achieve through this staff development approach. These outcomes are summarized in Table 1.

**Table 1. Staff Development Outcomes for Preliminary Set of Modules.**

Module 1. Career Development Theory

1. Identify current practices in your career guidance program that reflect each of the eight career or vocational development theories.
2. For each theory, list at least one additional activity you would consider adding to your program.
3. State the assumptions on which your current guidance program is based.
4. Produce a written plan that, when implemented, will result in a statement of the philosophy and assumptions underlying the career guidance program you will plan through the course of these modules.

Module 2. Program Development Model

1. List at least three common guidance problems the approach described here can help provide solutions to.

## Table 1 (Continued)

2. Describe the essential characteristics of the career guidance program improvement approach discussed in the module and list several of its advantages and disadvantages.
3. List the essential skills to be developed in this staff development program.
4. Identify the skills *you* want to develop in the staff development program.

Module 3. Assessing Desired Outcomes

1. Understand and state the value of assessing the desired outcomes of a program.
2. Specify the tasks and considerations in assessing a program's desired outcomes.
3. Perform basic skills involved in assessing a program's desired outcomes, including
   a. Defining the population(s) and selecting the sample(s).
   b. Selecting and developing assessment instruments.
   c. Administering instruments.
   d. Summarizing and translating data into data outcomes.
4. Develop a plan for defining the desired outcomes of your program.

Module 4. Assessing Current Status

1. Define "current status assessment," state its emphasis, and explain how it fits into the needs assessment process.
2. State the human, financial, and technical resources of a guidance program.
3. Adapt and/or use an instrument for determining how resources are being used currently.
4. State what techniques are available for assessing current status.
5. Review and select instruments and items from instruments for assessing the current status of students according to appropriate criteria.
6. Produce a plan for assessing the current status of your program.

Module 5. Establishing Program Goals

1. Define the phrase "program goal" and give an example of one.
2. Identify program needs by comparing desired outcome and current status information to determine the discrepancies.
3. Draft goals for a program based on the program needs and other relevant information.
4. Classify goals into a useful overall scheme.
5. Determine priorities for the goals of a program.
6. Define issues and techniques important in evaluating and reporting the activities involved in planning career guidance programs.
7. Produce a plan for developing program goals for your program.

Module 6. Specifying Student Performance Objectives

1. State the reasons for and importance of writing career guidance student performance objectives.

*(continued on next page)*

Table 1 (Continued)

---

2. Write an outcome stating an identifiable performance for a goal statement.
3. Write, or select and modify, a full objective for an outcome. Each such objective will contain the four components of a good objective.
4. Produce a sequenced list of all objectives pertaining to a given goal statement and target population.
5. Produce a plan for developing student performance objectives for your program.

---

Module 7. Selecting Alternative Program Strategies

1. Write a definition and give three examples of guidance strategies.
2. Write a set of your criteria for considering alternative strategies for guidance objectives.
3. State your decision rule for selecting a strategy to use to reach a guidance objective.
4. Produce a plan for selecting program strategies at your school.

---

Module 8. Specifying Process Objectives

1. List the advantages of writing process objectives.
2. List process objectives that must be performed in order to implement a given strategy.
3. Assign staff members to carry out process objectives by matching available staff skills with needed skills to accomplish the objectives.
4. Schedule process objectives by use of Program Evaluation and Review Technique (PERT) and by use of time, task, and talent analyses.
5. Incorporate process objectives into planning activities at your school or district.

---

Module 9. Developing Program Staff

1. Use skills checklists to write staff development objectives.
2. Create your own staff development strategies by combining available sources of help with possible delivery methods.
3. Use the criteria suggested in this module and/or your own criteria to select staff development strategies suited to your school or district.
4. Outline the planning and implementation tasks which would need to be completed in your school or district to carry out a given strategy of your choice.
5. Map out a plan for developing and administering your own staff development.

---

Module 10. Trying Out Activities and Monitoring

1. State the primary purpose of carrying out preliminary activity tryouts and describe at least two situations in which such pilot testing is useful and two in which it is a waste of time.
2. Verify the internal logic of a planned career guidance activity, given a written

## Table 1 (Continued)

description of such an activity covering its goals, student performance objectives, and process objectives.

3. Develop a relatively accurate estimate of the cost of implementing a career guidance activity.
4. Develop measures of attainment of the *process* objectives of a career guidance activity, given a written description of the activity and its process objectives.
5. Develop relatively objective, reliable, and valid measures of the *outcomes* of a career guidance activity.
6. Develop a plan for trying out activities and monitoring early implementation efforts at your school.

Module 11. Conducting Summative Evaluation

1. State the purposes and value of conducting a summative evaluation.
2. Select an appropriate evaluation design and sample, given an evaluation situation.
3. Select, adapt, or adopt appropriate measurement instruments given particular evaluation needs.
4. List the major considerations involved in administering evaluation instruments.
5. Propose appropriate methods of processing, analyzing, and presenting evaluation data.
6. State the considerations important in determining cost effectiveness.
7. State appropriate decisions based on evaluation results, given an evaluation situation.
8. Map out a plan for conducting a summative evaluation of your program.

Module 12. Communicating Evaluation Results

1. Explain how content, format, and level of sophistication can vary in an evaluation report.
2. Choose content, format, and level of sophistication appropriate for (a) decisions and the data they require, (b) audience characteristics, and (c) resources available for producing the evaluation report.
3. Specify how to use simple, logical organization in preparing evaluation reports.
4. Specify how to use concise language in evaluation reports.
5. Specify how to use clear, accurate presentation of data in evaluation reports.
6. Specify appropriate methods that contribute to an interesting, attractive presentation.
7. Tailor your writing and presentation of data to be appropriate for (a) the decisions and data needed for them, (b) audience characteristics, and (c) resources available.
8. Identify the reporting considerations for your own situation and develop a plan for reporting evaluation results using communication strategies appropriate to the considerations you have identified.

*In-Service Pilot Tests.* During the 1974-75 school year, this staff development approach was pilot-tested to collect feedback on each package and overall workshop procedures (for example, participant's selection of modules, coordinators' roles, module-testing activities) we were using to help participants work through the modules they chose.

The results of these trial attempts were positive. However, sufficient constructive reactions were obtained that a major revision cycle was warranted. We classified these reactions into two categories. The first group included concerns counseling participants had relating to their orientation to this type of individualized, competency-based, staff development workshop. This was a novel experience for them and not one for which they felt well prepared, as far as both knowledge and motivation were concerned. The second category of concerns focused on the delivery system we used in the workshops. The materials needed to be more palatable to the participants and more self-motivating. To respond to the first category, we decided to devote more effort interviewing potential participants before the initial day of the workshop and orienting those who wanted to participate and were then selected. This additional effort would attempt to convey fully the advantages and disadvantages of the program planning and evaluation model that this set of modules stresses, identify our staff development assumptions and convey them to participants before selection, explain just how much hard work is involved and the kind of commitment that this staff development approach demands, and select highly motivated participants.

On the other hand, to effect an improved delivery system we implemented a series of actions to revise module format and content. The general types of modifications included reducing the amount of reading; increasing the simplicity of the remaining text (including eliminating jargon); increasing the number of discussions and practice activities; improving the layout of all materials; expanding the use of tapes, slides, examples, and cartoons; and making fuller use of coordinators to communicate the basic purposes and procedures of each module.

AIR is continuing to produce competency-based staff

development materials for those working in guidance. While the twelve modules outlined earlier in this chapter are complete, an additional project developed and field-tested twenty-seven new ones.

This project, the National Consortium for Research on Competency-Based Staff Development in Comprehensive Career Guidance, Counseling, Placement and Follow-Through, coordinated the efforts of centers in four states: California, Maryland, Michigan, and Missouri. At each center, the state education department joined with a university (California State University at Long Beach, the University of Maryland, the University of Michigan, and the University of Missouri) to form a team of module developers and researchers. Each center, together with AIR, developed materials that focused on high-priority staff development needs in each state. Table 2 summarizes the content areas and numbers of these modules and the initial set of twelve (see numbers in parentheses in the AIR column). These modules were patterned after those described earlier, with activities designed to develop actual skills, and were field-tested on both an in-service and preservice basis.

At the same time, AIR has continued its search for competency-based materials useful for the development of personnel working in guidance. We expanded our catalogue to include new materials that became available, as well as those that we failed to discover through our initial search. Information on the revised catalogue as well as the additional modules is available from Youth Development Research Group, American Institutes for Research, P.O. Box 1113, Palo Alto, Calif. 94302.

## Problems with This Staff Development Approach

The most nagging concern we have faced throughout all aspects of our research and development in this area entails participant motivation. Most of our participants to date have experienced our approach in an in-service setting. Our current perceptions are that many such personnel are accustomed to staff development activities in which they do not have to be too actively involved, do not have to work too hard, can be enter-

Table 2. Competency Domain and Areas of Center Specialization.

| Competency Area | Competence | Centers | | | | |
|---|---|---|---|---|---|---|
| | | AIR | California | Maryland | Michigan | Missouri |
| Skills in using systematic planning and evaluation to improve career guidance programs for clients | 1. Knowledge and skills in *planning* improved programs based on an explicit career development theory and set of assumptions as well as needs assessment data. | 5 modules | | | | |
| | 2. Knowledge and skills in *developing* (structuring) improved programs. | 2 modules | | | | |
| | 3. Knowledge and skills in *implementing* improved programs. | 3 modules | | | | |
| | 4. Knowledge and skills in collecting *accountability information* to evaluate the costs and impact of such programs, employing *results management*, and using the data to make *key decisions*. | 2 modules | | | | |
| | 5. Knowledge and skills in establishing *program organizational procedures and patterns.* | | 1 module | | 2 modules | |
| Skills in meeting the career needs common to all clients | 1. Knowledge and skills to help clients in *personal assessment* (for example, using tests and other techniques to assess personal characteristics and needs). | 1 module | | | | |
| | 2. Knowledge and skills to help clients *clarify their values.* | | | | | |
| | 3. Knowledge and skills to help clients learn about and explore *career options* (for example, understanding the sociological history and psychological meaning of work, understanding occupational clusters, finding and using occupational information, benefitting from career exploration experiences, exploring available educational options, and becoming aware of leisure opportunities). | | | | | |
| | 4. Knowledge and skills to help clients acquire and practice *career decision making skills.* | 1 module | | | | |
| | 5. Knowledge and skills to help clients in *goal setting* and *career planning* (for example, establishing plans of action). | | | | | |
| | 6. Knowledge and skills to help clients in *career development* toward their goals. | | | | | |
| | 7. Knowledge and skills to help clients in career placement (for example, preparing resumes, interviewing for career options, securing job and educational placements). | | | | | 2 modules |

| Category | Skills | Modules |
|---|---|---|
| | through (for example, collecting data on graduates, helping them continue career planning and development, evaluating the effectiveness of placement procedures, evaluating previous educational and guidance programs). | 2 modules |
| Skills in meeting the unique career needs of special target groups | 1. Knowledge and skills in working with *girls and women.* | 1 module |
| | 2. Knowledge and skills in working with *ethnic minorities.* | 2 modules |
| | 3. Knowledge and skills in working with *physically and educationally handicapped* individuals. | 1 module |
| | 4. Knowledge and skills in working with adults. | 2 modules |
| | 5. Knowledge and skills in working with the *elderly and aged.* | 1 module |
| | 6. Knowledge and skills in working with *postsecondary education students.* | |
| | 7. Knowledge and skills in working with *elementary school children.* | 2 modules |
| Skills in using and evaluating innovative intervention techniques | 1. Knowledge and skills in *human relations* in using *interpersonal communication* techniques (for example, relating effectively with verbal and nonverbal skills, creating and maintaining rapport, respect, fairness, support). | |
| | 2. Knowledge and skills in *individual counseling* (for example, conceptualizing cases, teaching personal problem-solving strategies, applying behavior assessment and analysis techniques, applying behavior modification strategies, using social modeling, engaging in behavioral rehearsal, writing case reports, terminating counseling contracts, evaluating counseling impact, making referrals). | |
| | 3. Knowledge and skills in *group guidance and counseling* (many of the specific skills listed under individual counseling may also be used in group guidance and counseling). | |
| | 4. Knowledge and skills in using *paraprofessionals* and appropriate *technology* (for example, computers and other data processing equipment, audio-visual equipment, instructional counseling units). | 2 modules |

*(continued on next page)*

# Table 2 (Continued)

| Competency Area | Competence | Centers | | | | |
|---|---|---|---|---|---|---|
| | | AIR | California | Maryland | Michigan | Missouri |
| | 5. Knowledge and skills in designing, establishing, staffing, maintaining, and evaluating *career centers*. | | 1 module | 1 module | | |
| | 6. Knowledge and skills in identifying, incorporating, and utilizing *community resources*. | | | | | |
| | 7. Knowledge and skills in studying *futurism*, developing future projections, and communicating such projections to career deciders. | | | | 2 modules | |
| Skills in maintaining and improving the educational system and its environment on behalf of clients' career needs | 1. Knowledge and skills in providing *consultation* to staff, parents, administrators, and community representatives. | | | | | |
| | 2. Knowledge and skills in *client advocacy* (for example, monitoring and intervening in the educational system and its economic, political, and social environment to help clients meet their needs, including clients in decision making). | | | | | |
| | 3. Knowledge and skills in maintaining *public relations* needed to support client programs. | | | | | 1 module |
| | 4. Knowledge and skills in *educating and counseling parents* to help their children solve problems. | | | | | |
| | 5. Knowledge and skills in *conducting and using research* (for example, institutional and local descriptive research, experimental investigations of client-intervention interactions, identification and use of published research results). | | | | | |
| | 6. Knowledge and skills in conducting updated *in-service staff development* and articulating this with preservice education. | 1 module | | | | |

*Note:* Italicized numbers refer to the twelve modules focused on planning and evaluation discussed in this chapter. Roman numbers refer to the twenty-seven modules, more broadly focused, developed through the National Consortium.

tained by powerful speakers and glossy audiovisual and printed materials, can spend a lot of time talking in group discussion, have few reading and product development tasks requested of them, can follow workshop leaders who assume a controlling role, and are not expected to show measurable changes in behavior as a result of workshop experience. As we hope it is obvious from the preceding sections of this chapter, the delivery system of our staff development approach contradicts most of these preferences. This approach attempts to engage participants in a learning process that emphasizes individualization; learner responsibility for personal growth; more independent, self-instructional activities than many participants desire and have been accustomed to; participant generation of specific products that will have transfer value to their practical settings after the workshops; few didactic presentations and lectures and more reading and self-study activities; a facilitator, rather than a leader, role for workshop coordinators; and performance assessment of gains participants make in their knowledge and skills as a result of these learning experiences.

Needless to say, we have experienced motivational problems with many of our participants. In response, we have modified our delivery system, as was indicated in the preceding section, as much as we feel is possible and still maintain the learning principles we continue to accept. At the same time, we are committed to a mission of trying to gradually change participants' staff development expectations to what we believe are more specific, measurable, and higher goals than they have adopted in the past.

*Instructional Time.* A related problem with our delivery system is the amount of participant instructional time it requires. This type of modularized approach to learning reinforces individualization of learning experiences to the needs and characteristics of learners but, because it is designed and evaluated on the basis of measurable objectives, it also requires that participants receive the learning resources to achieve agreed-on performance levels. The instructional materials and procedures have to "deliver." Therefore, participant time for exposure to appropriate learning experiences becomes a very important ingredient. We began with modules that necessitated ten to fifteen hours of learner time. Even though we have tried to extinguish all attempts to present our program-planning and evaluation model as a lockstep series of sequentially related activities, we have had to deviate from this goal in our staff development. We know that participants who are beginning their experience with this model must first be exposed to certain fundamental concepts before they work on some of the more sophisticated skills. This meant that each participant agreed to take three or four modules. The total time commitment became impossible in many school settings where staff could be released for a maximum of three or four days of workshops. As a result, we have reduced the module time for the typical participant; the average time is now six hours per module. However, for in-service education we continue to ask each participant to commit him- or herself to at least three modules. As a result this staff-development approach is not feasible for guidance personnel who cannot devote at least four days of learning time.

*Disinterest in Evaluation.* Participants were often reluctant to engage in evaluation activities aimed either at helping them assess changes in their performance levels or at assisting us to improve the staff development materials and procedures. Usually, they have been more supportive of the second evaluation purpose than they have of the first one. A central concept in our approach is a dedication to specifying instructional objectives and measuring progress toward them. However, many of our participants have not shared that dedication. Some of them seemed to have been threatened particularly by any preassessment activities intended to help them assess changes in their performance. They were demoralized by their entry level assessment results and frustrated that our items were tailored far too closely to module content. As a result, we have abandoned the preassessments and are focusing more attention on criterion-referenced evaluations at the end of and after the workshop. Other participants, anxious to emphasize learning experiences that had immediate application to their practical job settings, felt evaluation activities diverted them from this main purpose. As a result, we have reduced the number and extent of the evaluation instruments and procedures but also have reaffirmed our dedication to trying to stimulate participants to adopt more positive attitudes to the aims, process, and results of the evaluation of any staff development approach.

*Measuring Skill Improvement.* The most important aspect of evaluation of our staff development is the measurement of changes in participants' competencies. Solid criterion-referenced evaluation requires that skill-based objectives be assessed by instruments and activities that ask participants to demonstrate their performance of competencies outlined in those objectives and the products that result from this performance. Since our approach stresses the acquisition and practice of competencies that are transferable beyond the staff development setting and into each participant's practical job setting, pencil-and-paper measurement items will not suffice. Indeed, we gave up our earlier emphasis on assessing each participant's competence in solving contrived problems we presented through simulation experiences. One reason for this change was participants' concern about the artificiality of the simulations and their preference for more personally relevant assessments. We are now concentrating on the personal application plans, described earlier in this chapter, and postworkshop follow-up evaluations of the degree to which such plans are implemented. However, this tactic incurs the participant time problem again and is expensive to conduct. Obviously, we have not resolved this evaluation problem.

### Adapting this Approach to Preservice Settings

It is our desire to produce staff development that is equally appropriate for preservice and in-service settings. Thus far, most of our efforts have concentrated on in-service education. However, we are fully aware of some critical issues that are involved in generalizing our staff development approach to college and university programs that attempt to shape the learning experiences of professional and paraprofessional personnel in the counseling and guidance field. Some of the strategies that need to be worked out to facilitate such applications include

strategies for conducting *task and competency analyses* for determining generic human service skills. Also, strategies are
needed for conducting *competency assessments* to determine
what students to admit to counselor education programs at the
graduate and undergraduate level and how to develop individualized programs of study tailored to the interests and needs of
each student accepted. There is also a need for consistent procedures and formats to be used by all department members in the
*competency staff development* of these students and for strategies for *performance evaluation* of student progress on individualized programs of study. Strategies need to be worked out for
changing state credentialing requirements to be compatible with
a competency-based certification model developed through such
an educational program. This issue introduces a host of questions. Perhaps a few of them should be noted here. Should a
college's or university's programs be tied to credential standards
that are either self-imposed or established by an outside regulat-
ing body (such as a state agency or examining committee)? If
so, what group or agency should assess the performance of each
candidate to determine which standards he or she satisfies?
What should be the performance evaluation process? If an external body handles the credentialing, would in-house examinations, administered at the college or university, become meaningless? Some type of collaborative assessment and monitoring
process combining the resources of the preservice institution
and an outside regulatory body seems most desirable to us.
However, other alternatives and their possible consequences
need to be systematically investigated. Furthermore, strategies
are needed for implementing information management services
to support such competency-based learning and for follow-up
evaluation of graduates' job performance and, therefore, of the
counselor education program. Finally, there is a need for maintaining recurrent task and competency analyses to ensure that
such programs focus on *current* competencies appropriate to
practical settings. The counseling profession must not expect to
develop these strategies without a heavy commitment. All of us
must see this as a long-range project.

## Other Staff Development Approaches

Effective planning and evaluating of guidance programs are important to their improvement. But it is not the only area in which innovations in counselor education can contribute, particularly from the point of view of developing in counseling personnel usable skills, as opposed to the more traditional cognitive and affective outcomes. Recognizing this, the project that put together the staff development approach described above also undertook the task of conducting a national search for other competency-based approaches.

The search proved an interesting venture. The first problem was one of defining its precise focus. After an extensive ERIC documents search, we came up with a total of two references to competency-based counselor education. So we decided to make the focus broad enough to gather in any staff development materials, even if not specifically designed for counselors. To be precise, we asked for "competency-based staff development materials in career guidance." We wrote to every institution of higher education with counselor education programs, all publishers active in educational fields, all state departments of education, all members identified on American Personnel and Guidance Association (APGA) mailing lists provided by various division presidents in five areas (school counseling, rehabilitation, group counseling, higher education, and corrections), all state vocational research offices; all federal regional educational laboratories, all relevant research and development centers, and selected sources chosen from a search of Stanford University's data bank of *teacher* competency-based education programs. In addition to staff development materials, we asked for statements of counselor competencies, as such lists are usually the products of the first step toward competency-based programs. We sent out over 1,200 letters to every state and territory in the United States, and held our breath. The response was underwhelming. In spite of the fact that a prepaid, preaddressed, multiple-choice postcard was included to provide a simple statement of the status of the respondent relevant to the development of competency-based approaches, only about 60 percent responded. A sizable proportion of those did seem quite impressed with the project and, while they had never heard of competency-based education, wondered if *we* could send *them* information on it. Professional jealousy proved a problem; one gentleman in Nevada replied he would show us his if we would show him ours. Through some yet unexplained foul-up, a number of respondents who received follow-up letters had failed to receive the original letter, and many called collect to register their confusion and ire. But when the dust settled, 120 respondents had sent materials. The majority of these were competency statements, but there were thirty-one actual sets of counselor education materials. These varied considerably in focus, length, and quality.

After observing this wide range of materials, we decided to limit our focus to those dealing with necessary competencies for counseling personnel. Therefore, we eliminated materials whose chief concern was in counselor education institutions, competencies for trainers of counseling personnel, or other slightly different aspects of counselor education. The remaining materials either summarized staff development programs or presented lists of competencies. The next step was to review and classify programs according to the general types of competencies on which they focused. These six categories resulted in programs to develop competencies in:

1. Using systematic planning and evaluation to improve career guidance programs.
2. Meeting the career needs common to all clients.
3. Meeting the unique career needs of special target groups.
4. Using and evaluating interventions techniques (direct and indirect).
5. Maintaining and improving the educational system and environment.
6. General counselor competencies.

To catalogue the information on each program, we developed a general description of it and indicated its format, contact person, needed outside resources, and price (whenever possible).

Next, lists of competencies were reviewed and summarized. These were grouped into the same six competency categories. Once again, our summaries noted the format and contact person, but, since most competency lists were available at no charge, price information was excluded unless a charge existed.

One problem in this cataloguing activity entailed the difficulty of defining the term *competency based.* Some of our respondents apparently use this to describe any educational procedure that even talks about what counselors do. Others demand that before the term *competency based* can be applied, participants be involved in real-life situations, performing skills in question with real clients in their own settings. A middle position assumes that participants must be able to perform a skill in order to produce a product for the definition to be satisfied and that this skill be transferable to a practical setting. Even this raises problems. Where does one draw the line between cognitive abilities and skills? Are there not cognitive skills, such as writing behavioral objectives or designing needs assessment? No two program developers agree on precise definitions of *competency based.* While we had our own (defined earlier), we were reluctant to impose it ruthlessly and eliminate from consideration most of what we received. In addition, few competency-based programs by *any* definition are currently available. All this should be understood to provide the correct perspective on the programs described here.

For this chapter, we selected five of the programs that will illustrate the variety of responses received in terms of the following variables: level of training (paraprofessional, professional); nature of the source (federally funded projects, universities, commercial publishers); target audiences (manpower counselors, school guidance personnel, occupational guidance personnel); and types of competencies (as indicated in six categories listed earlier). Each description will attempt to briefly summarize authors, format, goals and objectives, target audiences, training personnel, methods used, availability of evaluation information, price, outside resources needed, and contact person or agency. The selection does not pretend to be comprehensive; neither is it intended as an evaluative statement. Many other approaches exist; often they are comparable to the ones described. What *is* hoped is that these descriptions will provide an overview of some of the efforts and directions currently being pursued in competency-based development of guidance and counseling staff around the country.

## Program Descriptions

1. *Occupational Specialist Training Program*

   *Author:* Florida State Department of Education.

   *Format:* Handbook for students (162 pages) plus fifteen instructional modules (ranging from 20 to 130 pages each).

   *Description:* This program is planned to train paraprofessionals as occupational specialists. It was developed and field-tested by the Florida Department of Education in cooperation with state education personnel, thirty-eight local school districts, and 132 working occupational specialists. It is designed to improve specific skills within the context of a more general local training program and may be implemented as a whole or only in areas where skill development is necessary to meet local needs.

   The program consists of a series of fifteen performance-based components, or areas of objectives. These are:
   1. State and local policies, procedures, and organizational structures.
   2. Nature and scope of vocational education in Florida.
   3. Utilization of community resources.
   4. Communication skills.
   5. Employment opportunities and job requirements.
   6. Public and private vocational and technical programs.
   7. Apprenticeship programs.
   8. The decision-making process.
   9. Administration and utilization of standardized tests.

10. Identification of the potential and actual early school leaver.
11. Identification and securing of job placements.
12. Career education information center.
13. Planning and implementation of career education activities.
14. Assessment of career guidance services.
15. Conduct of follow-up studies.

Program materials consist of a training handbook plus fifteen instructional modules. The handbook details objectives within each component, and contains lists of suggested resources; pre- and postassessments, plus feedback for the postassessments; and evaluator's instruments. The instructional modules (which generally but not precisely parallel the components) are bound separately as Appendices A through P and contain much of the resource material in themselves, plus details of learning activities. Keys for postassessments are also included in many modules; those not included are contained in the final appendix.

*Evaluation Information:* Evaluation and revision went on during the process of module development.

*Outside Resources Needed:* Coordinator, a few outside readings.

*Price:* $18.00.

*Contact:* Panhandle Area Educational Cooperative
P.O. Drawer 190
Chipley, Fla. 32428

2. *Basic Attending Skills: An Introduction to Microcounseling and Helping*

*Authors:* Norma B. Gluckstern, Allen E. Ivey.

*Format:* Leader manual; participant manual; eleven videotapes, lasting two-and-a-half hours.

*Description:* This training program is a video system for

teaching single counseling skills to beginning helpers, particularly at the paraprofessional level. The material provided is sufficient for fifteen to forty-five hours of training to groups of twenty or less. It focuses on six specific helping skills:

1. Attending.
2. Open questions.
3. Minimal encourages.
4. Paraphrasing.
5. Reflection of feeling.
6. Summarization.

The videotapes illustrate use of the skills in model interactions by the authors, often focused on male-female issues in current society. Videotaping of trainees is then utilized to aid their own skill development. No evaluative criteria are specified; these are at the leader's discretion.

The leader manual gives step-by-step activities and suggestions for developing workshops of varying size and format. (It is recommended that workshops be supervised, if not led, by professionals qualified in psychological or counseling services.) The participant manual contains sections on various listening skills and emphasizes behavioral contracts. Encouragement is given throughout for trainees to teach helping skills to others.

Other material available from this organization on this topic includes a videotape on *Microcounseling: An Introduction* and Ivey's book *Microcounseling: Innovations in Interview Training* (1975).

*Evaluation Information:* Research results and participant response are both available on this program.

*Outside Resources Needed:* Leader; videotape system.

*Price:* Five-day rental of *Basic Attending Skills* videotapes: $185.00. Purchase price: $325.00 on three reels, $425.00 on eleven reels.
Leader manual: $9.75.
Participant manual: $3.75.

Rental and purchase prices on other material available from supplier.

*Contact:* Microtraining Associates
Box 641
North Amherst, Mass. 01059

3. *A Competency-Based Training Program for Manpower Counselors*

*Authors:* Manpower and Community College Counseling Program of Northwest Regional Educational Laboratory, School of Education at Oregon State University, and the United States Office of Education.

*Format:* Trainee's manual (200 pages); resource manual (250 pages), *Implementing Competency-Based Counselor Preparation; Instructor's Key; Core Counseling Competencies: A Manual for Self-Growth* (relevant reading materials, not yet available).

*Description:* This program is a cooperative effort of the three authoring institutions. It is designed for use in a one-week group training program for manpower and community college counselors and is an "attempt to develop both theory and practice" in techniques for manpower counselors. It also attempts to bridge the gap between those with counseling background but little experience in manpower counseling, and those experienced in manpower programs but without training in counseling practices as such.

The training is based on eight broad competency areas:
1. Counseling techniques (for use with individuals and in groups).
2. Staff relationships and the correlation of counseling and administrative functions.
3. Client information and referral services.
4. Populations served by manpower programs.
5. Assessment.
6. Career development.
7. The labor market.

8. Evaluation of counseling effectiveness (planning, research, and evaluation competencies).

Each competency area consists of statements of learning objectives, usually five to ten; descriptions of learning
activities; and statements defining criteria for accomplishment (called *evidence of learning*). Each objective is a general
statement of the desired knowledge or skill; the learning activities and evidences of learning are more specific and behavioral. Activities (including readings) are often based on actual
situations in the Portland area.

The manual also includes thorough preassessments for
each objective: Some are self-evaluations, some are objective
tests, and some are case studies which ask the trainee to recommend and defend a course of action. A glossary of terms is
also included. Written resources cited are extensive and practical: legislative acts; books and articles on current career
availability and on general aspects of career selection; Department of Transportation and other government publications;
journal and magazine articles; and works on specific counseling skills.

*Evaluation Information:* The manual underwent four revisions; however, specific evaluation
information is not included in the
manual and was not available to
catalogue compilers.

*Outside Resources Needed:* Instructor, extensive books, articles, use of local agencies for
some activities.

*Price:* Trainer manual: $8.00.
Resource manual: $9.00
Instructor's key: $7.00.
Price not established for *Core Counseling Competen-
cies* manual.

*Contact:* Manpower and Community College Counseling Program
Northwest Regional Educational Laboratory

Lindsay Building
710 S.W. Second Ave.
Portland, Oreg. 97204

4. *Preparation Program for Educational Staff Associate Certification of School Counselors*

*Authors:* Consortium of Pacific Lutheran University, Tacoma Public Schools, and Tacoma Alliance of Education.

*Format:* Booklet (92 pages).

*Description:* The state of Washington currently has nine functioning consortia of universities plus local school districts, which are implementing competency-based counselor training programs. While each curriculum is unique, the Pacific Lutheran University-Tacoma consortium is a representative example.

The document describing this curriculum specifies competencies, assessment instruments, and levels of achievement for counselor certification at two of the three certification levels in the state: preparatory and initial. Those for the third level, continuing, are not yet fully developed. The program emphasizes both knowledge and experience and includes practicum experiences as well as classroom work. Candidates must complete field work of nine hours weekly for one semester in a school or agency, with an accompanying seminar. In addition, the candidate must take four "mini" practicums, which last a semester each and involve different counseling experiences and competencies, such as training in empathic behavior, counseling sessions with actual clients, and utilization of special skills such as play therapy.

The program has these characteristics:
1. Individualization and flexibility to meet the needs and interests of each candidate.
2. Self-evaluation on the part of the candidate.
3. Feedback from peer-group members, clients, and supervisors.

Included in the program are specific competencies for seven different areas:

1. Personal characteristics.
2. Counseling skills.
3. Individual assessment or inventory.
4. Information services.
5. Research and evaluation.
6. Consultation.
7. Placement.

Each area is broken down into an overall role statement, learning experiences, and assessment tools. Evaluation instruments are included for the rating of characteristics by clients, peers, supervisors, and the candidate. Some objectives are met by written tests or papers, some by performance. Usual criteria are 70 to 80 percent positive evaluation for accomplishment of an objective.

Extensive resource lists are also contained in this document, including state and federal publications and commercially available materials for counselors, teachers, and students, plus their sources and prices. Actual course offerings planned for the development of each competency are not specified.

The other state consortia are:

1. Central Washington State College (plus three school districts and three education associations; contact Dr. James Green, Department of Psychology, Central Washington State College, Ellensburg, Wash. 98926).
2. Gonzaga University/Spokane School District/Spokane Education Association (contact Dr. Terry Peterson, Gonzaga University, Spokane, Wash. 99202).
3. Northwest Adventist Consortium (Dr. Dale O. Wagner, Walla Walla College, College Place, Wash. 99324).
4. Seattle University/Highline School District/Highline Education Association (contact Dr. Marylou Wise, Seattle University, Seattle, Wash. 98122).
5. Southeastern Washington Counselor Consortium

(contact Deal Van De Grift, Walla Walla High School, Fern and Abbott Road, Walla Walla, Wash. 99362).

6. University of Puget Sound/Tacoma School District/ Tacoma Education Association (contact Dr. James Roy, University of Puget Sound, Tacoma, Wash. 98416).

7. Western Washington State College/Seattle Pacific College/Edmonds School District/Edmonds Education Association (contact Jacqui Reid, Meadowdale High School, 6500 168th S.W., Lynwood, Wash. 98036).

8. Whitworth College/Mead School District/Mead Education Association/Spokane School District/Spokane Education Association (contact Dr. Nick Faber, Whitworth College, Spokane, Wash. 99218).

*Evaluation Information:* None available to catalogue compilers.

*Outside Resources Needed:* Since this is a university curriculum, extensive written and audiovisual resources are utilized.

*Price:* $3.94.

*Contact:* (For document) Pacific Lutheran University Bookstore
Pacific Lutheran University
Tacoma, Wash. 98447

(For further information) Joseph Fletcher
School of Education
Pacific Lutheran University
Tacoma, Wash. 98447

5. *Helping Skills: A Basic Training Program*

*Authors:* Steven J. Danish, Allen L. Hauer.

*Format:* Trainee workbook (122 pages); leader's manual (62 pages).

*Description:* Six basic helping skills are the focus of this program. The program was initially developed for paraprofessional guidance workers and human service and social service personnel but is applicable to any group serving in a basic helping role. The program requires approximately twenty-five hours of group training, generally carried out in sessions of two-and-a-half hours each. The training is directed toward attainment of these stages of helping skills:

1. Understanding one's needs to be a helper (attempting to develop the basic awareness of self necessary for genuine helping).
2. Using effective nonverbal behavior.
3. Using effective verbal behavior (in an empathic, nondirective manner and also in a more influencing manner).
4. Self-involving (confrontation) behavior.
5. Understanding others' communication.
6. Establishing effective helping relationships.

The definition of each skill and the training process to achieve it are broken into seven discrete steps:

1. The skill is defined in behavioral terms.
2. The rationale for the skill is discussed.
3. A skill attainment level is specified.
4. Models are used to demonstrate both effective and ineffective examples of the skill.
5. Opportunities are provided for extensive supervised practice of the skill.
6. Homework is assigned to assist in the generalization process.
7. An evaluation is conducted using behavioral checklists and peer and trainer feedback.

The leader's manual is designed to help trainers avoid as many pitfalls as possible in the training program. It describes necessary trainer skills, program logistics, skills for introducing the program, and possible procedural problems. Suggested readings are also included.

*Evaluation Information:* Several formal evaluations have been conducted of changes in trainee performance; their skills were assessed before, directly after, and seven months after training. Some evaluation results were published in professional journals; for further information, see *Contact.*

*Outside Resources Needed:* Leader.

*Price:* Leader's manual: $2.95.

Trainee workbook: $4.95 for one copy, $3.95 each for 10 or more copies, $3.50 each for 25 or more copies, $2.95 each for 50 or more copies.

*Contact:* Steven J. Danish
S1-A Human Development Building
Pennsylvania State University
University Park, Pa. 16802

### Progress Toward Competency-Based Staff Development

Although only a few approaches to competency-based counselor education have been reported in this chapter, they reflect an impressively large shift in training methods and materials. As encouraging as this trend may be, there are at least three obstacles impeding its growth. First, there is a lack of evidence on the effectiveness of competency-based staff development. It is disheartening that there is so little solid data on the benefits of training programs that are converting to a competency-based orientation.

Second, there is a difficulty of identifying the desired competencies on which such programs should focus. The specification of counseling tasks is well illustrated in the literature. Such references demonstrate that it is relatively easy to identify *tasks,* but they do not help solve the problem of specifying the *competencies* required for successful task performance. Third, limited sets of materials for developing competencies are available. There is a critical need for instructional methods, materials, and sequences that train participants to learn predetermined competencies. One alternative that is gathering momentum as a possible solution to this problem is individual-ized instruction through training packages, kits, or modules such as those described in this chapter. However, such a solu-tion is still in the infant stage. It—and alternative answers to the other two problems—require the concentrated attention of the counseling profession over the next few years.

Let us close with a hopeful thought. The possibilities to which human service programs can look, given imaginative lead-ership and hard work, are boundless. The services they can pro-vide are invaluable. Although the problems discussed at the beginning of the chapter are real and pressing, at no time in the past has the potential been more limitless. The approach de-scribed in this chapter represents one attempt to help meet these pressing challenges and allow the fulfillment of that po-tential. To those interested, we offer it as a tool in that effort. If it can help even a few people engaged in the endeavor of im-proving human services, our work will be well rewarded.

# 14

# Training Models
# for Tomorrow

## Bonnie S. Brooks

In light of the varied career opportunities available for human service professionals now and in the future, it is vital that consideration be given to alternative modes of recruitment, training, and professional recognition. Counselor education has come a long way since the days of Frank Parsons (Gianz, 1974). The number of training sites has expanded from 1 in 1908 to well over 400 in 1977. Each year we are preparing some 1,500 Ph.D.s, 17,000 master's level graduates, and an untold number of bachelor's- and associate-level people in the fields of counseling and counseling psychology (Jones, 1976). And our sister fields of psychology, sociology, criminal justice, adult education, gerontology, social work, and so on are similarly preparing individuals who aspire to careers related to mental health.

But progress should not be measured by numbers alone. Where have we been, and where are we going, and what are some of the major issues that arise as part of that process? The professional training of mental health practitioners is experiencing growth and diversity; experimental and innovative programs are appearing in all areas of the country and at all professional levels, from paraprofessional to terminal degree and beyond. This chapter will briefly sketch our ancestry, describe conditions bringing about the need for a change in emphasis, and summarize current trends and issues in the recruitment, training, certification, and licensure of persons engaged in the field of mental health.

## The History of Counselor Education

Early counselor education programs, reflecting existing career opportunities for their trainees, were school oriented. Individuals who were recruited or who "selected themselves" for admission to training programs came primarily from the field of education. Since standards for admission were not articulated, a somewhat random group of trainees appeared, from diverse backgrounds and teaching fields. With articulation of the needs of school children, and roles of the school counselor, the term *guidance* emerged as an umbrella term, representing the specific functions that counselors were to assume within the school setting. These functions were identified by many as counseling, testing, information, placement, and follow-up. Looking back, it appears that in the 1950s counselors came nearer to articulating and agreeing on their roles and functions than they have been able to do since.

Counselor educators, then, developed programs and strategies for the preparation of guidance workers in that framework. What eventually emerged were the first set of standards for the preparation of school counselors (Association for Counselor Education and Supervision, 1964), outlining recommended admission standards, program design, and implementation. The 1964 *Standards* provided a source of direction and focus for new and existing programs; however, they were never officially adopted, nationwide. What developed, instead, were minimum standards for the certification of counselors, originating with state departments of education. As a result, requirements varied; a counselor certified in the state of New York, for example, might bear little if any resemblance to a counselor certified in the state of New Mexico.

By 1971 all states had developed certification standards for school counselors, and although each set of standards was unique certain common characteristics emerged:

1. Most states required some teaching experience (one to three years).
2. Most states required a teaching certificate.
3. Some states required employment experience outside the field of education.
4. Most states specified a certain number of semester hours of approved counseling-related coursework; specific graduate course requirements varied from twelve to thirty or more hours; and most states spelled out the subject matter.
5. Most states required a master's degree.

Colleges and universities involved in the training of counselors operated within the framework of their particular state departments of education and offered the coursework that would prepare their graduates for the necessary credential.

Partly as an outgrowth of the 1964 *Standards* and partly because of the reality of graduate admission requirements in American higher education, certain standards for admission to counselor education commonly appeared. These were (1) Intellective predictors of success (for example, Graduate Record Examination, Miller Analogies Test, and grade-point average) and (2) Nonintellective predictors of success (for example, interview, letters of recommendations, autobiography, statement of philosophy, and measures of personality).

Attempts to define admissions standards, program content, and ultimate certification requirements occurred in concert with the biggest boom we have witnessed thus far in counselor education. With the passage of the National Defense Education Act in 1958, floods of potential school counselors were recruited, new training programs emerged, and schools were given the monetary impetus to develop more and better guidance services for our nation's youth. The money flowed in,

guidance and counseling institutes thrived, and all was well in
counselor education, at least for the period of the late 1950s
and early to mid 1960s.

## The Change in Emphasis

Toward the end of the 1960s, a number of social issues
emerged, many of them having a direct bearing on the counseling function. All across the nation, students pleaded for and
even demanded more voice and participation in the educational
process. Cries rang out that education was not "relevant," that
needs of minorities and other special groups were not being
met. Faced with gross destruction of lives and property, the
general public began directing questions to educators who
should have been knowledgeable about student behavior, student needs, and student management. Where had counselors
gone wrong? A 1971 Gallup poll on education reported that,
given sixteen proposals for economizing, the public chose the
removal of counseling services as fourth in priority (Gallup,
1971). School systems faced with diminishing financial support
began consistently cutting back on counseling services, reflecting the attitude that counseling is an "unnecessary frill" (Pine,
1975).

Thus the message was clear that school counselors were
not performing at a sufficient level of effectiveness to meet the
needs of school children, or to convince the public that their
role was vital. Perhaps the "traditional" guidance services that
had been offered were missing the mark by focusing only on the
normal developmental problems of youth. Many counselors
who had been trained in the traditional programs felt threatened and unequipped to meet school crises. Some responded by
actively seeking out additional training and experimenting with
new approaches; others responded by withdrawing further
into the security of their offices. Feelings of incompetence on
the part of practicing school counselors, then, called for a restructuring of not only the content but also the process of
counselor training programs.

*Emergence of Nonschool Mental Health Service Roles.*
Subsequent to the era of student unrest and continuing to the
present, additional concerns emerged, including drug abuse, student discipline, sexual mores, needs of minorities, and juvenile
offenders. Federal and state monies have been and continue to
be spent in support of programs designed to deal with these
issues. Other chapters in this volume have described new non-
school employment opportunities and professional roles that
have been created as a result. All of these call for a "new breed"
of mental health practitioners, a species that is adequately prepared to effectively deal with new and innovative career roles.
With these developments, it also becomes clear that counselor
education programs cannot focus exclusively on the school setting, if they wish to prepare people for these new roles.

*The Call for Accountability.* The impact of federal, state,
and local funding has been double-edged. On the one hand, new
human service programs have emerged. At the same time, the
spending of funds carries with it the need to be accountable.
Counselors cannot be content to blithely cite their successes in
terms of making people "happy," or "more self-actualizing," or
"more fully functioning human beings." Effectiveness must be
documented; success must be measurable; costs must be justified. Those employed in the mental health field must be prepared to respond to matters of accountability, not simply because it is mandated but, more importantly, because it has
direct bearing on the effectiveness and viability of mental health
services as a whole. Thus, accountability is another area to be
stressed in the education and training process.

*The Information-Technology Explosion.* With advancing
research, experimentation, program evaluation efforts, and so
on, the field of mental health is producing a great deal of information. What programs and treatments have been effective? With
what specific populations? What are some possible reasons for
the successes and failures? How can the employment market be
extrapolated to five, ten, or twenty years hence? What new
human needs do we see emerging, for what special subgroups
(for example, the elderly, the handicapped, and women in

middle life)? With the assistance of modern technology, information storage and retrieval systems, modeling and simulation, and systems theory, we are beginning to accumulate masses of data on which to develop and test hypotheses, reach tentative conclusions, and provide more meaningful services. We can use the information-technology explosion to our advantage, or we can be overwhelmed and baffled by it. At the same time, we must preserve privacy and human dignity and not allow individual uniqueness to be overrun by the system. Human service specialists will need to deal with these issues and are entitled to some training and experience in the information-technology area as part of their preparation.

*Efforts of Counselor Educators.* Counselor educators themselves have provided impetus for change. The literature is focusing more and more on descriptions of innovative programs for the preparation of mental health workers, the kinds of outcomes realized, and recommendations for further change. At their professional meetings, trainers are sharing information and encouraging trainees to do likewise. Special meetings and colloquia are being held, bringing together people from diverse backgrounds to address the issue of contemporary training needs. As an example, in 1973 the Western Interstate Commission for Higher Education (1973, p. 2) published findings of the task force on *Preparing Tomorrow's Campus Mental Health Professionals.* This report described current training programs and proposed that future training programs should adopt the following form.

| Current Training Characteristics | Proposed Training Characteristics |
|---|---|
| 1. Unidisciplinary. | 1. Multidisciplinary. |
| 2. Terminal (diploma). | 2. Ongoing (certification for different levels). |
| 3. Traditional service based (reactive). | 3. Future service based (proactive). |
| 4. Remedial orientation. | 4. Preventive orientation. |
| 5. Emphasis on the individual. | 5. Emphasis on person-environment transactions. |
| 6. Individual practitioner. | 6. Team collaborator. |

7. Selection on academic performance.
8. Self-serving.



9. Pathology oriented.
10. Didactic emphasis.

11. Theory based.


12. Credit oriented.

7. Selection criteria diversi-
   fied, include performance.
8. Consumer oriented and
   sociopolitical, awareness of
   implications for mental
   health programming.
9. Growth oriented.
10. Experiential and didactic
    integrated.
11. Theory and demonstration
    master teacher.
12. Competency oriented.

The Vail Conference (see Ivey and Leppaluoto, 1975), cited by
other authors in this volume, stands as a landmark in changing the
direction and emphasis for the training and practice of applied
psychologists.

In summary, a number of developments including changing expectations of school counselors, emergence of nonschool
mental health service roles, a call for accountability, the impact
of the information-technology explosion, and efforts of counselor educators, have contributed to new developments in counselor training. What follows is a description of some of the
major changes that have been witnessed over the past decade
and the trends that seem to be emerging.

## Changes and Trends in Counselor Education

The first major shift in emphasis occurred in 1971, when
the South Carolina State Board of Education approved an
undergraduate training program for school counselors. Change
from the old certification requirements (including a B.A., two
years of teaching, and an M.A. in guidance and counseling)
seemed in order, because not enough students were choosing
counseling as a vocation to meet the demands of the public
schools in the state. The new undergraduate program called for
a full-time, one-term internship, directed by a full-time certified
counselor in a school setting, with supervision jointly shared by

the master counselor, members of the staff of the training institution, and state department of education guidance consultants.
This latter internship provision replaced the two-year teaching
requirement.

Following the South Carolina lead, several other states
took similar steps in recognizing and supporting bachelor's-level
guidance workers. An an example, the state of Texas approved a
model that was conceptualized by counselor educators at North
Texas State University (Dameron, 1972) and that was based on
the concept of differentiated staffing. This concept, presented
as follows, had been utilized in many other professional and scientific fields; however, it represented a unique proposal for the
guidance profession, calling for the systematic programming of
support personnel roles not previously articulated. Its proponents stressed the notion that appropriately prepared support personnel, working under the supervision of professional
counselors, can contribute significantly to the work of the profession and can make the total guidance endeavor more accountable and viable.

The career ladder in Figure 1 presents three distinct levels
of functioning. One rung of the ladder might lead to the next,
but this may not always be the case. The paraprofessional level
is characterized by individuals who enjoy people, are effective
in human relations, and are willing to be trained. These might
be adults: middle-aged women seeking renewed meaning in life,
elderly people who wish to maintain purposeful human contact.
They might also be students: school-age people who wish to be
helpers and who want to become involved in the guidance function. People in the paraprofessional category would start on the
career ladder as intern guidance aides, serving in the capacity of
receptionists, clerks, librarians, field trip coordinators, or general office workers for a period of one or two years with or without salary. Following the initial period of service, and after
thorough evaluation by the professional guidance staff, they
may be given contracts as guidance aides or assistants. In some
cases, the contract guidance aide may be expected to complete
additional college-level work, adult education courses, or possibly on-the-job training experiences. Evaluation would be
ongoing, and contracts would be renewed on the basis of job

**Figure 1. Career Ladder for Guidance Personnel.**

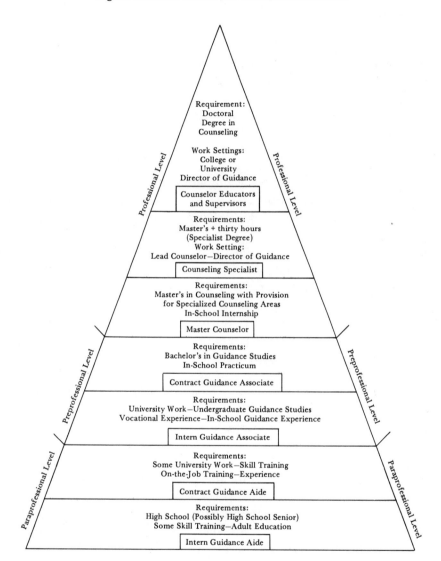

competency and personality attributes. Most individuals would
be expected to remain at the paraprofessional level; however,
those who show the desire and possess the ability may choose
to seek the next rung of the career ladder. This may be especially true of the students, whose successful involvement might

lead to an interest in seeking further training at the college level. Thus, there is an opportunity for the profession to recruit from a large reservoir of potential talent.

Moving up the ladder, the preprofessional level represents individuals who have obtained formal training in guidance at the university level. The first rung of this level is the intern guidance associate, who has entered an undergraduate training program in guidance studies and has completed a significant portion of the curriculum leading to the bachelor's degree in education with guidance representing a teaching field. At the junior and senior level, the guidance studies experiences are integrated with on-the-job experience in the form of an in-school internship in public school guidance offices under the supervision of the professional counseling staff, taking the place of the student teaching program.

On successful completion of the bachelor's degree program in guidance studies and on recommendation by the public school professional counseling staff, the individual might be employed as a contract guidance associate, represented on the state salary schedule as being equivalent to a first-year teacher. What has been described, then, is a pool of individuals at the pre- and paraprofessional levels, available to assist in the delivery of guidance services, allowing the master counselor to focus on those functions for which he or she is professionally prepared.

It should be noted that it is only at the professional rung of the ladder that the term *counselor* appears. In order to advance to this level, the individual must possess a master's degree in the field of guidance and counseling and must receive the professional endorsement by the state education agency. It is expected that the professional counselor, by virtue of his or her advanced training and support personnel, will be able to assume coordinating, consulting, and such other innovative roles that have not previously been feasible within the school structure.

What has been the outcome of the career ladder concept and the implementation of undergraduate guidance associate training programs in Texas? Obviously, new programs of study take time and effort to conceptualize and implement. Course titles, descriptions, content, and materials must be developed;

faculty and institutional (and, in many cases, state board) approval must be sought. Resistance from faculty who are not convinced that the new program is viable, from administrators whose concerns relate to program cost, and from practicing counselors who express fears that their jobs may be jeopardized and their training considered obsolete—these are only some of the difficulties that were met. Nevertheless, some seven or eight colleges and universities pursued and implemented guidance associate training sequences. The first thirty guidance associates in Texas were graduated in the spring of 1974.

A follow-up survey conducted in the spring of 1976 and originating in the Texas Education Agency was sent to all bachelor's-level people who had received their degrees in Texas and who could be located; a total of thirty-nine responded to the questionnaire. In response to the question, "Are you presently employed and where?," the thirty-nine respondents were distributed as follows: 7 guidance associates in public schools, 2 guidance associates in community colleges, 1 teacher aide, 8 teachers, and 11 other fields (6 secretaries, 1 carpenter, 2 salesmen, 1 policeman, 1 medical assistant). Responses indicated that the major strengths of the guidance program are that:

- The program provides students with a strong guidance and counseling foundation, which is beneficial in any area of education.
- Students are better prepared for the graduate-level counseling programs.
- The program teaches students how to deal with all kinds of people on a personal basis.
- Students achieve greater self-understanding.
- The practicum (internship) provides firsthand experience.
- The program is new and up-to-date with current educational practices.

Responses also indicate (Clark, 1976) that the major weaknesses of the guidance associate program are that:

- There is poor acceptance of guidance associates by the major-

ity of administrators and school staffs; this may be partially
due to a lack of statewide publicity, explaining the training
and functions of these bachelor's-level people.
• Without special funding, few schools consider hiring guidance
associates; so consequently there are few jobs.
• Many counselors feel threatened because guidance associates
have received better, up-to-date training than they have had.

The Texas plan, then, has not yet received wide acceptance. From the point of view of the trainees, their training and
experience were perceived as being very positive; further, the
counselors who have been directly involved in working with
guidance associates have a much more positive attitude about
them and the program in general than do counselors who have
had no direct contact. Nevertheless, the employability of bachelor's-level people seems to be in jeopardy at the present time,
according to observations in Texas. This may be partially due to
the generally depressed job market and state of the economy.
Also, it may be premature to attempt the evaluation of such a
young program.

What is the situation nationwide? A survey of counselor
education programs conducted by Sheeley discovered that although only thirty counselor education departments were offering an undergraduate major or minor in counseling education,
fifty-six departments were giving consideration to the establishment of either or both in the future. Total responses numbered
160. Thus, although many counselor educators are giving some
thought to the introduction of bachelor's-degree programs, it
does not appear that a significant proportion have gone as far as
implementation. That may turn out to be fortunate, considering
a general lack of demand for people with undergraduate training
within the public schools.

*Competency-Based Training and Certification.* A second
major trend appears to be even more far-reaching, in that competency-based training models are appearing all over the country. Again referring to the Association for Counselor Education
and Supervision (ACES) survey (Jones, 1976), approximately
three quarters of all counselor education programs have made a

commitment toward converting to the competency-based mode of instruction. Why is this approach being adopted by such large numbers? The answer is not an easy one.

Some have made the move because of state or federal mandate. Many funding sources have "pulled" mental health practitioners and the trainers of mental health workers into systems such as management by objectives or outcome-referenced competency assessment. The message is clearly sent: "Get with the program, or your funds will be withdrawn." Although the statement was eventually rescinded because state courts ruled it a threat to academic freedom, one state commissioner of education announced that "Institutions with approved programs [for teacher and counselor education] should in cooperation with local education agencies and with professional organizations, begin the immediate phasing in of competency/performance-based programs. All presently approved programs must be converted to competency/performance-based programs by September 1, 1977." That type of statement certainly forces individuals into action. Accountability pressures are mounting; competency-based programs may represent responses to those pressures. In these cases, it seems important to take a close look at programs that emerge. "Do they represent a mere listing of competencies appended to the traditional course syllabus, or has a new course been created?" (Jones, 1976, p. 169).

Others have made the move because traditional approaches to counselor education are believed to be ineffective for today's requirements. A number of exemplary programs, addressing themselves to new ways to improve the preparation of helpers, have thus emerged. Motivations behind such programs are obviously serious and sincere; the results have been laudable.

Common characteristics of competency-based preparation programs might be summarized as follows:

1. Trainees go through a process of preassessment in which their previously acquired counseling skills and knowledge are thoroughly evaluated.
2. Individualized, sequential learning experiences, commonly

referred to as *instructional modules,* are planned for trainees,
based on preassessment outcome.

  a. Each module specifies targets of service and related skill
     requirements.
  b. Each module recommends a variety of educational ap-
     proaches for use in helping the trainee acquire the desig-
     nated skill.
  c. Methods of evaluation are designed to assess level of com-
     petency for each module objective, with provision for re-
     cycling.
3. Trainees typically proceed through the program at their own
   rate; time required for completion depends on the speed with
   which the trainee is able to master tasks.
4. Grading systems are normally pass/fail, or A/incomplete. Penalties are not assessed for failing to meet performance standards; the awarding of credit is merely delayed until the
   trainee is able to demonstrate competency.

Typically, counselor education programs have defined
their goals and expectations of students on the basis of the
training and theoretical orientations of the faculty. Therefore,
graduates have identified themselves as having come from a
Rogerian, or Gestalt, or behavioral program of training. The
introduction of a competency-based mode requires that counselor educators arrive at carefully defined, agreed-on skills and
performance criteria for their trainees. Menne (1975) surveyed
experienced counselors, asking them to rate a list of 132 competencies. Through a process of factor analysis, twelve dimensions
of counselor competency were defined. The results of his survey
indicated that significant differences in the level of importance
assigned to the clusters occurred on nine of the twelve dimensions. We are far from reaching consensus as to what common
core of competencies might be expected, as illustrated by the
brief descriptions of selected competency-based programs that
follow.

The program developed by Brammer and Springer at the
University of Washington (1971) identifies six clusters: identification of potential clients, solicitation of information, goal
identification, modes of interacting, types of informational ex-

change, and evaluation procedures. In contrast to this process-oriented model, the Stanford plan calls for a more problem-oriented approach, requiring the counseling graduate to demonstrate skills in dealing with child, family, and social problems; interpersonal and social skills problems; sex, avoidance, and addiction problems; decision-making and academic problems; and problems of minority students (Hendricks, Ferguson, and Thoresen, 1973, p. 421). Variety in number of components ranges from eighty-five subsystems at Michigan State (Winborn, Hinds, and Stewart, 1971) to nine components required in the Learning Development Consultant (LDC) Model described by Stilwell and Santoro (1976), to as few as four major clusters described by Hosford (1972).

Adding fuel to the fire of the generic counselor competency debate, states are beginning to enact statements and standards for competency-based certification. The Jones (1976) survey, sent to all state supervisors of guidance, revealed that 53.6 percent of the states have based, or intend to base, the certification of counselors on specific competencies acquired in university coursework. Thus, for example, the state of Texas expects its counselors to be competent in three general areas, with specialized competencies related thereto, diagrammed as follows:

Professional Competencies

Counseling     Consulting     Coordination

Career Education

Individual Assessment and Inventory

Placement and Follow-Up

Referral

Research and Evaluation

Planning and Implementation

On the other hand, a counselor in the state of Washington must be competent in:

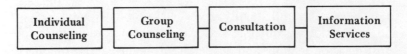

| Individual Counseling | Group Counseling | Consultation | Information Services |

Thus, the debate goes on.

Proponents of the competency-based design point to advantages (Hartwig, 1975, p. 16) such as the potential to:

- Increase motivation of student interest through realistic and relevant experiences.
- Measure skills and concepts already mastered.
- Help bridge the gap between everyday life and the relative abstractness of some curriculum topics by providing real-life experiences.
- Establish an opportunity for the student to use imagination, problem-solving and creativity skills.
- Encourage students' responsibility for their own learning through interaction with a continuous learning process.

Stilwell and Santoro (1976, p. 326) stress the accountability advantage in such models. Assessment data on collected program objectives and teaching strategies are specified, and follow-up evaluation data are available with which to make future decisions and develop program modifications.

On the other hand, competency-based training programs pose problems. Although Jones (1976) found a large percentage of counselor educators committed to the concept of competency-based training (76.1 percent), the proportion who had actually made the shift was only 7.1 percent! He concluded that "This fact, along with comments written in by the respondents, suggests that a significant number of counselor education institutions may be having difficulty implementing the approach" (Jones, 1976, pp. 168-169).

One obvious problem has centered around difficulties in converting the evaluation of competencies, achieved in small increments, to a traditional university grading system. Even though registrars and administrators might be coerced into going along with the idea of awarding only pass/fail or A/incomplete grades on a particular campus, the difficulty of transferring credits to other institutions may pose problems. Related to the grading issue, academic tradition expects the student to devote a specified amount of time to the completion of courses, credits, and eventual degrees. The system is designed to handle such things as class scheduling, registration, and faculty teaching loads on a quarter or semester system, or on some other kind of academic calendar. Acceptance of the concept of an open-entry, open-exit, field-centered system of granting academic credit for competency (even the possibility of earning a master's degree in four months!) interposed on such a system is very problematic.

Beyond the academic traditions, there are difficulties inherent in the training itself. What the system requires is a good deal of one-to-one, tutorial interaction between faculty and student. Thus the role of the professor must change—from that of preparing lectures and meeting classes on time to one of planning, preparing, updating, coordinating, and evaluating a variety of learning resources. In addition his or her time priorities must shift—from allowing time for research, clinical practice, or consulting to a continuous commitment to laboratory- and field-based learning management and program evaluation. We are aware that most educators teach in the same manner in which they were taught. Expectations that counselor educators will wholeheartedly buy into such a radically different scheme may be unrealistic. Reward systems (such as tenure decisions, merit and promotion criteria, and graduate faculty membership status) will similarly require modification of the traditional benchmarks of excellence. Many counselor educators, too, are opposed to the notion of narrowly defined, behaviorally oriented objectives being applied to the humanistic "art" of helping people.

Students, too, must perform differently. The system requires that one take responsibility for one's learning; self-motivation and sustained effort are paramount. The opportunities for peer-group interaction through large group instruction are fewer because learning packages are designed individually. Some people function well under such a system; others do not.

So we have a number of pros and cons. There is no doubt that accountability is with us. Competency-based counselor education may develop into a very strong and viable process wherein the selection of training techniques and the resulting trainee behavioral outcomes can be measured and documented; or it may be a passing phase.

*Systematic Counselor Skills Training.* Systematic training models, particularly for one-to-one counseling, are becoming more prevalent. Such systems are usually quite narrow in scope, presenting one carefully defined skill at a time and remaining with that skill until mastery is achieved. Movement to the next skill is predicated on accomplishment of adequate performance at each successive stage. Throughout the process, written and videotaped materials are presented that simulate "live" models after which to pattern oneself. Such systematic approaches have achieved relatively wide acceptance, since they are adaptable not only to the competency-based program model but also to the more traditional programs. The microcounseling approach presented by Ivey (1971) has been demonstrated to be effective (Gluckstern, 1973; Haase and DiMattia, 1970). Likewise, other new training technologies, including human relations training (Carkhuff, 1969; Egan, 1975) and interpersonal process recall (Kagan, 1972), have achieved positive results.

Systematic models for the training of skills in group counseling have not been as prevalent, although they too are beginning to appear. Since group work is a relatively new function of the counselor, studies investigating the kinds of skills (both cognitive and experiential) needed by group counselors are generally nonexistent. Nevertheless, counselor educators are recognizing the importance of including group counseling skills as part of the student's preparation. Lechowicz and Gazda (1975) reported an early attempt at systematizing the training of group counselors by conducting successive surveys of group "experts" and developing a list of cognitive and behavioral objectives in order of priority. These objectives should prove useful in developing systematic models for the training of group counselors. Undoubtedly, future research will be designed to measure the degree of internalization of systematically introduced counseling skills, over time, and the general cost effectiveness of such programs.

*The Extension of Training.* Mention has been made of bachelor's-level programs. What is intended here is a brief discussion of training extensions at both the lower and upper levels. Training programs for paraprofessionals can increase their effectiveness; such training need not include advanced psychological concepts. Research has shown that twenty to forty hours of empathy training suggested by Carkhuff (1973) and by Delworth and Moore (1974) produces sufficient levels of perceptiveness and understanding to effect client improvements. It has also been found to be important that paraprofessionals be carefully screened and selected. Those directly involved with paraprofessionals also emphasize that supervision should be continuous, beginning with close supervision in the early stages of the paraprofessionals's work and decreasing when knowledge, skills, and understanding are demonstrated. Much more work and research needs to be done in this area.

The mental health profession can benefit from increasing efforts at training and using paraprofessionals effectively. Parents may be trained; schools might explore ways of conducting workshop-format programs, sensitizing interested parents and retired people to psychological needs; community mental health units may wish to recruit volunteers who are interested in growth-producing activities. All of this suggests a shift in emphasis from the usual credit- and degree-granting training format to a more informal, skill-oriented, workshop-format approach. Although the task would require time and effort, effective use of community resources may be well worth it.

At the other end of the continuum, we are witnessing a possible trend in the direction of continuing education programs for the upgrading of professional mental health practitioners. Some professional fields (such as nursing) have a tradition of requiring its members to seek further training on a regular basis in order to maintain their licenses. That trend seems to be emerging in the field of mental health as well, calling for professionals to maintain "an active and aggressive pursuit" of the latest developments in their profession. Currently six states require continuing education (CE) units for the relicensing of psychologists, and over twenty-five states require CE for relicensure of physicians. The American Personnel and Guidance Association is sponsoring workshops on special topics of current interest to the profession, and, for many of these, continuing education credits are available. With the concern for licensure looming, the counseling and mental health profession may be well advised to take a closer look at continuing education possibilities. Questions relating to determining what continuing education will be accredited, who should do the accrediting, what vehicles might be used for the recording and transmitting of CE credits to various states, how funding for CE will be obtained—all of these must be addressed if professional upgrading is to become a reality.

Some of the major trends that we are witnessing in counselor education, then, can be summarized as (1) bachelor's-level training, (2) competency-based models, (3) systematic models, and (4) extension of training. All of these observed trends are not without problems and issues to be addressed. Other issues likewise are unresolved.

## Unresolved Issues

Who should be recruited and admitted to counselor education programs? McKee (1973) conducted a nationwide survey of admissions policies and procedures among master's degree-granting programs. Based on his 298 responses, he found that admissions policies and procedures have not changed appreciably since the early 1950s. McKee's findings are remarkable, inasmuch as graduate admission policies have been recognized as a problem of the counseling profession since the early 1950s (for example, see Cottle, 1953). Further, the problem has been studied extensively; the literature related to the issue of selection policies of graduate counseling departments is abundant.

While it has become a matter of government policy to encourage the hiring of representatives of ethnic and linguistic minorities, McKee's study suggests that graduate departments have made little provision for adapting admissions requirements to the educational realities of those minorities. The literature contains extensive evidence that mental health programs and practices in this country are almost exclusively associated with white, middle-class values (see, for example, Sue, 1977). These serve as a barrier to the establishment of rapport with culturally different clients. The reader is referred to Julius Menacker's chapter in this volume for a more complete discussion of counseling minority groups. The important concern as it relates to training is that there seems to be a lag between research and application. We realize that minority groups are underusing mental health services because their needs are not being met; yet we seem to be slow in translating that knowledge to our recruitment and admissions practices in counselor education.

Moore (1969) says that among the untapped talents of the poor and undereducated is the ability to "empathize, understand, and accept other human beings." In the same vein Carkhuff (1969, p. 7) says, "Indications are that, in general, lay counselors are less intelligent, as measured by traditional intellective indexes, less educated, and from lower socioeconomic classes than professional counselors and therapists." And yet he also says that, following training, "lay trainees function at levels essentially as high or higher (never significantly lower) and engage clients in counseling process movement at levels as high or higher than professional trainees" (Carkhuff, 1969, p. 5). In other words, a wide variety of people may have much to offer the counseling profession, and if selection criteria are used that do identify those people who are most likely to succeed *as mental health workers* a broader range of people might be tapped and encouraged to apply for and be accepted in counseling programs. Any such programs ought to have a built-in evaluation component that offers a check on the validity of whatever admission criteria are used.

*Licensure.* It would require at least a chapter to adequately present the licensure and certification controversy that has recently captured the attention and concern of mental health service providers. Since the issue has direct implications for training, those concerns that are primarily related to training will be presented here. What lies at the root of the problem is the need for a definition of who is qualified to provide mental health services and how qualifications should be measured and by what authority. Licensure addresses itself directly to this need, since it controls not only the title but also the practice of a profession.

The question of licensure was not a concern of the counseling profession as long as counseling was considered to be primarily a school-related activity. States had certification standards, and, although they varied, these served as the benchmarks on which to evaluate an individual's qualifications to provide services to the general school public. Now the situation is different, since mental health professionals are pursuing non-school employment, some in private practice. In addition, there are people who are "setting up shop," calling themselves *group therapists,* or *sex therapists,* or *marriage and family experts,* who do not have the necessary training or qualifications. This poses an ethical, as well as a legal, question for the profession. Another important consideration has to do with third-party representatives (that is, insurance companies) who are generally unwilling to reimburse clinicians whose names do not appear on a nationally approved list. The counseling profession does not have such a roster, listing those who are deemed qualified to provide mental health services. Finally, there have been a number of counselor-trained persons who have sought licensure through their state boards of psychology and who have been turned down simply on the basis that their degrees were awarded in education or educational psychology as opposed to psychology. So the debate touches very close to home, particularly as it regards counselor preparation and training.

Where do counselor educators stand on the issue, and what might be some alternatives? In February 1976, a subcommittee of the Association for Counselor Education and Supervision Licensure Commission surveyed the ACES membership (close to 4,300 persons). Based on the responses of the 40 percent who returned the questionnaire, it was concluded that licensure is definitely an issue of contemporary concern. For example, respondents said (Carroll, Griggs, and Halligan, 1977):

- They were concerned about the controversy over whether counselor educators and supervisors who are trained outside university departments or divisions of psychology should be licensed for private practice in counseling, consultation, psychological diagnosis, and therapy (93.5 percent).
- They thought individuals who are trained outside university departments or divisions of psychology should be licensed for private practice (87.8 percent).
- They felt that ACES should institute a process whereby the association becomes actively involved in program approval of counselor-training programs (90.8 percent).

A number of suggestions have been made as to how the profession might respond to the licensure issue. Some of the proposals are presented as follows. Each has its merits and its problems.

First, counselor-trained persons could work within the confines of current state psychology licensing boards and could seek licensure based on those standards that have been defined by psychologists. With the exception of Virginia, which has enacted a counselor licensure law, this is the situation that exists now in the great majority of the states. If people wish to prepare themselves to pass state psychology board exams, then training programs should be geared in that direction. Many counselor education programs are doing that very thing, providing an option with two tracks or more, one track—consisting of coursework that is "primarily psychological in nature"—that leads toward licensure as it is defined in whatever state the training program is located.

The majority of those who are seriously motivated to obtain the license would probably be allowed to take the licensure examination, since in many states counselors have managed to develop good working relationships with psychology examining boards and since the phrase "primarily psychological in nature" has been loosely defined. In fact, of the 27.5 percent of the ACES respondents who did apply, 75 percent were permitted to take a state licensure exam. Twenty-five percent ($N = 97$) reported they were refused the exam, and almost two thirds of the refusals came from ten states. With civil suits or additional effort at public relations activities, those ten state psychology boards might be wooed into taking a more liberal position with regard to counselor-trained persons.

On the other hand, some people feel strongly that the counseling profession should not measure its standards against those designed for another profession. The personal experience of Dale Wachowiak (1977) is cited as an example of that point of view: "As I was sitting there applying my test-taking wisdom to the standardized exam used in most states for psychological licensure, it was clear to me that it was designed to exclude a certain type of person. . . . The test seemed designed to eliminate those who weren't heavy in research design, statistics, scaling, learning theory, and so on. . . . The test seemed designed to sort out the person who may have come to 'psychological practice' by some route other than the traditional psych-major avenue. Yet the majority of the people taking the exam will use the license as a certificate of competency as a counselor or psychotherapist" (Wachowiak, 1977, p. 222). In other words, if counselor-trained people aspire to and will be expected to engage in counseling, of what value is a traditional psychology examination in measuring counseling effectiveness?

A second option or combination of options would be to develop standards of licensure that relate to the counseling field, and to push for state or national licensure bills that apply to counseling alone or that apply to counseling and are subsumed under a larger umbrella board for the behavioral sciences, as was accomplished in Virginia. It seems that most counselors favor this option. Responding favorably to a questionnaire is one thing; being willing to provide the necessary money and effort to enact passage of a state law is another. A licensure questionnaire in Texas, for example, reported overwhelming support for the state personnel and guidance association to introduce and lobby for a licensure bill for counselors in Texas.

Yet, when asked to what extent respondents would be willing to finance such an effort through a special assessment, the overwhelming majority was willing to spend $25 *or less*!

Beyond matters of strategy, the task of defining minimum requirements for a counseling license is a difficult one. Who will set the standards? If it is a national organization, then matters of regional uniqueness in terms of client needs and resulting training strategies become an issue. At what level of training would persons qualify for a license? The profession is currently divided on this issue, with some arguing that nothing less than doctoral-level qualifications should be acceptable and others pushing for a multilevel system, beginning with paraprofessionals and moving through the entire career ladder (Association for Counselor Education and Supervision, Licensure Commission, 1976).

Finally, there is disagreement as to how competence should be evaluated. When asked this question, respondents to the ACES survey indicated that the licensing law should specify degree titles (11.1 percent), competencies (63.3 percent), both degree titles and competencies (25.6 percent). The assessment of competencies, if it is to go beyond a mere reporting of on-the-job behavior, represents a very expensive and time-consuming task. As has been experienced in the state of Washington, the process of setting up regional examining boards for the purpose of reviewing videotapes and evaluating competencies in a number of areas is not an easy one to accomplish. Competency-based assessment presupposes agreement on the specific competencies to be evaluated, a matter discussed earlier in this chapter. We seem to be a long way from achieving consensus.

A third option might be to eliminate the individual licensure of counselors altogether and instead work toward national recognition and/or approval for training programs. This point of view, espoused by Mackin (1976), emphasizes that valid licensing examinations probably will not be developed in the near future, and in the meantime, "Greater control over training schools and programs could be exerted by professional organizations. Professional associations could suggest ways to change existing courses and even teacher qualifications. The result might be that people who were able to succeed in their training, regardless of their ability to pass a posttraining test, would be eligible to be licensed" (Mackin, 1976, p. 511).

In conclusion, there are a number of stands that could be taken with respect to the licensure issue. The American Personnel and Guidance Association is currently involved with assessing the stance of its membership and providing guidelines and support systems for state organizations wishing to pursue licensure within their state legislative bodies. It seems apparent that the need for standardization of requirements for certification or licensure of counselors and mental health practitioners is clearly shown, thus providing for more uniformity of professional services throughout the country.

It is clear that other issues are unresolved and that trainers have their work cut out for them. The need for further expansion of training to include interdisciplinary emphases, such as assessment and analysis of social needs, organizational patterns, consulting skills, the process of change agentry, the use of technology, and staff training and development, need to be further developed. Continued experimentation and innovation, with a built-in emphasis on the evaluation of new training models, must be carried out. Training sites must be expanded— beyond the traditional classroom setting and into the realm of field placement, allowing trainees to experience, firsthand, human needs and issues that are prevalent. And special attention must be given to the needs of special groups (minorities, women, the elderly, children in daycare centers, the handicapped, and the urban dweller) as an integral, meaningful part of the training process.

The period of affluence is over. Federal funding is being cut. Innovation is being considered wasteful by many who control the purse strings. Not fewer services, but more services with fewer dollars is our challenge—a challenge that speaks directly to counselor educators. The real problem now is what we are going to do, how we are going to demonstrate increased effectiveness, and how we are going to accomplish these tasks within the confines of the resources that we are allotted. The task is immense.

# 15

# External Degree Programs in Counseling

## Frederic M. Hudson

This chapter reports some of the ways that now exist to educate professional clinical and counseling psychologists outside of the mainstream university doctoral programs. In the past ten years, a number of new schools known as *free-standing graduate schools* have emerged as alternatives to the dominant model, with which most of us are very familiar: getting admitted to graduate school, passing the basic and elective courses, taking the general or comprehensive examinations, passing the field or specialized examinations, forming a doctoral dissertation committee, preparing a proposal, conducting research, writing a dissertation and defending it, completing an internship, obtaining the Ph.D., starting postdoctoral professional experience, passing a licensing examination, and entering into professional practice.

The new schools have been created largely by faculty and students from mainstream graduate schools who wanted to

351

design new models for learning and teaching. These faculty and students, who emerged with their creative dissatisfaction in the late 1960s, were frustrated by their inability to conduct significant reforms at their established institutions. During the 1960s, "innovation" was an educational slogan, and the spirit of the times encouraged new frontiers through social reform. Educational reform did take place, on every level, including graduate schools. But the nature of the reform was primarily "experimentation" with innovative ideas, which in retrospect has had little effect on the basic model of graduate education at mainstream institutions. Innovations there were, such as individualized study programs and special programs for older students, but they were and still are tiny barnacles on the huge bulwark of an old hulk. Some students and faculty wanted to change the design of the ship itself, along with the nature of the crew and the journey it was to take. The new schools sought to transcend mere tinkering with minor revisions. They were born with visions of new ways to educate psychologists. So, during the late 1960s and early 1970s, a number of new, small graduate schools were born out of the dissatisfaction with traditional graduate education and out of the visions about how to conduct postbaccalaureate teaching and learning differently. Although some of the new schools are opportunistic attempts to peddle cheap diplomas apart from a solid graduate experience, most of them are honest and sincere efforts at reforming the very basic model of graduate education itself. Each school is so small that its integrity can quickly be established by an astute observer. In fact, almost anyone who takes the time to visit these schools can determine their character and qualities. The ultimate contribution of these new schools will be to provide clear, workable "models" for alternative ways to conduct graduate education.

I propose to examine how some of the new schools prepare professional psychologists. My fundamental criticism of established university programs in psychology at the doctoral level is their lack of significant diversity. These programs dwell within the same academic constraints and programmatic guidelines that control most academic disciplines functioning at the graduate level, such as sociology, English, and biology. In fact, the Carnegie (1971) and Newman (1971) reports on graduate education that documented the monolithic character of post-baccalaureate education in the United States were themselves stimuli for the founding of the new schools. At mainstream graduate schools, each discipline or field is guided by a "body of literature" and by a faculty that is highly specialized in some cognitive area and capable of guiding research. Yet counseling and clinical psychology are professions, not merely academic disciplines. The practice of professional psychology utilizes many competencies in addition to the cognitive abilities stressed by the dominant university model. Unfortunately, the traditional model has evolved throughout academe in the United States with amazing uniformity as a research model, primarily servicing the professional needs of educational and research institutions.

I do not quarrel with the fundamental excellence of the research model and with its ability to produce well-trained professors (in subject matter areas) and researchers. My quarrel is with the stranglehold that this model maintains over the graduate education of psychologists and other professionals whose *primary* work is not research. I seek a diversity of models, not merely modest innovation within the dominant model. Although there is considerable talk about "flexibility" and "innovation" within doctoral programs in psychology—with the inclusion of field experiences, internships, training programs, and part-time "professional" faculty appointments—the basic research model, with its singular focus on cognitive skill development, remains dominant.

The new schools are not opposed to cognitive development. What they want is a different focus. What would happen if we described the professional characteristics of competent professional psychologists and then devised a graduate education that would foster those behaviors? Instead of imitating established graduate routines that have evolved to produce academicians and researchers, we would create graduate experiences that develop clinical and counseling psychologists as persons and as professionals.

The salient characteristics of the model advocated by the

new schools, in stark contrast to the current practice at mainstream schools, are described succinctly in the 1973 report of the Western Interstate Commission for Higher Education's task force on *Preparing Tomorrow's Campus Mental Health Professionals* (see listing in Chapter Fourteen).

Since quite a few of the new schools offering graduate degrees in psychology call themselves *professional schools,* let me say a few words about what is meant by *professional.* The new schools are interested in a practical outcome—a person with real, functioning abilities that serve real human needs. They are not seeking to abandon "education" for "training," nor are they abandoning research as a significant skill. The focus on "professional" outcomes is a curricular focus on abilities, competencies, and skills within a given career context (Anderson, 1974). The new schools want most of the instruction that relates to the practice of psychology to be taught by exemplary professionals who currently practice psychology for a living. And they want training and internship contexts for learning professional practice starting early in a student's graduate program.

The new schools are not clear as to whether this new emphasis on "professional" abilities implies a new doctoral-degree nomenclature, such as the Psy.D. (Doctor of Psychology). The Vail Conference of the American Psychology Association (APA) recommended in 1973 that the following distinction be made between the Ph.D. and the Psy.D. in psychology: "We recommend the completion of doctoral-level training in explicitly professional programs be designated by award of the Doctor of Psychology degree (Psy.D.) and that completion of doctoral level training in programs designed to train scientists or scientist-professionals be designated by award of the Doctor of Philosophy (Ph.D.). . . . Where primary emphasis in training and function is upon direct delivery of professional services and the evaluation and improvement of those services, the Psy.D. degree is appropriate. Where primary emphasis is upon the development of new knowledge in psychology, the Ph.D. is appropriate." Simple and clear as that recommendation may seem, it has not been received evenly across the ranks of either practicing or academic psychologists. Also, not all licensing bodies in the various states have indicated in their codes and practices that they will honor the Psy.D. degree. More basic, however, is the reluctance to dilute the emphasis on research that is stressed in Ph.D. programs. And, since most of the current practicing psychologists have Ph.D.s, the Ph.D. remains the most desired and socially acceptable degree, and research remains a significant component in such programs at the new schools.

The new schools seek to locate and design their graduate programs in environments consistent with the professional behaviors they are seeking as educational outcomes. "Freestanding" graduate schools are not attached to large campuses. They do not have large classroom buildings. The environments for learning include apprenticeship with other psychologists; utilizing available libraries, local research resources, training and internship settings; and utilizing of other graduate school learning opportunities. It is important to recognize that the new schools are not replacements for the traditional model. They do not replace the academic resources; rather, they seek to utilize academic and training facilities that are available throughout the social setting of the student. The new schools use learning opportunities located throughout society, and their professors are largely practicing professionals. Although these schools differ considerably among themselves, they tend to share certain characteristics.

There are two types of free-standing graduate schools: those that offer internal degrees and those that offer external degrees. The former have specific geographic locations where the educational programs are conducted. Students at these schools must live within commuting distance. For the most part, internal degree schools offer "courses" that their students take, which materialize in "units" that relate to graduating. Their learning environment differs from that of most mainstream graduate schools in several ways. First, at most of the new schools the average student is between thirty and forty years of age, and already involved with a career in professional psychology. This is a very important point, often overlooked by critics of the new schools. The new schools are really extensions of the adult education movement into the important realms of higher degrees and credentialing. They are centers for lifelong learning, for serious learners in the middle of their careers who want to improve themselves and their standing. The students attending the free-standing graduate schools represent a clientele that has been ignored by the mainstream schools. These students are middle-aged professionals who, for one reason or another, did not obtain the final degrees in their field when they were younger. They are productive professionals who cannot or will not drop out of their jobs and rooted lives to return to a conventional campus program. What they want is an opportunity to do first-class graduate study without wrecking their life-styles and work settings.

A second characteristic of the internal degree, free-standing school is that most of the instruction takes place on evenings and weekends, since so many students work to some extent during the weekdays. Third, although students are asked to reduce their work schedule in order to make room for graduate study, the employment setting of the student, or some other work environment, is utilized as a part of the curriculum. A member of the faculty may evaluate the effectiveness of the student at his or her place of employment. Fourth, the "classrooms" are, for the most part, informal settings—living rooms, group rooms at a professor's office building, or small seminar rooms. Classes are informal and interactive. Fifth, the professors are largely practicing psychologists, professional "models" who teach part-time. These are supplemented with a core faculty of facilitators and researchers. Sixth, there is considerable curricular flexibility, so students can cross departmental and discipline lines. Interdisciplinary research is encouraged within a focus on professional improvement. The emphasis is on upgrading a professional in midstream rather than on preparing a young person for a first job. Three good examples of free-standing graduate schools with internal degrees are the Wright Institute (Berkeley, California), the California School of Professional Psychology (San Francisco, California) and Rosemead Graduate School of Psychology (Los Angeles county).

The California School for Professional Psychology (CSPP)

is a model for graduate training that is being replicated in many cities throughout the country. The educational content of the curriculum is conventional, but the way educational services are distributed is not. In other words, they conduct classes in conventional subjects, but the classes are arranged where and when they are convenient for the students and faculty. Since most of the faculty are part-time, much of the instruction is done away from the headquarters of the school. Moreover, since most of the faculty hold positions in critical mental health facilities, training opportunities and internships can be facilitated. In fact, CSPP has been politically involved obtaining recognition for its model of graduate education from accrediting bodies, licensing bodies, and from APA.

The Wright Institute is less conventional than CSPP. Wright stresses interdisciplinary thinking, especially between the behavioral and social sciences. Its founder, Nevitt Sanford, casts a long shadow of respectability and erudition on the school, and Wright attracts students who are change agents. While Wright stresses professional impacts as educational outcomes, it would not narrow its focus to clinical and counseling psychology. Wright is more of a "think tank" than CSPP and less of a linkage to credentialing.

The external degree schools have the same six characteristics as the internal degree schools, plus several more. For one thing, the primary location for learning at external degree schools is where the student is—mostly away from the campus. That is what *external* means. Students conduct learning programs where they live, travel, and work, utilizing available resources throughout society. In addition, each student has an individualized "contract" that describes his or her study program. External degrees are program based, not "course" based. Students design coherent learning programs according to their own goals, abilities, and interests, utilizing available resources in their life situations. One of the most available resources utilized by external degree students is mobility, getting to where the special events and experts are. The school negotiates with each student's proposed study program until individualized contracts have integrity for both parties involved. Contracts address themselves to the cognitive and professional "gaps" a student has, rather than to a comprehensive coverage of a field. Contracts are amendable, yet very definite. The faculty in an external degree program function more to provide assessment of competencies than to provide basic instruction. Students entering such programs usually have master's degrees in the field, plus years of experience. The emphasis is on student demonstration of knowledge and ability, not on how he or she obtained the knowledge or ability. Students may take courses at other schools, often with tuition vouchers from the external degree school, or they may learn through informal tutorials with experts outside of school settings. Most external degree schools offer seminar or workshop instruction, in various geographic locations, for short periods of time. The chief function of the faculty, however, is to evaluate the competencies of students: as scholars, as researchers, and as effective psychologists. Students and faculty form "clusters" in the various geographic areas where they live and work. The notion of clusters arose out of the need of some students to have regular contact with other students and faculty. Frequency of cluster meetings varies, and belonging to a cluster is usually voluntary. Some external degree schools use "external examiners" to review the scholarly attainments of their students. Such external examiners would be experts in the student's field, persons who do not know the student but who would be capable of evaluating his or her work. In this way, the school as well as the student is evaluated. Two examples of external degree, free-standing graduate schools are Union Graduate School (Yellow Springs, Ohio) and the Fielding Institute (Santa Barbara, Calif.).

I want to examine with considerable detail one phase of the external degree school model so the reader can discern how it differs from the mainstream model. I will describe an admissions process that culminates in a doctoral contract.

The admissions process at mainstream graduate schools is much the same for all fields, disciplines, and professions. Students are admitted in relation to their academic readiness. Most applicants are in their twenties, recent graduates of baccalaureate or master's programs. They come bearing transcripts with grades and grade-point averages. The applicant is expected to have demonstrated cognitive acquisition of the prerequisite fields.

The admissions question I want to raise is "what is the relationship of the prerequisite academic performance of applicants to their postgraduate professional performance as counseling psychologists?" I know of no positive correlation between good academic performance in prerequisite cognitive areas and the abilities of the graduate as a clinical or counseling psychologist.

How can we minimally correlate our entrance requirements with our exit expectations for professional practice? For example, if one exit expectation of graduates who are professional psychologists is that they should be capable of demonstrating maximum autonomy, then some sort of entrance review of their autonomous behavior deserves central, not peripheral, consideration. This is a line of reasoning shared by many of the new schools and is a major reason why some of them have invented "workshop" environments for concluding the admissions process.

The admissions process I know best is that of the Fielding Institute, an external degree graduate school. Fielding looks for self-motivated learners who already possess master's degrees and considerable experience in the field. The average student is about forty, and slightly more than 50 percent of the student body is female.

Applicants first complete portfolios that include previous academic work, the master's thesis, descriptions of employment functions as a counselor, a record of their own experience of receiving counseling, and a general statement describing their proposed doctoral program of study. Interviews are then conducted by professors and students in the field, and about thirty applicants are invited to attend a six-day doctoral contract workshop.

The workshop is a selection device aimed at choosing those students who demonstrate the basic proficiencies of counseling psychologists. Approximately seven faculty, three current students, and two administrators join the thirty selected applicants for the full week, residing together in a retreat setting where face-to-face relationships are natural. Applicants have an opportunity to examine the graduate program carefully before they commit their lives and money to it.

Applicants are divided into three groups for three days, to explore their abilities as counselors as well as to provide an opportunity for discharge. The faculty, along with student leaders, model their own leadership in the groups and then let the applicants "lead." By the end of the third day, a considerable amount of self-selection and peer selection has already taken place informally. The faculty then meets to make the final selection, having in hand all the applicant records plus three full days of personal experience. The intent is to choose students who demonstrate the basic abilities of the profession and then to become their advocates throughout the doctoral program. At the end of two and one half years since we began these workshops, two thirds of the applicants attending the workshops have entered Fielding programs. Of those who entered, 93 percent have remained enrolled. The workshop provides a counseling environment for the selection of counselors. It also provides a good beginning for new students and faculty to establish relationships that are more than casual and role playing.

After students are admitted at a workshop, they write "doctoral contracts," which are comprehensive outlines of their total study program. Each contract is an individual statement of how a student will come closer to his or her personal and professional goals by obtaining new knowledge and training at the doctoral level. A contract is a future-oriented document having to do with the behavioral improvement of a student. When the newly admitted student leaves the workshop, he or she has a final draft of a doctoral contract that his or her faculty adviser has reviewed.

Since each student writes his or her own contract, he or she is responsible for its fulfillment. The school functions as a facilitator, an assessor, and a validator of student attainments. This concept of graduate education works only with highly competent students who have demonstrated their research and counseling abilities. Built into each contract is how the students will demonstrate their abilities in each contract area. The graduate school "assesses" each student in an ongoing way, through progressive reviews of contracts. In fact, an external degree graduate school represents an ongoing tracking system that at its best is a series of positive reinforcements. Students utilize the faculty as they need and want to do so; seminars, workshops, training and internship opportunities, research assistance, and other "school" resources are made available, but not required.

When a contract is completed at Fielding, the student has been assessed in twelve knowledge and skill areas comprising a core curriculum, completed 300 to 600 hours of new training, concluded a supervised internship, and finished a doctoral dissertation that has been successfully reviewed by an external examiner who is an expert in the topic area.

External degrees are not for everybody, but they do represent an alternative model for educating clinical and counseling psychologists. They upgrade an existing cadre of productive professionals, and they encourage students to become change agents in higher education and in the ranks of professional psychologists.

The most critical issue for the new schools is what is called *quality control* or *standards*. Most of the new schools emphasize ongoing assessment of student learning, in contrast to the "hurdle" concept of a few, stressful examinations that form the backbone for assessment at so many mainstream graduate schools today. Quality control is the key issue on which the new schools and the old schools will be judged. The new schools may be in the goldfish bowl of academic surveillance by their peers at the mainstream schools, but both kinds of schools are in the swirling ocean that is under surveillance by government officials, consumers, licensing boards, and practicing professionals. The ultimate measure of graduate schools of psychology will be the abilities of the graduates themselves.

# 16 ✤ᵰᵱᵰᵱᵰᵱᵰᵱᵰᵱᵰᵱᵰᵱ✤

# Directions for Tomorrow

## Bonnie S. Brooks

Counseling psychology is growing rapidly, expanding far beyond its traditional roles. There is an exciting variety—in types of clients served, work settings, methods, attitudes and skills, and in techniques for outcome assessment. It is now our professional responsibility to search among these innovations and to determine tomorrow's emphases and directions.

People *do* experience crises in their lives and may turn to a counselor for help with marital difficulties, communications breakdowns within the family, or feelings of ineptness in coping with children. Others seek help in overcoming drug dependence, feelings of alienation, or despair. Children may feel confused about conflicting value orientations between what is expected of them in school and what they are experiencing in the "real life out there." Some may feel victimized by what they perceive to be unrealistic or unfair treatment. Adults may experience loss of esteem and self-worth when retirement is forced on them, and many feel useless and powerless living in a life of poverty, loneliness, depression, and guilt. These are very real

accompany loss through death or other

medical model response to these problems
ough validly criticized for being basically
a rather standardized service format, it
y. Efforts should be made to improve this
ather than simplistically rejecting it.
s in overall direction have taken place. It
ize that there are many other potential
oblems have not grown to crisis propor-
s, clients who are unaware that potential
. Such clients might be characterized as
ren in classroom groupings whose devel-
anticipated and worked through as part
e program, or special human groupings
e handicapped, and low-income groups)
whose unique circumstances and needs can be identified and
dealt with on a systematic basis. They may be groups of parents
who receive specialized education and skills in "parenting"
*before* problems develop, or they may be congregates of couples
who work through attitudes and feelings about marriage and its
alternatives during the early stages of their relationships. Also
included may be groups of teachers who are given the opportunity to learn more effective skills in dealing with students, as
well as populations of students who are regularly exposed to an
expanding world of career and employment opportunities. People at all stages of life may benefit from opportunities to look
at their feelings about death and dying, reduction of income,
institutionalization, loss of loved ones, use of leisure time, and
so on *before* these eventualities appear.

Organizations may also be clients. Effectiveness of counseling programs can be significantly increased if the range of
services is extended to include the general environment in which
people live and work. Attention should go to the concept of
"the organization as client," wherein all features of a particular
institution (human and nonhuman) might be taken into consideration in assisting the organization to mobilize its own
forces to function more effectively.

Programs in community psychology, usually housed in

university departments of psychology, have declined markedly in the last five years. Counseling psychology, on the other hand, has sharply increased its activity in the community, and this is where its greatest new opportunities lie. This is especially true in business and industry—the work environment. The Federal Manpower Development and Training Act and other government-sponsored programs provide companies with both requirements and incentives to include counseling programs. The effectiveness of recruiting and retraining disadvantaged minorities depends on education and counseling services. Industry's cost-effectiveness analyses have shown that a critical proportion of absenteeism, turnover, and low worker productivity is caused by alcoholism and drug addiction. Further, most line management members share a common work ethic, which is not as strong a motivation for younger workers. Most large organizations do incorporate personnel counselors into their system, but the creative possibilities here are only just beginning to be tapped.

The ultimate extension, then, is to look on the environment as the total context in which human behavior takes place and to consider the multitude of transactions that occur among all elements at the time and place of their occurrence. The "client," in that frame of reference, is an extremely broad range of potentialities. The change in practices for counselor roles recommended by the Professional Affairs Committee of Division 17 (Counseling Psychology) of the American Psychological Association has taken place. The educative and developmental role becomes primary, with the preventative role in the secondary portion. The traditional remedial and rehabilitative role is not abandoned, but it is no longer the primary and exclusive direction.

As client characteristics and needs vary, so do the settings in which needs are addressed. Counselors have little difficulty imagining themselves functioning in a pleasant office located in the student services area of a high school, or in a community mental health complex, or in an office building where they expect clients to come to them for assistance. They might even concede that the office does not necessarily *have* to be envisioned as "pleasant," since they are aware that mental health practitioners have been able to function quite effectively (by traditional standards) in less than adequate surroundings, such as school book rooms or janitorial closets; private, out-of-the-way cubicles in dormitory complexes; and converted residences. Yet the implicit expectation in all of these more traditional orientations is that the client *will seek us out.* The overriding message that is presented in this volume is the need for flexibility. Counselors must leave their pleasant or semipleasant offices, and base their offerings in locations that are more readily accessible for the clientele being served. Thus, mental health service practitioners might imagine themselves functioning in a high school locker room, in a corporation president's conference room, on the front steps of a tenement, in a data-processing laboratory, in a storefront recreational facility, in a meat-packing plant, at a hospital bedside, or in the quiet solitude of a cemetery. Likewise, they may begin the day at 7:00 a.m. or 8:00 or 9:00, or maybe not even until noon; and they may have no set schedule whatsoever.

Professionals must begin to speak clearly and distinctly to administrators and program directors to change the current stereotyping of counselor functions. University educators in counseling must begin to work with their counterparts in the master's degree programs in administration to reeducate administrators in training.

Chapters in this volume have described a range of settings as well as a range of work schedules; the variety is extensive. Direct involvement with clients has been described in a number of contexts. Group work is prevalent, including use of structured, problem-oriented group approaches (for example, there are groups for assertiveness training, sexism, divorce, weight control, parenting, retirement, and death). Chapter descriptions and bibliographic references have provided sources and evaluations of a number of prepackaged, field-tested group programs. Authors have described procedures for developing their need-specific approaches, which readers might consider applying toward their particular clientele and locale. Discussions centering on specialized needs, such as those of urban dwellers, minor-

ity groups, the handicapped, the elderly and children with behavioral problems, will be of interest to readers who wish to
expand their knowledge and/or their repertoire of services to
specific subgroups within the purview of their settings.

The traditional concept of "group guidance" has been
contemporized to include career education; psychological education; increasing teacher awareness and sensitivity to human
differences and individual needs; computerized simulation experiences; and competency-based, modular systems for the education and training of human relations skills as they apply to mental health service consumers and providers.

Two chapters are specifically addressed to the issue of
education and training needs of contemporary and future mental health service practitioners. It is readily apparent that value
orientations are in need of modification—from the gratification
(and indirect power) that results from seeing one's clients pro-
gressing and leading more productive lives as a partial result of
direct human interventions, to a feeling of satisfaction that results from more indirect approaches, which may not provide as
much interpersonal involvement but which may touch the lives
of many, many people. No longer can counselors expect people
to emerge from "traditional" training programs possessing the
confidence and competence required by emerging and not-yet-
conceptualized role expectations. The new roles will require
greater interdisciplinary emphasis in training, such as assessment
and analysis of social needs, organizational patterns, consulting
skills, the process of change agentry, and an openness to new
technology. It also means more extensive practicum placement
systems that get trainees out of the university and into the community, where they are closer to the human needs and issues of
the majority of the population.

Finally, the matter of program evaluation and accountability is addressed. The theme is clear, "We've come part of the
way, but we have a great deal *more* to do." Counselors in the
past have generally not had the need to concern themselves with
evaluating the results of their efforts, and what evaluation has
been done has usually focused on qualitative criteria, as opposed to quantitative (that is, on facilities). With current calls

for accountability, mental health services are turning their attention to more careful and systematic evaluative efforts, focusing on matters of cost-effectiveness, criterion-referenced, outcome measures based on predetermined needs assessment and goals statements. The era of lavish and relatively unmonitored federal and state spending is over. Increasingly, counselors will be required to do more with less. Stiffer evaluation requirements are a part of almost all grant applications, and agencies have become more aggressive in seeing that these commitments are carried out. Further, federal granting agencies have shown a disturbing willingness to apply their evaluation techniques to counseling programs if program staff do not spend time to devise an effective system of their own: They say "Do it or we will do it for you."

An overview of what has been presented reveals a number of recurring unresolved issues to which attention should be directed. One is the concern for *reeducating* the various publics to these emerging mental health service models. It seems that the first step should be that of reeducating and retooling among our own ranks as professionals. Systems of in-service education and training need to be developed; professionals should be encouraged to update their skills and understandings; and there should be built in a reward system for those who contribute their time, effort, and personal resources in obtaining additional education. Our constituents must be made aware of changes and trends in mental health services. Many of the innovations described here have been housed in sympathetic and supportive environments; some were funded through special experiential grants; and in some instances participants were "instructed from above" to become involved. It is important to recognize that not all attempts will receive such support, and it behooves us to make widespread efforts in public relations and public education activities if we hope to be successful with innovation and change. For without public support very little can be accomplished.

The issue of professional ethics and control was touched on in many of the chapters. With rapid expansion and experimentation, with new programs, new services, new orientations, how is it possible to ensure that the public is being provided with *quality* services? The goal is to somehow ensure quality but still to maintain enough flexibility in the system so that innovations can produce new growth. Much of medicine and psychiatry have pursued the first objective, but have received considerable recent public criticism for failing in the second. Clinical psychology is in the midst of a substantial internal dispute now over whether or not inclusion in national health insurance will tend to produce a more closed, guildlike profession. Counseling psychology has generally recommended standards and guidelines, placing less emphasis on control issues. It will not be able to progress much longer without more serious attention to this area. Meeting the goal of quality and flexibility is difficult, but that is not a reason to evade facing the problem.

Basic concepts regarding "mental health," including "acceptable" and "unacceptable" behavior, are undergoing significant change. Standards and norms for human behavior are being reevaluated in light of human uniqueness, and mental health workers are encouraged to sharpen their levels of awareness and sensitivity to individual needs. Counseling systems based on implicit expectations that individuals must conform to the system are being replaced by those which advocate changing the system in order to make human existence more rewarding, or at least more palatable. Stereotypic role definitions (such as, "The functions of a social worker are. . . ."; "A counselor serves as. . . ." "A paraprofessional is useful with. . . .") are beginning to crumble, and are being replaced by broader, more holistic orientations. Interdisciplinary efforts are being advocated, and teamwork based on solid professional relationships is being regarded as essential. The time for jealously guarding one's so-called territory is over; professionals must go beyond mere technical gimmicks and develop more thorough foundations in related fields, such as sociology, anthropology, economics, and political science.

What all of this calls for is a new orientation—a reevaluation of the past, a critical assessment of the present, and careful planning for the future. The field is expanding and innovating, providing more options for clients and practitioners. In meeting the many challenges and controversies, perhaps we should take a lesson from the experience of the alternative counseling centers and remember that creativity and innovation is our most valuable key to tomorrow.

# Bibliography

Adams, D. K. "Foreword." In P. H. Klopfer, *Behavioral Aspects of Ecology*. Englewood Cliffs, N.J.: Prentice-Hall, 1962.

Alinsky, S. "Of Means and Ends." In F. Cox and others (Eds.), *Strategies of Community Organization*. Itasca, Ill.: Peacock, 1970.

Alinsky, S. *Rules for Radicals*. New York: Random House, 1972.

Allport, G. W. "The Open System in Personality Theory." *Journal of Abnormal and Social Psychology*, 1960, *61*, 301-309.

Alschuler, A. *Developing Achievement Motivation in Adolescents: Education for Human Growth*. Englewood Cliffs, N.J.: Educational Technology Publications, 1973.

Alschuler, A., Tabor, D., and McIntyre, J. *Teaching Achievement Motivation*. Middletown, Conn.: Education Ventures, 1970.

American Association of Marriage and Family Counselors. *Marriage and Family Counseling: A Manual of Accreditation of Graduate Training Programs and Approval of Clinical Training Programs*. Claremont, Calif.: American Association of Marriage and Family Counselors, 1975.

American Personnel and Guidance Association. "Ethical Standards." *Personnel and Guidance Journal*, 1971, *40*, 206-209.

American Psychological Association, Division of Counseling and

371

Guidance, Committee on Counselor Training. "Recommended Standards for Training Counseling Psychologists at the Doctorate Level." *American Psychologist,* 1952, *1,* 175-181.

American Psychological Association. *The Counseling Psychologist,* 1971, *1* (4, entire issue).

American Psychological Association. "Levels and Patterns of Professional Training in Psychology: The Vail Conference." Washington, D.C.: American Psychological Association, 1973.

Amos, W. E., and Grambs, J. D. (Eds.). *Counseling the Disadvantaged Youth.* Englewood Cliffs, N.J.: Prentice-Hall, 1968.

Anastasio, E. J., and Morgan, J. S. *Study of Factors That Have Inhibited a More Widespread Use of Computers in the Instructional Process.* Princeton, N.J.: Educational Communication, Interuniversity Communications Council, 1972.

Anderson, G. L. "ERIC/Higher Education Research Report No. 7." *Trends in Education for the Professions.* Ann Arbor: University of Michigan, 1974.

Andrus Gerontology Center. "Health and Physical Fitness in Retirement." Los Angeles: Andrus Gerontology Center, University of Southern California, 1974a.

Andrus Gerontology Center. "Is My Mind Slipping?" Los Angeles: Andrus Gerontology Center, University of Southern California, 1974b.

Andrus Gerontology Center. "Nutrition for Health and Enjoyment in Retirement." Los Angeles: Andrus Gerontology Center, University of Southern California, 1974c.

Andrus Gerontology Center. "Getting Ready for Retirement." Los Angeles: Andrus Gerontology Center, University of Southern California, 1975a.

Andrus Gerontology Center. "Sex, Romance, and Marriage." Los Angeles: Andrus Gerontology Center, University of Southern California, 1975b.

Andrus Gerontology Center. "What About the Generation Gap?" Los Angeles: Andrus Gerontology Center, University of Southern California, 1975c.

Ansbacher, H., and Ansbacher, R. R. (Eds.). *The Individual Psychology of Alfred Adler.* New York: Basic Books, 1956.

Arbuckle, D. S. "Counselor, Social Worker, Psychologist: Let's Ecumenicalize." *Personnel and Guidance Journal,* 1967, *45,* 532-540.

Ard, B. N., Jr. *Treating Psychosexual Dysfunction.* New York: Aronson, 1974.

Ard, B. N., Jr., and Ard, C. C. "Laws Regarding Marriage Counseling." In B. N. Ard, Jr., and C. C. Ard (Eds.), *Handbook of Marriage Counseling.* Palo Alto, Calif.: Science and Behavior Books, 1969.

Arkin, A. M. "Notes on Anticipatory Grief." In B. Schoenberg and others (Eds.), *Anticipatory Grief.* New York: Columbia University Press, 1974.

Ash, P. "Pre-Retirement Counseling." *Gerontologist,* 1966, *6* (2), 97-99.

Association for Counselor Education and Supervision. "Standards for Counselor Education in the Preparation of Secondary School Counselors." *Personnel and Guidance Journal,* 1964, *42,* 1062-1073.

Association for Counselor Education and Supervision Licensure Commission. "Current Status and Opinionnaire of ACES Members Concerning Licensure Requirements." Fairfield, Conn.: Division of Counseling and Community Service, Fairfield University, 1976.

Aubrey, R. F. "Misapplication of Therapy Models to School Counseling." *Personnel and Guidance Journal,* 1969, *48,* 273-278.

Bakan, D. "The Mystery-Mastery Complex in Contemporary Psychology." *American Psychologist,* 1965, *20,* 186-191.

Bakan, D. *On Method: Toward a Reconstruction of Psychological Investigation.* San Francisco: Jossey-Bass, 1967.

Banks, W., and Martens, K. "Counseling: The Reactionary Profession." *Personnel and Guidance Journal,* 1973, *51,* 457-462.

Barnes, E. K., Sack, A., and Shore, H. "Guidelines to Treatment Approaches." *Gerontologist,* 1973, *13* (4), 513-527.

Barnette, E. L. "I Came Not to Praise Caesar (Nor to Bury Him)." *The School Counselor,* 1970, 249.

Bateson, G., and others. "Toward a Theory of Schizophrenia." *Behavioral Science,* 1956, *1,* 251-264.

Bell, D., 'Kasschau, P., and Zellman, G. *Delivering Services to the Elderly Members of Minority Groups.* Santa Monica, Calif.: Rand Corporation, 1976.

Benedict, R. "Anthropology and the Abnormal." *Journal of General Psychology,* 1934, *10,* 59-82.

Bessell, H. *Methods in Human Development.* El Cajon, Calif.: Human Development Institute, 1970.

Blank, H. R. "Anticipatory Grief and Mourning." In B. Schoenberg and others (Eds.), *Anticipatory Grief.* New York: Columbia University Press, 1974.

Blonsky, L. E. "Formation of a Senior Citizen Tenants Council." *Social Work,* 1973, *18,* 76-83.

Bohn, M. J., Jr., and Super, D. E. "The Computer in Counseling and Guidance Programs." *Educational Technology,* 1969, *9,* 29-31.

Borton, T. *Reach, Touch and Teach: Student Concerns and Process Education.* New York: McGraw-Hill, 1970.

Bottome, P. *Alfred Adler.* London: Faber and Faber, 1957.

Bower, E. M. *Early Identification of Emotionally Handicapped Children in School.* Springfield, Ill.: Thomas, 1960.

Brammer, L., and Springer, H. C. "A Radical Change in Counselor Education and Certification." *Personnel and Guidance Journal,* 1971, *49,* 803-808.

Braun, S., and Pollock, S. W. "Teaching Disturbed Pre-Schoolers: Making Observations Operational." In *Curriculum is What Happens: Planning is the Key.* Washington, D.C.: National Association for the Education of Young Children, 1970.

Brody, E. M. *A Social Work Guide for Long-Term Care Facilities.* National Institute of Mental Health, DHEW Publication (ADM) 75-177. Washington, D.C.: U.S. Government Printing Office, 1974.

Brody, E. M., Kleban, M., and Lawton, M. P. "Help for the Mentally Impaired Aged Person—The Treatment of Excess Disabilities." In J. Segal (Ed.), *Mental Health Program Reports.* Vol. 6. National Institute of Mental Health, DHEW Publication (ADM) 75-256. Washington, D.C.: U.S. Government Printing Office, 1974.

Brotman, H. "Income and Poverty in the Older Population." *Gerontologist*, February 1977, *17* (1), 23-26.

Brown, B. *New Mind, New Body*. New York: Harper & Row, 1974.

Brown, G. *Human Teaching for Human Learning: An Introduction to Confluent Education*. New York: Viking, 1971.

Bruyn, S. T. *The Human Perspective in Sociology: The Methodology of Participant Observation*. Englewood Cliffs, N.J.: Prentice-Hall, 1966.

Bry, A. *The T.A. Primer: Transactional Analysis in Everyday Life*. New York: Harper & Row, 1973.

Bry, A. *T.A. Games: Using Transactional Analysis in Your Life*. New York: Harper & Row, 1975.

Burnham, R. W., Johnson, D. H., and Youst, D. B. "Some Applications of Educational Media in a Support System for Educational and Career Planning." In W. M. Lifton (Ed.), *Educating for Tomorrow: The Role of Media, Career Development, and Society*. New York: Wiley, 1970.

Burnside, I. M. "Acute and Chronic Brain Syndrome." In I. M. Burnside (Ed.), *Nursing and the Aged*. New York: McGraw-Hill, 1976.

Butler, R. N. *Why Survive? Being Old in America*. New York: Harper & Row, 1975.

Butler, R. N., and Lewis, M. *Aging and Mental Health*. St. Louis, Mo.: Mosby, 1973.

Byrne, R. H., and others. *Final Report: The Elementary School Project*. Interprofessional Research Commission on Pupil Personnel Services. Washington, D.C.: Regional Research and Demonstration Center, University of Maryland, 1968.

Campbell, R. E. "Applications of the Systems Approach to Career Guidance Programs." *Focus on Guidance*, 1972, *4*, 1-11.

Canfield, J., and Phillips, M. *A Guide to Humanistic Education*. San Francisco, Calif.: Association of Humanistic Psychology, 1971.

Caplan, G. *The Theory and Practice of Mental Health Consultation*. New York: Basic Books, 1970.

Carkhuff, R. R. *Helping and Human Relations*. Vols. 1 and 2. New York: Holt, Rinehart and Winston, 1969.

Carkhuff, R. R. *The Development of Human Resources.* New York: Holt, Rinehart and Winston, 1971.

Carkhuff, R. R. *The Art of Helping.* Amherst, Mass.: Human Resource Development Press, 1973.

Carnegie Commission on Higher Education. *The Future of Higher Education: How To Get There From Here.* New York: McGraw-Hill, 1971.

Carroll, M. L., Griggs, S., and Halligan, F. "The Licensure Issue: How Real Is It?" *Personnel and Guidance Journal,* 1977, *55,* 577-580.

Carter, R. D. *Help! These Kids Are Driving Me Crazy!* Champaign, Ill.: Research Press, 1972.

Chandler, J. R., and Plakos, J. "Spanish-Speaking Pupils Classified as Educably Mentally Retarded." *Integrated Education,* 1969, *7,* 28-33.

Clark, J. "Results of Guidance Associate Survey." *Guidelines: Newsletter of the Texas Personnel and Guidance Association,* 1976, *25,* 1.

Clark, T., and Jaffe, D. *Toward a Radical Therapy: Alternative Services for Personal and Social Change.* New York: Gordon and Breach, 1973.

Cohen, J. "The Way the Poor Live." In D. W. Smith, G. D. Spiesman, and F. M. Swartz (Eds.), *Dependency and the Poor.* Monograph No. 1 (December). Tucson, Ariz.: Community Resources Project, Rehabilitation Center, College of Education, University of Arizona, 1969.

Coleman, J. *Equality of Educational Opportunity.* USOE OE 38001. Washington, D.C.: U.S. Government Printing Office, 1966.

Comfort, A. *The Anxiety Makers.* London: Panther Modern Society, 1967.

Commission on Computer-Assisted Guidance Systems, National Vocational Guidance Association. *Toward Guidelines for Computer Involvement in Guidance.* Washington, D.C.: U.S. Government Printing Office, 1971.

Cottle, W. C. "Personal Characteristics of Counselors." *Personnel and Guidance Journal,* 1953, *31,* 445-450.

Dameron, J. D. "Futuristic Training Models: The Texas Plan." *Impact*, 1972, *2*, 50-56.

Darby, C. A., Jr., Korotkin, A. L., and Romashko, T. *Survey of Computing Activities in Secondary Schools*. Silver Spring, Md.: American Institutes for Research, 1970.

Deibert, A. N., and Harmon, A. J. *New Tools for Changing Behavior*. Champaign, Ill.: Research Press, 1973.

Delworth, U., and Moore, M. "Helper Plus Trainer: A Two-Phase Program for the Counselor." *Personnel and Guidance Journal*, 1974, *52*, 428-433.

Dewey, J., and Bently, A. *Knowing and the Known*. Boston, Mass.: Beacon Press, 1960.

Dinkmeyer, D. *Developing Understanding of Self and Others*. Circle Pines, Minn.: American Guidance Service, 1972.

Doubleday Multimedia. "Careers in the 70s Series" (Film Series). Santa Ana, Calif.: Doubleday Multimedia, 1970.

Dreikurs, R., and others (Eds.). *Adlerian Family Counseling: A Manual for Counseling Centers*. Eugene: University of Oregon Press, 1959.

Dreikurs, R. *Psychology in the Classroom*. New York: Harper & Row, 1964.

Dreikurs, R. *Social Equality: The Challenge of Today*. Chicago: Regnery, 1971.

Dreikurs, R., Grunwald, B., and Pepper, F. *Maintaining Sanity in the Classroom*. New York: Harper & Row, 1971.

Drew, J. H. "The Effectiveness of an Ombudsman." *Personnel and Guidance Journal*, 1973, *51*, 317-320.

Drum, D. J., and Figler, H. E. *Outreach in Counseling*. Cranston, R.I.: Carroll Press, 1973.

Drum, D. J., and Figler, H. E. "Achieving Total Outreach Potential: A Seven-Dimensional Model." *Impact*, 1974, *3*, 5-17.

Dumont, M. *The Absurd Healer*. New York: Science House, 1968.

Dworkin, E. "Implementation and Evaluation of Clergy and Interagency Mental Health Consultation Programs." Paper presented at the annual American Psychological Association convention in Montreal, September 1973.

Dworkin, E. "Implementation and Evaluation of a Clergy In-service Training Program in Personal Counseling." *Journal of Community Psychology*, 1974, *2* (3), 232-237.

Dworkin, E., and Dworkin, A. "The Activist Counselor." *The Personnel and Guidance Journal*, 1971, *49* (9), 748-753.

Dworkin, E., and Dworkin, A. "A Conceptual Overview of Selected Consultation Models." *American Journal of Community Psychology*, 1975, *3* (2), 151-159.

Dworkin, E., and Walz, G. "An Evaluation Model for Guidance." In D. Cook (Ed.), *Guidance for Education in Revolution*. Boston: Allyn & Bacon, 1971.

Egan, G. *The Skilled Helper: A Model for Systematic Helping and Interpersonal Relating*. Monterey, Calif.: Brooks/Cole, 1975.

Eisenberg, L. "If Not Now, When?" *American Journal of Orthopsychiatry*, 1962, *32*, 781-793.

Ernst, M., and Shore, H. "Sensitizing People to the Processes of Aging: The In-Service Educators Guide." Denton, Tex.: Center for Studies in Aging, School of Community Service, North Texas State University, 1975.

Eysenck, H. J. "The Effects of Psychotherapy: An Evaluation." *Journal of Consulting Psychology*, 1952, *16*, 319-324.

Eysenck, H. J. "The Effects of Psychotherapy." In H. J. Eysenck (Ed.), *Handbook of Abnormal Psychology*. New York: Basic Books, 1961.

Faust, V. *History of Elementary School Counseling: Overview and Critique*. Boston: Houghton Mifflin, 1968.

Flanagan, J. C. "The Role of the Computer in PLAN." *Journal of Educational Data Processing*, 1970, *7*, 1-10.

Foster, H. L. *Ribbin', Jivin', and Playin' the Dozens*. New York: Ballinger, 1974.

Freed, A. *T.A. for Tots (and Other Prinzes)*. Sacramento, Calif.: Jalmar Press, 1974.

Frostig, M. "Education of Children with Learning Disabilities." *University of Southern California Summer Session Notes*, 1962, no. 1.

Fuller, F. F., Brown, O. H., and Peck, R. F. *Creating Climates for Growth.* Austin: Hogg Foundation for Mental Health, University of Texas, 1967.

Gallese, L. R. "Counseling Increases in Elementary Schools Despite Teaching Cuts." *The Wall Street Journal,* January 2, 1976, p. 1.

Gallup, G. "The Third Annual Survey of the Public's Attitude Toward the Public Schools." *Phi Delta Kappa,* 1971, *57,* 33-48.

Ganschow, L. H., and others. *Practical Career Guidance, Counseling, and Placement for the Noncollege-Bound Student: A Review of the Literature.* Palo Alto, Calif.: American Institutes for Research, 1973.

Gelwicks, L. E., and Newcomer, R. J. *Planning Housing Environments for the Elderly.* Washington, D.C.: National Council on Aging, 1974.

Georgia Center for Continuing Education. "New Wrinkles on Retirement" (Film Series). Athens: Georgia Center for Continuing Education, University of Georgia, 1972.

Gianz, E. C. *Guidance: Foundations, Principles, and Techniques.* Boston: Allyn & Bacon, 1974.

Glasscote, R. M., and others. *The Alternate Services.* Washington, D.C.: American Psychiatric Association, 1975.

Gluckstern, N. "Training Parents as Drug Counselors in the Community." *Personnel and Guidance Journal,* 1973, *51,* 676-680.

Godwin, W. "Considerations in the Design of Automated Guidance Systems." In A. Y. Scates (Ed.), *Computer-Based Vocational Guidance Systems.* Washington, D.C.: U.S. Government Printing Office, 1969.

Goldfarb, A. I. *Aged Patients in Long-Term Care Facilities.* Rockville, Md.: National Institute of Mental Health, 1973.

Goodman, P. *Compulsory Mis-Education.* New York: Vintage, 1964.

Gordon, E. W. "The Socially Disadvantaged Student: Implications for the Preparation of Guidance Specialists." In College Entrance Examination Board, *Preparing School Counselors in*

*Educational Guidance.* Princeton, N.J.: College Entrance Examination Board, 1967.

Gordon, E. W. "Social Status Differences: Counseling and Guidance for Disadvantaged Students." In D. Schreiber (Ed.), *Profile of the School Dropout.* New York: Vintage, 1968.

Gordon, E. W., and Smith, P. M., Jr. "The Guidance Specialist and the Disadvantaged Student." In D. R. Cook (Ed.), *Guidance for Education in Revolution.* Boston: Allyn & Bacon, 1971.

Gordon, T. *Parent Effectiveness Training: The Tested New Way to Raise Responsible Children.* New York: Wyden, 1970.

Gordon, T. *Teacher Effectiveness Training.* New York: Wyden, 1975.

Gordon, W. J. *Synetics.* New York: Harper & Row, 1961.

Gramlich, E. P. "Recognition and Management of Grief in Elderly Patients." *Geriatrics,* 1968, *23,* 87-92.

"The Graying of America." *Newsweek,* February 28, 1977, pp. 50-65.

Grayson, L. P. "Costs, Benefits, Effectiveness: Challenge to Educational Technology." *Science,* 1972, *175,* 1216-1222.

Graziano, A. "Clinical Innovation and the Mental Health Power Structure: A Social Case History." *American Psychologist,* 1969, *24,* 10-18.

Grossman, H. J. "Do School Districts Need an Ombudsman?" In W. R. Hazard (Ed.), *Education and the Law.* New York: Free Press, 1971.

Guerney, B. G., Jr., and Flumen, A. B. "Teachers as Psychotherapeutic Agents for Withdrawn Children." *Journal of School Psychology,* 1970, *8,* 107-112.

Guidance and Counseling Task Force. *A Plan for the Improvement of Guidance Services in California.* Sacramento: California State Department of Education, 1973.

Gum, M. F., Tamminen, A. W., and Smaby, M. H. "Developmental Guidance Experiences." *Personnel and Guidance Journal,* 1973, *51* (9), 647-652.

Gunther, B. *Sense Relaxation: Below Your Mind.* New York: Macmillan, 1968.

Gurin, G., Veroff, J., and Feld, S. *Americans View Their Mental Health.* New York: Basic Books, 1960.

Haase, R., and DiMattia, D. "The Application of the Microcounseling Paradigm to the Training of Support Personnel in Counseling." *Counselor Education and Supervision,* 1970, *10,* 16-22.

Hanson, N. R. *Patterns of Discovery.* Cambridge, England: Cambridge University Press, 1958.

Harris, J. E. "Analysis of the Effects of a Computer-Based Vocational Information System on Selected Aspects of Vocational Planning." Unpublished doctoral dissertation, Northern Illinois University, 1972a.

Harris, J. E. (Ed.). *Computer-Assisted Guidance Systems.* Washington, D.C.: National Vocational Guidance Association, 1972b.

Harris, J. E. *The Computer: Guidance Tool of the Future.* Villa Park, Ill.: Willowbrook High School, 1973.

Hartman, W. E., and Fithian, M. A. *Treatment of Sexual Dysfunction.* Long Beach, Calif.: Center for Marital and Sexual Studies, 1972.

Hartwig, J. E. "A Competency-Based Approach to Adult Counseling and Guidance." *Counselor Education and Supervision,* 1975, *15,* 12-20.

Hatcher, C., and Himelstein, P. (Eds.). *Handbook of Gestalt Therapy.* New York: Aronson, 1976.

Hendricks, C. G., Ferguson, J. G., and Thoresen, C. E. "Toward Counseling Competence: The Stanford Program." *Personnel and Guidance Journal,* 1973, *51,* 418-424.

Henry, J. *Culture Against Man.* New York: Vintage, 1963.

Herr, E. L., and Cramer, S. H. *Vocational Guidance and Career Development in the Schools: Toward a Systems Approach.* Boston: Houghton Mifflin, 1972.

Hersch, C. "The Discontent Explosion in Mental Health." *American Psychologist,* 1968, *23,* 497-506.

Hess, R. D. "Educability and Rehabilitation: The Future of the Welfare Class." *Journal of Marriage and the Family,* 1964, *26,* 422-429.

Hillhaven Hospice. *Training Manual.* Available from Valley House Health Care, 5545 East Lee, Tucson, Ariz. 85712.

Holland, J. L. *Making Vocational Choices.* Englewood Cliffs, N.J.: Prentice-Hall, 1973.

Holleb, G. P., and Abrams, W. H. *Alternatives in Community Mental Health.* Boston: Beacon Press, 1975.

Hosford, R. E. "Systems Approach and Operations Research: Appropriate for Evaluating and Improving Counselor Training." *Counseling Psychologist,* 1972, *3,* 58-63.

Huber, G. P., and Ullman, J. C. "Computer Job Matching: How and How Well." *Manpower,* 1970, *2,* 2-6.

Hudson, J. W. "Value Issues in Marital Counseling." In B. N. Ard, Jr., and C. C. Ard (Eds.), *Handbook of Marriage Counseling.* (2nd ed.) Palo Alto, Calif.: Science and Behavior Books, 1976.

Hunter, W. W. *A Longitudinal Study of Pre-Retirement Education.* Ann Arbor: Division of Gerontology, University of Michigan, 1968.

Impellitteri, J. T. "Implementation Problems: Counselor Acceptance of Systems." In A. Y. Scates (Ed.), *Computer-Based Vocational Guidance Systems.* Washington, D.C.: U.S. Government Printing Office, 1969.

Ivey, A. *Microcounseling: Innovations in Interview Training.* Springfield, Ill.: Thomas, 1975.

Ivey, A. E. *Professional Affairs Committee Report* (Division 17—Counseling Psychology). Washington, D.C.: American Psychological Association, 1976.

Ivey, A. E., and Alschuler, A. S. (Eds.). "Psychological Education: A Prime Function of the Counselor." *Personnel and Guidance Journal,* 1973, *51* (9), 585-691.

Ivey, A. E., and Leppaluoto, J. R. "Changes Ahead! Implications of the Vail Conference." *Personnel and Guidance Journal,* 1975, *53,* 747-752.

Jackson, P. W. *Life in Classrooms.* New York: Holt, Rinehart and Winston, 1968.

Jacobson, D. *Progressive Relaxation.* Chicago: University of Chicago Press, 1938.

Jacobson, D. *You Must Relax.* New York: McGraw-Hill, 1962.

Jaffe, D. T. "Transition People and Alternative Services." *Journal of Applied Behavioral Science,* 1973, *9* (2-3), 204.

James, M., and Jongeward, D. *Transactional Analysis for Moms and Dads: What To Do With Them Now That You've Got Them.* Reading, Mass.: Addison-Wesley, 1975.

Jarvick, L., and Cohen, D. "A Bio-Behavioral Approach to Intellectual Changes with Aging." In C. Eisdorfer and M. P. Lawton (Eds.), *Psychology of Adult Development and Aging.* Washington, D.C.: American Psychological Association, 1973.

Jencks, C., and others. *Inequality: A Reassessment of Family and Schooling in America.* New York: Basic Books, 1972.

Jersild, A. T. *When Teachers Face Themselves.* New York: Columbia University Press, 1955.

Johnson, L. B. "Address to the Nation, July 27, 1967." In *Report of the National Commission on Civil Disorders.* New York: Bantam Books, 1968.

Jones, G. B., and others. *Manual for Developing Career Guidance Programs.* Irvine, Calif.: Educational Properties, 1974.

Jones, L. K. "A National Survey of the Program and Enrollment Characteristics of Counselor Education Programs." *Counselor Education and Supervision,* 1976, *15,* 166-176.

Kagan, N. *Influencing Human Interaction.* East Lansing: Instructional Media Center, Michigan State University, 1972.

Kahl, A. "Special Jobs for Special Needs: An Overview." *Occupational Outlook Quarterly,* 1976, *20,* 2-5.

Kamin, L. *The Science and Politics of IQ.* New York: Wiley, 1974.

Kaplan, H. S. *The New Sex Therapy.* New York: Brunner/Mazel, 1974.

Kelly, J. "Ecological Constraints on Mental Health Services." *American Psychologist,* 1966, *21,* 535-539.

Kelly, J. "Towards an Ecological Conception of Preventive Interventions." In J. Carter, Jr. (Ed.), *Research Contributions from Psychology to Community Mental Health.* New York: Behavioral Publications, 1968.

Kelly, J. "Naturalistic Observations in Contrasting Social Environments." In E. Williams and H. Raush (Eds.), *Naturalistic*

*Viewpoints in Psychological Research.* New York: Holt, Rinehart and Winston, 1969.

Kelly, J. "Antidotes for Arrogance: Training for Community Psychology." *American Psychologist,* 1970a, *25,* 524-531.

Kelly, J. "The Quest for Valid Preventive Interventions." In C. D. Spielberger (Ed.), *Current Topics in Clinical and Community Psychology.* New York: Academic Press, 1970b.

Kerckhoff, R. K. "The Profession of Marriage Counseling as Viewed by Members of Four Allied Professions." In B. N. Ard, Jr., and C. C. Ard (Eds.), *Handbook of Marriage Counseling.* (2nd ed.) Palo Alto, Calif.: Science and Behavior Books, 1976.

Kimber, J. A. "Psychologists and Marriage Counselors in the United States." In B. N. Ard, Jr., and C. C. Ard (Eds.), *Handbook of Marriage Counseling.* Palo Alto, Calif.: Science and Behavior Books, 1969.

Kirschenbaum, H., Simon, S., and Napier, R. *Wad-ja-get: The Grading Game in American Education.* New York: Hart, 1971.

Koff, T. H. "Social Rehearsal for Dying." *Journal of Long-Term Care Administration,* 1975, *3,* 42-53.

Kohl, H. *36 Children.* New York: New American Library, 1967.

Kohlberg, L. "Moral Development." In D. Sills (Ed.), *International Encyclopedia of the Social Sciences.* New York: Crowell, Collier, and Macmillan, 1968.

Kohlberg, L. "Stage and Sequence: The Cognitive Developmental Approach to Socialization." In D. Goslin (Ed.), *Handbook of Socialization Theory and Research.* Chicago: Rand McNally, 1969.

Kohlberg, L., LaCrosse, R., and Ricks, D. "The Predictability of Adult Mental Health from Childhood Behavior." In B. Wolman (Ed.), *Handbook of Child Psychopathology.* New York: McGraw-Hill, 1971.

Kolton, M., and others. *Innovative Approaches to Youth Services.* Madison, Wis.: Stash Press, 1973.

Koltveit, T. H. "Counselor-Consultant as Quasi-Ombudsman." *Personnel and Guidance Journal,* 1973, *52,* 198-200.

Kosa, J. "The Nature of Poverty." In J. Kosa and I. K. Zola

(Eds.), *Poverty and Health: A Sociological Analysis.* Cambridge, Mass.: Commonwealth Book Fund, 1975.

Kozol, J. *Death at an Early Age.* Boston: Houghton Mifflin, 1967.

Kroeber, T. C. "The Coping Functions of the Ego Mechanisms." In R. White (Ed.), *The Study of Lives.* New York: Atherton Press, 1966.

Krumboltz, J., and Krumboltz, H. *Changing Children's Behavior.* Englewood Cliffs, N.J.: Prentice-Hall, 1972.

Kubler-Ross, E. *On Death and Dying.* New York: Macmillan, 1969.

Kuriloff, A. H., and Kuriloff, P. J. "Gaining Entry to the Organization." In A. H. Kuriloff (Ed.), *Organizational Development for Survival.* New York: American Management Association, 1972.

Kuriloff, P. "Toward a Viable Public Practice of Psychology: A Psychological Model." Unpublished doctoral dissertation, Harvard University, 1970.

Kuriloff, P. J. "Law, Education Reform, and the School Psychologist." *Journal of School Psychology,* 1975, *13* (4), 335-345.

Lawson, J. S., Rodenburg, M., and Dykes, J. A. "A Dementia Rating Scale for Use with Psychogeriatric Patients." *Journal of Gerontology,* 1977, *32* (2), 153-157.

Lawton, R. "Life Space Counseling." *Personnel and Guidance Journal,* 1970, *48,* 661-663.

Lechowicz, J. S., and Gazda, G. M. "Group Counseling Instruction: Objectives Established by Experts." *Counselor Education and Supervision,* 1975, *15,* 21-27.

Lenn, P. D., and Maser, T. F. *Computer Assisted/Programmed Instruction on the Law.* San Francisco: American Analysis Corporation, 1971.

Leslie, G. R. "The Field of Marriage Counseling." In H. T. Christensen (Ed.), *Handbook of Marriage and the Family.* Chicago, Ill.: Rand McNally, 1964.

Lewis, J. A. (Ed.). "Women and Counselors." *Personnel and Guidance Journal,* 1972, *51,* 84-160.

Lewis, L., and Streetfield, H. *Growth Games: How to Tune In to Yourself, Your Family, and Your Friends.* New York: Harcourt Brace Jovanovich, 1971.

Lewis, S. L. "The Characteristics of Different Media." In W. M. Lifton (Ed.), *Education for Tomorrow: The Role of Media, Career Development, and Society.* New York: Wiley, 1970.

Linton, T. E. "The Educateur Model: An Alternative and Effective Approach to the Mental Health of Children." *Journal of Special Education,* 1969, *3,* 319-327.

Linton, T. E. "The Educateur Model: A Theoretical Monograph." *Journal of Special Education,* 1971, *5,* 155-190.

Linton, T. E., and Menacker, J. "The School Counselor as Child Advocate: Towards a New Thrust in Mental Health Services for Children." *Canada's Mental Health,* 1975, *23,* 3-4.

Lippitt, R. "Dimensions of a Consultant's Job." *Journal of Social Issues,* 1959, *15,* 5-12.

Lippitt, R. "Directions for Change." In *Task Force 6 Report.* Chevy Chase, Md.: Joint Commission on Mental Health of Children, 1969.

Lippitt, R. "On Finding, Using, and Being a Consultant." *Social Science Education Consortium Newsletter,* 1971, *11,* 1-2.

Lippitt, R., and Jung, C. "The Study of Change as a Concept in Research Utilization." *Theory into Practice,* 1966, *5,* 25-29.

Lippitt, R., Watson, J., and Westley, B. *The Dynamics of Planned Change.* New York: Harcourt Brace Jovanovich, 1958.

Longhary, J. W. "The Computer Is In!" *Personnel and Guidance Journal,* 1970, *49,* 185-191.

Lowe, R. "Goal Recognition." In A. G. Nikelly (Ed.), *Techniques of Behavior Change.* Springfield, Ill.: Thomas, 1971.

Lowe, R. *Dreikursian Principles of Child Guidance: Guide to Enrollees.* Eugene: University of Oregon Press, 1974.

Lowen, A. *Physical Dynamics of Character Structure.* New York: Grune & Stratton, 1958.

Luborsky, L., and others. "Factors Influencing the Outcome of Psychotherapy: A Review of Quantitative Research." *Psychological Bulletin,* 1971, *75,* 145-185.

McClelland, D. "Toward a Theory of Motive Acquisition." *American Psychologist,* 1965, *20,* 321-333.

McClelland, D. C., and Winter, D. G. *Motivating Economic Achievement.* New York: Free Press, 1969.

Mace, D. R. "Marital and Sexual Counseling: The State of the Art." In D. W. Abse, E. M. Nash, and L. M. R. Louden (Eds.), *Marital and Sexual Counseling in Medical Practice.* (2nd ed.) New York: Harper & Row, 1974.

McKaness, W. "A Biographical Study of the Life of Rudolf Dreikurs, M.D." Unpublished doctoral dissertation, University of Oregon, 1963.

McKee, J. E. "Master's Degree-Level Admission Policies and Procedures in Counselor Education Departments." Unpublished doctoral dissertation, Indiana University, 1973.

Mackin, P. K. "Occupational Licensing: A Warning." *Personnel and Guidance Journal,* 1976, *54*, 507-511.

McLuhan, M., and Fiore, Q. *The Medium is the Message.* New York: Bantam Books, 1967.

Magoon, T. "Project Upstream." Paper presented at the North Eastern Counseling Center Directors Conference, Durham, New Hampshire, 1974.

Malamud, D., and Machover, S. *Toward Self-Understanding: Group Techniques in Self-Confrontation.* Springfield, Ill.: Thompson, 1965.

Malone, C. A. "Safety First: Comments on the Influence of External Danger in the Lives of Children of Disorganized Families." *American Journal of Orthopsychiatry,* 1966, *36,* 3-11.

Martin, A. M. *A Multimedia Approach to Communicating Occupational Information to Noncollege Youth.* Pittsburgh: Center for Media Studies, University of Pittsburgh, 1967.

Maslow, A. H. *Motivation and Personality.* (2nd ed.) New York: Harper & Row, 1954.

Masters, W. H., and Johnson, V. E. *Human Sexual Inadequacy.* Boston: Little, Brown, 1970.

Melhus, G. E. "Computer-Assisted Vocational Choice Compared with Traditional Vocational Counseling." Unpublished doctoral dissertation, Illinois Institute of Technology, 1971.

Menacker, J. *Vitalizing Guidance in Urban Schools.* New York: Dodd, Mead, 1974.

Menacker, J., and Linton, T. E. "The Educateur Model: An Ef-

fective Alternative for Urban Pupil Personnel Services."
*School Counselor,* 1974, *21,* 336-340.

Menne, J. M. "A Comprehensive Set of Counselor Competencies." *Journal of Counseling Psychology,* 1975, *22,* 547-
553.

Meranto, P. J. *School Politics in the Metropolis.* Columbus,
Ohio: Merrill, 1970.

Mercer, J. "Institutionalized Anglocentrism: Labelling Mental
Retardates in the Public Schools." In P. Orleans and W. R.
Eliss (Eds.), *Race, Change and Urban Society.* Los Angeles:
Sage, 1971.

Mercer, J. *Labelling the Mentally Retarded.* Berkeley: University of California Press, 1973.

Merton, R. K. *Social Theory and Social Structure.* New York:
Free Press, 1957.

Miller, A. L., and Tiedeman, D. V. "Technology and Guidance:
The Challenge to More Elastic Experience amid Accelerating
Obsolescence." In E. L. Herr (Ed.), *Work in the Comprehension of Man.* Washington, D.C.: National Vocational Guidance Association, 1973.

Miller, G. "Psychology as a Means of Promoting Human Welfare." *American Psychiatrist,* 1969, *24,* 1063-1075.

Miller, W. *The Cool World.* Boston: Little, Brown, 1959.

Minor, F. T., Myers, R. A., and Super, D. E. "An Experimental
Computer Based Educational and Career Exploration System." In J. Whiteley and A. Resnikoff (Eds.), *Perspectives
and Vocational Development.* Washington, D.C.: American
Personnel and Guidance Association, 1972.

Mitchell, A. N. *The Orange County, California, Vocational
Guidance Research Study: An Evaluation of Career Guidance
Films.* Santa Ana, Calif.: Doubleday Multimedia, 1972.

Molnar, A. P. "Media and Cost Effectiveness." *Transactions,*
1970, *11,* 291-298.

Moore, G. D. "Beyond Professionalism or Professionalism Reconsidered." *Counselor Education and Supervision,* 1969, *9,*
42-48.

Moorhouse, W. F. "Computer Information Systems: A New
Tool in Guidance." In W. F. Moorhouse (Ed.), *Implications
of New Technology for Counselor Education: A Committee*

*Report.* Washington, D.C.: Association for Counselor Education and Supervision, 1969.

Morrill, H., Oetting, E., and Hurst, J. C. "Dimensions of Counseling Intervention." Technical Report No. 1. Fort Collins, Colo.: Rocky Mountain Behavioral Science Institute, 1972.

Mosher, R. L., and Sprinthall, N. A. *Counseling Psychologist,* 1971, *1* (4, entire issue).

Mudd, E. H., and Fowler, R. C. "The AAMC and the AAMFC: Nearly Forty Years of Form and Function." In B. N. Ard, Jr., and C. C. Ard (Eds.), *Handbook of Marriage Counseling.* (2nd ed.) Palo Alto, Calif.: Science and Behavior Books, 1976.

Myers, R. A., and others. *Educational and Career Exploration System: Report of a Two-Year Field Trial.* New York: Teachers College, Columbia University, 1972.

Nagler, S., and Cooper, S. "An Intervention Model for Community Psychologists in Planning for Prevention." Paper presented to University Park Conference on a Developmental and Preventive Emphasis in Pennsylvania's Community Mental Health and Mental Retardation Program, University Park, Pa., 1969.

National Council on Aging. "Myths and Realities of Life for Older Americans." *Perspectives on Aging,* 1975, *4* (2, entire issue).

National Vocational Guidance Association. "The Role of Computers in Guidance." *NVGA Newsletter,* 1971, *10* (2), 6-7.

Newberg, N., Borton, T., and Gollub, W. "Research Report Summary." Available from Affective Development Program, 21st and the Parkway, Philadelphia, Pa., 1971. (Mimeograph)

Newman, F., and others. *Report on Higher Education.* Washington, D.C.: U.S. Government Printing Office, 1971.

Nichols, W. C., Jr. "Marriage and Family Counseling: Legislative Considerations." In B. N. Ard, Jr., and C. C. Ard (Eds.), *Handbook of Marriage Counseling.* (2nd ed.) Palo Alto, Calif.: Science and Behavior Books, 1976.

Nyler, D., Mitchell, J. R., and Stout, A. *Handbook of Staff Development and Human Relations Training.* Washington, D.C.: National Institute of Applied Behavioral Science, 1967.

Palomares, U. "Nuestros Sentimientos son Iguales, la Diferencia es en la Experiencia." *Personnel and Guidance Journal,* 1971, *50,* 137-144.

Parks, C. M. *Bereavement.* Middlesex, England: Penguin, 1973.

Parnes, S. *Creative Behavior Handbook.* New York: Scribner's, 1967.

Peirce, C. S. *Collected Papers.* Cambridge, Mass.: Harvard University Press, 1931.

Peirce, C. S. "How to Make Our Ideas Clear." *Selected Writings.* New York: Dover, 1958.

Perrone, P. A., and Thrush, R. S. *Vocational Information-Processing Systems: A Survey.* Madison: University of Wisconsin, 1969.

Peterson, A. *Motivation Advance Program.* Rosemont, Ill.: Combined Motivation Education Systems, 1972.

Pfeiffer, J., and Jones, J. *Structured Experiences for Human Relations Training.* Vol. 1. Iowa City, Iowa: University Associates Press, 1969.

Pfeiffer, J., and Jones, J. *Structured Experiences for Human Relations Training.* Vol. 2. Iowa City, Iowa: University Associates Press, 1970.

Pfeiffer, J., and Jones, J. *Structured Experiences for Human Relations Training.* Vol. 3. Iowa City, Iowa: University Associates Press, 1971.

Pfeiffer, J., and Jones, J. *Structured Experiences for Human Relations Training.* Vol. 4. Iowa City, Iowa: University Associates Press, 1973.

Pfeiffer, J., and Jones, J. *Structured Experiences for Human Relations Training.* Vol. 5. Iowa City, Iowa: University Associates Press, 1975.

Pfeiffer, J., and Jones, J. *Structured Experiences for Human Relations Training.* Vol. 6. Iowa City, Iowa: University Associates Press, 1977.

Pine, G. J. "Quo Vadis, School Counseling?" *Phi Delta Kappa,* 1975, *61,* 554-557.

Prediger, D. J. *Validation of Counseling—Selection Data for Vocational School Students.* Iowa City, Iowa: American College Testing Program, 1970.

"Prepare to Free Forgotten Patient After 44 Years." *Chicago Sun Times,* November 8, 1971.

Price, G. E. *A Comparison of Computer and Counselor Effectiveness in Assisting High School Students to Explore and Select Courses.* Unpublished doctoral dissertation, Michigan State University, 1971.

Public Law 94-142. *Federal Register.* Washington, D.C.: U.S. Government Printing Office, November 29, 1976.

Raimy, V. (Ed.). *Training in Clinical Psychology.* Englewood Cliffs, N.J.: Prentice-Hall, 1950.

Rexford, E. "Antisocial Young Children and Their Families." In L. Jessner and E. Pavenstedt (Eds.), *Dynamic Psychopathology in Childhood.* New York: Grune & Stratton, 1959.

Rhodes, W. C. "The Disturbing Child: A Problem of Ecological Management." *Exceptional Children,* 1967, *33,* 449-455.

Rhodes, W. C. "Utilization of Mental Health Professionals in the Schools." *Review of Educational Research,* 1968, *38,* 497-509.

Riley, M. W., and Foner, A. *Aging and Society.* New York: Russell Sage Foundation, 1968.

Rogers, C. R. "The Interpersonal Relationship: The Core of Guidance." *Harvard Educational Review,* 1962, *32,* 416-429.

Ross, L. L. *The Effectiveness of Two Systems for Delivering Occupational Information: A Comparative Analysis.* Eugene: Oregon State University, 1971.

Rosser, D. S. "What You Should Know About New Computer-Based College Selection Services." *Nation's Schools,* 1969, *84,* 47-49.

Royko, M. "How to Handle Jammed Classes." *Chicago Daily News,* October 23, 1972.

Rutledge, A. L. "The Future of Marriage Counseling." In B. N. Ard, Jr., and C. C. Ard (Eds.), *Handbook of Marriage Counseling.* Palo Alto, Calif.: Science and Behavior Books, 1969.

Sarason, S. B. *The Creation of Settings and the Future Societies.* San Francisco: Jossey-Bass, 1972.

Scates, A. Y. (Ed.). *Computer-Based Vocational Guidance Systems.* Washington, D.C.: U.S. Government Printing Office, 1969.

Schaar, K. "*MACOS*: The Controversy Continues." *APA Monitor,* 1975, *6* (7), 1-5.

Schiff, A., and Schiff, J. "Passivity." *Transactional Analysis Journal,* 1971, *1,* 1.

Schmuck, R., and Miles, M. *Organizational Development in Schools.* Palo Alto, Calif.: National Press, 1971.

Schuckit, M. A. "Geriatric Alcoholism and Drug Abuse." *Gerontologist,* 1977, *17* (2), 168-174.

Schultz, W. *Joy.* New York: Grove Press, 1967.

Seidman, E., and others. "The Elementary School Counselor as Psychologist—An Experiment." Paper presented at American Psychological Association convention, New York City, 1966.

Seidman, E., and others. "Functions and Outcomes of Child Development Consultants Compared with Elementary School Counselors—Report of Three Years Research." Paper presented at American Personnel and Guidance Association convention, Detroit, 1968.

Seidman, E. "Proliferation or Reconstruction?" *School Counselor,* 1969, *17,* 89-93.

Seligman, M. "Submissive Death: Giving Up on Life." *Psychology Today,* 1974, *7,* 80-83.

Shaw, M. "Role Delineation Among the Guidance Professions." *Psychology in the Schools,* 1967, *4,* 3-13.

Sheeley, V. L. Unpublished survey of Counselor Education Programs. Available from Department of Education, Western Kentucky University, Bowling Green, Ky. 42101.

Shore, H. "Group Work Program Development." In M. Leeds and H. Shore (Eds.), *Geriatric Institutional Management.* New York: Putnam's, 1964.

Shore, H., and others. "Chai—Eighteen Years at Golden Acres, the Evolution of a *Life* Philosophy, a Report to the Board of Directors of the Dallas Home for Jewish Aged." Dallas: Dallas Home for Jewish Aged, 1971.

Simon, S., Howe, L., and Kirschenbaum, H. *Values Clarification.* New York: Hart, 1972.

Singh, J. P., and Morgan, R. P. *Computer-Based Instruction: A Background Paper on Its Status, Cost-Effectiveness, and Telecommunications Requirements.* St. Louis, Mo.: Washington University, 1971.

Skinner, B. F. "Token Economy: Behaviorism Applied" (Film). Del Mar, Calif.: CRM Educational Films, 1972.

Smith, D. E., and Luce, J. *Love Needs Care.* Boston: Little, Brown, 1971.

Smith, T. W. "Development of a Research-Based and Computer-Assisted Guidance System." *California Personnel and Guidance Association Journal,* 1969, *2,* 27-33.

Snyder, L. H. "Ebenezer: Ancient Symbol of a Safe Haven." *Innovations,* 1977, *4* (1), 6.

Sprinthall, N. A., and Mosher, R. L. *Studies of Adolescents in the Secondary School.* Monograph 6. Cambridge, Mass.: Center for Research and Development, Harvard University, 1969.

Stewart, M. "Will Counselors Find a Friend in the Machine?" *Occupational Outlook Quarterly,* 1969, *13* (3), 20-26.

Stiller, A. "The Changing Role of the Guidance Counselor in the Emerging School." In W. M. Lifton (Ed.), *Educating for Tomorrow: The Role of Media, Career Development, and Society.* New York: Wiley, 1970.

Stilwell, W. E., and Santoro, D. A. "A Training Model for the 1980s." *Personnel and Guidance Journal,* 1976, *54,* 322-326.

Streib, G. F., and Schneider, C. J., Jr. *Retirement in American Society.* Ithaca, N.Y.: Cornell University Press, 1971.

Sue, D. W. "Counseling the Culturally Different: A Conceptual Analysis." *Personnel and Guidance Journal,* 1977, *55,* 422-425.

Sulzer, B., and Mayer, R. G. *Behavior Modification Procedures for School Personnel.* McLean, Va.: Dryden Press, 1972.

Super, D. E. (Ed.). *Computer-Assisted Counseling.* New York: Teachers College, Columbia University, 1970.

Super, D. E. "Computers in Support of Vocational Development and Counseling." In H. Borow (Ed.), *Career Guidance for a New Age.* Boston: Houghton Mifflin, 1973.

Sussman, M. "An Analytic Model for the Sociological Study of Retirement." In F. M. Carp (Ed.), *Retirement.* New York: Behavioral Publications, 1972.

Swope Ridge. "Information packet." Available from Swope Ridge, 5900 Swope Parkway, Kansas City, Mo. 64130.

Szasz, T. S. *The Myth of Mental Illness.* New York: Dell, 1967.

Tamminen, A. W., and Miller, G. D. *Guidance Programs and*

*Their Impact on Students.* St. Paul: Minnesota Department of Education, 1968.

Taylor, C. "Developmental Conceptions and the Retirement Process." In F. M. Carp (Ed.), *Retirement.* New York: Behavioral Publications, 1972, 74-114.

Tharp, R., and Wetzel, R. *Behavior Modification in the Natural Environment.* New York: Academic Press, 1969.

Thompson, A. S., and Super, D. E. (Eds.). *Professional Preparation of Counseling Psychologists.* Report of 1964 Greyston Conference. New York: Bureau of Publications, Teachers College, Columbia University, 1964.

Tickton, S. G., and Kohn, S. D. *The New Instructional Technologies: Are They Worth It?* Washington, D.C.: Academy for Educational Development, 1971.

Tondow, M., and Betts, M. *Computer-Based Course Selection and Counseling.* Palo Alto, Calif.: Palo Alto Unified School District, 1967.

Tyler, L. "Minimal Change Therapy." *Personnel and Guidance Journal,* 1960, *38,* 475-479.

U.S. Department of Labor. *Dictionary of Occupational Titles.* Washington, D.C.: U.S. Government Printing Office, 1965.

U.S. Riot Commission. *Report of the National Advisory Commission on Civil Disorders.* New York: Bantam Books, 1968.

Venn, G. *Man, Education, and Manpower.* Washington, D.C.: American Association of School Administrators, 1970.

Vincent, C. E. *Sexual and Marital Health.* New York: McGraw-Hill, 1973.

Von Bertalanffy, L. *General System Theory.* New York: Braziller, 1968.

Wachowiak, D. "Rites of Passage." *Personnel and Guidance Journal,* 1977, *55,* 222-223.

Walz, G., and Miller, J. "School Climates and Student Behavior: Implications for Counselor Role." *Personnel and Guidance Journal,* 1969, *47,* 859-867.

Wasser, E. "Protective Practice in Serving the Mentally Impaired Age." *Social Casework,* 1971, *52,* 510-522.

Weinstein, G. "The Trumpet: A Guide to Humanistic Curriculum." *Theory into Practice,* 1971, *10,* 196-203.

Weinstein, G. "Self Science Education: The Trumpet." *Personnel and Guidance Journal,* 1973, *51* (9), 600-606.

Weinstein, G., and Fantini, M. *Toward Humanistic Education.* New York: Praeger, 1970.

Weiss, D. J. *Computer-Assisted Synthesis of Psychometric Data in Vocational Counseling.* Research Report 12. St. Paul: Adjustment Project, University of Minnesota, 1968.

Wells, H., and Canfield, J. *About Me: A Curriculum for Developing Self-Motivation.* Rosemont, Ill.: Combined Motivation Education Systems, 1970.

Wertheimer, M. *Fundamental Issues in Psychology.* New York: Holt, Rinehart and Winston, 1972.

Western Interstate Commission for Higher Education. *Preparing Tomorrow's Campus Mental Health Professionals.* Boulder, Colo.: Western Interstate Commission for Higher Education, 1973.

White, R. "Motivation Reconsidered: The Concept of Competence." *Psychological Review,* 1959, *66,* 297-333.

White, R. "Competence and the Psychosexual Stages of Development." *Nebraska Symposium on Motivation* No. 7. Lincoln: University of Nebraska Press, 1960.

White, R. "Sense of Interpersonal Competence: Two Cases of Some Reflections on Origins." In R. White (Ed.), *The Study of Lives.* New York: Atherton Press, 1966.

White, R. "Can Community Mental Health Work Be Done with Competence?" Address on the fiftieth anniversary of the Judge Baker Guidance Center, Boston, April 14, 1967.

Wilkinson, G. L. "Needed: Information for Cost Analysis." *Educational Technology,* 1972, *12,* 33-38.

Willingham, W. W., Begle, E. P., and Ferrin, R. I. *Career Guidance in Secondary Education.* New York: College Entrance Examination Board, 1972.

Winborn, B. B., Hinds, W. C., and Stewart, N. B. "Instructional Objectives for the Professional Preparation of Counselors." *Counselor Education and Supervision,* 1971, *10,* 133-137.

Winick, A. "New York's Automated 'Bloodhound.'" *Manpower,* 1970, *2,* 7-9.

Wolpe, J., and Lazarus, A. *Behavior Therapy Techniques*. Elms-
ford, N.Y.: Pergamon Press, 1968.
Wrenn, G. G. *The Counselor in a Changing World*. Washington,
D.C.: American Personnel and Guidance Association, 1962.
Yawney, B. A., and Slover, D. L. "Relocation of the Elderly."
*Social Work*, 1973, *18*, 86-95.

# Index

## A

Abrams, W. H., 200, 204, 205
Accountability, 288-289, 329, 342, 366
Achievement motivation, in psychological education, 139
Ackerman, N., 106
ACTION, 229
Activist counseling/-ors, 5, 63-92, 174-176, 197
Adams, D. K., 48
Adler, A., 146-170
Advocacy, 17; for aged, 221-222, 240; student, 7-8, 171-198
Aged. *See* Elderly
Aging, 8-9, 219-247
Alcohol, elderly and, 246-247
Alinsky, S., 66
Allport, G. W., 45
Alschuler, A. S., 6, 126-145
Alternative counseling centers, 8, 199-218; examples, 213-217
American Association of Marriage and Family Counselors (AAMFC), 98-99, 102, 103-104
American Association of Sex Educators, Counselors, and Therapists (AASECT), 104
American College Testing Program (ACT), 274
American Institutes of Research (AIR), 290, 302, 303
American Medical Association, free clinics and, 212
American Personnel and Guidance Association (APGA), 124, 181, 344, 350
American Psychological Association (APA), 111, 124, 145
Amos, W. E., 177
Anastasio, E. J., 264, 276
Anderson, G. L., 354
Andrus (Ethel Percy) Gerontology Center, 372
Ansbacher, H., 148
Ansbacher, R. R., 148
Arbuckle, D. S., 111
Ard, B. N., Jr., 6, 93-107
Ard, C. C., 98
Arkin, A. M., 244
Ash, P., 227

397